Assault on Green Island

At 01:38 hours, Lieutenant Bar ordered his men to remove their air pipes and slowly rise out of the camouflaging depths. From beneath the tower and walkway, twenty figures emerged from the Red Sea, raising the barrels of their Uzis and AK-47s upward toward the sentries. As Lieutenant Bar and the remainder of the force clutched their weapons anxiously, Ilan Egozi suddenly noticed a sentry approaching. Instinctively, he recoiled his arms, raised the Uzi, and dropped the sentry with a quick burst of fire. Immediately, Green Island was ablaze with fire and engulfed in the deafening blasts of automatic fire. The naval commandos hurled smoke grenades toward Egyptian machine gun nests, blinding their sights while the first wave made it out of the water to engage the enemy. . . .

Books by Samuel M. Katz

The Night Raiders: Israel's Naval Commandos at War
Fire & Steel
The Elite

Published by POCKET BOOKS

THE NIGHT RAIDERS

RAIDERS

ISRAEL'S NAVAL COMMANDOS AT WAR

SAMUEL M. KATZ

POCKET BOOKS
New York   London   Toronto   Sydney   Tokyo   Singapore

An *Original* Publication of POCKET BOOKS

POCKET BOOKS, a division of Simon & Schuster Inc.
1230 Avenue of the Americas, New York, NY 10020

ISBN: 0-671-00234-1

First Pocket Books printing May 1997

10 9 8 7 6 5 4 3 2 1

Front cover photo by IDF Spokesman

Printed in the U.S.A.

Dedicated to the anonymous warriors who traveled to destinations unknown and depths uncharted, and who sacrificed their lives so that others could live . . .

Author's Note

As a writer who has spent nearly a decade covering both military and law enforcement special forces around the world, from the NYPD's Emergency Service Unit to the Royal Jordanian Special Forces, I have had the privilege and honor of having a secretive world opened to me. Sometimes, I was allowed directly into that world—certain units embraced me with open arms, considering me a friend and a trusted confidant, and I was even allowed to come along on ops. Other times, as in certain European nations that will remain anonymous, I have been treated as a nuisance, "the ugly American," the temporary intruder, who was to be provided with only the bare minimum. When I began my research on Flotilla 13, a unit that continues to live in the cloak-and-dagger world of covert special ops, I was neither embraced nor mistreated (not initially, at least). I simply became a resident of the never-never world of Israel Defense Forces bureaucracy—my request was caught between the responses of "No way, we'll never authorize this" to "Maybe, we'll try, you never know." I was always a phone call away from waiting another day not to find out!

My experiences with the Israelis, of course, should have been different from a project, let's say, with the French GIGN or the New Zealand Special Air Service. I have been

AUTHOR'S NOTE

writing on the Israel Defense Forces for nearly ten years, written over a dozen books and articles and documentary scripts on the Israel Defense Forces, and had thought of myself as well versed in the art of dealing with the IDF maze as could be expected. I had already been ingratiated in what can be coined as the Israeli routine and had happily accepted it—the "routine," it has been said, is part of the national charm.

There are many in the Israeli naval special warfare community who were instrumental in the production of this book. First and foremost, I am grateful to Rear Admiral (Ret.) Ze'ev Almog for his time, his trust, his friendship, and his faith in this project. Ze'ev Almog is the type of commander that "workers" love, soldiers respect, and slackers, those just along for the ride, tend not to get along with at all— especially those in his command. The true test of his mettle as a special operations officer, beyond any reputation, is the fact that the unit's most decorated, heralded, and successful officers revere him simply as "the flotilla," an inseparable element of the unit's past, its present, its character, and the scale of professionalism that the unit strives to maintain long after Ze'ev's retirement. Thankfully, I was able to interview many of these remarkable warriors, and I owe them a debt of gratitude for letting me into their world. I would like to thank Herzl Lavon; Yisrael Asaf; Yisrael Dagai; Izzy Rahav; Uzi Livnat; Ilan Egozi; and the late Yochai Bin-Nun, the first commander of both Flotilla 13 and the IDF/Navy.

Obviously, there are a great many individuals who deserve thanks but because of the nature of their work (past and present) must remain anonymous. They know who they are, and I am indebted to their kindness and trust.

I am also grateful to Rear Admiral (Res.) Ami Ayalon, a warrior of incredible courage, skill, and guile who, like his mentor Rear Admiral Almog, would go on to command the flotilla and the IDF/Navy (as well as the Israeli Secret Service), for authorizing this project. I owe a special word of thanks to Colonel Irit Atzmon at the IDF Spokesman's Office, as well as to Major Natan Rotenberg, IDF Spokesman Assistance Branch, for their gallant, incessant, and successful efforts on my behalf. To borrow a term from the NYPD, Natan is "good people" and someone I consider a good friend.

AUTHOR'S NOTE

I would also like to thank the crew at the IDF Censor's Office for the review of the manscript. I know this wasn't easy for them. There was a time, in the not-so-distant past, that the words "Flotilla 13" were considered state secrets of the highest order and the only materials published on the unit were "according to foreign report" blurbs in magazine articles and history books. In 1992, when I published an article on Flotilla 13 for the U.S. Naval Academy's *Proceedings Magazine,* I am sure I caused a flurry of angina attacks in the censor's office. There were those who told me then that "if it were up to them, they wouldn't have permitted the article to be published." Others, namely a certain Major Y. who was an officer though certainly no gentleman, were less cordial (again, part of the Israeli routine). Thankfully, there were enough individuals in the censor's office to see that the times have, indeed, changed, and public knowledge in Israel (and the Arab World for that matter) no longer has to be treated as state secrets as far as the rest of the world is concerned.

I would also like to take this opportunity to thank Rear Admiral Irv "Chuck" LeMoyne at USSOCOM for his time and efforts, Lieutenant Commander (Ret.) Mike Walsh, U.S. Navy SEALs, for his unique insight and incredible expertise, Major M., British SBS, for his tutorial help in the A-to-Zs of naval special warfare, as well as officers (you know who you are) in the U.S. Navy SEALs, German KSK, Argentine Buzos Tacticos, and Norwegian Marinejægers for their kind assistance. Thanks also to noted novelist and Hollywood screenwriter Steve Hartov, for his insight and friendship.

I owe a very *special thanks* to my agent, Al Zuckerman, for his faith in me and my work, and for taking me to the "next level," and my editors Paul McCarthy and especially Tris Coburn for making sure that the "next level" got published.

Finally, a very special word of thanks and appreciation to my wife, Sigi, a true inspiration and the definition of love, friendship, patience, understanding, and support.

All opinions and conclusions, however, are my own!

Samuel M. Katz
New York, May 1996

THE NIGHT
RAIDERS

Introduction

"What we are about to study is one op in a long war that rewrote the way people like us do business. These blokes not only transcended the art of surprising the enemy, they . . . basically . . . proved that guts and determination are the most important tools that operators can bring to bear on an op. What we are about to study is one of the most important missions in the history of underwater commando warfare. As important and significant as the Italians, and their Pigs, in Alexandria harbor in 1941. These men proved that they were like no others. I wouldn't want to be a sentry in their sights, or on their list of potential targets. If we can come close to replicating their actions on that night we'll prove that we are the world's best."

— Major B.,* instructor at the British Special Boat
Service (SBS) School at Poole, lecturing a class on
the Israel naval commando attack on Green
Island on July 19–20, 1969[1]

IN THE PARATROOPS, THEY ARE KNOWN AS PATHFINDERS, THE first brave soldiers to leap out of an aircraft and determine whether or not a DZ is hot. In naval special warfare, in the

Samuel M. Katz

cruel world of the operational vernacular, pathfinders are more commonly referred to as "trip-wires." They are the commandos who come ashore first, lightly armed, and determine whether or not an innocent-looking beach is a proper landing zone or an ambush—and disaster—waiting to happen. Unlike their comrades who usually are a klick offshore in a Zodiac or Cigarette speedboat, the trip-wires swim to the LZ. They deploy their body's enormous power to slice through the murky waters and navigate through the darkness to reach the right point on a map and ensure that the mission, whatever that mission may be, commences as planned.

Trip-wires, as they like to point out, have an unforgiving job—they are the first to swallow and the last to spit out. Usually deployed in small teams (the exact size of which is considered classified top-secret by the IDF/Navy) where the heaviest weapons they carry are AK-47s, they have to test an enemy beach, many miles from friendly lines, in search of any trip-wires, sentries, or unwanted troop presence. It doesn't matter if the mission that night is a reconnaissance foray against a terrorist training camp, a covert patrol, or the placement of explosives under a bridge. It all begins—and can end—with the trip-wires. They know that being the first ones to emerge onto a hot beach is a dangerous way to earn a living. In the good-case scenario, they encounter absolute fear and a brain-swelling rush of adrenaline powerful enough to tug a locomotive. If need be, they'll eliminate a sentry with a well-placed slice of their dagger across an unknowing guard's carotid artery, or launch a 9mm round from a silenced weapon into the center of an enemy soldier's brain. In the bad case scenario, and there are many bad case scenarios in this line of work, they'll find themselves up against overwhelming firepower fighting for time—and desperately little else—until an escape plan can be formulated before the ammo runs dry. Since they are usually on secretive missions meant to be absolutely deniable, the larger forces waiting in the waters at 500 meters or so away cannot always come to their aid. Since their missions are deniable—and missions that got fucked are

2

more deniable than others—it is likely that their bodies won't be returned for a proper Jewish burial; if they are unfortunate enough to be taken as prisoners (special forces personnel usually are honored with specially brutal brands of torture), it will be years—if at all—before their government will be able to secure their release.

Trip-wires live by a three-tier set of standard operating procedures: *Don't get caught, don't get killed, and pray that the intel is accurate!*

If trip-wires hate anything, it's a last-minute mission on a moon-filled night. On such a night, when the lunar glow illuminates much of the Mediterranean coast, a team of trip-wires emerge from the Mediterranean surf. It is cold, freezing in fact, and the LZ is a rocky enclave where the surf literally chisels the rock into grotesque series of sharp-angled figurines. The sound of the waves crashing against the rocks is perfect cover. It masks the noise of the men removing their weapons from their waterproof sealers and muffles the digitized beeps and squelches of highly sophisticated and highly classified communications gear making contact with the force waiting offshore. Black neoprene wet suits adorn their short, lanky physiques, and buoyancy vests, communications and night-vision gear, and waterproof web gear are tightly fastened to their torsos. The frigid waters, uncharacteristically cold even by Mediterranean standards, makes the pulmonary systems of the pathfinders race much faster—hearts pound louder and chests inflate beyond their normal girth taking in all the oxygen possible.

The lead trip-wire, a stocky sergeant in his early twenties whose blue eyes shine through the slots of the black neoprene balaclava covering his face, removes a pair of night-vision binoculars from his web gear and gazes across the rocky landscape. The cloudy green image produced by the device reveals a quiet LZ. No enemy soldiers, no hot trails of lit cigarette butts or traces of a jeep engine still warm from a sergeant's ride around the compound, not even a barking dog. It looks good. Slowly the trip-wires spread out. One remains close to the beach, a 40mm grenade launcher attached to his Soviet-built AK-47 7.62mm assault rifle at the ready in case any "heavy" fire-support is required.

Another crawls forward along a path where rock and sand converge and aims his AK along a 270-degree field of fire ready to strike down any unwelcome visitor. Other trip-wires crawl on their guts in search of mines or trip-wires that will ignite a claymore or set off a barrage of flares.

None are found though ordnance hidden in the moist sand beach can be hard to find and act in a temperamental fashion.

Seven minutes have passed since the trip-wires came ashore. The commander, determining that the LZ is cold, removes a blinker light from his pouch and flashes it westward, toward the sea. "It's a go," moans the mission CO from his perch inside a black Zodiac rubber inflatable bobbing up and down in the choppy sea. "Let's move it!" The outboard engines are fired up, safeties dully switched to semi-automatic, and weapons clutched tight, raised and aimed toward the approaching beachhead. The two Zodiacs make it to the shoreline in less than two minutes. The spray of the craft hugging the waves at twenty knots has immersed the commandos in a shimmering film of sea water, and goggles are worn to protect everyone's eyes from the blinding salt spray. Even before the Zodiacs have reached the rocks, the commandos find themselves already in the water, racing in with the waves onto the LZ already secured. The mission commander, a cocky captain of few words and built like the chiseled rocks defiantly standing guard on the shore, marches at a brisk pace inland. He never looks back. Never utters a word. He just races inland, followed by a contingent of men in black, some carrying RPG-7 anti-tank rockets. Each commando carries approximately twenty kilos in gear and equipment on his back. It is a cumbersome load, especially while wearing soaking-wet fatigues in the cutting winds of a night-time temperature hovering around 44 degrees Fahrenheit. But there is nearly a kilometer and a half to negotiate and terrain is rocky and rough. Barbed-wire concertina covers much of the inland route, as do trenches and pillbox batches of anti-personnel mines.

Tonight's operation is an ambush. A statement of resolve meant to deter terrorist traffic along the coastal highway, and at the same time possibly even snare a terrorist chieftain traveling to his barracks or returning from a rendezvous with his Syrian or Iranian handlers. The AK-47s and FN MAG light machine guns carried by the force are enough to turn any vehicle into a peppered remnant of its pristine showroom appearance—7.62mm rounds can do that to the aluminum bodies of Mercedes sedans and Toyota pickups. One force of operators positions itself up on a rocky embankment, about twenty yards from the coastal highway, in perfect concealed firing position. Two RPGs are trained at the roadway, as are two FN MAGs— they are to fire at any vehicle deemed a definite target (a tank, APC, or 4x4 in camouflage markings). A squad of operators lies closer to the roadway ready to assault any vehicle deemed suspicious—civilians are to be avoided at all costs and not harmed under *any* circumstances. Laser designators indicate whether the shots will miss or hit their mark. An operator caressing the wooden stock of his FN MAG 7.62mm light machine gun depresses the trigger just enough so that one more milligram of pressure will begin the evening's festivities.

Once the operators are in place and ready for anything, the sound of a jeep's ignition being fired up cuts through the silence. It is Lieutenant Commander R., the section's CO, and the grin on his face, as he glances at his digital stopwatch, indicates a measure of dissatisfaction. It is thirty-three minutes *and counting* since the trip-wires came ashore and fifteen minutes since the Zodiacs have touched down on the beach and the operation's simulated assault has scored its first kill. "Not bad," barks the squadron commander, "but certainly not good, either." His voice, one sanded coarse by nicotine and saltwater, has a confident soft-spoken cadence. No words other than those absolutely necessary are spoken. "You have all done this before in Lebanon and you know what it takes. We need to be in position before there is even a hint of our presence. Without being able to just simply appear, we will never have the chance to just disappear. We've got two hours more until daylight, and seven more hours before we head south for the parachuting exercise. Do it again and let's get it right before we become a spectacle to the first buses heading to Haifa."

It's been just another early morning work out at a place where early morning is midnight. Welcome to Atlit! One of the most remarkable places in the world and the Mecca for Israeli naval special warfare.

Atlit is the type of geographic landmark that appears on very few maps. Most Israeli tour maps don't mention the small seaside town, and it isn't the location that the Ministry of Tourism—or the Ministry of Defense for that matter—wants many people to visit. Although it is nestled along the southern approach to Haifa, Israel's bustling port on the Mediterranean and the nation's third largest city, Atlit isn't as much a suburb as it is a curious footnote. On the road to Haifa from Tel Aviv, in fact, as one can look on to the west to view the roaring Mediterranean, the approach to Atlit isn't indicated by numerous traffic signs or billboards offering seaside seafood at bargain rates. The approach to Atlit is a series of military watchtowers, impassable rows of barbed-wire concertina, and a foreboding seabanking series of cliffs that invite the rush of the sea to hit the rocks with incredible, almost angry, ferocity. Atlit, as those who know it will grudgingly admit, is a place where man comes to be one with the sea.

Atlit is one of those many places on the Israeli landscape that seems to be home to lots of military traffic, and little else. The small interchange off the main highway is usually bustling with sandy-gray painted military trucks ferrying supplies in and out, staff cars racing to and from staff meetings and training maneuvers, and the odd helicopter flight slicing through the salty air en route to a landing strip well-obscured from public view. Occasionally, young soldiers, wearing the khaki Class-A fatigues and navy blue berets of the IDF/Navy, will stand on the main coastal highway near the interchange attempting to hitch a ride to the mysterious location. If picked up by a motorist, the hitchhiking soldier will, by element of incessant training, not divulge anything about his military service—what unit he is in, exactly where his base is, and what's he's been doing for the past six months. Even a novice to the Israeli roadways and the Israeli military realizes that this is no ordinary "sailor." Parachutist wings are worn over his right breast pocket, an odd-looking bat-wing insignia adorns the space above his left breast pocket. The "sailor" is not armed with the American-made M-16A2 5.56mm assault rifle that has become a mainstay of the IDF, but rather he carries a weapon in the AK-47 family, perhaps a weapon made in the former Soviet Union or perhaps made in North Korea. There is an elite status to be owned by a soldier who serves in a unit where the weapon issued is one captured from the clutches of the dying hands of a vanquished enemy. There is a certain charisma that the soldier possesses. A definite confidence most soldiers just can't carry. It is clear that he is part of an elite class of warrior.

It is the *worst*-kept secret in Israel but Atlit is the home base of *Shayetet Shlosh-Esrai*, the Hebrew name for the IDF/Navy's special warfare unit, known in English as "Flotilla 13." In fact, Atlit has been the epicenter Israeli naval special warfare for nearly fifty years. One does not think of the State of Israel as a great naval power, nor should the fact that the fledgling Jewish State had—on paper—a navy before it had any seaworthy warships convince anyone to think otherwise. For a military, that during its fight for independence in 1948 had soldiers without uniforms and commandos without guns, to even contemplate a sea arm was an impressive example of optimistic-induced fantasy. But what the born-in-battle Israeli military did have, in surprising abundance, was a multitude of young men willing to volunteer for missions that, even on a good day, were kamikazelike. Israeli built its navy on the courage of a few men who were determined to compensate for a lack of ships and equipment with sheer guts and dedication. Those men were the seeds from which Flotilla 13 blossomed. Flotilla 13 became an example which the entire Israeli Navy would emulate. Although the IDF/Navy HQ was in Tel Aviv, and its largest port was Haifa, Atlit became the Mecca for Israeli sea power—a hidden alcove along the Mediterranean coast where special men could be trained and special missions could be prepared far from prying eyes.

Samuel M. Katz

As home base to one of the premier units in the Israeli
military (and, according to one operator, "The best damned
infantry force Israel ever fielded"[2]) and one of the trailblazing special warfare units in the world, Atlit is strikingly
modest. When compared to the sprawling Coronado NAB
in the wake of the San Diego coast, home to the U.S. Navy
SEALs, or the quaint splendor of Poole, home base to the
British SBS, Atlit is anticlimactic. It is a place dedicated to
the business of naval special warfare and little else. On its
compact grounds, a foreboding enclave of rock and sand
facing the shimmering waters of the Mediterranean, the
sounds of automatic fire and explosions are constantly
heard. War is conducted 365 days a year at Atlit. Squadrons
of operators hone such unique skills as cold-killing of
sentries, waterborne assaults, and night-time insertion and
extraction operations. Operators, wearing black neoprene
outfits, often enter the icy depths of the *Yam Ha'Tichon* (the
Hebrew name for the Mediterranean) carrying odd-looking
gear resembling the booty taken at a James Bond yard sale
only to emerge exhausted hours later at a point several
klicks away from the base. The roar of truck and jeep
engines are often muted by the whining power of Zodiac
craft and specialized Cigarette speedboats. Helicopters often hover above the base and its off-limit waters, as do
Dabur patrol craft and larger Sa'ar-class missile boats.

For the soldiers who serve in and support Flotilla 13, Atlit
is an island a world away from the rest of Israel—a universe
unto itself where the smell of diesel fuel and gun grease
competes with the saltwater mist flowing about with the
southern winds. The overall picture of the IDF is largely
ignored in Atlit, as is the larger picture of the Middle
Eastern geopolitical map. Atlit is concerned with its little
slice of the map of special ops and little else. As a result, gut
wrenching pulses of anxiety and stress permeate throughout
the base. Atlit is on a permanent war footing. It isn't the
full-scale-war footing that was evident at Pearl Harbor or
Portsmouth, during the Second World War, where men and
vessels are constantly entering and exiting their port. Atlit's
war is low-key, it's constant and permanent. The kind of
conflict waged late at night by a small group of men who

8

score a big victory when news of their actions never makes it to a wire-service story or CNN World Report.

As a result, Atlit isn't the type of base where wives and girlfriends often come to visit, and there are never the children of the unit personnel coming to visit Daddy at work. Instead, visitors to Atlit tend to be deputy defense ministers, generals, intelligence operatives, and other anonymous cloak-and-dagger faces carrying attaché cases, rolled up maps and charts, and hand-tooled Jericho 9mm automatics tucked into waist holsters. Also visiting Atlit on a fairly common basis are small and select group of operators who carry AK-47s and carry the unmistakable swagger of men in possession of a life's supply of confidence and *chutzpah*. Yet these men wear the olive khakis of the regular IDF, the ground army, and the red beret and red jump boots of the Israeli Parachute Corps. Sometimes, even, the visitors will be men of lanky construction who speak neither Hebrew nor English, yet seem to share a common language with the operators of Flotilla 13. And, according to USSOCOM officers, those who pass through the heavily fortified front gate are English-speaking musclemen sporting American accents and who wear the Trident on their Class A's, and call places like Little Creek NAB, Coronado, Fort Bragg, and MacDill home.

Since the early 1950s, Israeli naval commandos have been calling Atlit home, and remarkably there have been "Israeli" naval commandos operating in the waters of the Mediterranean (plus the Red Sea, Sea of Galilee, Dead Sea, and others) for over fifty years. The unit has evolved from a semi-guerrilla sabotage unit into the most battle-experienced naval special warfare unit in the world. Flotilla 13's history has mirrored the turbulent history of the State of Israel, its actions, courage, and sacrifice have made history. There isn't a war or campaign in Israel's forty-eight years of existence that has evaded the grasp of the men whose calling card is a bat-wing insignia. During the struggle against the British, British-sanctioned Jewish frogmen were trained for strikes against the Axis. During the 1948 War, a fledgling commando entity within the even more fledgling Israeli Navy not only managed to field a rather technical force of operators in the Mediterranean, but managed to sink the Egyptian Navy flagship in the process. In 1956, they fought in Sinai, in the years to follow, they charted the beaches of "unfriendly" coasts along the Mediterranean from Minat el-Biada to Alexandria. In the 1967 War, they "attempted" to wage war against Arab shipping lanes; during the 1967–70 War of Attrition, the flotilla rewrote the book on how naval commando units operate, perform, and wage a war "deep" behind enemy lines. During the 1973 War, Flotilla 13 took the war straight to the enemy—attacking enemy harbors in mission-impossible raids that resulted in the destruction of dozens of enemy craft—from patrol boats to missile corvettes. From 1974 to 1996, from the coast of Tyre to "reportedly" the plush suburbs of Tunis, Flotilla 13 has been the world's dominant counter-terrorist commando force. In the words of one former member of the U.S. Navy's SEAL Team SIX, who had trained and worked with the flotilla on several occasions, "There isn't a unit like them in the world. They have seen it all and done it all, and done it better than anyone else!" And, it should be remembered, SEALs tend to shy away from complimenting anyone not wearing the trident on his chest.

While the U.S. Navy SEALs might have had Vietnam as a certified baptism of fire to inaugurate its special brand of naval special warfare into the fold, it did so with an entire fleet and massive infrastructure behind it. The Second World War might have been the testing ground for the canoe-paddling commandos of the SBS, but the unit was brought into existence as part of a military organization, the Royal Marines, that were in existence since the mid-1600s and had an army, navy, and Royal Air Force to support it and help it deploy. Flotilla 13 never had such luxuries at its creation. It had no Israeli fleet behind it because there was no Israeli Navy when the unit was born; there was no Israel at the time. Flotilla 13 was born out of the guerrilla struggle against Hitler in the dark days of German victories in the Middle East, the Mediterranean, and North Africa in 1941 and the Jews' struggle for an independent state against the British at war's end. Flotilla 13 is probably the only naval special warfare unit in military history to boast such a meager and unimpressive starting point.

Those humble beginnings, many unit veterans say, are part of Flotilla 13's charm and character. Others, however, note that it is a symptom of a commando unit forced to fight and die with little else than a dagger, homemade explosives, and balls larger than life! It is a unit that from its inception has been at the cutting edge of the nation's covert operations and special warfare capabilities. It is a unit that from day one has never known a moment's peace.

Israel's history, like that of many units in the Israel Defense Forces, can be measured by the wars it has fought. Flotilla 13's history is not as simple to categorize. It is as busy in peace (the Middle East version of peace, that is) as it is in war. Rather, Flotilla 13 is an entity that can be chartered by the character of the men who don the wet suits and slice their way toward enemy harbors in swimmer-delivery vehicles for the last fifty years, and by two periods of time, thinking, and operational expertise: the years before Ze'ev Almog and the years after. From its inception as an underwater sapper force to the 1967 War, when a frogman team was captured in Alexandria by Egyptian forces prior to them mounting a raid on the harbor, Flotilla 13 was viewed as nothing more than an underwater sabotage unit. Its men were adventurous, courageous, and capable, but they were misunderstood and underutilized by the IDF/Navy and the IDF General Staff. When Ze'ev Almog was appointed the commander of Flotilla 13 in 1968, he was adamant, almost meticulous, in his master plan of transforming the unit into the IDF's busiest and most capable special operations force. He was the first unit commander to politic and lobby the General Staff for work for his men. He created an aura of professionalism and adherence to detail in the unit meant to foster a discipline and tightly rung force of men who would swim faster, shoot better, and perform miracles under the most impossible of situations. If the chief of staff said it couldn't be done, the Flotilla 13 commander was determined to volunteer for the mission. Lieutenant Commander Almog knew how to harness talent and how to deploy it. From Green Island in 1969 to the coast of Tyre in 1996, he provided the unit with a soul, its stubborn iron will, and its unflinching mission.

In October 1993, during the opening ceremonies for Flotilla 13's fiftieth anniversary celebration held at Atlit (one of the few "parties" held at a base built for business) veterans from all of the unit's wars and operations gathered under a cool autumn sky for a night of reminiscing, boozing, and tearful memories. There were veterans from the 1948 fighting, survivors from the failed 1967 Alexandria raid, and men who, as a result of their operations behind enemy lines with the flotilla, now sport glass eyes, prosthetic limbs, and hearing aids. Before the first round of beers was drunk, at the onset, Rear Admiral Ami Ayalon, the IDF Navy commander and former commander of Flotilla 13, came to the podium in a striped polo shirt and with the apprehensive shyness of a man whose entire career has been out of the spotlight. Looking at the men assembled for the festivities, some of whom he had fought with years ago, his desire to get off the stage and not give a speech became obvious. "I had hoped that it would rain tonight and this evening would be canceled," Rear Admiral Ayalon brought out, as he sought an opening for what he wanted to say. "All I have to say," Ayalon continued as he tugged at his muscle bound neck and swept back his bald head, "Command at sea in naval special warfare and the essence of Flotilla 13 is but one man and that is Ze'ev Almog. And that's all I have to say." The commander who didn't want to say anything had simply said it all. The assembled men burst into applause. As Captain (Ret.) Gadi Shefi, former commander of Flotilla 13, said, "It was Ze'ev that put the unit on the map."[3]

In the profession of naval special warfare, being on the map is reserved for an elite group of warriors who have paid their dues in sweat and in blood. But just as the unit's history can be examined by the period preceding and following the War of Attrition, it is the men of the unit from the flotilla's inception to the present day, that have carved out the force's incredible battle record and legacy. Throughout its history, there have been standout individu als who have come to earn Israel's highest decorations of valor and have risen through the ranks of the IDF/Navy and beyond. More than mere veterans, the men gathered at the celebrations were survivors. They had survived the grueling flotilla selection process, survived the nearly two years of intensive back-breaking training, and they had survived operations where anyone less than "the best" would not make it. They had good reason to feel proud. Good reason to kick back and let loose with their emotions and memories.

The outdoor party was decorated with flowers, hanging color lights, and adorned by the sounds of champagne bottles being cracked opened. A cloud of cigarette smoke raced toward the darkened star-filled sky, just as on many dark nights years ago on nameless shores far from home, clouds of smoke and cordite engulfed the air and the spray of water and blood splashed around.

The drinking, reminiscing, and storytelling went on well into the night. Before the last bottle was put to bed and the last "Remember when we tossed the grenade down the bunker shaft in Lebanon" was uttered by past generations of the flotilla, the current generation was waking up. It was time to go to work. Prepare, train, study, and head off into the Mediterranean for a training assignment or a real op, a mission, far from the national boundaries. As the last stalwart storytellers stumbled over the last bottles of bad Israeli vodka, the sounds of three Bell-212s flying overhead produced a moment of introspection as they recalled when they were back in the fold waking up groggy-eyed after a two-hour night sleep for a raid against an Egyptian fort or a Palestinian terrorist compound. "The bat wings become a badge of your soul," claimed one teary-eyed veteran. "You are never really out of the unit, even years after you are too old for reserve duty, because this unit becomes a big part of you, part of your skin, part of your brain, part of your existence!"

For the last fifty years, Israelis have, in one form or another, been safeguarding their elongated frontier with the Mediterranean and professing Israeli security interests with a small navy spearheaded by an energetic, courageous, innovative, and most capable naval special warfare element considered to be among the world's finest—clearly the world's most battle-tested. They have, through trial and error and the ballistic impact of fire-fights and detonating enemy shipping, written the book on how naval commandos should be deployed during a full-scale war and during the less certain and more volatile times of "peacetime" covert ops. Flotilla 13's first fifty years have been characterized by remarkable achievements, remarkable technological tools, and some remarkable men.

This is their remarkable story—out of the shadows and out of Israel's top-secret files.

14

CHAPTER ONE

The Early Years

Israeli Naval Commandos: 1940 to 1953

PALESTINE IN 1941 WAS A PRESSURE-COOKER WAITING TO EX-
plode. Overwhelming panic didn't electrify the air, but the
numbing sense of anxiety and desperation gnawed at every
one's gut, from British servicemen to Jewish refugees to
Arab freedom fighters. The Second World War had come
dangerously close to the Holy Land, and it appeared as if
but a matter of time before the German and Italian armies
would march through the gates of the Old City of Jerusalem
en route to conquering the entire Middle East. The Vichy
French controlled Lebanon and Syria, General Erwin
Rommel's Afrika Korps was advancing unhindered through
the vast Egyptian desert, Italian warships routinely attacked
British shipping along Palestine's Mediterranean coast, and
warplanes from Mussolini's air force regularly bombed
refineries in Haifa and power plants near Tel Aviv. With
tens of thousands of Allied troops in Palestine (Brits,
ANZACs, Poles, Indians, Czechs, French, and South Afri-
cans), the small sliver of land between the Suez Canal and
the Jordan River became less a base of operations for the
Allied Middle East war effort and more of a pocket of a last-
ditch defense that was growing smaller by the day. Many
high-ranking British officers began preparing the evacuation
of Palestine through a boat armada escaping from Haifa.

The second coming of Dunkirk, many joked, with a Levantine flair.

Palestine in 1941 was also embroiled in an underground civil war between Arabs and Jews over ownership of that tiny sliver of land. As civil wars go, it was a vicious bloodletting with the added element of religion and legitimacy thrown in. From 1936 to 1939, full-scale rioting broke out between the small Jewish population, who sought an independent Jewish State of one sort or another in their biblical homeland, and the Palestinian Arabs, who wanted to eradicate their land of the foreign Jewish presence imported from Eastern Europe half a century ago. Both sides had official promises from the British, lord and master of the territory following the First World War, that *their* side was right and would be granted independence, and both sides had fought the British to prove that *their* claims were right. There were no winners, only losers and suffering. The intransigence of ancient beliefs, claims, and fears.

Yet Palestine in 1941 was also a refuge of last resort for thousands of Jews fleeing Nazi tyranny in the first actual stages of the Final Solution. Jewish migration to Palestine accelerated in 1933 with Hitler's rise to power. Between 1936 and 1939, tens of thousands of German Jews fled Nazi Germany for sanctuary in any country that would have them—few wanted them. These Jews made it to the United States, to some countries in Western Europe, and many made it to Palestine—*illegally!*

Bringing the Jewish refugees to British Palestine, under the restrictive immigration protocols of the infamous White Paper (a governmental decree meant to placate the Arabs by cutting off Jewish entry) required skill, courage, guile, and the ability to find holes in the enemy's security—the same prerequisites needed to be a commando. Volunteers from *Haganah,* mainly from the seaside Kibbutzim (agricultural collectives), were mobilized for these nightly attempts to smuggle a boatload of refugees onto the shores of Haifa, Atlit, Ness Ziona, and Tel Aviv—many only seconds ahead of Royal Navy guns and British military patrols. Working the refugee ships was dangerous work. Getting caught could mean a fifteen-year prison sentence or deportation. It could also mean a death sentence. Therefore, the cornerstone of each operation was simple: *Don't get caught!*

Because these *Haganah* ferrymen were lightly armed (one Turkish-era Mauser in a ten-man squad was considered a heavily armed formation) and could not hope to engage British forces and "survive," silence became their most effective weapon. Special buoyancy vests made of raincoats and scrap rubber were pieced together in Kibbutz workshops, to help bring the wooden rafts and small vessels to the refugees faster, and they could double as life vests in case exhausted refugees found themselves chest high in the Mediterranean. The ferrymen conducted elaborate reconnaissance patrols of virtually all the beach-front property in Palestine in order to select only the most advantageous landing zone possible. Once ashore, the *Haganah* operators would have to assume protective details and ensure that the human wave of refugees coming ashore would vanish into the night before arriving British forces could make arrests.

These smuggling vessels would, inevitably and so remarkably, become the cornerstone of the future Israeli Navy. The need for such ships acquainted the *Haganah,* Israel's pre-independence underground army, with the experience of ship procurement, plotting sea routes and covert drop points, and, inevitably, a hands-on look at the most professional navy in the world, the Royal Navy. "We Jews didn't have a great seafaring tradition," recalled Rear Admiral (Ret.) Yochai Bin-Nun, the first commander of the IDF's frogmen squad. "We weren't like the Lebanese who could trace their routes to the Phoenicians, nor were we Spaniards or English with a history of sea exploration. We were Jews and we made do with what we had—rickety boats and a few courageous men!"[1]

The British always possessed a grudging respect for the *Haganah*'s "naval" effort. The boats were piloted by brave SOBs who, if they were smarter, would never have boarded the rust-buckets in the first place. British sentiment followed, the men and women who met the vessels in midwater were of equal gumption. But, they were the enemy. And, if encountered, they were to be arrested and possibly shot.

17

In the months following the start of World War II, however, when Great Britain's interests in the Middle East suddenly became center stage, the Jews were no longer pesky nuisances with a cause—they were potential allies. Britain needed fearless men eager to participate in the war effort and capable of achieving a lot with very little. The *Haganah*, quid pro quo, was eager to get in on the war effort, too. They were eager to get combat experience for their men, get them arms and training, and to gain legitimacy and a bank account's worth of favors from the British that they could withdraw from at a later date. The marriage between the British and the *Haganah* was a natural.

Many senior British commanders in the Middle East were dead set against any cooperation with the *Haganah*—the Jews and the Arabs were the enemy, pure and simple, and not foreigners to be coddled like other elements of the colonial effort mobilized against the Axis. Such sentiments were even stronger in the ranks of the Royal Navy—they considered the Jews nothing more than pirates and criminals. Yet Britain's covert war in the Middle East was not run by stuffy shirt admirals and generals, but by eccentrics, professors, visionaries, and commandos. The Special Operations Executive (SOE) was the body running much of the intelligence and special operations war in the region, and Britain's spies had a lot of work for the *Haganah*.

In early 1940, the British SOE set up shop in a small pension in the Mediterranean port city of Haifa as an espionage OP (observation post) of sorts to begin gathering and analyzing data on the Germans and Italians in the Mediterranean. Great Britain at the time was in the middle of one its most disastrous seasons of the Second World War—defeat, retreat, and the Battle of Britain were the currency of the day. The war in Europe had headed south to the outer perimeter of the British Empire in North Africa and the Mediterranean, and it was clear to the British High Command that the Middle East would become an inevitable battleground in this global conflict. For the British, the loss of the Middle East, and the Suez Canal, meant loss of empire. Should the Germans reach Palestine, for the Jews this contingency signaled the end of a race. Although the

Jews of Palestine and the British had been at odds as a result of migration prior to the outbreak of the war, both parties had obvious reasons to set aside regional issues and concentrate on the task of survival. To the British, there was the paramount realization that everything that could be done in the fight against the advancing German forces *needed* to be done. The British, for so long masters at manipulating strategic alliances in order to advance the interests of the empire, were now thinking in terms of weeks and months. Whitehall realized that there would be trouble later on and that training and arming the *Haganah*—officers from which were rounded up by the authorities only days earlier—was a double-edged sword that might come back to haunt the empire in biting fashion. But British commanders on the ground, especially intelligence officers in the SOE and Foreign Office, realized that the Jews were the sole indigenous ally that the British had from the Mediterranean to the Persian Gulf. Of the Arabs, King Farouk of Egypt was a German sympathizer who hoped for a Nazi victory and the liberation of his country. Haj Amin al-Husseini, the Grand Mufti of Jerusalem, spent the war in Berlin as a guest of Hitler and the Waffen-SS; in Jerusalem, the Palestinians openly awaited their liberation by Abu Ali, the affectionate Arabic name for General Erwin Rommel, the Desert Fox.[2] Only Emir Abdullah of Trans-Jordan and his nephew Abdul-Illah of Iraq remained staunchly pro-British.

The Bedouins of Trans-Jordan, however, could not pose as Europeans or even German soldiers in a fifth-column effort should Palestine become the epicenter of the Middle Eastern theater of operations. The British needed the *Haganah,* and, as a result, and only as a result of this desperate need, a new and uncomfortable alliance was born.

From their modest hotel room with a view (eventually expanded into a suite and then a floor) atop Mt. Carmel in Haifa overlooking the bustling port of Haifa, the SOE set up shop; their objectives, to assemble intelligence, catch German espionage agents from the *Abwher,* and harass nearby enemy lines. The SOE crew dispatched to Palestine was an eccentric lot, to say the least; many *Haganah* officers

who worked with them viewed them as nothing short of
odd. They included Arnold Lawrence (T. E. Lawrence's
brother), almost as eccentric as his legendary brother,
"Lawrence of Arabia"; Nicholas Hammond, a Greek history professor at Cambridge; and Henry Barnes, an eccentric
soul with a wild and expansive imagination. From their
hotel room, the three, and the staff they'd soon assemble,
attended to their intelligence-gathering tasks by interviewing the thousands of recent refugees from Europe who
provided these trusting souls with insight into German rail
stations and seaports, as well as a virtual library of travel
documents and forms—all of which would later be replicated by MI-10 (British Military Intelligence) and the SOE
to be used by Allied agents that would later be transplanted
into Europe. The SOE officers also established a special
training camp, code-named Me-102, where German-
speaking Jewish agents could be trained for later infiltration
back into Nazi-occupied Europe.

Another one of the primary SOE objectives during those
early dark days of World War II was to harass the Vichy
French occupation of Lebanon and Syria. To achieve this
objective, the SOE established a powerful transmitter atop
Mt. Carmel from where French-speaking de Gaulle loyalists
spread propaganda into the barracks of Vichy troops serving in Beirut, Tyre, Tripoli, and Damascus. On the operational level, the SOE sent French and Arabic-speaking
Haganah operatives into the Levant to gather intelligence,
sabotage roadways, and set up the basis for a pro-Allied fifth
column. There were tremendous fears inside the policy-
making hallways at Whitehall in London that the Afrika
Korps would sail into the port of Beirut and move on
Palestine in a thrusted pincer movement from the north
and south. Operations in Lebanon became a British priority, though they couldn't be overt military moves that would
raise red flags in Berlin. A covert war was needed, and that
meant the Jewish operatives.

Two men who would engineer the military and intelligence cooperation between Jewish and British special oper-
ns elements were as diverse and separate on the
tine equation as could be. One was Yitzhak Sadeh,

Haganah special operations commander and burly Crimean who was known as much for his egalitarian genius as he was for his tall tales of wrestling bears in the Crimean forests. His partner was the SOE officer in charge of Palestine, RAF Squadron Leader Major William Parkins. Both men were of similar suspicious mindsets: Sadeh, born in Czarist Russia, had mistrust born into him; Parkins, a card-holding member of the "Old Boys' Network," wasn't the type to trust a man like Sadeh (not to mention to invite him to the officer's club for a glass of sherry). Nevertheless, the two men knew that they shared a common foe and that each needed the other—future considerations of a fight for independence were not even considered.

Among the most pressing priorities facing the SOE was the crippling of the Vichy economy—an economy driven (and war machine fueled) by the massive oil refinery along the coast at Tripoli. But Tripoli wasn't solely an economic target. It had ultrastrategic military importance as well.

At the time the raid on Tripoli was being planned, German intelligence agents had played a major role in the bloody coup of April 3, 1941, in Iraq in which the pro-Nazi Rashid Ali al-Gailani seized power in Baghdad. Pro-Nazi Iraqi rebels attacked British forces in country and fierce battles broke out throughout the country, especially surrounding the ultrastrategic Habaniyah air base where the British found themselves surrounded. The coup also presented the Germans with unique opportunities in creating a second front in the Near East against the British. Agents of the *Abwher,* German military intelligence, were parachuted into Iraq to help spread and intensify the armed resistance, and the Luftwaffe began bombing British fuel dumps, ammunition stores, and airfields. The British High Command feared that if the Luftwaffe could obtain the use of an airfield, such as one in Palmyra or Damascus, and obtain a localized supply of fuel, such as those pumped out by the Tripoli refinery, British forces in Iraq and British interests in Persia could be severely threatened.

Since Britain and Vichy France weren't yet involved in full-scale fighting (let alone small-scale hostilities), a sabotage raid, one perpetrated by deniable frogman, seemed ideal. Since the fall of 1940, the SOE had been training a small force of Jewish frogmen in Tel Aviv's Exhibition Park, situated just north of the city center. The training was rudimentary and fairly primitive, though designed for both intelligence and sabotage operations. British instructors, dive masters from both the Royal Navy and Royal Marines, taught these Jewish volunteers the A-to-Zs of naval special operations—long-range swimming, canoeing, underwater demolitions, cold-killing, map work, navigation, as well as other aspects of espionage activity. As Palestine was awash with espionage agents from all sides (from *Abwher* agents to Arab mercenaries to Polish military intelligence agents who were proactively anti-Jewish), the training at Exhibition Park was carried out with incredible security. Only those involved with the project were allowed in and out of the facility, and the Jewish volunteers participating in the training were forbidden from telling family members where they were and obviously what they were doing—even though many of the volunteers lived but a few blocks from where they were being trained.

In all, forty men were trained for the raid on Tripoli. They were eager, zealous, and capable. The brunt of their instruction was in the demolitions sphere; the planting of explosives, the hiding of explosives, even the improvised production of explosive materials. These men were to be *saboteurs* in the classic sense of the word. They were to come ashore secretly, reach their targets, plant explosives charges, and return to their mother vessel before the installations blew up. Classic sabotage. Classic World War II commando work. But not formally being part of an army and not being in uniform, these men risked a very certain fate if captured by Vichy forces. They were all indoctrinated in the type of torture they'd receive and all knew that capture meant certain execution. Although never confirmed, some reports indicate that they were issued cyanide caplets "just in case" capture was imminent.

It is believed (still never confirmed by the British, though) that this force was not being trained solely for operations against Vichy targets in Lebanon—the frugal British tended not to invest such sums in forces with only a limited regional operation ability. Instead, the frogmen were being prepped for operations in the Adriatic (with the British Special Air Service) and even possibly for western and northern Europe. There could be no future missions without one in the bag, and the raid on Tripoli was slated for the spring of 1941 at the height of the Allied covert offensive in Lebanon. The British were adamant about the use of indigenous forces for the operation to somehow convince the Vichy and Germans that a guerrilla and fifth-column army was laying in wait.

For the British High Command, the "forty" were a convenient and expendable force. Little rumblings would be made in Whitehall should the force be eliminated, and sending Jewish volunteers was a lot more cost effective than sending Royal Marines or other Commonwealth units. For the *Haganah,* however, this was an opportunity to perform, experiment, and strike a blow against the Axis Powers. It was an opportunity not to be missed.

The officer in charge of the "twenty-three boatmen" was a striking English officer and a gentleman, Major Anthony Palmer, a rising star in the SOE. Palmer was everything the *Haganah* volunteers were not. Oxford-educated, Palmer was polish to the volunteers' swagger and zeal. Palmer could always be located at the Exhibition Park training ground by the sweet aroma drifting out of his mahogany pipe, and he worked twenty-hour days supervising the instruction and meeting with SOE representatives concerning intelligence reports obtained about possible targets in Tripoli. Affectionate of the Jews and their energies, Palmer didn't consider the *Haganah* volunteers a footnote at all. He admired their desperate energy. It was an energy he felt was contagious.

For the forty *Haganah* volunteers on this dangerous and secretive duty against the Axis, working with Palmer and the British was nothing new. Since the riots of 1936, when Palestine erupted into a civil war of Arab guerrilla raids, Jewish proactive responses and the Commonwealth forces stuck in the middle, a covert arrangement existed between the Jewish and British forces that the Palestinian Arabs, for lack of better words, were a common enemy that needed to be dealt with through unconventional means. Unconven-

tional means for the British meant Captain Orde Wingate, a
veteran of the Eritrea campaign and a man with a lust for
the eccentric and a genius for the covert that made the
British think him just mad enough to want him to work in
Palestine; his dedication to the bible, and the Children of
Israel, would convince *Haganah* commanders, mistrustful
of even their own, that this bible-thumping British officer
was truly a friend. Wingate, in fact, became known as
Ha'Yedid, "The Friend," and with British funds and rifles,
he organized a joint British-Jewish retaliatory patrol known
as the Special Night Squad, or SNS. The SNS was a
remarkable creation—a joint counter-terrorist task force
with the British Army and the underground *Haganah*. But
Wingate was a remarkable man—as Churchill would say of
him, "A man of genius who might very well have become a
man of destiny." Chaim Weizmann, Israel's first president,
called him "Lawrence of Judea."[3] He was an odd chap with
strokes of insanity laced with zealous biblical devotion who
was one of the most underrated military thinkers of his
time. His superiors, more than anything, thought of him as
bizarre and a loose cannon. Even Jewish leaders were wary
of his marked penchant for eccentric behavior; Jewish
Agency diplomat Abba Eban even writes of a formal meeting in which he found Wingate, sitting in his hotel room
stark naked, stroking his body down with a coarse hair
brush.[4] The British, however, knew that only Wingate was
able—and willing—to work with the Jews, and with tacit
British approval, Wingate trained his men in the art of light
infantry strikes and decisive offensive action. He instilled in
them the very fabric needed to comprehend commando
thought, and an ethic of command that was forged in fire
into the heart of many young *Haganah* commanders, the
men who would guide the IDF through its first thirty years.
Wingate taught his troopers to use the enemy's weakness as
the attacker's strength—an emphasis was placed on nighttime operations. Platoon commanders were given incredible independence under Wingate, and all units were to be
led into battle with the highest-ranking officers charging at
the helm; Wingate's principles would become IDF law years
later. For the *Haganah*, Wingate's SNS and the commando

operations mounted achieved two all-important military objectives—they made a quantitative disadvantage on the battlefield evaporate into a qualitative edge, and they instilled fear and trepidation in the heart of the enemy.

Among Palmer's forty volunteers were many veterans of the SNS.[5] Palmer wasn't as eccentric as Wingate, and not as charismatic. But he was a British officer who possessed the respect and admiration of the men he commanded. Although the raid on Tripoli was to be the first strike in the commando force's operations, Palmer did test out his combatants with several smaller sabotage missions in Greek ports, and against German shipping in Crete.[6] The missions in the Aegean were meant to see firstly if the Jewish frogmen were up to the task at hand and secondly to see if any of the men he saw as owning unique potential were also equipped with the elements of command. The operations in Greece and Crete also served as a "hot LZ" dress rehearsal for the men. If these missions could succeed, then so, too, could Tripoli. In fact, rather ambitious plans were thought of for the SOE's force of Jewish frogman. An energetic plan to have the Jewish seaborne sappers disrupt German supply efforts was penciled in, calling for the force to sink a Romanian freighter in the Danube. Other plans called for Palmer's force to act as kayak-racing squads inflicting a sabotage spree against river targets throughout German-occupied Europe. For the mission against Lebanon, Palmer knew he had to check his notes and calculations carefully. Equipped with an old coast-guard launch, the H.M.S. *Sea Lion* was large enough to barely hold twenty-four men.

British intelligence and operations staff analysis called for the raid to be carried out sometime in May 1941—D-day was set for May 18, 1941. In the weeks prior to the raid, the training intensified, too. Swimming trials went from pushing the envelope of endurance to smashing through it. Small arms training began to intensify, as well, as did instruction in how to remove a sentry with a dagger, boulder, piece of wood, or fist. French was taught at a brisk pace, as was Arabic with a specific Lebanese flair; most of the volunteers already spoke the colloquial Arabic as well as their Palestinian neighbors. The training was provided to all involved—

25

even the H.M.S. *Sea Lion's* "pilot," Katriel Yafa, a first-generation seafarer and *Haganah* captain, and the ship's machinists and engine drivers, became full-fledged commandos.

A week before the ship was set to depart Palestine, Yitzhak Sadeh was secretly smuggled into their training facility to see the men—many of whom he knew he'd be seeing for the last time. The group, wearing their filthy fatigues stained with perspiration, grease, and gunpowder residue, assembled in the typical Israeli circle, sitting on the ground with their legs crossed, with Sadeh, affectionately called "The Old Man," standing in the middle. As he caressed his scraggly white beard, Sadeh looked into the eyes of the volunteers, caressed the revolver he wore on his hip, and then said, "Firstly, you aren't connected to any group or organization. You are going out without any identity cards or documents. If, God forbid, you get caught, you mustn't reveal who you are or who sent you. The British Army will deny any knowledge of you and will not stand up for you. You will not become POWs. You will be considered spies, and suffer with what we all know happens to spies in wartime."[7]

Sadeh was a boisterous man whose speeches were usually interlaced with jokes, some off-color, and macho calls to arms. This time, however, he was somber and deadly serious. Spies arrested were tortured, beaten, then shot or hung. No trials, no prison, no POW camps and Red Cross package. The silence in the room was such that the sound of a cigarette's paper burning was the only noise heard. All eyes focused on Sadeh with a tunnel vision reserved for only the most dire situations. "We are not children and everyone knows here what the dangers are," Sadeh continued, "but we all know the importance of the operation. If we succeed, it will be a harsh blow to the Germans and at the same time prove our military abilities. Conditions in the field will be as rough as they can be but the order is to carry out the mission successfully and that's exactly what you'll do and what we expect you to do."

For the next two days, the twenty-six-year-old Palmer

made his final selection—only those who could swim the fastest, shoot the best, and were most comfortable with the idea of carrying around with them ten-kilogram packs of TNT were selected. Secrecy was absolute and security around their departure facility the tightest it had ever been at the Haifa facility. It bothered many of the volunteers that they couldn't write home, or even hop in a lorry for a quick ride home to say goodbye to their parents, siblings, and sweethearts; some, even, lived only a few blocks away in the northern suburbs of Tel Aviv. It cast a cloud over the mission and created a morale problem. Less than twenty-four hours before the *Sea Lion* was to set sail for the shores of Tripoli, Sadeh returned to Haifa. He ordered each of the twenty-three volunteers into a conference hall and interviewed each of them individually. "The chances of returning from the mission you are about to embark on are minimal. Do you still volunteer?" Sadeh received twenty-three responses of "I volunteer."

The H.M.S. *Sea Lion* set sail for the Lebanese coast on the night of May 18, 1941. It departed the Palestine shoreline silently and slowly and with no fanfare. It never made it to Tripoli, it never radioed in a mayday, and it was never heard from again. SOE operations officers, following the charted progression of the vessel, were aghast with anxious fear about what happened to Major Palmer and his Jewish frogmen. At first, they feared the boat had exploded as a result of an accident involving the load of high explosives carried by the frogmen. Then, as the days stretched into weeks, the fear came over the SOE's Palestine HQ that the ship had been boarded and the operators seized. Indeed, rumors soon filtered through the Levantine pipeline that several Palestinian Jews and a British officer were tried and executed in a Gendarmerie facility in Tripoli. The most logical explanation of the *Sea Lion*'s disappearance was that an Italian submarine, patrolling the shores of Palestine (as Mussolini's Navy often did), encountered the ship and simply placed a torpedo across its bow.

For months, the families of the twenty-three were kept in the cruel world of military secrecy. They were not informed that their loved ones were missing, nor were they even informed that the men were no longer in Palestine. They were told nothing and expected to remain silent. Only in November 1942, more than eighteen months later, were the families discreetly told that the men were considered missing. Even to this day, what exactly happened to the twenty-three Jewish commandos and Major Palmer remains a mystery historians are still trying to figure out. Although no remains were ever found, there were reports that twenty-three Jewish sailors were seen in the southern Italian POW camp by other Allied prisoners. Following the Allied invasion of Sicily, the POWs were moved north and then transferred to the hands of the German military, who, it is believed, murdered the surviving members of the crew. While this remains only a theory about what happened to Major Palmer and his crew, it is supported by evidence—including eyewitness accounts. Two years after the ship disappeared, the head of the political office of the Jewish Agency, Moshe Sharett, wrote his liaison in British intelligence a letter that included the following:

"SEA LION" OPERATION.

A Maltese soldier, of the name of Thomas CASTOR, who was a prisoner-of-war in Italy and escaped, arrived in ALEXANDRIA about three to four weeks ago and inquired there whether there were any Palestinian soldiers from TEL AVIV about. He met a Palestinian Jew, of the name of Ezra ROZEN, who is serving with the Royal Navy in ALEXANDRIA, and told him that in this prisoner-of-war camp where he was detained, No. 65 H.P.M. 3454, there were twenty-one Palestinian sailors who, for some reason, wore civilian's clothes, and were treated with considerable more harshness than the other prisoners. In particular, they were allowed no contact with the outside world, either through the Red X or any other method. CASTOR gave also a detailed description of the senior member of that party, and the description tallies with that of the Skipper of the "SEA LION" 10.6.43.[8]

The saga of the *Sea Lion* was a bitter beginning for the *Haganah*'s naval effort and one that remains a source of great mystery to this very day. The courage of the crew and the boldness of the mission cannot be lost in the fact that Israel's first attempt at naval special warfare had ended disastrously.

The chapter of the twenty-three boatmen is a sad one laced with mystery, and it is especially tragic in light of the fact that two days before the men set sail for Tripoli, Yitzhak Sadeh announced the creation of the *Haganah*'s elite "Strike Companies," or *Pal'mach*, as they were known in Hebrew. The *Pal'mach* was everything that Major Palmer's commandos weren't—an "overt" statement of Jewish and British special forces cooperation against the Axis powers. The British, fearing defeat in Egypt, had begun to contemplate Palestine becoming the next major Middle Eastern battleground. The men—and women—of the *Haganah*, on the other hand, had very specific skills that the British couldn't replicate and motivations the British could hardly imagine.

One of the reasons why Major Palmer's forty-man team was such a secret was not as much a security measure to keep the unit covert from the Germans, but rather to keep it a secret from the Palestinian Arabs—most of whom, incidentally, had very pro-Nazi sympathies. As lords and rulers of Palestine, Great Britain faced a thankless task—especially in light of the greater world conflict. To keep peace in a most troublesome colony, the British needed to placate the Arabs in order not to risk a Palestinian front in the midst of a war in which forces could not be tied down policing meddlesome factions. With so many forces in the Middle East, however, from Iraq to Egypt, the Arabs were a far more important voice to consider than that of the 400,000 Jews in Palestine. In 1939, to placate Arab fears about a massive tidal wave of German Jews seeking a safe haven in Palestine, the British government issued its infamous White Paper, severely curtailing all Jewish entry into the region at the time when it was needed most. Radicals inside the Jewish community of Palestine considered the White Paper a declaration of all-out war against the Jewish

29

people, and underground groups like the Stern Gang even offered their services to the German and Italian intelligence services.

By May 1941, just as the H.M.S. *Sea Lion* was prepared to set sail, the British High Command in Palestine realized that the White Paper was buying them more grief than strategic depth. The Germans were nearing the gates of Cairo, the *Abwher,* German Military Intelligence, was parachuting agents into the Judean desert equipped with gold bars and explosives to start an indigenous Palestinian fifth column primed for an Afrika Korps invasion, and Haj Amin al-Husseini, the Grand Mufti of Jerusalem, was a guest of Hitler in Berlin. British officers were sanctioned to prepare evacuation plans for the garrison in Palestine, and an airfield atop Mt. Carmel and the nearby port of Haifa were primed as staging points for a Holy Land Dunkirk departure.

The British needed to buy time; they needed help and they realized that they needed the Jewish fighters of the *Haganah.* The Jewish Agency, the quasi-political body overseeing affairs in Palestine, had lobbied the British for a full-fledged Jewish Brigade—a conventional trained force that could assist the forces of the crown in the defense of Palestine. The British, not wanting to train an army they might have to face after the war, balked, though agreed to sponsor, train, and equip a Jewish guerrilla force that could defend the "Jewish interests" in Palestine from Arab and Nazi attack. The force would become known as the *Pal'mach,* the Hebrew acronym for "Strike Companies," and was formed on May 14, 1941. For both the British and the *Haganah,* it would become a truly Middle Eastern marriage of convenience. The British would have at its disposal a force of highly motivated individuals who, because of their superb language abilities, could become scouts, spies, and saboteurs, and the *Haganah* would get the military training, experience, and background needed later for the fight for Israeli independence. The *Pal'mach* would train three times as many men and women as the British authorized, and for every weapon issued, the *Pal'mach* would steal two from British armories; additional weapons were liberated from Free French bases, as well as from Commonwealth units, like the Australians, who were fond of the Jewish cause and whose friendly and gregarious nature made them favorites of the locals.

The man who was charged with leading the *Pal'mach* was Yitzhak Sadeh, and Sadeh designed the "Strike Companies" along guerrilla lines—the largest *Pal'mach* unit was to be a company with six companies altogether. *Pal'mach* commandos were trained in lightning assaults, demolitions, cold-killing, reconnaissance, and espionage work. Less than a month after the Strike Companies were formed, they found themselves in the vanguard of the British invasion of Syria and Lebanon, preceding the Allied effort with nighttime reconnaissance and sabotage forays to destroy bridges and other Vichy communication lines. When, on June 8, the Allied invasion of Lebanon was launched, the *Pal'mach* was attached to the Australian 7th Division and served with distinction as scouts, translators, and demolitions experts. Many of Israel's future leaders began in the *Pal'mach,* including Moshe Dayan, who lost an eye to a Vichy rifle round.

The *Pal'mach* would also field special operations units within its framework—language-based units meant for daring missions deep behind enemy lines. These units included *Ha'Machlaka Ha'Aravit,* or "Arab Platoon," a force of volunteers made up of Jews from throughout the Middle East who were taught to act, think, behave, and operate like Arabs. Their mission was intended to be deep-cover and dangerous. A "German Platoon," *Ha'Machlaka Ha'Germanit,* was formed to serve as a fifth-column force and consisted of fair-haired recent arrivals from Germany, Austria, and Switzerland—anyone who spoke German as his native tongue and who didn't look Jewish. Operators in the German Platoon were to infiltrate behind German lines dressed as Afrika Korps (even SS) personnel, in order to gather intelligence and sabotage key installations. In their Jezreel Valley training facility, the operators spoke only German—speaking Hebrew or any other language was grounds for being booted out of the unit. The men trained solely with German weapons such as the Mauser rifle and MP-38 submachine gun, and were taught Wehrmacht slang with religious conviction, and expected to know everything about being a soldier—from rank and insignia to salary wages and even the location of the most popular brothels in Germany. For many in the *Haganah,* it was odd to sanction these Jewish refugees disappearing into the woods for a few weeks only to have them come out as *Deutscher Soldaten,* but the novel approach was wildly successful. Some of the brightest pupils of the "German Platoon" went on beyond the borders of Palestine. They served with Captain David Stirling's SAS and Long Range Desert Platoon in the North African desert conducting hit-and-run commando attacks, intelligence-gathering raids, and even an audacious plot to blow up Field Marshal Rommel's desert HQ. Other "German Platoon" volunteers were sent to Allied POW camps where they were mingled with actual German soldiers in order to gather intelligence on German units and troop locations.

A "Balkan Platoon" was also formed and it saw action alongside British SAS and SOE units operating in the Aegean Sea and in Yugoslavia. A "Romanian Platoon" was also rumored to have existed, sanctioned specifically and solely for a commando raid against the massive Ploesti oil fields.

As the *Pal'mach* grew and expanded, so, too, did the scope of Yitzhak Sadeh's growing overt underground army. By 1943, the *Pal'mach* had managed to train over 1,000 fighters and equip them with issued, confiscated, and stolen weapons. It was clear to many in the *Haganah* hierarchy that the *Pal'mach* had become a military elite and an embryonic seed of what would eventually become the Israeli military. The *Pal'mach,* therefore, needed to be nurtured and expanded into a multipurpose arm. A fledgling air arm of the *Pal'mach* was created in 1943; known as the *Pal'Avir,* the small volunteer force consisted of glider pilots and a few Palestinian-Jewish RAF pilots. A naval arm of the *Pal'mach* was also sanctioned. Known as the *Pal'yam,* or "Sea Companies," the force had no warships or coastal artillery. In fact, the *Pal'yam* wasn't a defensive entity at all.

It was a strike unit designed to hit at sea with the only muscle the Jews had at the time—brave men armed with explosive charges. They had no underwater equipment to speak of, and wet suits were heavy woolen sweaters and knickers coated with a concoction of thick motor oil and hardened chicken fat. They also had no conventional explosives that they could deploy in battle; their equipment was a potpourri of homemade gear and volatile ideas put together in basement bomb factories. *Pal'yam* commanders had hoped for missions against German and Italian targets throughout the Mediterranean. Instead, in 1943, the British, no longer needing the Jewish strike companies in a war the Allies were now winning on their own in a theater of operations that had suddenly taken a back seat, ended their relationship with the *Haganah* and demanded that the *Pal'mach* return all its arms. An underground—hence illegal—organization, the *Pal'yam* braced itself for the inevitable war of independence it would be waging against the British and the Arabs. The cut of its mettle would be tested against the mightiest navy in the world at the time—the Royal Navy.

When dealing with a state yet to be born, and an army yet to be established, the leaders of the *Haganah* realized that the best they could do in 1943 was to lay the foundations of a conventional military entity on paper and in the field, and let due course and divine intervention take care of the rest. A naval service was needed, as Palestine's elongated coastline dictated that a future Jewish State would need to have a powerful navy to safeguard the coast from Gaza to Rosh Haniqra slicing into the Lebanese border. But navies needed ships, and the *Pal'yam* had but a few seagoing vessels; it was a volunteer force, but according to one of the founding members of the force, Izzy Rahav, "If they needed you, you were volunteered into the unit."[9] It was a meager start, but the *Haganah* would learn an invaluable lesson about naval warfare by the very fact that it was pitted, in the subsequent campaign to smuggle in refugees under British blockade, against the Royal Navy.

If there is one trait that the "have nots" all have in common is that they know how to maximize their meager resources in an efficient, effective, and innovative manner. In this aspect, the *Haganah* was truly a "have not" that was eager to learn. *Haganah* commanders realized that the Royal Navy would have to be neutralized on two important fronts once the Second World War ended—easing their blockade against Jewish immigration and finding gaps in their defenses, so that ships carrying arms and ammunition could make it to Haifa harbor. It was a daunting task and a challenge that the German Navy, the *Kreigsmarine,* had not done effectively, and, *Haganah* commanders pondered, the Nazis had scores of submarines. Studying the naval campaign of the Mediterranean as best they could, *Haganah* officers soon realized that there was only one Axis navy to successfully deploy special warfare operators against the Royal Navy and that was the Italian's famed Underwater Sabotage Unit, the legendary *Decima Flotiglia MAS.* The 10th Flotilla MAS became legendary and *Pal'yam* officers began studying their tactics and abilities with great interest. Ominously and luckily for the *Haganah,* the *Pal'yam* had opted to emulate one of the world's most innovative and effective naval special warfare units to ever strike against conventional shipping in the history of modern naval warfare.

By March 1945, the war in Europe was grinding to its inevitable end as German forces were pushed east by the advancing British and American armies in Belgium and Holland, and west by the unstoppable legions of the Soviet Red Army. The horrors of the Nazi Final Solution soon began to become evident as concentration camps, death camps, and forced labor camps were liberated. The survivors, those liberated from the doorstep of death and now called "Displaced Persons" (or DPs) by the Allies, sought any and all routes away from western Europe. Many found refuge in the United States, many more sought for a stake in the building of a Jewish homeland. A homeland in Palestine.

On V-E day, as hundreds of thousands gathered in London to hear Prime Minister Churchill announce the end of the war in Europe, David Ben-Gurion, in London for a

Jewish Agency Executive Council, marked the day as a very sad one.[10] Of the seven million Jews who had lived in Nazi-occupied Europe during the war, only one million had survived and there was little being done by the Allies to bring the survivors to Palestine. Ben-Gurion demanded that the British grant emergency entry visas to 100,000 of the survivors, but his call fell on deaf ears.

The only way to get the refugees into Palestine was by guile, by stealth, and by breaking through the British blockade. That meant the use of force. Former wartime allies were about to become enemies.

World opinion supported the Jewish survivors in their quest to reach Palestine, but Great Britain wasn't as concerned about world sympathy as it was with its crumbling empire, especially as chunks of the realm disintegrated into independent entities on virtually a daily basis. Palestine, to the British, wasn't as strategic as it was a tinderbox, and the British were determined to keep the 100 million Arabs in its empire complacent. Complacency, of course, meant that Jewish refugees were not permitted entry in Palestine and this policy of exclusion needed to be public. Destroyers, cruisers, and coast guard craft of the Royal Navy sealed off the Mediterranean shores of the mandate with a virtually hermetic blockade. Ships, or rickety contraptions of welded steel and paint meant to pass themselves off as ships, chartered by the *Haganah* to ferry the survivors to Palestine were often intercepted on the high seas, boarded, and usually forced to land in Cyprus. In Cyprus, the refugees were huddled into outdoor detention camps, closed in by barbed wire and guards carrying rifles and patrolling perimeters with dogs, where conditions cruelly resembled the geographic characters of Auschwitz, Bergen-Belsen, and Dachau. Warehousing the survivors in concentration-camp-like conditions outraged the *Haganah* High Command and it prompted them to take immediate and decisive action. *Pal'mach* founder Yitzhak Sadeh, "The Old Man," had thought of mounting attacks against patrol craft in Haifa, in the north, and in Jaffa, just south of Tel Aviv. Sadeh did not want the *Pal'mach* operators to carry any side arms or even knives (just in case they were stopped by a British patrol), just homemade incendiary devices that would destroy a ship. Two volunteers entered Jaffa harbor, found a small spot to enter the water where a searchlight or guard was not watching, and placed an improvised explosive device near the stern of two British patrol vessels. The job complete, they emerged from the water and went to the trendy "Kasit" cafe on Tel Aviv's fashionable Dizengoff Street to report the success of the mission to their local commanders.

The next morning, radio reports confirmed the destruction of two vessels in Jaffa harbor. Sadeh was so pleased with the raid that he ordered the *Pal'mach* and *Pal'yam* to raise an underwater sabotage unit. On November 2, 1945, with no swimmers, no fast boats, no underwater gear, and an improvised explosive factory that even the most optimistic *Pal'mach* officers were sure would blow up at any minute, the *Pal'mach* entered the naval special warfare business on a full-time basis.

On the shores just due south of the old Roman city of Caesarea, located south of Haifa along the Mediterranean coast, the *Haganah* established a special sub-unit of the *Pal'yam* that would, in essence, declare open warfare against the Royal Navy. War against the Royal Navy meant sabotage, and that meant men brave enough to pit themselves against the mightiest navy in the world. The unit that the *Haganah* secretly created on paper was known as *Yechidat Ha'Habala Ha'Yamit* (or "Underwater Sabotage Unit"), and the one man brave enough not only to attack British shipping, but also lead the unit that would conduct a naval campaign of sabotage and destruction against the Royal Navy, was a tall and lanky foot soldier named Yochai Bin-Nun.

Yochai Bin-Nun was born to lead, many of his contemporaries would later comment. He was quiet, confident, and capable—the prerequisite in the *Haganah* criteria for a man destined to go places. Born in Haifa in 1924, Bin-Nun volunteered for *Haganah* service at a very young age and was a full-fledged operator in the *Pal'mach* in 1942 serving in the upper Galilee area and Jezreel Valley. In 1944, upon his release from active duty while en route home to his flat in Jerusalem's Beit Ha'Kerem neighborhood, a friend convinced him to "try out" for a new unit being formed along the beach near Caesarea. A week later, a man who had been deemed to be one of the most capable infantry squad leaders in the *Pal'mach,* but more importantly, as Bin-Nun would later recall, "I was a sapper with a keen knowledge of explosives." He would leave the relative comfort of nighttime raids and fire-fights to soon immerse himself in grease and oils, learning how to protect his body against the frigid bite of the cold sea. He was a man who had been converted and would remain in "naval service" for the next thirty years, rising to the rank of commander of the IDF/Navy.

The "Underwater Sabotage Unit" was a motley assembly of fishermen, swimmers, and adventurers—the adventurers, some in the *Haganah* hierarchy would observe, bordered on the insane in terms of the risks they were willing to take. The men assembled under great secrecy and with little logistics, and even fewer supplies. Nearby *kibbutzim* supplied them with food. Local clothing manufactures, nearby fishing villages, and stolen supplies provided them with their rafts, suits, and basic underwater equipment, and *Haganah* weapons and explosives workshops provided them with improvised explosive devices—the tools of the trade by which the war of revenge and respect would be waged against the Royal Navy. Anti-shipping limpet mines, the kind that Italian and British frogmen had successfully used during the Second World War, were not stored in Palestine by the British Army, and as a result could not be stolen by unit operators "foraging" British bases for supplies. Limpet mines were such a select item that *Haganah* agents working in Europe, had trouble in stealing them, as well. As a result, the explosive devices to be used by the unit had to be built by scratch, prepared in *Haganah* workshops by part-time volunteers who in their regular civilian jobs might have been anything from accountants to bakers. The traditional limpet was a remarkable example of destructive ingenuity. A metal plate fastened to six small magnetic legs (many called them "explosive cockroaches"), limpets were to be attached, by their six small magnetic legs, to the hull of a ship and then activated, with a delayed acetone fuse, for later detonation. The Americans, British, Italians, and

Germans—and every other nation that built limpets—
employed facets of industry to produce the devices under
safe and regulated circumstances. "The *Haganah* was just
happy to find enough explosives and material to produce
the damn things," once commented the IDF's chief historian. "Safety checks and product control was not even a part
of the equation."

Bin-Nun was less concerned about the safety of the
devices as he was about their reliability; danger was, after
all, an element of the job that each of the divers knew and
understood. Reaching a Royal Navy vessel and evading
British sentries was half the battle and placing a device on
the bow of a destroyer only to have it not explode was a
scenario to be avoided at all costs.

Although officially a sub-unit of the *Pal'mach's* 4th Battalion, the one reserved for special operations and
intelligence-gathering, the underwater sabotage unit was by
pure definition an independent entity. Training for the
twenty-man all-volunteer unit was lengthy, excruciating,
and remarkably primitive. With very primitive civilian-
purchased underwater equipment, unit divers had to endure the unforgiving surf of the Mediterranean and swim
great distances in order to reach *Pal'yam* vessels off shore
being used as practice targets. In order to add a sense of
realism to the training exercises, as if swimming underwater
with ten kilograms of unstable explosives wasn't realistic
enough, Bin-Nun ordered the maneuvers in waters that
British coast guard craft routinely patrolled. Knowing that
the Royal Navy was usually nearby gave the divers increased incentive to stick to the operational plans and to
reach their target quickly and undetected. To add to the
masquerade, the "target" ship was actually a fishing vessel.
Fish caught that day in training were later eaten back at
Caesarea. It was all very pragmatic—all very *Haganah*.

As Bin-Nun and company trained and perfected their
skills, the British scored a major success against the growing
number of Jewish refugees being smuggled into Palestine
when the Royal Navy seized the *Haganah* ship *Berl Katzen-
elson,* a rickety old freighter that had seen better days and
surely an easier cargo. The British brought the ship to Haifa

and then transported its human cargo, nearly 2,000 refugees, to interment camps in Cyprus. The 4th Battalion responded by attacking British police and radar facilities, but the attacks only strengthened the British resolve to seize more ships and intern more refugees. By the summer of 1946, the number of Jewish refugees being interned by the British in Cyprus swelled to nearly 20,000; almost weekly, Royal Navy vessels were stopped, turned around, and brought to Cyprus. The successful transport of the illegals *(Ma'apilim)* to Palestine required breaking through the British naval blockade, a task assigned to the *Pal'yam*. A major training facility was established at Kibbutz Sdot Yam near Caesarea to instruct *Pal'yam* personnel to operate refugee ships, as well as counter British ships attempting to intercept them. Many ships were intercepted, and their "human" cargo interned in detention camps in Cyprus. Nevertheless, the *Pal'yam* crews displayed exemplary skill and courage, especially against British boarding parties, and succeeded in bringing to Palestine thousands of future Israelis. The *Haganah,* the Jewish Agency, and the *Mossad Le'Alyiah Bet,* the clandestine organization that supervised the smuggling of Jews into Palestine, had purchased and chartered vessels throughout the southern Mediterranean and had filled them to capacity and beyond with refugees eager to reach the shores of Palestine. But with the Royal Navy so successful against any attempt to breach the blockade, dispatching the ships was pointless. Pressure had to be brought to bear against British naval forces, but in the rear, where they felt safe and impervious. Bin-Nun got the order. Attack the Royal Navy.

At first, ground targets were mounted to drive a small wedge into the now almost hermetic British blockade of the Mediterranean. On June 17, 1946, the *Pal'mach* mounted an incredibly audacious nationwide operation when it blew up thirteen bridges connecting Palestine to the rest of the mandate. At the same time, Bin-Nun's squad was called upon to blow up a rail tunnel in southern Lebanon used by the British military traffic heading to northern Israel.[11] Bin-Nun had mobilized the men that would be called upon for the job, he had prepared indigenous explosive devices to be used to collapse a tunnel, and he had figured out a way to sail up the coast in order to reach the target. But, unfortunately for Bin-Nun, the raid was eventually scrubbed.

The "Night of the Bridges," as the raid of June 17 was known, sparked the British into full-fledged action. On what became known as "Black Sabbath," British forces and police agents arrested most of the *Haganah*'s top leadership, virtually crippling underground activity against the British-mandate forces. The only unit still operational was the *Pal'yam* (whose leaders had evaded the roundup) and Bin-Nun's underwater unit. After all, as one of the squad would later say, just because the top bosses were in prison didn't mean that the survivors wouldn't be coming.

With the help of increased naval assets assigned to the eastern Mediterranean and additional radar stations built along the coast, the Royal Navy was scoring increased successes against the *Haganah* refugee ships. In August alone, they stopped and captured four ships and interned nearly 10,000 refugees. They had even mobilized a massive naval flotilla, made up of surplus American-made "Liberty" ships, to transport the refugees from Haifa to Cyprus on an around-the-clock ferry service.

Attacking bridges and radar stations was good for getting the British garrison commander upset and for warranting nasty telegrams from Whitehall, but to stop the explosion of the refugees required a proactive and decisively inventive naval response. At first, the unit tried to damage a British ship by having arrested refugees smuggle explosives on board and detonate the device far from the civilian holding areas. The first ship targeted was the H.M.S. *Empire Heywood,* but the amount of explosives carried on board was small, and the damage virtually nonexistent. The failed attack angered Bin-Nun and it caused the British to take notice. The Royal Navy realized that it was only a matter of time before the Jews, a foe whose ingenuity and resourcefulness they truly—though grudgingly—respected tried something a bit more innovative. Overnight, security around Royal Navy vessels in Haifa grew from routine to stringent. Royal Marine commandos, in their characteristic green berets, patrolled the port and dock areas with orders to shoot on sight any signs of suspicious characters swimming in the nearby waters or walking near Royal Navy vessels. Even the Royal Navy's legendary underwater EOD dive-master, Lieutenant Colonel Lionel Crabb,* was rushed to Palestine to help secure the fleet.[12]

The "naval" campaign in the waters off Palestine was pure tit-for-tat. The heightened British security response and the failed attack on the *Heywood* only strengthened Bin-Nun's resolve to strike out at a significant British naval target. Scanning the port for their perch midway up on Mt. Carmel in the Hadar section of Haifa, Bin-Nun noticed a Liberty ship, a large vessel of 12,000 tons, moored a bit away from the remaining ships close to the opening to the sea. The ship, that intelligence would later reveal to be the H.M.S. *Empire Rival,* was just isolated enough to be sabo-taged without compromising the security of the frogmen that would pull the assignment; unit divers "went" on each and every operation with the knowledge that there was a 99.9 percent chance that they would not be returning.[13]

The *Empire Rival* was clearly an ideal target—the suc-cessful destruction of which would clearly rock British confidence, morale, and its ability to carry on unhindered with the expulsion campaign. Making it even a more attractive target was the fact that a Royal Navy destroyer had moored aside it and was there for the taking, as well. But attacking a fully manned destroyer, an attack with almost as many political implications as the bombing on July 22, 1946, of the King David Hotel by Menachem Begin's *Irgun* underground, was a decision left for the politicians. High-ranking Jewish Agency and *Haganah* offi-cials were dead-set against sinking a British destroyer—such an act was deemed far too risky. *Pal'mach* commander Yigal Alon, however, thought enough of the intriguing planned operation to invite Nachum Sarig, the *Haganah* deputy commander, to do a personal reconnaissance overview of the *Empire Rival* from their midcity observation post overlook-ing the port. Sarig did not authorize the mission, but Alon was eager to see if the newly formed unit was worth its salt. "Go ahead," he said, "I take full responsibility."[14]

One of the unit's scroungers, a necessary position to fill

when forming any special operations force, was the legendary Haim Zinger, who was known as the man of a thousand patents in the unit; he was also an expert in building explosive devices and obtaining the raw materials for pyrotechnics and explosives. For this mission, though, Zinger, by hook and by crook, was able to get his hands on an actual "genuine-article" British-produced Royal Navy limpet mine. Limpet mines were scarce and Zinger warned Bin-Nun "not to waste it."

The two-man team selected by Bin-Nun to carry out the *Empire Rival* attack consisted of Moshe Lifson, a hearty soul who enjoyed being challenged by the elements and by British patrols, and a young firebrand named Izzy Rahav. Confident, strong, and with a will that was considered stronger than iron, he was one of those volunteers in the sabotage unit that many in the *Haganah* considered "far too motivated." Motivation was a plus, but capability is what saw missions through and Bin-Nun had the absolute confidence in Rahav's ability to lead an operation and to return from it alive.

On the night of August 21, 1946, Rahav and Lifson, along with Reuven Pinchas and Bin-Nun, left the unit's battered fishing vessel close to the entrance of Haifa harbor and entered the murky muck-filled depths of the port area. Both men had placed *Kefiyeh* Arab headdresses on their heads, they hadn't shaved in several days and tried to impersonate local Arab fisherman to the best of their abilities. The masquerade worked. The British patrols scanning the plush waters of the Mediterranean at the entrance to the base paid little attention to the Arabs playing with their nets returning from a disappointing evening out on the water. It was all very routine. The results weren't, however. The limpet mines were World War II surplus and the magnetic-plate mechanism had already been eaten through by saltwater. The device placed on the hull of the *Empire Rival* managed (miraculously) to remain on the hull, but it appeared as if the detonation mechanism was faulty. Nevertheless, the device was fastened and set for detonation for early the following morning—for an hour before most of the British sailors would board for the 8:00 A.M. inspection.

42

The operators returned to their fishing vessel and then returned to safehouses in Haifa for a few hours of shut-eye. They had hoped to awake the next morning for the early headlines of a blast in the port area and the sinking of a British naval vessel, but there was nothing. No blast, no alert. The limpet was a dud.

Undaunted and angered by their failure, Bin-Nun dispatched his men out into the waters off Haifa harbor the following night. This time, he reached out to the Technical Platoon of his unit and requisitioned a "speedboat"—in reality a small rowboat from the Kibbutz E'yin Ha'yam's fishing fleet. Using an indigenously produced "Zinger" mine, the two-man team of Lifson and Rahav would once again affix the device to the hull of the *Empire Rival* and this time pray for better results. British alertness that night was a bit more stringent than on the night of previous operations, and sentries even walked around with their weapons in hand, not slung across their shoulders. Nevertheless, Rahav and Lifson entered the water and began their 200-meter swim to the *Empire Rival* being careful to swim fast and silent. They reached the ship unhindered, but working underwater without any breathing gear had taken its toll on the swimmers and they needed to come up more frequently for air. As Rahav raised his head above the water line to inhale deeply, he heard a noise coming from up above and puddles of vomit raining down upon him. A British sailor, drunk and aching, had used the rail of the *Empire Rival* to hold himself up as he let loose with the remnants of a night's drinking in a Haifa pub. As the sailor completed his part in keeping the waters of Haifa harbor pollution-free, he saw a disgusted face in the water staring back at him. The sight of the saboteur was enough to wake the sailor out of his stupor and he immediately sounded the alarm. Searchlights soon illuminated the waters and cries of "Shoot the bastard!" were heard being shouted by angry patrol sergeants.

Rahav immersed himself back in the water and expected a fusillade of depth charges and grenades being thrown at him. He quickly regrouped with Lifson, scraped the hull of the *Empire Rival* with enough gusto to quickly fasten the magnetic mechanism of the device, and he quickly raced to the motorboat with whatever energy he had remaining. Lifson, the better swimmer, followed behind Rahav just to make sure his partner made it to the ship. The *Empire Rival* was scheduled to detonate in four hours.

The road back to the Haifa safehouse was a hairy one. Royal Navy launches pursued the motorboat and fired at it with a Bren gun mounted near the pilot's perch. Over thirty 7.62mm holes were sliced through the boat, though none striking the four *Pal'mach* divers. They abandoned the boat approximately fifty meters in front of a breakwater south of the port and swam toward shore while the launch gingerly approached the abandoned craft.

The following morning, as the men clutched Mauser pistols expecting a raid by British CID officers, they heard the radio report confirming the destruction of the *Empire Rival*.

Besides their success in the sinking of the H.M.S. *Empire Rival*, Bin-Nun's unit had also scouted British naval locations throughout the Mediterranean coast (in search of targets), and had a small army of *Haganah* personnel working in the nearby shipyards able to supply invaluable intelligence about the layout of British naval facilities. The largest Royal Navy base was in Haifa, the port city in the north, and it was here that the unit dedicated its resources and operations. The unit mounted small-scale attacks against shipping and port facilities, and frequent reconnaissance forays to gather intelligence. Most important, perhaps, the reconnaissance sorties gave the unit operators a feeling about what it was like to operate in enemy territory.

Unlike other operational units fighting for Israeli independence at the time, the "Underwater Sabotage Unit" was not what the British used to term as instigators. They responded to British actions and retaliated. They were meant to be a means by which the problem of illegal Jewish immigration to Palestine could be addressed militarily. British authorities disposed Bin-Nun's underwater sabotage unit not because of the destruction they caused (Menachem Begin's *Irgun* was hated for its cold-blooded attacks), but because they were known as the "Teflon Terrorists." The British were unable to either capture any of Bin-Nun's men or seize any of their explosives. Kibbutz S'dot Yam, Bin-Nun's operating base, became a constant hub of British military activity. The base, at one time or another, was under military curfew; at one point, it was even surrounded by a full battalion of British paratroopers. Desperate and hoping to strike a raw nerve among many of the survivors from Nazi Europe, the British even brought in dogs to try and locate hidden explosives. Their searches always yielded little except ill will and a desire to strike back.

Attacks usually followed the seizure of a refugee vessel by the Royal Navy. In the winter of 1947, the Royal Navy seized the refugee ship, the *Haim Arlozorov* and its cargo of 1,348 refugees. It was moored off the coast of Haifa for several days as the logistic arrangements were made to ferry the refugees to British craft for the return voyage to Cyprus. A *Pal'yam* operation of retaliation was forthcoming.

It was decided that the first target of the unit would be a Royal Navy launch moored in the port of Haifa—it wasn't a sexy target, Bin-Nun would later recall, but it was a target that was accessible. Rahav and his partner, Lifson, would slip into the murky waters in Haifa harbor and attach a homemade limpet mine to the bow of a launch. Since the port area was heavily defended by sentries, augmented by roving patrols with armored cars, the only access for entry and escape was the oily filth of water that kept the boats afloat in the port area. Although the British maintained a strict curfew both in the city of Haifa and in the surrounding waters, Bin-Nun and his motley assortment of commandos moored a fishing vessel approximately 200 meters south of the port area, in an alcove where they were not seen and hopefully not heard.

February is not a good time for any nighttime naval operations off the coast of Haifa—the waters reach an uncomfortable temperature of 45 degrees Fahrenheit, the winds race in from the northeast slicing off of Mt. Carmel and then ending up in a bone-chilling whirlwind across the coastline. Bin-Nun's crew did not possess any dry suits—they only had one wet suit, in fact, and that was not suitable for "mobility." So the divers had to opt for the poor-man's neoprene—buckets of grease that they applied to their shivering naked bodies. The grease insulated their bodies somewhat and allowed them to still swim fast. It was, however, uncomfortable as hell and took forever to remove. Nevertheless, near midnight on February 12, 1946, as British sentries carried their Lee Enfield rifles slung over their shoulders, two men disrobed on the deck of a creaky fishing vessel registered to a Kibbutz off the coast of Caesarea, and began the masochistic ritual of rubbing gobs of machine grease across their naked bodies. Rahav and his partner were ready for the mission—they had trained for the past week in the waters of Caesarea reaching their targets underwater, evading depth charges and fragmentation grenades hurled into the waters by sentries, and had felt confident that they were up for the task. Yet moments before the two were about the leap into the water, Yochai Bin-Nun came running across the pier with a worried look on his face. He had just checked with a *Pal'mach* informant working the port and discovered that the British were expecting an attack. Added patrols were roaming the perimeter, and tugs, cutters, and other small craft were tossing hand grenades into the murky waters. The mission was scrubbed.

Disappointed and faced with the task of removing five kilograms of grease from a hairy body, the two saboteurs found some solace with the fact that Bin-Nun was not the type of officer to cancel an operation—only postpone it. Twenty-four hours later, on an even colder night, both Rahav and Lifson were once again greased up and ready to go. This time, with British vigilance lax, Bin-Nun was able to position the unit's fishing trawler approximately 200 meters from the two ships to be attacked that evening. All was clear for the mission to proceed. No goodbyes were said, no words exchanged. The two divers took their improvised limpet mines on their backs and jumped into the frigid waters.

Luckily for the two divers, each tasked with placing their charges on the bow of one ship, the targets were illuminated by deck lights; the British, apparently having survived a night when the attack was "supposed" to transpire, had lowered their guard. Unluckily for the divers, the illuminated decks meant that the waters, too, were lit and anyone crazy enough to be swimming in the ice-cold filth would be spotted by even the most unalert sentry. That meant that they had to swim mostly submerged and that meant a slow swim—in cold water, that was a recipe for disaster. Soon, Rahav lost the feeling in his arms and then his legs. Each of the divers carried two of the "Haganah-produced" limpets, attached to one another by a sturdy piece of rope; the second limpets were spares in case one should be lost or damaged en route to the target. The "pencil," the timer and detonator rod that went into the limpet mine and was to commence the mechanism of the acetone timer, had already been activated once the divers entered the water so there was no turning back—no aborting the mission.

For Rahav, the bone-snapping cold had truly affected his physical abilities. His hands were numb and he found it difficult to free the other limpet mine from the rope. He tried loosening it, he tried hacking the rope with his blade. Nothing worked. Making matters worse, he couldn't affix the limpet mine to the steel hull of the coast guard launch because the weight of the second mine kept pulling the other one off its magnetic adhesion. With no choice but to affix them to the anchor, Rahav set the mines in place, prayed that the timer wasn't premature, and headed back to the fishing boat. Lifson, too, had met with difficulties as a result of the cold water but had managed to overcome the tremendous chill that swept through his body and affixed the homemade mine to the hull of the second Royal Navy coast guard launch.

Both men returned to the fishing vessel forty-five minutes after entering the waters off of Haifa harbor. They were close to passing out from hypothermia, and both operators began to shiver and emit sounds of frigid pain that they thought would give away their positions to nearby British patrols. Bin-Nun ordered that both receive towels, a secure spot atop the warm engine, and a quick wipe-off of the grease that was supposed to keep them insulated from the water's cold grip.

Once the two men had recovered, they got dressed, and the four men left the vessel with a day's catch of fish, their nets, and poles, then walked calmly and slowly down the pier as if they had just returned from a day out at sea. As they neared the exit, a British policemen pulled out his Webley revolver and confronted the four who, by their appearance and fragrance, appeared to have legitimately been out at sea all day. "Don't you know that there is a curfew?" the policeman asked the fisherman. *"Shwaye,"* or "slowly," Bin-Nun responded in a heavily accented Arabic, as if to say that "We are Arabs, we don't speak English, and we don't care about the curfew meant for Jews." The policeman was convinced that the four were the genuine article and waved them past. Bin-Nun and crew hopped into an awaiting Arab-owned taxi cab, completing the deception, and sped off into the night.

An hour later, at 02:00 hours, Rahav's target erupted in a huge blast that engulfed the night with a bright orange glow and a cloud of smoke, debris, and flying shards of metal and wood. As emergency crews raced toward the sinking vessel, Lifson's boat blew up, as well.

British forces later issued a communiqué that Arab fisherman had sabotaged two of their craft.

Bin-Nun's underwater sabotage unit did not restrict its operations to the physical boundaries of British-mandate Palestine and "overseas" missions were the responsibility of one of the most remarkable men ever to "operate" in the Mediterranean. Yosef "Yosele" Dror volunteered into the *Pal'mach* in 1942 and set his sights exclusively on a naval career. He successfully completed a sailor's and master seaman's course during the Second World War, and immediately following V-E day, he was dispatched to Europe to pilot in *Haganah* ships smuggling refugees into Palestine. His track record was a good one, and as a commander he was considered something of a renaissance man—intellectual, well-read, humorous, and highly charismatic. With his lanky form and untrimmed beard, he looked the part of the daring commando. But, as many men in Bin-Nun's unit would comment, "There wasn't a man they'd rather be with on a dark night up against a heavily armed enemy."

Because of his renaissance-man qualities, Dror was the ideal candidate to be operating "outside" the boundaries of Palestine. He looked just as comfortable working a fishing vessel off the coast of Haifa as he did sitting in a cafe in Bari, Italy, with an attaché case full of explosives tucked between his legs. Because British security efforts in and around Haifa harbor became so vigilant following the sinking of the *Empire Rival*, and because the island of Cyprus began to swell with interned Jewish refugees, something a bit more aggressive was needed to get the message home to Whitehall. On April 2, 1947, a limpet mine was attached to H.M.S. *Ocean Vigour* off the Cyprus coast by Dror; it exploded hours later inflicting irreparable damage. Considering that the divers wore wet suits which didn't keep out the water or cold, and were deployed with dubious homemade explosives, the operation far from the Israeli coast was a remarkable feat.

The *Pal'yam*'s special units also found itself operating on land in missions that supported the landing of Jewish refugees along the Palestinian coast. While soldiers from the *Pal'mach* defended the landing beach until the *Ma'apilim* had finished wading through the water and had been met on the shore by squads of *Haganah* personnel who were awaiting with blankets and trucks and false identity papers. Security prohibited the mentioning of a landing zone until mere hours before the landing, and as a result, *Pal'mach* security details were required to march long and far in order to reach any proposed landing site within hours. Once the immigrants had been loaded on *Haganah* transports, the *Pal'mach* would initiate its British-taught guerrilla tactics to delay pursuing British forces, while *Pal'yam* sappers set off charges along the shoreline to act as diversions.

The unit's final mission, ominously, came in September 1947 when Bin-Nun and company once again struck against the *Empire Rival*, which had been repaired and brought back to the coast of Palestine to continue removing refugees to Cyprus. But, by the fall of 1947, the British had washed their hands of the Palestinian question—it was a matter for the newly formed United Nations to decide and resolve. The British would be withdrawing and *Haganah* commanders knew that Arab armies and terrorist bands would soon be attacking the Jewish population of the soon-to-be-formed Jewish State. Bin-Nun's underwater sabotage unit did not single-handedly push the British out of Palestine, but their actions were instrumental in destroying British military assets and British military morale. In many ways, the unit was in the vanguard of the campaign to attain Israeli independence. All knew it would be just as instrumental in the coming fight for Israeli survival.

The declaration of the State of Israel on May 14, 1948, and the subsequent invasion of the newly created Jewish nation by the combined armies of Lebanon, Syria, Iraq, Trans-Jordan, and Egypt turned the fighting into a conventional military struggle. Although the *Pal'mach* had by now been fully incorporated into the newly created *Tzava Haganah Le'Yisrael,* or Israel Defense Force (formally established on May 31, 1948), the notion of spectacular operations conducted by highly specialized elite units was not lost. Yitzhak Sadeh, commander of the newly created *Pal'mach's* 8th Armored Brigade, sanctioned the creation of a mechanized "commando" battalion to be based loosely along the lines of the LRDG. The unit was designated the "89th Assault Battalion" and was commanded by Moshe Dayan.

The Israelis weren't commando geniuses by choice—it was their pragmatic solution to being so outmatched numerically by the conventional armies of the bordering Arab nations. When compared to the combined Arab armies, Jewish forces were outnumbered a hundred to one and that insurmountable gap needed to be addressed somehow. Sneak attacks, small unit strikes, and sabotage sorties helped convince the Arabs, both conventional armies and irregular guerrilla forces, that the Jewish fighter was not only some kind of superman, but that there were more of them than met the eye. Had they had their choice, it is obvious that the *Haganah,* and later IDF High Command would have much rather fielded a division of M4 Sherman tanks than a squad of *Pal'mach* sappers equipped with homemade satchel charges. On the land front, the conventional Israeli army was pitifully equipped—rifles and vehicles were few and substandard, and heavy artillery and other essentials were nonexistent. In the air, a few biplanes dropping everything from Molotov cocktails to empty seltzer bottles. It was all that the infant *Heyl Ha'Avir* ("Air Corps") could fly until a shipment of Czech-built Avia S199 fighters, indigenous copies of the Luftwaffe's Messerschmitt Me-109 could arrive. On the naval front, the situation wasn't even desperate—it was considered beyond hope. A national army whose infantrymen didn't carry more than a handful of bullets couldn't be expected to send a fleet of destroyers and battleships to sea. Israel's "navy" in those dark and tumultuous days surrounding Israeli independence meant naval special warfare.

The Israeli Navy was formally created on March 17, 1948, when *Haganah* commander Yisrael Galili issued directive No. D 18/9 ordering the creation of the *Sherut Ha'Yami* ("Sea Service") transferring all *Haganah* and *Pal'mach* sea assets to the Sea Service for the overall naval defense of the Jewish State. The man that David Ben-Gurion, the Israeli political leader, and Yisrael Galili, the *Haganah* chief of staff, both chose to command the Sea Service was Gershon Zaq, a no-nonsense Ukrainian-born *Haganah* officer who was less a diplomat than a "doer." He had a rough road ahead of him. *Pal'yam* personnel, owners of a rather elite status among *Haganah* circles, who were adamant against becoming part and parcel of a conventional force; especially one they knew that would be on the short end of the equipment, budgetary, and manpower set of equations that a new army would be forced to establish. By March 1948, however, two full months before the declaration of Israeli independence, full-scale war had overtaken Palestine. British forces, set to depart the mandate on May 14, 1948, had abandoned many strategic targets throughout Palestine, hoping to avoid getting their forces embroiled in the inevitable bloodletting. And, as British commanders knew would happen, the moment the Union Jack was lowered from city centers and military installations, Jewish underground forces and Arab irregular units began to battle

51

it out—sometimes, especially in urban environments, with horrific body counts.

When the ultrastrategic port of Haifa was liberated in early April 1948, the Sea Service had a base of operations and even some ships—several abandoned British vessels that soon received a new paint job, some Hotchkiss heavy machine guns, and the flag of the as-yet-to-be-announced Jewish State. Zaq was not a popular figure and, indeed, *Pal'yam* officers and sailors mutinied and joined up with ground units, especially with the elite 4th Battalion, in order not to be part of the new "regular" navy. But Zaq, to his credit, realized that a small navy with more powerful enemies might need a special operations force of its own, and he created a "Landing Unit," even though the Sea Service didn't possess any landing craft. The "Landing Unit" would be commanded by Yochai Bin-Nun and would evolve into one of the most remarkable special operations forces to emerge out of the 1948 War for Israeli independence.

Even though Zaq had to encounter turmoil amid his ranks and had very few seaworthy ships to work with, on the naval front, many *Pal'yam* veterans, now full-fledged "operators" with the *Pal'mach's* 4th Battalion, executed a remarkable and truly audacious commando operation against Syrian shipping interests in the Mediterranean. Known in the *Haganah* log-book as Operations *Shalal* ("Loot") 1, 2, and 3, the operations were conducted in three different stages against a single target: a large shipment of arms that the Syrian Army had purchased from Czechoslovakia—a shipment of rifles, machine guns, pistols, ammunition, and explosives that could equip an entire division, and very well turn the tide of fighting on Israel's vulnerable northern frontier.

"Operation Loot 1" was the search at sea for the Italian ship S.S. *Lino,* a merchant vessel chartered by the Syrian military to transport the Czech weapons shipment. Once located, the true heart of the operation would go into effect to prevent them from reaching the intended destination of Beirut, where the supplies were to be unloaded and then ferried overland to Damascus. On the night of April 2, the

Haganah ship S.S. *South Africa,* a beaten-up freighter, headed out toward Rhodes with a handful of frogmen formerly from Bin-Nun's underwater sabotage unit. The ship searched for the *Lino,* but after three days received word that *Lino* had dropped anchor in the Italian port of Bari. This intelligence was handed over to *Rechesh* (*Haganah* intelligence squads that roamed the world in search of weapons), and agents from the *Mossad Le'Aliyah Bet* (the clandestine body that helped arrange the smuggling of Jews into Palestine throughout the world) in Italy, who acted immediately. Knowing who to bribe and who not to ask, the small army of *Haganah* intelligence operatives in search of the elusive ship manned a determined stakeout on the ship, studying its security ring, and at the same time making friends with guards and hookers who carried out their business on the piers of Bari. Getting to the *Lino* wouldn't be a problem—compared to what many of these drivers and operators had been used to in their fight against the British, security was not tight. Yet armed guards did patrol the ship, and they had orders to shoot on their own discretion at any sight of intruders.

The plan for the destruction of the *Lino,* now code-named "Loot 2" was simple enough—a limpet mine would be attached to the bow of the freighter and hopefully sink the ship in the harbor's deep waters. On the night of April 9–10, the mission commander, Yosef Dror, and his second-in-command, Benny Kravitz, attached limpet mines to *Lino's* stern. They entered the water from a nearby breakwater and found the swim an easy effort. The mine was attached with little difficulty, and an hour later, following a tremendous blast that woke up all the bars and whore houses along the shore, the *Lino* sank. The Italian government had tactically supported the *Haganah* throughout their postwar struggle to smuggle Jews into Palestine and they had turned a blind eye to the fact that the *Haganah, Rechesh,* and the *Mossad Le'Aliyah Bet* had turned Italy, especially its port cities, into nerve centers of underground activities. Jewish hit teams, in fact, remnants of the Jewish Brigade of the British Army that fought in Italy in the Second World War, openly roamed the hills of northern

Italy in search of Nazis evading the Allied dragnet. This time, however, the Italian government was eager to avoid an international incident and to avoid having Arab and Jewish agents battling out in the streets of its cities. The Italian authorities couldn't save the damaged ship, with a ten-foot-wide hole in its bow, but it did succeed in salvaging the *Lino*'s precious cargo and returned it to the supervision—and protection—of the Syrian Army. The Arab League dispatched Syrian Colonel Mardam Ba'i, a professional soldier considered to be a future candidate for the post of chief of staff, to oversee the transfer of the weapons to a newly commissioned Italian cargo ship, the S.S. *Argero,* and its safe passage "not" to Beirut, since that destination was considered compromised, but rather to Alexandria, Egypt, where the invaluable cargo would be safer.

It was already the summer of 1948, and the conventional war between the newly declared State of Israel and the combined Arab armies was underway and the war was not going well for the newly created Israel Defense Forces (IDF). In Jerusalem, the center point for Jewish existence, the Trans-Jordanian Arab Legion had completely cut off the city and were besieging its Jewish inhabitants. In the north, the Syrians and the Iraqis were fighting close-quarter battles in Galilee against the outnumbered Israeli defenders, and in the south the mighty Egyptian Army, the largest Arab fighting force, was moving through the Negev Desert attempting to strike at both Jerusalem and Tel Aviv. For the newly established Israel Defense Forces, it was a desperate situation growing more precarious each and every passing hour. The balance of power was such that the IDF was barely surviving. Anything to shift that unsteady balance against the fledgling Jewish army could have disastrous effects. The *Argero*'s cargo was to be kept away from Alexandria at all costs. Yet senior officers in both the IDF General Staff and in the newly establish *Heyl Ha'Yam* (or "Naval Corps") thought it a pity to simply sink the Italian boat in the middle of the Mediterranean without making at least a noble attempt in stealing its precious cargo.

"That" phase of the operation was known as "Loot 3." One morning in early August 1948, as the crew of the *Argero* was having breakfast and maintaining the ship near the coast of Crete, a fishing vessel flying the Italian flag moved in. The sailors wore Italian coast guard uniforms and carried Italian pistols, but they were, in fact, *Pal'yam* officers David Ben-Horin and Oved Sadeh. They demanded to board the *Argero* under the guise of carrying out a surprise customs inspection, and while they examined the cargo and inspected the crew, two Sea Service warships, the I.N.S. *Wedgewood* and *Haganah* moved in for the "kill." While the *Pal'yam* officers managed to disarm elements of the *Argero's* crew and detain Colonel Ba'i, sailors from the two warships began to unload the precious cargo. It was a difficult task lasting nearly a week. On August 29, 1948, 8,000 rifles and 8 million rounds of ammunition reached the port of Haifa.

Colonel Ba'i was later executed for his incompetence.

Soldiers in the *Haganah* and the *Pal'mach* were, more than anything else, expert tinkerers. They could fix anything, repair the most desperate wreck, and make the unworkable function. They had to. Any army whose weapons had firing pins produced from recycled household items and bullets stolen from drunken Australian soldiers on leave, had to be mechanically inclined to make their very little do an awful lot. Tinkerers are by their very nature imaginative and inventive, and some of the best inventors to be found in the newly formed Jewish State were members of Bin-Nun's inner circle of naval special warfare operators. Although they hadn't been schooled in Sandhurst or West Point, these men were brilliant tacticians and strategists who, for the lack of any resources, were able to dissect military situations into their most basic equations and come up with unique and highly innovative technical solutions. During the campaign against the British, Yochai Bin-Nun had attempted to come up with a whole host of means to reach their targets undetected and to deliver a massive punch of explosive destruction—these ranged from floating gas tanks fitted with timers to wooden fishing boats laden with gasoline. Stealth was the means and explosive punch was the key and all sorts of hair-brained schemes were

drawn up and talked about. One idea that stuck was that of
a semi-guided torpedo that an operator could control by a
remote control device and drive toward a target until it
detonated upon impact. The inventor of that idea was a
Pal'yam technician named Uzi Sharoni, who developed his
brainchild in the fish pool at Kibbutz Ma'oz.[15] The torpedo,
the *Pal'yam* decided, was to be called the "Shark." Sharoni
had, in his own Kibbutz workshop, developed a remote-
controlled model airplane that could carry a payload, and
the Shark was a novel extension of this idea.

The Shark had to be many things—it had to be seaworthy, it had to be quiet, and it had to pack enough explosives
to destroy whatever it hit. It also had to be cancelable, as it
was designed, after all, at the height of the British campaign
against the *Haganah* and its underwater saboteurs. Therefore, the Shark also had to be built in sections that could be
put together quickly and it had to be operable from a
medium-size fishing vessel so it could be aimed toward its
target in midwater. Bin-Nun, Sharoni, and virtually half of
the unit worked on the Shark the entire winter of 1946 and
1947. Trials were held in the Sea of Galilee off of Kibbutz
Ma'oz, and then later in the Mediterranean off the shores of
Kibbutz S'dot Yam. The final variant, two were built,
weighed in at 300 kilograms, required eight men to operate
it, was run by electric propulsion and guided by a lengthy
electrical cord that flew off as the device raced toward its
target, and had a warhead with an impressive eighty kilograms of explosives.[16]

Bin-Nun and his crews had hoped to use the Shark
against the British, and an opportunity for such a deployment came on July 18, 1947, when the *Haganah* ship
Exodus and its cargo of 4,554 refugees was seized by the
Royal Navy near the coast of Haifa. The *Exodus*, a dilapidated river ferry, had tried in vain to outrun the British
destroyers, and when Royal Navy boarding parties finally
swarmed on board, the refugees fought back with all they
had. They used fists and handbags, the British used truncheons and pistols; three refugees were killed in the fighting
and over a hundred were wounded. The chapter of the
Haganah ship *Exodus,* happening less than a week after

Menachem Begin's Irgun hung two British sergeants in an olive grove, incensed the British, most notably Foreign Secretary Ernst Bevin. To make a point that would sear the minds of any future Jewish attempts to smuggle refugees into Palestine, the *Exodus* passengers were to be deported not to Cyprus, but to Germany. The *Haganah* vowed revenge, and Bin-Nun was asked to come up with a contingency operation.

Several days after the *Exodus* was moored into Haifa harbor, Bin-Nun's unit had set up its lethal ambush. The fishing vessel hiding the Shark was in place and the target, a British destroyer, was well within range; the sea, too, was cooperating, as the waves were small and the sea calm. Less than a half-hour before the Shark was to be lowered into the sea and set en route for the hull of the destroyer, *Pal'mach* commander Yigal Alon, who was personally observing and commanding the operation, received word from David Ben-Gurion that the mission was a scrub—the political leadership of the Jewish Agency viewed the sinking of a British warship as too provocative a move. "The Shark," recalled Yochai Bin-Nun, "remained untested and a virgin yet to see battle."[17]

Most navies didn't have to rely on the inventiveness of simple sailors for weapons systems designs, but few navies had to resort to pirate tactics and steal the enemy's weapons and ammunition, as well. Operations Loot 1, 2, and 3 had been highly successful and displayed the Israelis' now apparently inherent indigenous skills for special operations. But the raid also displayed another inherent trait of the Israeli fighter—desperate lack of equipment and munitions. What imagination couldn't dream up and local workshops couldn't produce, the agents of *Rechesh* (literally "Acquisition"), a quasi-espionage arms-buying section of the Jewish Agency, were meant to buy. They were military surplus consumers with limited funds and a frugal eye for bargains. They purchased whatever the newly formed defense forces needed that could be found for a bargain price in junk piles in Europe and North America. It was through the auspices of *Rechesh* agents that the just-formed *Heyl Ha'Avir* ("Israel Air Force") obtained surplus B-17 bombers from the United States and Avia S199s from the Czechs; *Rechesh* agents bought IDF infantrymen their Mauser K98 rifles and the ammunition needed to fire them, and they bought the first M4 Sherman tanks deployed against in the Negev Desert against the Egyptian military.

One of the favored stomping grounds for the frugal buyers of *Rechesh* was Italy. Italy was close to the shores of Israel—close enough to make shipping charges inexpensive and shipping times brief. Italy was also a black-market paradise—a Mecca for bargains in anything and everything: from intelligence to 81mm mortars. Italians had been surviving the war on a black-market currency since 1943, and they were masters at the trade. There were remnants of the war in just about every major roadway, junkyard, and former battlefield. Italian firms such as Fiat, Pirelli, and Beretta had prospered during the war, and afterward. With the Italian penchant for workmanship, quality, and low price, and with dozens of still-functioning ports eager for business, Italy was turning itself into an arms-buyer's bargain basement—from revolutionaries in Greece to North Africa. Italy, too, was a country where the authorities were, for the most part, friendly to the Jewish cause; "For us this was a moral obligation," said Giulio Andreotti, secretary to the Italian prime minister in 1946, "an attempt to atone, as it were, for the Fascist political chapter which was so alien to the traditions of our people."[18]

Italy was also a convenient base of operations for the *Haganah* and later the Israel Defense Forces since it was a country that possessed a precious natural resource—an overabundance of former military men eager to earn a few extra lira engaged in covert operations.

At the time, *Rechesh* agents in Italy were working for the Sea Service in search of motorized landing craft that could bring a force of approximately sixty commandos to an enemy position. While searching the junkyards for boats and other miscellaneous items, they came across one such former Italian military man that forever changed the course of Israeli naval special warfare history.

The Italians produced one legend during the Second World War and that was the exploits of their naval comman-

do force, the *Decima Flotiglia MAS*, or 10th MAS Flotilla.
Although one of the premier fleets in the Mediterranean (in
1940, it consisted of four battleships, eight heavy cruisers,
fourteen light cruisers; 128 destroyers, 115 submarines, and
sixty-two torpedo boats), an element of Italian naval strategy had always been light attack craft deployed in lightning-
fast hit-and-run attacks.[19] Before the war, in the mid-1930s,
Italian naval officers had toyed with the idea of an underwater swimmer delivery vehicle when two sub-lieutenants, T.
Tesei and E. Toschi, had submitted plans for the building of
a prototype human torpedo.[20] The idea centered on a slow-
moving torpedo piloted by two frogmen. The steerable
torpedo would be able to slip into harbor undetected and
would provide a long-range ability far beyond the physical
abilities of even the most gifted swimmers. When the two
men would reach their target, they would simply remove the
delayed-action warhead from the torpedo, affix it to the hull
of a ship like a limpet mine, and then head back to a
warship and await the destruction of their target. The
frogmen deployed a self-contained breathing apparatus,
called the Amphibian Mk. I, that was light in weight and
self-contained; it was also closed-circuit, and as a result it
did not emit any telltale exhaust bubbles. There was also an
explosive motorboat concept, the MTM, pioneered by the
Italians that were driven in the water and aimed at a target
in the open seas, once the driver was close enough to the
target to ensure his craft scoring a hit, he would jump into
the water and be retrieved by a mother craft. When the 10th
MAS Flotilla was formed in August 1940, it was divided
into three divisions—surface, underwater, and free-
swimming frogmen. Operators in the unit were parachutist-
qualified and taught to operate under the most adverse and
desperate of conditions.

From 1941 until 1943, the 10th MAS Flotilla waged a
campaign of terror and mayhem against British shipping in
the Mediterranean. Though the unit suffered heavy casualties, they did succeed in almost destroying the British
destroyer H.M.S. *York* in Suda Bay, and they disabled the
battleships H.M.S. *Valiant* and H.M.S. *Queen Elizabeth* in
Alexandria harbor. The unit also waged a relentless cam-

paign against British shipping in Gibraltar, often deploying from sunken Spanish ships resting on the ocean bottom in the nearby waters. On the night of July 26, 1941, eight MTM craft of the 10th MAS Flotilla mounted one of its most audacious attacks ever—a strike at the British Mediterranean hub in Malta. The attack failed miserably. The commandos were detected by British naval vessels and subjected to murderous cannon and machine-gun fire, RAF fighter-bombers were summoned and decimated the force. Fifteen Italians were killed and eighteen were captured—including a firebrand sergeant named Fiorenco Capriotti.

Capriotti was the type of man that legends were made of—boisterous, confident, and courageous to the end; he was, claims a former member of the unit, a rogue warrior in the Dick Marcinko mold of a naval special operator.[21] Yet the majority of his war was spent in POW camps—one year in Great Britain and four years in the United States, including two years in Honolulu, Hawaii. In 1946, he returned to Italy, seeking employment and found a steady, though boring, job serving as an instructor to the postwar Italian Navy, and then a job in business in the private sector. At the same time, the *Rechesh* operative in Milan, Ephraim Eilin, came across word that there were six World War II surplus MTM craft for sale; the boats, in pristine condition, even came with instructions. Eilin also made contact with Capriotti and asked him if he was interested in heading off to the newly formed State of Israel to serve as an instructor to the newly formed Israeli Navy, to which Capriotti simply nodded his head in agreement and asked, "Are you still fighting the British?"[22] Sea Service commander Gershon Zaq had to receive special authorization from David Ben-Gurion to bring Capriotti to Israel. While there were many Jewish—and Gentile—military veterans from the United States, Canada, and South Africa flocking to Israel to help the fledgling Jewish State in its hour of need, Caprioti wasn't a Jew. He was quite the other thing—a diehard Fascist and Mussolini loyalist. Ben-Gurion was adamant about not employing "Gentile mercenaries," especially from the Axis powers. He would be allowed to train the naval commandos, but he could not participate in any of the fighting. He was to be an observer, and the moment his services were no longer needed, he was to be on a boat headed back to Italy. Zaq agreed. Days later, Fiorenco Capriotti landed in Haifa.

Throughout the first few months of the war, most of Bin-Nun's original cadre of naval special warfare operators were in Europe, involved in various activities—from the sinking of the *Lino* and the hijacking of the *Argero,* to other operations in support of intelligence agents moving about the ports of Europe. When the fighting broke out in May 1948, Bin-Nun and company were sure that the time had come for them to finally be deployed out in the open and en mass. They were partly correct. Following everyone's return from Operation Loot, the top commanders of the newly formed IDF/Navy held a meeting in their headquarters in Tel Aviv's San Remo Hotel. They called together many of the veterans of the *Pal'yam* strike unit for what was termed a reunion, but it soon became clear to everyone in the room it was really a redeployment. The new navy would have three commando entities—an underwater frogman force, a force of combat operators deploying explosive craft, and Izzy Rahav's "Shark Unit." Yosef "Yosele" Dror, the *Pal'yam* master diver and saboteur, received command of the frogman force, while Yochai Bin-Nun was named as commander of the "Explosive Boat Unit."

Both Dror's "Frogman Unit" and the Shark element were busy preparing for action most knew would not involve their services; the 1948 War was a ground war, a battle of men climbing hills and surviving brutal hand-to-hand encounters. Nevertheless, Dror trained a class of seasoned seamen in underwater tactics and demolitions (including a woman, a remarkable French survivor of the camps), and Izzy Rahav, in charge of the Sharks, prepared his Sharks for what he hoped would be their baptism under fire. Only Bin-Nun had a hunch that his unit would be called upon in the fighting, and he relished the challenge of striking the enemy—no matter how. And, having been faced with swimming in hostile waters with limpet mines and improvised devices that might or might not explode, the MTM craft were a blessing. The 5.2-meter-long and 1.9-meter-wide wooden boats were lethal on the seas when in the hands of a courageous SOB. Incredibly seaworthy, they could fly on fairly rough seas reaching a speed of up to thirty-two knots.[23] The most charming aspect of the boat, of course, was its punch—a walloping 300-kilogram warhead that could literally blow most warships out of the water. To be an explosive boat driver required, as one former commando would say, "balls of rusty steel." While frogman are supposed to reach their targets quietly, employing darkness and stealth, the MTM boats made noise and were above surface. By the time the driver made his attack run, it was likely that every weapon on a warship would be aimed at a very visible target. The operator aimed the craft at his target, and then, at a point where the speeding wooden boat was heading dead center for its mark, he'd pull a shaft located alongside the controls and eject, like a pilot, into the sea, and be picked up by a mother ship. According to the Italian tactic, the MTM craft were like kamikaze weapons—if the operator managed to survive the endeavor or even be captured, then God's speed to him. The Israeli approach was somewhat more pragmatic. They added the element of another speedboat, an MTM with its explosives removed, that was responsible for plucking the MTM boat drivers out of the water. The operators were also fitted with "indigenous" helmets with infrared reflectors so that the operators racing about on the pickup boat, equipped with special night-vision glasses, could locate the "ejected" operators in dark waters and pull them in to safety. To make the strikes safer, the navy's technical department also developed special explosives to be fitted into the MTM's warhead that would not detonate when struck by a bullet.

It was a neat package of destruction and speed and, at the time, the most secretive weapon in Israel; after all, they were brought to Israel in crates marked "Taxi Cabs."

Capriotti, with the help of an interpreter, set up his course on the shores of the Sea of Galilee, where in a very short time Bin-Nun and his crew learned the A-to-Zs of the MTM—its operation, its abilities, its envelope, and true secrets. Capriotti was a masterful teacher, but he seemed disappointed by his surroundings. He expected to find himself at a naval base somewhere—not a Kibbutz. There were few trappings of command in Bin-Nun's unit. There weren't even ranks or salutes; the officers placed the difference between their salaries and the NCOs in a cookie jar for "later use." It was simple, egalitarian, though deadly serious. The one aspect of military tradition that force was not willing to sacrifice for frugality was an emblem—the unit's symbol was a ship broken in two imposed over a hand grenade adorned by two standing branches. Ominously, it was a symbol taken directly from the emblem of the *Pal'mach,* which by 1948 had been incorporated as a brigade within the IDF. Slowly, and with great affection, Capriotti became an admirer of the ragtag dozen. They were brave, ambitious, and adventurous. "I told the Israelis," Capriotti would later admit, "that if there were a few thousand men like them and Ben-Gurion in Italy, that country would look differently."[24]

Under a tremendous veil of secrecy, the unit trained on the Sea of Galilee, waiting to be called to action. Security at their training facility was tight. Curious fishermen tossing their nets into the early morning calm of the Galilee waters were told that this was an experimental rescue unit practicing in the art of rescuing downed pilots in the Mediterranean. The cover story worked, and the unit's official name was the "Rescue Boat Unit." The IDF bureaucracy was getting suspicious in its own right—especially when Bin-Nun requisitioned the Supply Department for a ton of high explosives. Even the Sea Service was kept in the dark about the activities of this mysterious force training near Tiberias. There was great fear at the time about "underground" units within the IDF loyal to one political affiliation or another, and the "Explosive Boat Unit" was held with great suspicion. When General Yigal Yadin, the IDF deputy chief of staff, visited the unit in Tiberias and saw their unit emblem, mistaking it for a *Pal'mach* coat of arms, he angrily denounced the gesture saying, "There won't be any *Pal'mach* or underground here anymore!"[25]

During a routine's day instruction in the fall of 1948, as Capriotti and Bin-Nun were observing the operators driving the boats toward a target, an urgent and secretive telegram was rushed to the commander's hands. Three MTM boats and a pickup boat were ordered to the Mediterranean port of Jaffa, just south of Tel Aviv, for a mission. Time was of the essence, and the unit was to be ready to go in a matter of days. Virtually bursting with excitement for the chance to prove that his craft could get the job done, Bin-Nun picked four men for the mission—Ya'akov Vardi, Zalman Avramov, Yitzhak Brockman, and Ya'akov Rituv. A flabbergasted Capriotti was left behind. "I thought I've come here to fight," Capriotti pleaded with Bin-Nun, but orders were orders and Ben-Gurion's directive was the law of the land.

In Jaffa, Bin-Nun's squad assembled in ramshackle quarters only a few kilometers from downtown Tel Aviv. Their four boats were loaded on the I.N.S. *Ma'oz,* a dilapidated ferry that was once a refugee transport ship, the *Ben-Hecht.* Slapped with a new coat of paint, a Hebrew letter and number *(Kuf-24),* she was transformed into an Israeli Navy support ship. Under a veil of secrecy, the *Ma'oz* slipped out of port early on the morning of October 21, 1948, headed for Gaza.

For days, a flotilla of Egyptian naval vessels had come dangerously close to the Tel Aviv shoreline—including the flagship of the Egyptian Navy, the R.E.N.S. *Emir Farouk*— a 1,441-ton Sloop-class cruiser launched by the British in 1926. Days earlier, the Sea Service's "Big Flotilla," as its squadron of five warships (actually converted ice-breakers, corvettes, and ferries), raced to the waters off of Tel Aviv to intercept the Egyptian ships. Although the *Emir Farouk's* six-inch main gun and four 20mm cannons outmuscled the Israeli fleet, the "Big Flotilla" commander, an American-Jewish volunteer named Paul Shulman, decided to engage the Egyptians with his most lethal weapon—his mouth. He grabbed a megaphone and ordered the *Emir Farouk's* commander to "scram!" The Egyptians, daunted by the gesture, did just what Shulman said. They set sail full steam ahead south to Gaza. A few days later, Shulman and fleet headed south just to show the Egyptians that Israelis, too, could linger off the enemy coast if they wanted to.

It was tit-for-tat behavior taking place amid the largest IDF attack of the war. The Egyptian-Israeli naval activity coincided with the commencement of "Operation Yoav," a major Israeli advance into the Negev Desert. The IDF General Staff viewed the *Emir Farouk* as a threat to the Israeli rear, and to the overall success of Operation Yoav. Decisive action was ordered. The *Emir Farouk* was to be sunk. It was no easy task, the *Emir Farouk* moved about with a mine-sweeper for an escort, a 215-ton B.Y.M.S.-class ship, and both usually stayed close to shore where they were within protective range of coastal artillery batteries. If the *Emir Farouk* was to be sunk, it was to be via nonconventional means. It meant Bin-Nun and company.

On the early morning hours of October 21, 1948, Bin-Nun and his four operators watched the coast of Jaffa and the Tel Aviv skyline disappear into the fog as they stood on the deck of the I.N.S. *Ma'oz* as they headed south for the coast of Gaza. They reviewed their tactics and checked, double-checked, and rechecked their boats. Nothing would be left to chance.

Bureaucracies being what they are, the I.N.S. *Ma'oz* set sail before the authorization was received to attack the *Emir Farouk.* Senior Sea Service officers had requested that Yigal Yadin, the IDF chief of operations and deputy chief of staff, rubber-stamp the operation, but he refused. Undaunted and with typical Israeli *chutzpah,* Sea Service commander Gershon Zaq drove to the private home of Prime Minister David Ben-Gurion in order to plead for governmental authorization for the mission. Ben-Gurion, however, exhausted after a week of touring the front lines, was taking a nap, and Mrs. Ben-Gurion refused to awaken her sleeping husband. Zaq's refused to allow a sleeping prime minister to ruin the Sea Service's golden opportunity to strike at the heart of the Egyptian fleet persisted to the point, according to legend, where Mrs. Ben-Gurion had to reach for a revolver in a nearby dresser drawer and order the navy commander to back off.[26] The ruckus awoke Ben-Gurion who rubbed his eyes, grabbed a pitcher of water, and agreed to grant a five-minute audience to the stubborn naval officer. At first, the Israeli prime minister was dead-set against the operation—sinking a flagship was a political statement of total war, he thought. Yet Ben-Gurion was concerned about the mission's chance for success. Zaq, fearing for his career, told the prime minister that chances of success "were good." Ben-Gurion began to like the idea better, the more Zaq talked. Bin-Nun would receive the green light minutes later on a wireless radio set aboard the *Ma'oz*.

As the *Ma'oz* zeroed in on the Egyptian vessels, Bin-Nun supervised as the MTMs were lowered into the choppy seas. Darkness was approaching and there was a looming amber sky drifting darker to the west. The coast of Gaza was visible, as were the silhouettes of the *Emir Farouk* and the mine-sweeper; the Egyptians were on battle-stations, but still beyond the range of engaging the Israeli flotilla, so a standoff ensued with both forces carefully eyeing the other. Bin-Nun's strategy was simple and cautious. He assigned Zalman Avramov to boat No. 1, tasked with destroying the *Emir Farouk*. Ya'akov Vardi, assigned to boat No. 2, was tasked with bringing down the mine-sweeper. Bin-Nun was the strategic reserve and would attack whichever target was proving difficult. Being the "reserve" boat was rough sailing. Bin-Nun would attack a ship only after both MTM craft had exploded; if he went into action, it meant that one boat had failed and the enemy would almost definitely be alerted to the impending attack—the ship, in turn, would train all their available weapons on any incoming targets. It was, in retrospect, a suicidal task, and that is why he chose to carry out the assignment personally. The Israeli ethic of command, dating back to the *Pal'mach*, was that the commander led from the vanguard. He was the one who walked through a door first, was let out of an aircraft ahead of his men, and was primed to take the first bullet. It was leadership through example and command through courage. Men were not expected to be asked to do anything that their commanders wouldn't do. In sending Avramov in boat No. 1, Bin-Nun was breaking that ethic, but he was ensuring that the most dangerous part of the mission would be his. Adding to the sense of danger and trepidation was the fact that the unit had not finished their course when they were summoned to action. They had mastered the theoretic of the craft, and the actual operating functions, but they had several weeks of technical instruction still ahead of them.

The ideal tactic of attack with the MTMs is simple and direct—sneak up on an enemy vessel at a 45-degree angle and then, a hundred meters from the target, aim the craft in for the kill at a 90-degree point of impact. The MTM, deploying a hydrastatic device, could also be set to detonate partially submerged. The operating mechanism provided for control of the ship and the removal of the safety catch which operated the ejection system. The operator sat beside a cushion that was in reality a flotation device. When he aimed his boat at the target and the ship began its 90-degree charge, he was to eject his cushion and it would in turn open up into the device. The operator was to jump out of the speeding craft ten seconds later; his leg was tied to the flotation device by a thick rope. By the time the MTM's 300 kilograms of high explosives detonated and the enemy target erupted in a ball of flames, the operator was "supposed" to be on the device to avoid suffering the effects of the explosion through the water at ten times its actual power.

The four boats assembled in the water for a final briefing, but their engines were already fired up and the men had trouble listening to Bin-Nun's instructions. Avramov went first toward his target. He raced alongside the *Emir Farouk* at a neat 45-degree angle, and then as he neared what is known in the trade as "the point of no return," he straightened out the MTM at a crisp straight line heading for the bow of the ship at a 90-degree turn. Avramov's ship worked perfectly—just as the Italians had designed and just as Capriotti had taught. After aiming the ship at a 90-degree angle of attack, he removed the craft's safety mechanism, ejected his flotation device, and then hurled his body overboard into the twirling waters. The *Emir Farouk* was struck thirty seconds later. The explosion lit the darkening sky with a bright orange glow, and it filled the air with a tremendous punch and engulfed the swishing sounds of the water entirely. The *Emir Farouk* was badly damaged by the impact, but Vardi, in boat No. 2, opted to aim his MTM at the *Emir Farouk*, as well. Bin-Nun, screaming at the top of his lungs to recall boat No. 2, couldn't figure out why Vardi would take it upon himself to attack a target already afire. Perhaps it was miscommunication. Perhaps it was the "legendary" fog of war. It was certainly overkill. Vardi's impact ripped the *Emir Farouk* into two. It sank eleven minutes later.

The sinking of the *Emir Farouk,* a tremendous victory for so small a unit, was only part of the operation—there was still the mine-sweeper moving about unmolested, and its four-inch main armament gun and batteries of 20mm cannons posed a definite threat to the I.N.S. *Ma'oz.* Without hesitating, Bin-Nun drove his MTM toward the mine-sweeper and began jockeying for the ideal attack position. All of the projector lights on board the mine-sweeper were now trained on the surrounding waters, and the Egyptian sailors began firing their heavy machine guns in a 360-degree field of fire in the hopes of hitting something. As Bin-Nun pursued the mine-sweeper in a 45-degree mark, a high-powered light picked up and illuminated the MTM in a bright yellow exposing glow. Tracer rounds began flying past Bin-Nun's boat and whizzed past his head. The MTM took several hits, but the warhead did not explode. "The sight of the rounds flying in toward me were terrifying," Bin-Nun would later recall, "but the target had to be taken out." He positioned his craft in a 90-degree angle of attack and then removed the safety from the MTM's 300-kilogram warhead.

Just as he'd been taught in Capriotti's impromptu classrooms, Bin-Nun ejected his flotation device but it refused to eject. Faced with the prospect of being neck-high in water about to absorb a 300-kilogram blast did not sit well in Bin-Nun's head—neither did driving his boat straight into the mine-sweeper's hull. At a hundred meters from the target he pulled the lever that ejected the wooden flotation system to which he was attached. His boat "wasn't" working as planned. He pulled and pulled until the handle snapped in two. He tried to free himself from the device, but the rope was too thick and tied too tightly around his waist. As he reached fifty meters from the target, Bin-Nun decided to chance it and leaped into the water, his leg still attached to the flotation device. At forty meters before impact, the pull of the rope jostled the flotation device free, though it sliced a deep gash in his side.

Seconds later, the mine-sweeper took a direct hit and erupted in a ball of flames. It sank, according to all accounts, seconds later.

The waters surrounding the battle zone were chaotic and horrid. Burning fuel filled the waters and the permeating stench of smoke and charred flesh was almost unbearable. The destruction had been complete. The *Emir Farouk*, about to ferry infantry reinforcements to Gaza, was carrying well over 500 men. Many of the infantrymen and regular soldiers did not know how to swim, nor were they issued with life jackets; many of the sailors, too, were amateurs and quickly drowned. Amid the cries of those still grasping for life and the burning patches of fuel, Ya'akov Rituv and Yitzhak Brockman sped about the water to pick up their comrades; Bin-Nun's helmet, with the infrared device, had been pulled off when he was dragged into the water, though he managed to signal his pickup by using a waterproof flashlight he had tucked into his shirt pocket. The five men returned to the *Ma'oz* changed by what they had done and what they had seen. Bin-Nun's unit had achieved the impossible, and it took time for the success of the mission to sink in. The IDF General Staff was ecstatic about the sinking of the *Emir Farouk*, though they only authorized the press to release word about the ship's sinking—not how it was accomplished. The Egyptians did not acknowledge their loss for several weeks—until anguished families lobbied the government to release word about their loved ones.

Eight and a half years after Major Palmer and his twenty-three Jewish volunteers disappeared at sea, there was a striking genesis to "Israeli" naval special warfare. The unit was on the map and had scored a remarkable victory. They had, in fact, outperformed the daring souls of Capriotti's beloved 10th MAS Flotilla. For the next few weeks, Bin-Nun and company were secretive celebrities in the upper echelons of power in the Jewish State. Bin-Nun was granted a private audience with "The Old Man," Prime Minister

Ben-Gurion, who was adamant about hearing every little detail about the raid "he" authorized. The five participants in the attack had their photographs taken with Ben-Gurion and were invited to a five-course meal by the prime minister. Bin-Nun, the modest and courageous commander of the unit and the attack, was awarded the *Itur Ha'Gvura*—Israel's highest award for courage under fire—for the sinking of the Egyptian Navy flagship.

Yosef Dror's Frogman Unit, too, was active. Like Bin-Nun's twelve-man force, Dror's underwater flotilla had been the recipient of some semi-modern diving equipment, courtesy of a *Rechesh* acquisition at the Pirelli plant in Italy. As the unit was no longer a facet of the underground, it could purchase explosives and underwater ordnance openly, and, as a result, it purchased reliable goods. The unit trained in the old port of Caesarea, and readied itself for a call to action.

The call came in November 1948.

A unit of *Mista'aravim,* or Arabists, the remnants of the *Pal'mach*'s famed undercover Arabic-speaking guerrilla and intelligence-gathering force, the Arab Platoon, had been dispatched to Lebanon to gather intelligence for their new bosses—IDF Military Intelligence; similar units operated in Syria, Trans-Jordan, and Egypt. In Beirut harbor, the squad came across a former German Navy ship that had, in fact, served as Hitler's private yacht, which was about to be requisitioned by the Royal Egyptian Navy. The ship, the S.S. *Igris,* was a 256-ton vessel capable of speeds in the upper twenty-knot range. Initially, the *Mista'aravim* wanted the job, and since part of their mission was as fifth-columnists and saboteurs, they possessed their own explosives and their own sappers. This was a naval target, however, and after great debate, it was decided to be a combined operation.

On the night of November 29, 1948, one year after the epic United Nations decision to partition Palestine into a Jewish and Arab state, the Israeli ship S.S. *Pal'mach,* a converted patrol craft, dropped off a squad of underwater sappers along the southwest shoreline of Beirut, near the

Bourj-el-Barajneh section of the city. The sappers made their way north, overland, toward the port of Beirut, and then they slinked pass a sentry and a group of fisherman in the port to enter the water far from view. They swam toward the target, and under the dangerous exposing light of a full moon, they affixed a limpet mine to the stern of the *Igris*. Confident that the device would detonate as planned, the sappers returned to the S.S. *Pal'mach* and headed back to Israel. But the Israeli intelligence agents still in place in Beirut reported no explosion. Another mission was planned, but, mysteriously and without explanation, the limpet mine "decided" to explode on December 17. The *Igris* was destroyed.

In Israel's bitter war for independence—a war in which 6,000 were killed and nearly 50,000 were wounded (remarkable when considering the Jewish population of the new state numbered only 600,000)—the fledgling navy had performed admirably. Toward the end of the war, Paul Shulman, the American volunteer who at the age of thirty had directed much of Israel's naval war effort, became the commander of the IDF/Navy. He was more a teaching commander than a "First Lord of the Admirality," and he functioned in the role of setting up a navy built on classic seamanship principles. He wasn't a naval tactician, but he knew a lot about ships and the type of men needed to sail them. In 1949, Shulman was replaced by General Shlomoh Shamir, an officer, a gentleman, and veteran of the British Army who was the first commander of Israel's legendary 7th Armored Brigade. He knew nothing about naval warfare, but he knew how to organize men into units, fill ledgers, and keep a massive bureaucracy running. He was exactly the type of man their navy needed—a force put together under chaos needed to be streamlined and consolidated into an effective fighting machine. The same thinking held true for the special warfare units.

Under General Shamir's command of the navy, Yochai's unit received the largest chunk of the special warfare budget—one couldn't argue with success and the sinking of the *Emir Farouk* was a masterstroke. Still employing Fiorenco Capriotti as their instructor, the unit continued to train in Tiberias alongside the Sea of Galilee, honing their skills and tactics. Yosef Dror's "Frogman Unit" also continued its training and equipment acquisition, but they were always the second-class citizens of the community—they could not compete with the legend of the MTMs and the sinking of the Egyptian Navy flagship. The "Shark Unit," a very small force of a handful of technicians and operators, was lowest in the Israeli naval special warfare pecking order. But all three forces possessed merit, and although they were rivals, Dror suggested to Bin-Nun that the three units merge into one large fighting force. They could obtain larger funding, Dror argued, they could attract better personnel, and combine their skills and equipment into a highly efficient and far-reaching commando force. Both Dror and Bin-Nun had spent a good part of their special operations careers abroad, in the neighboring harbors of the Mediterranean, and both agreed that the unit should recruit recent immigrants who could pass as foreigners. Dror even agreed that Bin-Nun, the more charismatic and capable of the two, should be the unit commander. Bin-Nun accepted the proposal; the IDF General Staff rejected it. They feared that the creation of a large and very elite fighting force might become a "partisan" unit answerable to no one. The General Staff thought it far safer to keep the specialized units small and separate from one another.

In typical Israeli fashion, however, Bin-Nun ignored the orders of the navy commander and of General Yigal Yadin, the deputy chief of staff, and went straight to David Ben-Gurion, who was used to getting visits from disgruntled army officers disillusioned with bureaucracy and small-mindedness. Ben-Gurion, still remembering the thrilling account of the *Emir Farouk's* sinking, asked Bin-Nun point-blank if there was "any future" to underwater special operations. With a quick and charismatic smile, Bin-Nun simply said, "Yes, sir, I truly believe there is."

The unit merger occurred weeks later. The three separate entities became known as "Flotilla 13." The number thirteen was considered special to the *Pal'yam* veterans because on the thirteenth day of each month, at lunch, they would raise a glass of wine to their comrades sailing about the Mediterranean. It was tradition and it mattered.[27] The "Explosive Boat Unit" joined the "Frogman Unit" in a new facility, located just south of Haifa, at an old British coast guard base near Atlit. The Shark, interestingly enough, became a tangible inspiration for what would later become a revolutionary wire (and optically) guided Israeli-produced surface-to-surface missile: the Gabriel. The "Shark Unit" became the corps surrounding which the newly formed flotilla would develop a highly-advanced think tank and production unit that would develop and produce innovative and ingenious equipment for the men of the unit.

Yochai Bin-Nun was the founding father of Israeli naval special warfare and the obvious choice to become the first commander of Flotilla 13. A kind and gentle man, known in his Kibbutz for his heart of gold, kind disposition, and will of forged iron, he was a likely candidate to volunteer and lead such a small and ragtag force. When looking at the odds they faced, from their campaign against the British to the sinking of the *Emir Farouk,* it took a special type of commander to lead such a force. When he took command of the unit, "Yochai" was already midway through a remarkable thirty-year career in Israeli naval special warfare. His body was like a map of the Middle East, commented a friend; it was decorated with scars and holes obtained in various parts of the region from a variety of enemy ordnance.

At first, Flotilla 13 adopted as its emblem the old "Explosive Boat Unit" symbol that resembled the *Pal'mach* coat of arms and had so infuriated Yigal Yadin in 1948. After infuriating Yadin once again with a reminder of the "partisan-like" free-thinking souls of the *Pal'mach,* the unit began toying with such varied symbols as a skull with a dagger in it (that was too much like the SS symbol), and a frog with bat wings (in honor of the British SBS). In the end, the unit's calling card would become a silver metal shield and sword with spread-out bat wings. The bat wings became the flotilla's symbol—the bat was a creature of the night much like the naval commandos. Both operated silently, both operated in pitch darkness, and both had the potential for lethal strikes. They wanted their enemies to simply refer to them as "The Batmen."

The Batmen, in 1950, were paper tigers. Flotilla 13 was beset by morale problems, equipment troubles, and the beginnings of what would become a love-hate relationship with the powers that be in IDF/Navy HQ. The true secret to its success, virtually everyone in positions of command knew, would be the caliber of men that the force could attract. It is the man that drives the machine, and quality and character had to be able to overcome the meager resources.

On a chilly May morning in 1954, a young and disillusioned corporal in an infantry unit, bored with the life of a foot soldier, attempted to realize his boyhood love for the sea and volunteer into the secretive flotilla. Appearing at the unit's home base in Atlit, south of Haifa along the Mediterranean coast, and soaking wet from a harsh winter's rain, Corporal Ze'ev Almog was determined to join this secretive unit, refusing to listen to the long list of reasons set forth by Major Yankele Náim, his infantry commander, about why he *shouldn't* volunteer, and why the horrid IDF bureaucracy would forbid him from volunteering. Izzy Rahav, the Flotilla 13 commander, just sat and stared at this motivated soldier. After Almog was sent by Major Náim to the adjutant's office to complete the paperwork, Rahav put down his cup of tea, turned to Major Náim, and said, "One day that man will be the flotilla's commander." He was right.

Flotilla 13 was on its way.

CHAPTER TWO

The Lean Years of Growing Pains and Misuse

Flotilla 13: 1953 to 1967

COMMANDOS IN A JEWISH NAVY ARE NOT SUPPOSED TO USE A weapon called a "Pig"—it just isn't politically correct. But for the operators in Flotilla 13, the acquisition of the Italian-produced World War Two era underwater warhead delivery system was a step ahead toward legitimizing a unit that had very simple beginnings.

Of all the units to emerge from the 1948 War, one would have thought that the newly ordained unit of "Flotilla 13" would have been at the top of the IDF's order of battle—a small unit of daring men who succeeded in sinking the enemy navy's flagship. Yet the IDF in 1950 was not an army proactively supporting small and secretive units in search of funding, legitimacy, and operational assignments. At the time, the IDF was a dirt-poor fighting force in complete disarray trying to successfully equip, train, and maintain itself. Israel in 1949 and 1950, in fact, was in a state of chaos, poverty, and confusion. The IDF had successfully fought off invasion and had fought to the bone to secure the establishment of the Jewish State. But the fighting took an irreplaceable toll on men and equipment—assets that

75

needed to be replaced. Of the 6,000 battlefield casualties, many were officers and commanders who had fought in World War II and against the British. They were experienced, charismatic, and self-sacrificing, and they had died by the hundreds. Equipment, too, had been destroyed faster than it could be replaced. The IDF was left with a victory following the war, and little else.

Building a professional army, even one with universal military service, was an incredible task for the already thinly stretched Israeli defense budget. They had to buy tanks, airplanes, cannons, ships, vehicles, bullets, uniforms, and radios to buy, let alone pay the salaries for conscripted soldiers and the benefits for professional officers and NCOs. There was also the question of where to house these soldiers and how they'd be fed. Exacerbating the budgetary limitation was the very real national task of building a country. The moment Israeli independence was declared and the British blockade no longer a factor, the refugee ships that had been turned away began to flood the new nation with those who had been interned in Cyprus. Once the war ended, Jews of the Middle Eastern Diaspora—from Iraq, Yemen, Morocco, Syria, and Egypt—all fled their native lands for the new Jewish homeland. The population of Israel doubled, then tripled, but the resources to house and employ these new immigrants were nonexistent. With few social institutions at the country's disposal, the IDF began being used as a melting pot. After all, why set up social services and Hebrew language learning centers when new immigrants could learn the language and citizenship in uniform?

Nation building and army building do not necessarily go hand in hand. The new immigrants, many of whom sold their uniforms and equipment for food money to send home to their extended families living in transit camps, proved to be an enormous burden for the fledgling defense forces to bear. The IDF's ability to produce an army of significant manpower to secure the just-fought-over-and-won frontiers was in doubt, as was its ability to absorb "used" equipment purchased abroad. The IDF could field a few brigades of infantrymen, one tank brigade, and a few dozen aircraft, but little else. It was not a military capable of serious offensive moves against its neighbors.

Flotilla 13 was one of the few commando units the IDF maintained in its order of battle in 1950, and it was a unit that was preparing for war. In 1949, in the final weeks of the War of Independence, the separate arms of the unit carried out their first fully conventional training courses. Bin-Nun's crew carried out—and was officially certified—to operate their exploding vessels along the shores of the Sea of Galilee, and Yosef Dror's squad was officially certified in underwater operations near Caesarea. In 1949, the first combined course opened up for new conscripts to the Israeli military at the unit's new training facility and home base at Atlit. Unlike the days of the *Pal'yam,* when whoever wanted to be in the unit was able to join if he could make the grade, this course was open to conscripts and active duty personnel, all volunteers, uninterested in being part of a national military, more interested in teaching Hebrew than striking at a sea of enemy states unwilling to accept the new Jewish State. From the entire conscription pool of 1949, of the tens of thousands of young men pressed into military service, Flotilla 13 received eighteen volunteers.

The majority of those eighteen volunteers accepted for training with the newly formed flotilla were all Kibbutznikim, and they had heard about the unit the way most had heard about the *Pal'mach* and the *Pal'yam*—word of mouth. In fact, the connection between Flotilla 13 and the *Pal'mach* was not lost to the unit commanders, those volunteering into the force, and those in the IDF hierarchy. Men like Bin-Nun, Dror, and Rahav wanted to capture the spirit of the *Pal'mach* into the backbone of the new unit—a motivated spirit of hard work, commitment, and maximizing in small numbers what others would take brigades to accomplish. The *Pal'mach* evoked a sense of elitism, a breed apart from the rest, and that was exactly what Bin-Nun and his commanders wanted for the flotilla. These men were, indeed, special—it took an elite brand of soldier to drive a wooden speedboat laden with 300 kilograms of high explosives and aim himself toward an enemy warship. Bin-Nun knew that his men needed to be elite, soldiers a cut above the rest, and it was operationally a prerequisite for the operators to live and breathe with that confidence.

The ethic of the *Pal'mach* was that of hard work and challenges. The training, termed "The Naval Commando Instructors Course" (so as not to let on as to the small number of pupils in the class)[1], was to push the participants beyond their limits—both in the water and in the classroom. Ocean training was conducted only in the roughest of seas. Recruits were often sent to swim by themselves, without instructors or safety officers, in order to endear them to the dangers and power of the water. Courses in diving, operating boats, explosives, exploding boats, and other tools of war were lengthy, arduous, and conducted with little time off. Classroom study was often interrupted by arduous forced marches along the Mediterranean coast—just like in the *Pal'mach,* there was virtue to long marches through the countryside. It built character.

But the IDF General Staff, eager to expand on an egalitarian spirit throughout the entire military, viewed the reaffirmation of the *Pal'mach*'s independent and elite spirit as dangerous. And Flotilla 13 expressed its independence at every step and turn—from not allowing senior IDF/Navy officers to enter the Atlit training base, to evading and sometimes confronting military policemen. "It was all very partisan," recalled Bin-Nun. "We were a separate entity tasked with some very dangerous and very critical work."[2] Even in 1950, many former commandos of the *Pal'mach* had urged their commanding officers to create a separate "Commando Corps" of special warfare specialists who would answer only to the Ministry of Defense; it would act as the executing arm for IDF Military Intelligence and the newly created *Mossad Le'Mode'in U'le'Tafkidim Meyuchadim,* Israel's foreign espionage service that the world would come to know simply as the "Mossad." Some envisioned this corps to number as many as 500 soldiers, and they would operate regionally—and internationally—to ensure Israel's strategic interests and territorial integrity. Bin-Nun envisioned Flotilla 13 as the vanguard of this entity, though all wanted Yigal Alon, the former commanding officer of the *Pal'mach,* to be the corps commander. For an army barely capable of equipping an infantry brigade, creating a 500-man unit was bold thinking. To many, however, this was also seditious thinking and it had to be wiped out.

Lieutenant General Yigal Yadin, the chief of staff, was one of those who was determined to rid the *Pal'mach* spirit from the IDF. He had locked horns with Bin-Nun in 1948 prior to the sinking of the *Emir Farouk,* and in 1950, during a visit to the flotilla's base, the confrontation would come full circle. Flotilla 13 still maintained as its emblem the "outlawed" *Pal'mach*-lookalike logo—it was supposed to be a secret symbol (after all, the unit and its base were off-limits to just about everyone in the IDF) for "in-house" only. After all, the unit motto used to be "We are so secret even we don't know what we are doing!" When Lieutenant General Yadin saw this emblem emblazoned throughout the Spartan-like grounds at the flotilla's training and headquarters facility, he went ballistic. IDF/Navy commander Shlomoh Shamir, a former British Army major and commander of the IDF's 7th Armored Brigade, could do little but try and pick up the pieces. Yadin wanted Bin-Nun and Dror out of the navy—Shamir helped diffuse the situation, though he could not save the commanders their jobs. Both were asked to resign their commands, though command of the unit was handed over to another *Pal'mach* and *Pal'yam* veteran, Lieutenant Commander Izzy Rahav. There was, at first, talk of having the unit mutiny and simply refuse to follow Yadin's edict; similar mutinies had occurred in the *Pal'mach* when an unpopular order was issued by the *Haganah.* But talk of mutiny remained just that—talk. Rahav assumed command without rumblings or court-martial-worthy actions. "Perhaps it was the unit's growing pains and perhaps it was the last bit of independence that needed to be removed from its spirit." What Yadin's purge did manage to do was set the unit on its path toward complete integration into poor, minimally equipped, poorly trained IDF. For better or worse, Flotilla 13 was part of the lackluster Israel Defense Forces.

Shlomoh Shamir was a professional soldier and a man

whose abilities were needed throughout the IDF—following his stint as commander of the IDF/Navy, he retired his white Class A's to assume command of the Israel Air Force (IAF). Shamir's replacement was Admiral Mocka Limon, only twenty-six years old when he assumed command of the fledgling fleet. Limon had no special warfare experience, though he had been a British naval officer during the Second World War, seeing action in the Mediterranean at Tobruk, Benghazi, Malta, and in the Indian Ocean. What he lacked in experience, he made up for in a dynamic ambition to get the job done. Having spent the war with the Royal Navy, he was afforded the opportunity to see how a professional navy got the job done in wartime. Working with the SBS, as well, he was also introduced into the small world, unique personality, and incredible capabilities of naval special operators. In Limon, Flotilla 13 would have the best type of friend a specialized unit could hope to find in a senior commander—one who would support it against the bureaucracy, and one who would also command with a hands-off approach, permitting it to grow as its commanders saw fit. And if Flotilla 13 needed anything in those early years, it was a chance to grow!

The unit base at Atlit looked little like a commando base, and more like a work camp. The uniform of the day was whatever the operator could find that would fit, few men shaved, long hair was common, and a salute was as rare to the facility as a pair of polished black boots. The sounds of explosions at sea were heard throughout the day, as were the sounds of beer bottles crashing against the hard jagged rocks along the shore. Many of the operators worked at the Haifa shipyards and port by day or whenever they could escape from their commanders, and commandos from one housing block often spent more time playing practical jokes on their comrades in the adjacent block than they did in the classroom or in the water practicing the application of a limpet mine to the hull of an enemy warship. If Yadin had hoped to expunge the partisan spirit by getting rid of Bin-Nun and Dror, he failed. The base looked like a guerrilla camp more than one of the most top-secret facilities in all of Israel.

One of the major problems facing the flotilla was the lengthy period of time it took to train an operator. The basic course, consisting of infantry training, dive training, explosives handling, and weapons and equipment proficiency lasted many months—half of the mandatory three years of conscripted service. A unit volunteer wasn't forced to sign on an additional two years of professional duty to his time of service, so by the time he finished his instruction and his probationary service, he had less than a year remaining in unit uniform. Faces changed at the base faster than the waves sweeping the shore. With little continuity in manpower, the unit was a way station for conscripts interested in an exciting alternative to the regular army; it was also a way station for soldiers eager for the moonlighting income of the nearby Haifa Shipyards.

There were almost no operational assignments, and little to do other than train and commiserate about how boring military service was. Morale was not good.

In professions such as that of naval commando, there has always been a debate about whether it is the machinery that drives the man, or the man that drives the machinery. The tools of the operator, their exploding boats, delivery vehicles, and even the still alive "Shark" guided torpedo project were integral parts of the unit's order of battle—as important, certainly, as the human element. Maintaining these devices, however, let alone improving and producing them, required a professional cadre of mechanics, designers, and ordnance experts (that could not turn over every time a three-year stint in the military). Luckily, the technicians proved to be a loyal and dedicated lot who remained in the unit year after year, enduring low pay and the bureaucracy of a frugal military in order to see their visions and designs through from the drawing board to enemy territory. Their professional ethic and their uncanny devotion to detail became an element of Flotilla 13's esprit de corps that would soon be translated on the training field and in operations behind enemy lines.

As flotilla commander, Limon refused to let the limitations of his surroundings limit the ambitious dreams for his unit. He realized that for the force to be able to act as a professional special operations arm of a conventional sea-going navy, it needed to learn from the best, and in 1953, the best meant Great Britain's Royal Marines and their elite commandos, the Special Boat Squadron (SBS).[3] Rahav petitioned Limon for permission—and the money—to send a representative or two from the flotilla to England, and he had also been in contact with the British for permission to accept two Israeli pupils. It was a longshot, he knew, for the British government to permit men, who years earlier had sabotaged its warships in Haifa, to learn more trade secrets from their premier commando force. But the SBS was also training commandos from West Germany's elite *Kamfschwimmerkompanie,* the postwar German Navy's combat swimmer company, and certainly the British had a worse history with the German Navy than it did with representatives of the *Pal'yam.* After much letter-writing and lobbying, two Israeli commandos were selected for the trip to Portsmouth, the SBS home base, where they would have the opportunity to train with the world's premier naval special warfare unit.

Coming from Atlit to Portsmouth was an eye-opening experience for two Israelis, Dov Shapir and Boaz Atzmon,[4] and their eyes saw the day-to-day operations of one of the most professional navies and marine forces in the world. The Royal Navy warships in Portsmouth harbor filled the horizon as far as the eye could see, and the level of order, discipline, and professionalism inside the SBS barracks was immaculate, unflinching, and all-encompassing. In Portsmouth, the two Israelis observed firsthand what they could have only dreamed about seeing in Atlit. The unit operated like a Swiss-designed piece of machinery. Discipline was the oil that greased the machine, determination was what powered it, and professionalism marked by courage was what ensured that the machine destroyed its target and made it back to base safely. Had Rahav been present in Portsmouth, he would have taken buckets of whitewash and disinfectant to Atlit and scrubbed the grime and apathy away personally.

Besides learning the A-to-Zs of professional military behavior at Portsmouth, the Israeli pupils also learned the art of fine-tuning the skills of a warrior. Intensive classes in cold-killing were given, as were lengthy instruction in marksmanship, sniping, and pistol-shooting. To the SBS, the term *commando* meant that the operator needed to know more than just what was needed to be done underwater. He had to know how to raid enemy harbors, kill sentries, and secure perimeters with fields of determined machine-gun fire until he could be rescued or find the means to escape. The limpet mine was studied and mastered, as were other explosive devices that could turn a 120-ton warship into a listing landmark of leaking fuel. Delivery vehicles were also studied and mastered—from the Zodiac rubber inflatable to the SBS calling card, the Klepper canoe. Flotilla 13 maintained its own small fleet of wooden kayaks, but the Kleppers were light, highly effective, and could be carried by its two-man crews. The Israelis learned how the SBS carried out beach reconnaissance raids, including the taking of soil samples; how they carried out intelligence-gathering assignments; and, even though the IDF/Navy had yet to purchase a submarine of its own, they learned the art of locking out of a sub with the Royal Navy.

In 1954, Mordechai Limon left his post as IDF/Navy commander to assume a more sensitive post in "special operations" with the Ministry of Defense. His replacement was Admiral Shmuel Tenkus, a *Pal'yam* veteran and "by-the-book" commander who was not so much interested in the special warfare aspect of the navy as he was with building it into a respectable and capable fleet. Two "Z"-class destroyers, aging relics of the Royal Navy from the Second World War, were purchased; one ship became the I.N.S. *Yafo*, and the other, deemed the flagship of the fleet, was designated the I.N.S. *Eilat*. In the first year as commander of the navy, Admiral Tenkus also cut through the budgetary restrictions he often faced for the purchase of several patrol craft and a few landing craft from France, but one of his major objectives was the acquisition of a submarine. Although it was doubtful that Israel would ever gather an underwater fleet with any significant strength, the ability to reach an enemy harbor undetected was a fleeting thought.

* * *

Along with dreams of a sub in 1954, came a new class of volunteer into the ranks of Flotilla 13. By 1954, the overall situation of the IDF had improved markedly and the IDF's morale and combat abilities reached proficient levels. Yigal Yadin, the chief of staff who professed an egalitarian ethic for the IDF, had been a powerful force in pushing the Israeli military past the traumatic 1948 War, but his views on elite forces were wrong. Elite units achieve many objectives other than blowing up targets behind enemy lines and instilling fear into the hearts of enemy sentries. Elite units are symbols, powerful icons of sacrifice and achievement that only a handful of men can hope to succeed at, but, more important, legions of soldiers can hope to emulate. An elite unit raises the capabilities—and morale—of an entire army, and that, in turn, raises the overall abilities of a nation to defend itself. Yadin's view that the presence of a few small and elite units in the new IDF would be a divisive distraction failed to take into account the fact that without a "best," everything is simply mediocre.

Even under Yadin's tenure as chief of staff, attempts to create and foster elite units existed in the Israeli military, but these were mainly "localized" efforts by regional commanders to shore up the gaping security holes in the frontiers they were tasked to defend. There was "Unit 300," a reconnaissance force of Bedouin, Druze, and Circassian volunteers that operated along the hills and wadis of Galilee; there was "Unit 30," a small intelligence-gathering and counter-intelligence force of reconnaissance commandos tasked with interdicting smugglers, armed infiltrators, and enemy espionage agents. There was even a small reconnaissance force of operators known as "Almond Unit" that patrolled the desert border with Egypt. Even in 1949, the IDF tried to conventionalize the concept of elite troopers with the formation of the *Tzanhanim* (or "Paratroops"). There had been Jewish parachutists serving British intelligence during the Second World War and an airborne unit of some kind was an accepted "conventional" force; there was, of course, no jump school in Israel at the time, and the airborne training was carried out at a former German SS barracks in the Bohemian countryside. A territorial brigade, known by the Hebrew acronym of *Na'ha'l* (short for *Noar Halutzei Lohem* or "Fighting Pioneer Youth"), made up of pioneer-spirited eighteen-year-old conscripts who combined agricultural and military service, was the true source of an elite mind-spirit within the Israeli military. Physically fit, politically motivated, and adept at service along dangerous frontiers, the soldiers of the *Na'ha'l* were the shining examples of the Jewish State. They were also quite used to self-sacrifice and, because they operated in small units, assuming dire responsibilities without direct contact with their immediate commanders. They were brave and independent thinkers and the perfect commando material.

The true rebirth of the elite spirit in the IDF was the creation of the legendary and famous (and some would say infamous) cross-border retaliatory strike force known as "Unit 101." In 1953, in response to an alarming number of cross-border raids by Palestinian guerrillas operating in the Gaza Strip and the West Bank, the commander of Jerusalem Brigade sanctioned Major Sharon, at the time a reservist studying in Jerusalem's Hebrew University, to create a small force of commandos who could bring the irregular war home to the enemy. Using Wingate's SNS as an example, Sharon built a small, rogue, unkempt, and completely loyal force of ex-*Pal'mach*niks, former French Foreign Legionnaires, and scouts from the *Na'ha'l* battalions looking for excitement. Unit 101 was a busy unit. It saw a lot of action and spilled a lot of blood, and many—Israelis and Arabs alike—consider it notorious. It did strike fear into the hearts of the Arabs and it did get a lot of press. Its actions elevated morale and the fighting spirit of the IDF. It was, though, a force whose high body counts made it a political liability. In 1954, six months after its creation, the unit was disbanded and incorporated into the paratroops. With Sharon's private army no longer in existence, many of the soldiers who used to flock to the Unit 101 camp in the hope of volunteering into the force soon made their way toward the Mediterranean, toward Atlit, where they petitioned and pestered officers of Flotilla 13 for the chance to join the Batmen.

By 1954, there were two true elite units in the IDF order of battle—the 890th Paratroop Battalion's reconnaissance company (*Sayeret Tzanhanim*) and Flotilla 13. Those wishing to jump and to march hundreds of kilometers into Syria, Jordan, or Egypt joined the red berets of the paratroops. Those wishing to jump, march hundreds of kilometers, and learn to become one with the sea volunteered for Flotilla 13. "The talent pool reaching Atlit was incredible at the time," recalled Yochai Bin-Nun, as he remembered many of the men he interviewed and put through the ringer. "These were kids more or less, but they were strong, motivated, and not willing to fail."[5] One of those volunteers was a young *Na'ha'l* infantryman named Ze'ev Almog. A soldier who, after being accepted into the unit, was already tagged with the mighty expectations of one day commanding the unit. As a twenty-year-old soldier in 1954, he was disillusioned with the average military service. Seeking adventure, a challenge, and an opportunity to be pushed, Almog was a leading representative in a growing number of soldiers seeking a challenge.

Some soldiers volunteered into the flotilla upon their conscription, but most were already serving elsewhere and had a friend, usually in a Kibbutz, who was in the unit. Reaching the front gate at Atlit because of a friend telling a friend telling a friend, was a common means for getting an interview with the flotilla commander. Many soldiers came to volunteer on their days off; some faked visits to the infirmary so that they could hitch a ride to Atlit, and some even went AWOL for the seventy-two hours needed to volunteer and try out. Senior flotilla officers tended to favor those who reached the base through bizarre and unscrupulous means. A "by hook or by crook" attitude showed initiative and mischievous spirit, something an operator needed.

Volunteering into the unit, of course, did not guarantee one's acceptance—no matter how noble or dishonest the effort was to get there. An attrition rate of 75 percent was common, and that number grew once the volunteers entered basic training and then the professional aspect of their underwater naval special warfare instruction. Getting into the unit meant having to pass a *Gibush*, a small series of mental and physical *"examinations"*—(the politically correct term for "torture")—designed to determine whether or not a volunteer had what it took to be a member of the unit. These ranged from vicious interviews and psychological challenges no human could pass, to small beatings and having to sit submerged in a pool of frigid water, hands tied, with a face mask painted black, while small sea creatures used the volunteers' body as a smorgasbord. The culmination of the *Gibush* was a three-day 200-kilometer-long forced march along the Mediterranean coast from the Lebanese border at Rosh Haniqra to the Egyptian frontier at Gaza. The march was a gauntlet of sinking sand, razor-sharp rocks, and steep dunes. It was also to be done nonstop—without stopping for food, bathroom, or sleep. Volunteers who were strong and sane dropped out once they hit Haifa. Those who were determined made it to Kibbutz Ma'agan Michael or even Netanya. The sturdy and slowly-to-be-determined-as-nuts made it to Tel Aviv. The "operators" made it to the Egyptian frontier.

Along the forced march route, flotilla commanders followed the limping bodies in a convoy of ambulances and jeeps. The commanders would try and convince the marchers that it was time to quit. "Hey, hop into the ambulance for a second to have your leg checked," a commander would yell at a volunteer. "We won't hold it against you!" Of course, the moment anyone stopped marching and dared go near the ambulance he was ejected from the *Gibush*. Many volunteers marched with bruises and fractures—some even with broken bones. There were those whose issued boots were so uncomfortable, causing such grotesque "bubbling" blisters, they simply marched barefoot. "The motivation of a man determined to succeed no matter what the price or pain is a weapon of such incredible power it cannot be measured," observed one officer at the time, who, like the men he pushed beyond the human envelope, had also undergone the infamous march. Many of the volunteers who would survive the hell of the *Gibush* were Kibbutzniks. For these men, service in an elite fighting formation wasn't just a personal achievement, it was a measure of their status in the closed Kibbutz society where being anything less than a fighter-pilot or commando was considered failure. "The Kibbutzniks saved the unit," reflects another officer who served in the flotilla at the time. "They provided the unit with a stubborn backbone that refused to back down to any challenge and any adversity."

Most important, the *Gibush* was a test in human endurance. "We weren't as interested in their physical strength and attributes as we were in their ability to suffer," reflected Izzy Rahav, the former commander of Flotilla 13. Indeed, many of the Kibbutzniks who made it to the gates of Atlit were incredible physical specimens—the realities of Kibbutz life meant that these eighteen-year-olds had been doing some sort of stressful physical labor since they could walk. Yet muscles, brawn, and a good physique are useless unless the brain of the individual can handle walking fifty kilometers with a sprained ankle. The best swimmer in the world is useless to the unit if he can only slice through the water in a heated pool. It takes a truly unique human specimen *not* to allow the frigid waters to press against bones to the point of excruciating and debilitating pain.

In the *Gibush,* commanders of Flotilla 13 were looking for exactly that type of specimen. They were seeking men who understood pain, but who weren't hindered by it.

Beyond the physical aspects, there was the character element. A volunteer might have tremendous physical skills and be able to endure a 200-kilometer march without so much as a wince, but questions arise: "Who is he?" "What type of man is he?" "Can he be relied upon when the shit hits the fan?" Flotilla commanders attempted, through their own investigations, to weed out those candidates who weren't flotilla material by interviewing their classmates and neighbors, their parents and schoolteachers. And it is because of this character element that so many of the first generation of Flotilla 13's commandos—and future officers—were from the Kibbutzim. "Kibbutznikim are healthier, stronger, and they lived in a closed society, like an army, and can follow orders without too much hesitation," recalled Izzy Rahav when looking back on some of the selection practices he installed as commander of Flotilla 13.

"We used to take a jeep to a candidate's Kibbutz, and ask . . . 'So, what about Moshe, is he any good?' If a man was good, we knew that the Kibbutz elders would come and plead with us *not* to take the eighteen-year-old into the unit because they realized that the moment we accepted him, he was out of the Kibbutz for at least five years [three years of mandatory service and (later) the two additional years of professional duty]. As a result, when we were told 'No, don't take, him, we really need him,' we knew that he'd soon be wearing the bat wings and join our family."[6]

Once in the unit, the volunteers were ushered into the paratroops for six months of infantry training concluding with jump instruction and then a one-year evolution from rough foot soldier to underwater operator. To get back something on its investment of money and time, and to ensure that the unit maintained a sense of inner cohesion, all those volunteering into the unit and passing the training regimen were forced to sign on for two additional years of service as professional soldiers.

Slowly, as the quality of volunteers improved and the level of training intensified, Flotilla 13 assumed a distinct and efficient order of battle divided into sections, subsections, and squads. There was, of course, the exploding boat section—now equipped with MTM craft upgraded and modified by the Flotilla 13 technical section. Not only did these semi-"indigenous" boats now boast a higher speed and greater maneuverability, but they also had a modified and highly improved ejection system designed to propel the operator away from the kamikazelike path without the struggle and possible Murphy's Law scenario that Yochai Bin-Nun experienced on October 21, 1948.

The most desired unit to get into was the frogman section. In 1950, Yosef Dror traveled to Italy and purchased a large quantity of Pirelli-produced diving equipment and wet suits; he also attended an in-depth naval frogman course with the Italian Navy. In operational terms, the frogman unit was the least active of the flotilla's forces, but it was considered the most physically challenging and the most dangerous. "In its first few years of existence," recalls

Herzl Lavon, one of the founding members of Flotilla 13 and in 1950 a new conscript, "the frogman unit was known as 'Eskimo's Suicide Squad'" [This was a reference to one of the unit's commanding officers and the precarious dangers involved in being a member of the force.][7] Deep-water diving instruction was almost as dangerous as the missions they were training for, and being able to boast about spending hours on end in the frigid waters of the Mediterranean was a bragging right of the highest order. Being a member of the frogman unit also enabled the operator to learn the A-to-Zs of the flotilla's primitive, though developing, swimmer delivery vehicle, "the Pig." Developed by the Italians during the Second World War, the "Pig," or *"Miale,"* as it was known by the 10th MAS Flotilla operators, was basically a torpedo taxi cab—a nonexploding torpedo fitted with a steering mechanism, two seats, and detachable compartments. It was a novel weapon and the genesis-notion behind every swimmer delivery vehicle used by naval commandos the world over to this day. The Pig—670 centimeters long and fifty-seven centimeters wide—was a two-man device driven by an officer or NCO from a seatlike perch in the center of the tube; the "No. 2," sitting behind him, was responsible for assisting in the navigation and other "en route" maintenance problems that could arise. The Pig was a hollow delivery system whose interior was laden with gears, engine cranks, cables to hook the warhead to a ship's hull, and other survival and navigational tools. It was a cumbersome device to lower into the water, but its technical glitches and slow speeds (it couldn't cut through the depths at a rate faster than 4.5 kilometers per hour) were limiting, and it was, in the words of one Israeli operator, a throw-to-me weapon, since its range could not breech an eighteen-kilometer envelope. The most important element of the Pig was a 300-kilogram warhead that could rip the hull off of just about any warship of the day. The Italians' tactical designs called for the operators to drive the Pig underneath the targeted ship, separate the warhead from the rest of the tube by means of a special latch, and then attach the warhead underneath the enemy vessel. The 10th MAS Flotilla had scored considerable

90

success with their Pigs in the Second World War with the attack against the H.M.S. *Queen Elizabeth* and H.M.S. *Valiant* in Alexandria. Another Italian tactical plan for their Pigs was for the operators to carry large supplies of limpet mines, and for them to simply travel underwater from hull to hull in placing their devices.

In the Israeli scheme of things, the Pig had additional uses as naval targets were limited and the Arab fleets were not as threatening as the Royal Navy's wartime Mediterranean fleet. The Pig, flotilla commanders saw, could be driven to a port's breakwater, hidden from view, and then the operators would return to the waters and attach a limpetlike device, carried on the warhead tubing of the Pig, to an enemy ship below the waterline. But the Pig had uses far greater than merely sabotage. Because the delivery vehicle relieved much of the physical exertion a combat swimmer would normally endure while slicing a path toward his target, Pig crews could be dispatched on intelligence-gathering assignments in enemy shoreline facilities without having to limit their capabilities as a result of fatigue.

The officer who assumed control and command of the Pigs was Herzl Lavon. A Romanian-born officer and *Pal'yam* veteran, Lavon was a tinkerer, a mechanic of incredible talent, and, most important, an innovative thinker whose mechanical appreciation for tools and design was nothing short of brilliant. Being a tinkerer in a small and poorly funded navy in need of tinkerers, Lavon and company made remarkable modifications to the original Italian design of the Pig. Flotilla technicians first shortened the Pig, then they widened the body in order to place the operators' two seats "inside" the craft to facilitate a more comfortable ride for the two-man team. An improved mechanical propulsion system was incorporated into the overall package, as was a more stable steering mechanism, one employing aircraftlike rudders and lifts. The front of the device was still capable of holding a 200-kilogram warhead, but limpet mines and other specialized explosive equipment carried for "special" demolitions work were carried in airtight containers underneath the operators' seats. Operators in the unit knew every section of the Pig, and where every nut and bolt went. They could dismantle the hydraulic steering system with their eyes closed, and they could also fix a glitch in the Israeli-produced navigational system with little more than a pair of pliers and a screwdriver. "Have the machine become an extension of you," Lavon bestowed upon his charges. "Make it your partner." Although the Israeli-produced modification of the Italian design "officially" took on the name of the "Herziliya," after the town north of Tel Aviv where many of the system's components were produced, it was always and solely referred to in Flotilla 13's circles as the Pig.

"It was of incredible satisfaction," Herzl Lavon would recall, to take a design, improve it, rebuild it, modify it, and play around with it and then see it lowered into the Mediterranean and perform above and beyond expectations in a training exercise."[8]

Augmenting the overall abilities of the Pig unit was the unheralded and sometimes overlooked Flotilla 13 technical section. In small and often poorly lit workshops, operators turned micromechanics produced a litany of equipment for use, ranging from improved limpet mines to special load-bearing packs for use with standard radio equipment. In fact, it was with the operators radio equipment that the small technical section made incredible advances. The most noted was a closed-circuit communications apparatus that allowed the two-man Pig team to talk to one another during a mission. Communications between partners is as important an asset on a covert mission as is a reliable delivery vehicle, and the element of surprise and the radio system proved itself first in training exercises and later while deployed far from friendly shores.

The Pig unit was the flotilla's smallest section, though one of its most important and certainly the most cohesive. Pig unit operators considered themselves to be the elite of the flotilla since their missions were both offensive (attacking enemy shipping and naval targets) and covert (working on intelligence-gathering assignments and sometimes with IDF military intelligence and other elements of the Israeli espionage community). It was also the most secretive section in the flotilla and thus, by the nature of secrecy in any military force, considered a distinct entity. It also had the distinction of being the only unit in the history of the IDF to receive a reprimand from the army's chief Rabbi. Although Lavon's Pigs were considered state secrets of the highest order that very few souls outside the gates of Atlit were to know about, word about a Pig reached Major General Shlomoh Goren who, incensed and fearing the laws of the mandatory Kosher diet enforced at *all* IDF bases had been violated, issued a formal complaint to the commander of the navy, Rear Admiral Tenkus.[9]

As the unit grew to nearly fifty men by 1955, the unit's budget and scale of training grew as well. The fact that each operator was jump qualified was a mixed blessing—Mussolini's 10th MAS Flotilla had sent its divers to jump school during the Second World War and operators serving in Britain's SBS were all jump qualified. All flotilla personnel were, of course, jump qualified, as well—they did their basic training with the paratroopers, after all. But as the unit grew and its organization became coherent as opposed to a sidetrack, operators soon trained in the art of airborne insertions—parachuting into the middle of the ocean. It was a difficult task, especially since the jumper had to free himself around five meters above the waterline in order not to get tangled in his chute once submerged. Flotilla 13 also trained in dropping kayaks into the sea along with the men to paddle them into action. At first, the Israel Air Force (IAF) C-47 Dakotas dropped the men with wooden kayaks, but the wooden boats often disintegrated upon impact, and fiberglass boats were later deployed.

For all their training and for all their abilities, the postwar version of Flotilla 13 was still a virgin. It had yet to see action, and in the words of one operator at the time, it was time to "break its cherry!"[10]

In 1955, the Middle East was inching its way toward another war. In 1952, an up-and-coming Egyptian army officer, Lieutenant Colonel Gamal Abdel Nasser had overthrown the regime of King Farouk and set in place a revolutionary council in power in Cairo whose mandate include a Pan-Arab revolution and the destruction of Israel. To implement the latter objective, one enthusiastically supported by the masses of Egyptians who cherished the thought of the Egyptian Army pushing the Jewish State into the sea, Nasser supported organized Palestinian terrorist squads that operated out of the Gaza Strip and the West Bank of the Jordan River and who attacked Israeli border settlements; the Palestinian fighters, known as *Fedayeen*, were supported and run by Egyptian military intelligence agents. Israel responded by unleashing its new airborne entity, the 202nd Paratroop Brigade, on deadly retaliatory raids into Gaza and the stretches of Egyptian-controlled territory. It was a brutal campaign of tit-for-tat waged with daggers plunged into the throats of sentries, and enemy fortifications bombarded with fragmentation grenades and automatic fire. Each incursion by either side threatened to escalate into a full-scale war. United Nations observers could do little but catalog the carnage and hope that the fighting stayed out of range of their own living quarters. Egypt, the largest Arab state with a half-a-million-man army, posed an incredible threat to Israel's security. When, in 1955, the Egyptian-Czech arms pact was signed, virtually turning the Arab world's largest army into a satellite of the Warsaw Pact, Israel stood alone against a daunting foe.

But Nasser, in keeping with his Pan-Arabist and anticolonial beliefs, also vowed to rid Egypt of any and all traces of Western imperialism. That meant only one thing—nationalizing the ultrastrategic British-French-owned Suez Canal, and that was something that 10 Downing Street and the Elysee Palace would simply not tolerate. Israel, out of the convenience of a common enemy, suddenly earned two of the world's most powerful military machines as allies. The piston-engine IAF soon became the recipients of Meteor and Ouragon jet fighters. Aging Sherman tanks were soon joined by "more modern" French-built AMX-13s, and operators from Flotilla 13 were told to pack their suitcases and board ships traveling to France. Israel's naval commandos were heading to Europe to train with the "big boys."

Senior naval commando officers knew that there was a lot to learn from other naval special warfare units around the region, and around the world, as well. They welcomed the opportunity to learn from the French, as well as take advantage of a spectacular opportunity to travel to the heart of Europe on the IDF's tab. The British, standoffish as always, were not willing to have a largescale Flotilla 13 contingent train with them, but they supplied Kleppers and other miscellaneous bits of special operations equipment (and advice) to the unit at regular intervals. The French, on the other hand, were a bit more open and eager to act as the teachers. There were several French "naval" special warfare units operational at the time—ranging from naval elements to army commando sections; there was a lot of heritage for France in special naval operations; the Naval Rifle Commandos *(Fusiliers-Marines Commandos)*, for example, was a French Navy unit tracing their lineage to the original *1ere Compagnie de la Mer* of 1622, and, in 1943, the force became *1er Bn. de FMC*, and in 1944 the unit fought in Normandy as part of "4 Commando" and performed with great courage and distinction in the first battle toward the liberation of their country.

In the day-to-day operations of underwater warfare, French naval divers have always been considered to be in a class by themselves and the Israelis found their disciplined professionalism eye-opening. According to Ze'ev Almog, "Few divers are as professional, cocky, arrogant, and capable as the French."[11] And, when the Israelis traveled to France, they didn't just get the cocky and arrogant French professionals from the legendary *Le Commando Hubert*, based in Toulon, and *Le Commando Jaubert*, a top-rate strike element specializing in both airborne and underwater commando strikes. They also got the wine-drinking, tattoo-adorned, whore-chasing mercenaries of the legendary *La Légion Étrangère*—the French Foreign Legion.

Because of its overseas deployments, namely to Indochina and Algeria, the French had developed a cutthroat fighting reputation—a much better one that they had earned (or lost) as a result of being overrun by the Germans. The French were not just divers, they were airborne shock troops and commandos just as comfortable on land as they were underwater. The French units favored amphibious assaults—coming up on a sentry, slitting his throat with a dagger, and then racing inland with weapons ablaze. With the Israelis, ground training was something delegated to basic training with the paratroopers and rarely studied again. "We were expert with the Pigs and with the limpet mine," reflected an operator who served in Flotilla 13 during the 1950s, "but we were 'wet behind the ears' with the Uzi and the Mauser."

In France, as well, the Israeli operators trained in locking out of submarines in the middle of the ocean, and operating covertly in the busy ports of Toulon and Marseille—the French and Israelis would form two-man teams and perform sabotage, reconnaissance and counter-sabotage assignments for their French commanders. "The French," Herzl Lavon recalled, "possessed an odd military ethic that translated successfully in how they taught us. They viewed their deployment in Europe not as an offensive cog in the NATO machine, but as a guerrilla force, a partisan unit in the resistance, trying to harass an occupying army." The Israelis found this ethic mind-boggling. Less than a decade following the end of the Second World War and their humiliating occupation and here the powerful French were once again readying themselves for a conventional military defeat.

The French also practiced airborne jumps into the water with their Israeli counterparts—something with comical and "almost tragic" consequences. In one exercise over the southern Mediterranean, Herzl Lavon was jumping out of a German Junker-52 transport, a relic of the Nazi occupation used by the *Commando Hubert* for training purposes, with a French partner—like in dives, the operators always jumped in twos. Unlike jumping from a C-47 Dakota, or even a French-built Nord Noratlass, the jump was not an automatic static-line glide to the sea. The operator had to pull his chord to open his chute, but commandos being commandos, both Lavon and his guide opted to play a temperamental game of macho at 7,000 feet over the Mediterranean. Both assumed a free-fall posture, and the two began talking in midair, going over the tourist attractions seen just below the horizon and seeing who would flinch first and pull his rip chord. Suddenly, however, Lavon realized that the sea was approaching—*and fast*—and he decided that the time was right to open the chute. Not used to the French chutes, however, Lavon prematurely released himself from his harness and shot like a missile approximately twenty meters into the turbulent blue waters. Lavon, shocked to be alive and even more surprised to be able to swim back to the reef, didn't bother waiting for his No. 2. The French officer, meanwhile, was clutching to his round-rig gliding down to earth when he saw Lavon's missilelike descent. Just as worried about what had happened to his partner as how he'd explain the death of a guest from Israel to an angry admiral, No. 2 was too busy worrying about his fate to take the time to look for his submerged buddy, and he rushed back to the breakwater. As he emerged from the water and sought out the lieutenant commander overseeing the exercise, he found Lavon standing with a group of French officers joking about his "thirty"-meter plunge. By the time the Israelis returned to Haifa following the month-long exchange, Lavon's drop height reached "fifty" meters. There are those in Toulon who still swear that Lavon plunged a hundred meters!

The French treated underwater special warfare as an amusing hobby, they brought wine along on their dives, and they were known to reconnoiter "targets" during maneuvers from port-side brothels, rather than from an improvised breakwater observation post. They would shoot ropes and grappling hooks to the anchors of moored ships, climb up silently, and use the anchor as an impromptu nighttime observation post. The operator and his partner would sit inside the anchor chamber all night, jotting down the comings and goings of enemy vessels, and only head back into the oily waters of the harbor at daylight, or when their supply of bread and cheese ran out. "The French were conceited sons of bitches, they were cocky and arrogant, but they taught *us,* the little *pishers* from Israel, to be cocky and arrogant, as well. We watched how a force of frogmen, equipped with the best and most expensive equipment that money could buy, could function like a force of underwater supermen. We had the most meager equipment money could *rent,* and we saw that we poor bastards had to function in an equally elite manner."[12]

French diving and naval special warfare equipment was considered state-of-the-art—from the now legendary Zodiac rubber inflatable craft to a whole series of wet and dry neoprene suits a class beyond the imagination of most of the Israeli operators. The trips to France were the first contacts that the Israelis had with the Zodiacs and their incredible potential. The French used to train attacking large harbors by racing into the port on their Zodiacs and tossing grenades and firing their MAS-49 machine guns. It was lightning-fast and highly effective. By the time the "enemy" sentries realized what was going on, another group of operators had succeeded in mining several enemy ships. From that first trip to France to the present day, the Zodiac has become the Flotilla 13's most durable workhorse.

Following the first few trips to France, the professional ethic and overall abilities of the unit increased tenfold. The operators took back to Israel newfound skills and tactics, and a bit of the bravado and swagger. In time, and with the French example engraved on their minds, the little *pishers* became cocky and confident. The atmosphere in Atlit was competitive, high-strung, and eccentric. Commandos played cruel practical jokes on one another, and anyone displaying thin skin only added to the fun. "It was just the right atmosphere needed for a unit like that at the time," reflected Herzl Lavon. "These men spent so much time together and knew each other's thoughts and actions so intimately that tension and means to relieve that tension were as important to the mental survival of the unit, as food and nourishment was to its physical sustenance." By 1956, the "little pishers" realized that being a commando was a mindset just as much as it was the skill and ability to twist the acetone timing device on a limpet. All they needed was work.

The IDF General Staff didn't exactly know what to do with its small fleet of aging destroyers and torpedo boats, and the IDF/Navy didn't know what to do with its flotilla of underwater warriors, but events would force the General Staff's hands. Israel was about to go to war.

There was great tension along both the Jordanian and Egyptian frontiers in 1956. Even though IDF retaliatory strikes followed each and every Palestinian incursion, the *Fedayeen* attacks continued. Both the Israelis and the Palestinians played a bloody game of tit-for-tat along the border, and each action grew in intensity, as well as in its chances of escalating the region into full-scale war. The region was about to explode anyway. The 1955 arms deal between Czechoslovakia and Egypt, in essence turning the Arab-Israeli conflict into a proxy of the cold war, also ensured inevitable bloodshed. Nasser ordered the Straits of Tiran, the only entrance to the Gulf of Aqaba and the port of Eilat, closed to Israeli shipping. Israeli ships, bringing fuel from Iran and goods from the Far East, now had to circumvent Africa in order to reach Israel's Mediterranean posts of Ashdod and Haifa. That act, under international law, was reason enough for Israel to go to war. A military relationship had developed with the British, but a full-fledged alliance with France, as demonstrated by the close-knit special forces relationship between the two nations, together with Nasser's nationalization of the Suez Canal ensured that hostilities would erupt before the year's end.

On October 21, 1956, Israeli Prime Minister David Ben-Gurion, Director General of the Ministry of Defense Shimon Peres, and IDF Chief of Staff Lieutenant General Moshe Dayan flew to Sèvres, France, to meet with French Premier Guy Mollet and British Foreign Minister Selwyn Lloyd to finalize the three-nation assault on Egypt. The three-party collusion called for the IDF to seize Sinai and race toward the Suez Canal—British and French forces would "intervene," looking after their interests near the waterway. The Sinai peninsula was a formidable obstacle, 130 miles wide at its largest stretch and 240 miles long; the landscape was mountain passes interspersed with pure and unforgiving desert. Egyptian forces in the Sinai Desert were defensive in nature, but well-equipped and, it was believed, well-trained.

There were many in the IDF General Staff, and indeed in IDF Military Intelligence, who thought that the "next" war with the Arabs would be on both the Jordanian and Egyptian fronts. Full-scale war between Israel and Jordan "almost" erupted on the night of October 9, 1956, when Arik Sharon's paratroopers attacked the Jordanian police fort in Qilqilya in response to a *Fedayeen* attack against a frontier settlement. In the raid, the largest of its kind, thirty Jordanian soldiers were killed. But Egypt remained the primary threat, and the Sinai Desert, the connective bridge between Africa and Asia, was seen as an ultrastrategic conduit that needed to be neutralized. As early as 1955, the IDF began conducting deep-penetration reconnaissance forays into the Sinai Desert to map out advance routes, locate possible drop zones, and fill a dossier for the General Staff and the IDF Operations Branch. On the naval front, as well, Flotilla 13 was summoned to reconnoiter the Mediterranean coast of Sinai, gather soil samples, and determine if any naval targets along the coast needed "special attention."

IDF planners realized that the Sinai campaign would be a land war, and that the Egyptian Navy, a small fleet, would not be able to play a significant role in the conflict but would need to be monitored just in case. As the march toward war proceeded, however, IDF/Navy Intelligence began to pay special attention to the Egyptian armada of six destroyers, four frigates, seven corvettes, and three submarines. Port activities were monitored by Israeli (and British and French agents) and reports rushed to naval headquarters in Haifa, but little activity was foreseen for the naval operators. Commander Izzy Rahav, the Flotilla 13 commander, had at his disposal only eighteen operators a week before the war broke out—some men were in advanced training, nearly forty members of the reserve had yet to be mobilized, and several commandos undergoing the mandatory NCO's course with the paratroops were gearing up for their soon-to-be-legend-making jump into the Mitla Pass in the first hours of the war. Rahav, nevertheless, wanted this conflict, one viewed without the fear and trepidation of the 1948 War of Independence and survival, to serve as a testing ground for the ability of his unit. Men like Arik Sharon and Meir Har-Zion, the soul behind Unit 101, had grabbed much attention and became national icons of courage. Now, he believed, it was the flotilla's time for some glory.

War erupted on October 29, 1956, at 21:00 hours when sixteen C-47 Dakotas ferrying the 395 men of Major Rafael "Raful" Eitan's 890th Paratroop Battalion flew over the Parker Memorial in the center of Sinai at the approach of the Mitla Pass to initiate Israel's first and only combat parachute jump; among the paratroopers was a young sergeant named Shaul Ziv, a Flotilla 13 operator, who would go on to command the unit in the years to come. IDF ground units, infantry battalions, and armored brigades punched across the frontier with Egypt and pushed south toward strategic road junctions and twisting desert passes. Israeli warplanes strafed Egyptian ground targets and flew cover for bombers heading toward the canal. British and French paratroopers, operating from bases in Cyprus, landed along the Suez Canal and attacked key Egyptian defensive positions along the strategic waterway. The second Arab-Israeli war was underway.

Commander Rahav lobbied the naval command echelons for an assignment and for the opportunity to execute a few innovative operations that senior commanders had been working on. The first planned Flotilla 13 mission of the war was "Operation Stork." IDF/Navy Intelligence reported that an Egyptian frigate was augmenting the naval artillery batteries at Sharm el Sheikh, situated at the southernmost tip of the Sinai peninsula, and could bombard IDF armor and infantry units pressing south along the coastal road. "Operation Stork" called for four operators, all divers from Herzl Lavon's "Pig Unit," to parachute into the Red Sea from a low-flying Dakota along with two wooden kayaks equipped with small motors. The four men would paddle their way toward the moored Egyptian frigate under the cover of darkness, plant several limpet mines to her hull, and then fire up their engines for a sail toward the Sinai coast. Equipped with several radios, Uzi submachine guns and enough ammunition to hold off a company of Egyptian infantrymen, the four would traverse a nearby peak and set up an observation post relaying back vital intelligence to the advancing Israeli units.

It was a bold plan, and one that the unit wanted badly. Rahav had spent his entire military career in the navy and knew and understood the bureaucracy involved in getting such a proposed operation authorized. To save time, he dispatched Lavon and his three subordinates to the main IAF transport base at Tel Nof, just south of Tel Aviv, along with the kayaks, the explosives, and their land warfare equipment. Once authorization was received, he'd speed toward the airfield in his jeep and give the four frogmen their final briefing. Three days after the war started, Rahav received his green light.

Because of the difficulties in flying low-level over water, Flotilla 13 had generally trained with a select group of IAF C-47 pilots—these aviators were the IAF's premier transport pilots and they have a cocky and confident bunch who became natural friends with the naval operators and the pilots. They worked well together and liked one another. Most important, the operators trusted the pilots to get them square over their mark when the chips were for real. Unfortunately for Lavon's squad, their flyers were busy on the day of "Operation Stork"—the squadron was airborne at the time, flying ammunition runs over Sinai. They received a C-47 crew that they had never seen before and that was unfamiliar with naval drops. Disappointed but undaunted, Lavon exchanged a few words with his commander before making sure that all the equipment was properly on board, and then, in the late afternoon of November 1, 1956, the Dakota lifted off from the misty Tel Nof tarmac.

The flight to Sharm el Sheikh should have taken three hours. The plane was on course for the trip south toward the Gulf of Aqaba at Eilat and then due south hugging the coastline of the Sinai peninsula. As Lavon checked his watch and readied his British-made parachute one final time, he sensed the plane rolling in circles, as if it were lost. Heading to the cockpit, he found out that the pilots could not find the target. "Don't worry, we'll get it," one of the pilots commented to an anxious Lavon. "We'll get you there." Feeling pressured, the co-pilot switched on the red light indicating that the jump time was near, and a jumpmaster unlocked the Dakota's side door. Herzl smiled at his mates, hooked up his line, and positioned himself in the door opening, his hands tightly clutching the exterior of the fuselage. "Where is that damn green light," Lavon thought. "We must be over it by now?" Lavon stood in the door for nearly three minutes until the pilot aborted the jump and canceled the mission. From his cockpit window and his navigational charts, the Dakota's pilot couldn't tell if he was near the Sinai or Saudi coast. The mission was a scrub.

Another Flotilla 13 operation, code-named "Pirate," called for a force of operators to make a nighttime parachute jump into the Red Sea, take over an Egyptian warship heading toward the Saudi coast, and commandeer it to Eilat. The plan was an ambitious assignment, and had been on the flotilla's operational books since the first operators earned their jump wings in 1954. Yet this, too, for reasons unknown, turned out to be an aborted mission.

Disappointed by the IAF's betrayal of their four operators, Flotilla 13's commander, Rahav, was willing to make a stink about the failures of Operations "Stork" and "Pirate" to his superiors, but the mood in IDF/Navy was not ripe for letting heads roll. Quite the contrary—there was a party atmosphere in the fluorescent-lit halls of IDF/Navy HQ. On the morning of October 31, 1956, the new flagship of the Egyptian Navy, the E.N.S. *Ibrahim el-Awal* had surprised the IDF/Navy and positioned itself within artillery range of the city of Haifa. Before most residents of the port city were awake, the *Ibrahim el-Awal* began an indiscriminate bombardment of Mt. Carmel. The Egyptians had successfully come through the back door, but they had entered alone. Unprotected by escort ships, the *Ibrahim el-Awal* was dangerously exposed to counterattack. When Israeli fighters began strafing the vessel, and Israeli destroyer boats zigzagged a path of attack toward the ship, the *Ibrahim el-Awal*'s commander, Captain Rushdie Ta'amzin, decided to surrender; it was seized, repainted, and pressed into Israeli service as the I.N.S. *Haifa*. One of the Israeli destroyers that reached the *Ibrahim el-Awal* first was the I.N.S. *Yafo*, commanded by Captain Yochai Bin-Nun. Bin-Nun, ejected from Flotilla 13 for trying to maintain an elitist atmosphere in the unit, had studied in Harvard from 1950 to 1954 and returned to the sea that he loved. He also loved his "child," the flotilla, and would return to serve as its commander in 1958.

Flotilla 13's level of inaction in the 1956 War was a symptom of the unit in its formative years. As Herzl Lavon would comment when talking about how the failure of "Operation Stork" created morale problems within the unit and within the navy, "With such bad luck and inept execution and faulty support, we couldn't expect great respect from our superiors. After all, respect in special operations circles is only as great as the success of your last operation!" Inactive compared to the remainder of the IDF, fighting a war against the Palestinian *Fedayeen,* the unit spent much of its time training and perfecting its skills for mounting covert operations behind enemy lines—even these operations were very few and far between. Even though the flotilla, under Rahav and Bin-Nun, obtained newer and more sophisticated equipment, including heavily armed speedboats to be used as mother ships and advanced underwater navigational gear, the operators were hungry. They wanted action.

Bin-Nun realized that without an operation, even one, the unit would endure a self-destructive period of self-doubt and malcontent. The unit needed work, and in 1958, Bin-Nun found a useful and convenient target to Israel's north that would, in time, become so familiar to the men of the unit that they'd consider it a second home.

Lebanon in 1958 was light-years away from the terrorist-controlled chaos that much of the world has come to known of that tragic nation. There weren't any Syrian Army checkpoints in Beirut in 1958, at the time the IDF didn't occupy a stretch of the south, and the Shi'ites were a poor and silent majority. French was the dominant language of the Lebanese capital, as its role as the "Riviera of the Middle East" was secured by Gulf State millionaires gambling in the city's casinos, spending money on the city's endless supply of liquor and prostitutes, and taking full advantage of the Christian government's liberal business regulations in order to use the Levant as the Middle East's business link to Europe. It was as far away from a participant in the Arab-Israeli conflict as could be found but still technically at war with the Jewish State, and that made it, in the eyes of the IDF, a target nation.

Lebanon was also the softest of the target nations. Its 16,000-man army was a minuscule force of poorly trained professionals tasked more with maintaining the current regime than launching sophisticated offensive strikes. The Lebanese Navy consisted of a few torpedo boats, and little more. Yet Bin-Nun knew that sending his men into an enemy port, even for a training exercise, would get the adrenaline pumping throughout the unit and also help get the force noticed in General Staff meetings, and most importantly by the IDF/Navy. Much to the unit's dismay, the IDF/Navy began to view Flotilla 13 as something of an anomaly who served no purpose other than to drain the overall naval budget. IDF/Navy Intelligence rarely provided Flotilla 13 with briefings or useful information; the IDF/Navy even refused to supply the flotilla with .50-caliber machine guns for use on the MTM boats modified for operator insertion/collection craft (the guns were "donated" by a battalion in the 1st Golani Infantry Brigade).[13] To reinstate the unit's abilities in everyone's eyes, including the operators, it was important to launch a mission away from the Israeli frontier. Bin-Nun lobbied the General Staff for authorization to mount a "training reconnaissance" sortie of Beirut harbor. Much to his shock and surprise, the mission was approved. It was code-named "Operation Affluent-3."[14]

The reconnaissance force, personally commanded by Captain Bin-Nun, was to reach the waters off Beirut courtesy of an IDF/Navy torpedo boat. Once their safe insertion into the territorial waters off the Lebanese capital was complete, two MTM craft used as insertion/collection craft would ferry the two two-man teams to a point where they'd be able to dive and reach the port area unnoticed. New "Oxygen" breathing apparatus gear, purchased from

France, allowed the operators to remain underwater for an astounding three hours.[15] In April 1958, Bin-Nun had covertly authorized a team of operators to mount a reconnaissance sortie against the Lebanese ports of Tyre and Sidon, and those missions were executed flawlessly and without incident. The divers for the two Lebanese sorties were Ze'ev Almog and Haim Shoham, two men who in tandem would rewrite many of the rules in the Flotilla 13 playback. Beirut was a bigger gamble, however. If any of the four was to be captured, the regional implications were enormous. At their final briefing, on the night of July 9, 1958, Bin-Nun told his men, "Don't get caught, and don't screw up and everything will be okay!" Listening in on the informal preoperational gathering was Admiral Shmuel Tenkus and Brigadier General Yitzhak Rabin, the IDF chief of operations. Rabin had fought with Bin-Nun in Jerusalem in 1948 and had been instrumental in getting General Staff approval for the Beirut mission.

Beirut, the Paris of the Mediterranean and the Middle East, was ablaze with colorful lights and the sounds of music—for a "military" target, the port was nicely silhouetted against the backdrop of lights and activity. Each MTM craft pulled to within a few hundred meters of the port entrance, but, to their horror, they found a large flotilla of Lebanese fishing boats crisscrossing the breakwater, either coming back from a day's haul or heading out for some nighttime net dropping. It would have been tragic for the four divers and the two two-man boat teams (one driver and one .50-caliber gunner) to have been discovered by a fisherman armed with nothing more than a pole, and the operators were ordered to take extra precautions to avoid any and all contact. One two-man team, consisting of Ami Amir and Amnon Ben-Tzion, were to reconnoiter the port area and the radar station; the other team, consisting of Ze'ev Almog and Ze'ev Ariel, were to hit the breakwater and monitor port activity at the other end of the harbor. They swam to their positions silently and unnoticed.

The two Ze'evs, as Murphy's Law would have it, encountered dire difficulties once they hit Lebanese soil. Ze'ev Ariel headed toward the eastern end of the breakwater closest to the port so that he, in the words of his partner, "could hear the hypnotic tunes of the Arabic music coming from a nearby cafe." A few minutes later, when the two music lovers climbed the ascending rocks, to reconnoiter the port they came across a Lebanese guard patrolling the breakwater. Both Almog and Ariel attempted to break contact, but Ariel slipped on some rocks. The guard came over to the two divers, a revolver in hand, to investigate the source of the suspicious noise. Almog had managed to return to the water, but Ariel soon found himself starring eyeball-to-eyeball with the Lebanese policeman who was aiming a pistol at his head; the Israelis were only armed with a dagger and their flares and had been ordered not to kill anyone; the raid was supposed to be deniable, and leaving behind a corpse made denial impossible. Soon another Lebanese guard appeared on the scene. Ariel responded with instinct and decided to begin yelling at the guards in English. "Who the hell do you think you are bothering me!" Ariel screamed in an authoritative voice. "I am a crewman from an American destroyer and you have no right to threaten me with a gun." Before the two dumbfounded Lebanese could respond or fire, Ariel and Almog had lurched their bodies back into the dark waters for the dive and swim across the harbor back to the MTM craft. Beirut harbor was soon abuzz with activity. Lights, sirens, and Lebanese Gendarmes firing bursts of machine-gun fire into the water. The Israelis made it back to their MTM craft in one piece and went quickly back to the torpedo-boat "mother ship." For good measure, Bin-Nun ordered the torpedo-boat commander to fire a few bursts of 20mm cannon fire over the heads of the fishing boats and against the Lebanese Gendarmerie vessels pursuing them outside port nearby "just to show that the Israelis meant business."

The "sortie" illustrated just how little accurate intelligence Flotilla 13 was getting.[16] The reconnaissance mission came in the midst of a revolt by forces loyal to Druze warlord Kamal Jumblatt in the Shouf Mountains to the east of Beirut. The Lebanese Army was on high alert, as was the U.S. Sixth Fleet moored off the coast of the Lebanese capital. One week following Operation Affluent-3, American President Dwight D. Eisenhower ordered 5,000 U.S. Marines ashore in Beirut.

Even though Operation Affluent-3 was a loud and compromised mission, the IDF General Staff was pleased with the ambitious venture. Several participants of the mission were decorated and Chief of Staff Lieutenant General Haim Laskov was so impressed by Bin-Nun's quest for behind-the-lines training missions for his men that two years later he was promoted to admiral and named commander of the IDF/Navy in March 1960.

From 1959 to 1967, Flotilla 13 was an enigma. Even though many of the unit's finest officers continued to serve and the level of training increased, the IDF/Navy and IDF Military Intelligence found very few assignments to give to the mysterious men from Atlit. "There is a norm in the IDF that the military doesn't do anything it doesn't deem as absolutely necessary," reflected Rear Admiral (Ret.) Ze'ev Almog, "especially if it involved morale-building."[17] It did very little, and as a result, the level of professionalism inside the unit, in all its different sections, suffered. There were several serious training accidents, including several fatal mishaps, and other elements of disgruntled men serving in a unit whose purpose and very need soon became a matter of doubt. In that dry period, two things saved the unit from complete collapse—the overseas training exchanges and the acquisition of the IDF/Navy's first submarine.

Following the 1956 War, Israel's military relationship with the French continued to flourish. Not only did flotilla operators continue to travel to Toulon and Marseille, but they soon traveled to Corsica for regular stints with the French. The French not only trained with the Israelis on French soil, but they took select groups of Israelis with them to Germany for NATO maneuvers. The French were an "odd" group of warriors who took nothing serious except the art of being French. When the French took the operators of Flotilla 13 on maneuvers in Europe, they would often take as much care in packing a lunch of baquettes, brie cheese, and wine, as they would in bringing the right quantities of explosives, the right maps, and enough ammunition to sustain a prolonged fire-fight. On one such mission, in the 1950s, when young Lieutenant Ze'ev Almog was paddling his way down the Rhine in Germany along with a French combat swimmer, he was shocked to see that the French commandos' canteen was filled with wine, not drinking water. "Aren't you worried about dehydrating?" the young Israeli lieutenant asked naively. The French operator smiled and took another gulp of wine from his kit, gesturing as if to say, "You won't be getting any of *my* wine!"[18]

Unfortunately for the Israelis, their French hosts were not only interested in the latest vintages from Bordeaux, they were also involved in changing the political map of Paris and seeking vengeance for what they viewed as treason by President Charles de Gaulle in his abandoning of Algeria in 1960. Many of the men in the *Commando Hubert,* the *Commando Jaubert,* and the Foreign Legion unit in Corsica were operational figures in the underground OAS. Some of the men that the Israelis had been trained by were killed in fire-fights with French security forces; many more were arrested. The French Ministry of Defense soon became apprehensive about its commando elements, and even more concerned about their contacts with elements abroad. Slowly, contacts between Flotilla 13 and the French evaporated.

At the same time, however, the Israelis had made contact with an old ally a bit closer to home. The successors to the 10th MAS Flotilla in the Italian Navy was a unit known by its acronym COMSUBIN, for *Commando Subacquei ed Incursori,* and they were as innovative and technologically imaginative as their predecessors from the Second World War. Operators and officers from Flotilla 13 visited Italy on an annual basis and found the exchanges most beneficial to their view of naval special warfare doctrine; the Italian COMSUBIN divers were less cocky and arrogant than the French, but extremely capable. They taught the Israelis how to tinker: how to breech the envelope of a weapon's capability by twisting a screw, adding a few more pieces of metal, and using one's imagination as a blueprint for the design and production of innovative weaponry—to turn a

109

torpedo into a guided weapon, and a limpet mine into a massive force of underwater explosive destruction. The French taught Flotilla 13 the bravado of being a commando; something that the Italians couldn't, by nature, export. "The Italians," responded Herzl Lavon, when talking about the French and Italian influence on Flotilla 13, "were great mechanical thinkers who always thought of an innovative approach when technology could solve a military problem. They had incredible foresight with gadgetry—even if it involved the design of a kitchen appliance."[19]

The Italians taught the flotilla the importance of technical prowess—all that was needed was some confidence in the top brass and some operational assignments to allow the personality and capabilities to gel on the battlefield.

An interesting footnote to the flotilla's "Italian connection" was the fact that the Italians were also secretly training Egyptian naval commandos in the art of naval special warfare. According to once-top-secret U.S. Naval Intelligence files, the COMSUBIN were also training Egyptian commandos in offensive techniques while deploying from the MSX-1 swimmer delivery vehicle (a 5.8-meters-long anti-magnetic metal successor to the World War II–era Pigs), and advanced underwater sabotage techniques. It was, perhaps, odd for the COMSUBIN base at La Speza to host both Israeli and Egyptian contingents, but the Italians attempted to be fair with their Mediterranean neighbors, even when it involved the proliferation of classified commando techniques and equipment.

The other international connection that the flotilla maintained at the time, though in more limited terms, was with the Royal Dutch Marines, and their elite NL SBS.[20] The motto of the Royal Netherlands Marine Corps is *"Qua Pater Orbis,"* or "Wherever the World Extends," and the Israelis were eager to learn from the rich Dutch naval history. Although a force of just over 3,000 men, the Royal Netherlands Marine Corps (RNLMC) was considered one of the finest combat units in NATO, with its special forces elements, especially the 7 NL SBS, receiving some of the most dangerous and covert assignments. Like the operators in Flotilla 13, the men of 7NL SBS are parachutist-trained combat swimmers considered among the world's best. In many ways, through their training, mandate, and sub-units, the Dutch SBS and British SBS are virtually indistinguishable. A Dutch SBS operator must first complete his service with the RNLMC before being able to volunteer into 7NL SBS; even though there is one year of mandatory military service in the Netherlands, all commandos in the RNLMC are volunteers, and volunteers that must prove their worth before being allowed to enter through the gates of the RNLMC's training center. Upon completion of a successful stint in the RNLMC, a commando is entitled to submit a formal request to volunteer into the 7NL SBS. Like the British SBS, a commando wishing to become a combat swimmer must first pass a grueling and extremely arduous selection process, and then (only about 30 percent pass this) endure a year-long training regimen; like his counterpart in the British SBS, the candidate can be removed from the course at any time. In terms of the 7NL SBS's infatuation with the Klepper canoe, the unit is virtually indistinguishable from its British counterpart. In fact, just like in the British SBS, the one and only Klepper is the 7NL SBS's main battle tank. It is used on virtually all 7NL SBS missions as the ideal means for infiltration and fast and stealthy insertion of two-man sabotage and recce squads into enemy territory, and the Israelis found this facet of the unit's abilities most interesting.

This overseas training, where professionalism and military proficiency was stressed, was complemented by some "bizarre" training back home. "In the middle of our *special warfare* training," Ze'ev Almog recalled, "Izzy Rahav sent us out to sea on a rickety old fishing vessel for a four month tour. The boat was a mess and it stunk, but we learned seamanship under the most arduous conditions, only the strongest survived, but it conditioned us. It also taught us how to masquerade as fisherman and how sneak into an enemy harbor. It was the most difficult period of training that I can recall!"[21]

The ascension of Rear Admiral Yochai Bin-Nun to the command of the IDF/Navy was a tremendous boost to the morale of the flotilla. "Finally," many in the unit thought, "an operator in command." Bin-Nun authorized additional trips abroad, purchased new breathing systems and diving equipment, implemented Yosef Dror's stymied vision of a decade earlier—the acquisition of a submarine. In 1958, Captain Yosef Dror took a small contingent of naval volunteers to Toulon, France, to conduct a French-run class in the art of submarine warfare. The Ministry of Defense and the General Staff had finally acquiesced to the lobbying of naval commanders pleading for the formation of a submarine fleet, but the budget was restrictive, and most submarines, even the obsolete ones, were beyond the price tag of the IDF/Navy. The IDF/Navy wanted to purchase a French sub—after all, the closest ties existed with Paris, and it was hoped that the French would see it was in their interests to help their allies out with a price break or even a grant of some kind. Shimon Peres, the director general of the Ministry of Defense, used his best diplomatic skills to try and persuade the French, but his efforts were unsuccessful. The only submarines within the IDF budget available were two British S-class World War II–era submarines. When the Royal Navy agreed to train the Israeli crews in Portsmouth, the deal was cemented.

On December 16, 1959, the I.N.S. *Tanin* (or "Crocodile") rolled into Haifa. "The dream of a submarine is finally a tangible reality," Admiral Tenkus proudly proclaimed at the sight of the first Jewish submarine in military history.[22] Two months later, the second S-class submarine, the I.N.S. *Rahav* (or "Swagger") reached Haifa as well. The initial lock-out training that the flotilla received in Portsmouth and Poole with the SBS, along with additional lock-out instruction that they received from the French, the Italians, and the Dutch, had suddenly become most useful. With two submarines at their disposal, the flotilla would no longer have to rely solely on mother ships to get them "close" to their targets. They now enjoyed a long-range stealth delivery means to ferry them anywhere in the region they needed to go. As commander of the IDF/Navy, Bin-Nun once told operators in the flotilla that it was imperative that they learn the two S-class subs to the best of their abilities—in the next war, he assumed, the submarine would play a pivotal role in any Israeli action against her Arab neighbors.[23] Tragically, he would be right.

Many analysts in the *A'man* (Hebrew acronym for *Agaf Mode'in,* or the IDF Intelligence Branch) predicted that a full-scale Arab-Israeli war would erupt sometime in the summer of 1969. It would be, their estimates argued, a full-scale total war and a conflict in which Israel's very survival would sorely be tested. The Arab states had been building up their arms supplies with feverish intensity, and the Arabs' numeric superiority was astounding. The IDF General Staff, by 1967 led by Chief of Staff Lieutenant General Yitzhak Rabin, were not men to panic and not men to overreact. They knew that the outcome of the next war depended on three primary factors: Israel maintaining its qualitative superiority (and a 500-plane air force of the best French fighters and bombers around was the personification of qualitative superiority); enjoying accurate and timely intelligence; and striking first!

Throughout 1967, however, tensions had escalated to the point where elements of Israeli intelligence, both military intelligence and the *Mossad,* reevaluated their initial predictions and estimates to assume that war would erupt before the end of the year. On April 7, 1967, near Tel Dan, the Syrian garrison atop the Golan Heights launched a massive artillery bombardment on Kibbutz Tel Katzir; 130mm shells ripped through nurseries, homes, and factories. Outraged by the bloody attack, Chief of Staff Lieutenant General Yitzhak Rabin ordered the air force into action to take out the Syrian gun emplacements that had harassed Israeli agricultural settlements in Galilee once and for all. A flight of Super Mystères was sent to take the guns out, and they, in turn, were intercepted by a flight of Syrian Air Force MiG-21s, which, in turn, was ambushed by a flight of French-built Mirage IIIC jets sporting the Star of David. The Syrian guns were removed and six MiGs erupted into balls of flame over the Golan Heights.

The dog-fight was the spark, and the hatred and desire for war in the Arab world proved to be a field of sizzling embers. Radicals in Damascus and Cairo urged for Israel's complete annihilation. Government radio in Damascus and Cairo openly called for the "infidel" Jewish State to be annihilated, and its "criminal inhabitants" to be pushed into the sea. As undisputed leader of the Arab world, Egyptian President Gamal Abdel Nasser was looked upon as the great Arab leader, one rivaling Saladin in his ability and charisma, to avenge the tragedy of 1948. On May 15, 1967, Nasser placed the nearly million-man Egyptian Army on full alert. On May 18, 1967, Nasser ordered that the 5,000 United Nations peacekeepers that had kept the Sinai peninsula demilitarized since 1957 evacuate their positions. Egyptian armored divisions quickly moved across the canal into the desert wasteland of Sinai and set up camp directly opposite strategic roadways leading into southern Israel, the coastal strip, and into the Negev Desert. On May 30, 1967, Jordan's King Hussein visited Cairo to sign a mutual defense pact with Egypt combining the armed forces of the two countries and placing the elite British-trained Jordanian military under overall Egyptian command. Exacerbating the chain of events was the Soviet Union, eager to extend its influence in the region, and an overwhelming euphoria of overconfidence in the Arab camp that promised victory in any conflict with Israel.

As the Soviet-advised Egyptian propaganda machine mobilized a nation toward war, Israel slowly prepared its military machine for war and its citizens for a total conflict. An emergency cabinet, including the political opposition, was established, and the unassuming Prime Minister Levi Eshkol named the charismatic Moshe Dayan, the former chief of staff and 1956 War hero, as his defense minister. The conscript army was placed on full alert, and volunteers, mainly women and schoolchildren, began digging ditches and defensive barriers along the plush cafe-and-tree-lined boulevards of Tel Aviv. Israel's war aims were clear— destroy the enemy before it could reach a numeric advantage and set forth a wave of motion and momentum across Israeli defenses. The Egyptian closing of the Straits of Tiran, once again, was an international *causus belli* for an Israeli attack. Armored divisions were rushed to the border with Egypt along the Gaza Strip, the air force was provided with an accurate list of targets (including every air base from the Nile to the Euphrates), and the IDF/Navy was placed on full alert.

War was no longer just a possibility. It was an unstoppable fact.

In May 1967, the commander of the IDF/Navy was Rear Admiral Shlomoh Erel, a Polish-born career naval officer. Unlike Bin-Nun, who held the post as naval commander for an astounding six years, Erel was a conventional sailor without any special interest or fondness for the swagger and special operations that Flotilla 13 could boast. He was a professional soldier and a man with an eye for the future—one of his pet projects was the Bin-Nun–initiated Israeli development of a surface-to-surface sea-skimming missile for deployment with a fleet of small attack craft the IDF/Navy was hoping to develop with the French. That missile, interestingly enough, was the Gabriel—an advanced development of the *Pal'yam*'s "Shark."

In terms of the naval theater of operations, the IDF/Navy was outnumbered and the only arm of the IDF to have inferior equipment than that of its Arab enemies. The Egyptian fleet was a massive deep-water navy complete with seven destroyers, two frigates, eleven submarines, dozens of torpedo and patrol boats, and, most important, twenty-four Soviet-built Osa- and Komar-class missile boats capable of firing the lethal Styx sea-to-sea missile.[24] The Styx SSMs outranged the heaviest guns carried on the Israeli destroyers I.N.S. *Eilat* and *Haifa,* and it was a daunting taste of high-tech reality that four Osa boats, with a moderately competent crew, could wipe out Israel's entire fleet. The only saving grace for the Israelis was the fact that the Egyptian fleet was split between the Mediterranean and the Red Sea. The Syrian Navy was a much smaller fleet, but one built around missile boats, as well.

To the IDF/Navy, the most pressing threat was the Arab fleets moving around the Mediterranean—the Egyptian fleet based at Alexandria and Port Said could threaten Tel Aviv, and the Syrian fleet threatened Haifa with a missile barrage. When the IDF would launch its preemptive strike, the IDF/Navy was tasked with neutralizing the enemy harbors. That mission fell to Flotilla 13.

The commander of Flotilla 13 in 1967 was Commander Dov Shapir, known by his nickname of *"Berele"* (or "Snail")—a young, cocky, and experienced commando officer. The unit, at the time, numbered only twenty-five regular operators, and with the mobilization of its reserve element, it never exceeded the "fifty-man" level. Additional manpower, at the time, was involved in either basic training with the paratroops, or squad and officers' courses. Commander Shapir's specialty was deep-water dives. He was one of the founders of a small IDF/Navy dive unit centering on underwater construction, repairs, and defensive tactics against intruding enemy frogmen; this force was given the mysterious title of "Unit 707." Shapir had been the commander of Flotilla 13 in the years 1960, through 1965, and he returned in 1967 following some turmoil and turbulence between the commander of the unit and the operators. Shapir realized that his assets were limited, but he was also the recipient of a unit whose quality was beyond reproach—energetic, innovative, brave, and dedicated operators, mostly Kibbutzniks, who felt indestructible. They relished the chance to strike out against the enemy and were determined to make a mark for themselves and the unit.

Even before the outbreak of the war, a sizable contingent of Flotilla 13 operators found itself on board the I.N.S. *Tanin* sitting in waiting "somewhere" in the Mediterranean, ready at a moments notice to attack the harbors of Latakia, Minat el-Biada, and Tartus in Syria, and Alexandria in Egypt. The I.N.S. *Yafo,* a World War II–era destroyer, also set sail south, toward Port Said, with a contingent of operators from Flotilla 13 and their exploding craft for an attack against the Egyptian naval station at the opening to the Suez Canal. Another small contingent of operators from Flotilla 13 were flown to Eilat, at the base of the Gulf of Aqaba, ready to attack Egyptian naval posts along the Red Sea ports in Sinai.

War erupted on the morning of June 5, 1967, at 07:45 hours when waves of Israeli aircraft bombed air bases throughout Egypt. Most of the Egyptian Air Force was destroyed on the ground, and the few fighters and bombers that managed to scramble under the unforgiving blitz were shot down by Mirage and Mystère pilots proving the military adage that quality will decimate quantity every time. By the time the order of *Sadin Adom,* or "Red Sheet," was issued, the code message ordering the offensive strike to begin against Egypt, Israel had complete air superiority, and Egyptian armor and infantry units in Sinai were helpless without air cover; IAF strikes destroyed the Jordanian, Syrian, and Iraqi air forces later that day. Israel's air victory had been achieved before the first tanks crossed the desert no-man's-land of Sinai.

Throughout those frantic early hours of the war, when IDF HQ in Tel Aviv was abuzz with electricity and engulfed in clouds of anxiety-inspired cigarette smoke, Rear Admiral Erel was busy pleading with the General Staff for the authorization to attack the Syrian and Egyptian ports. The boats were at sea and the operators ready, Rear Admiral Erel argued with anyone willing to listen, all that was needed was the green light. By midafternoon, Arel received his authorization, though, in retrospect, June 5 would prove to be an epic day for Flotilla 13—one marked by folly and tragedy.

The first target slated for Flotilla 13's attention was the Syrian naval installation at Minat el-Biada. A fishing vessel used by the IDF/Navy for covert insertions, under the command of Yosef Dror, was to insert a force of divers several kilometers away from the base, and they were to sabotage Syrian missile boats docked for the night. Already behind schedule, the operators dropped two Zodiac rubber inflatables in the water around midnight and headed toward the target in a slow and deliberate ride toward the rocky slopes near the entrance to the facility. From the onset, the mission went badly. The operators faced enormous difficulty in setting their navigational parameters on mark and reached the Syrian shoreline nearly 1,000 meters off course. By the time they figured out where they were and where they needed to go, they discovered three Syrian warships sailing precariously close to their positions. The logistical and navigational delays were costly. The operators reached the entrance to the port with only two hours of complete darkness remaining. The sortie, the commander decided, would have little chance for success since there was only two hours left of darkness, and the pickup, of the operators and their Zodiacs, would have to take place in full daylight, and that would have jeopardized the operators and the mother ship. The operation was scrubbed.

Another raid, slated for the same time against the Syrian naval position at Tartus, literally never hit the water. The raid, led by Rear Admiral (Res.) Yochai Bin-Nun, called for a squad of Pigs to be ferried to its target courtesy of a civilian research vessel. The Pigs would infiltrate the harbor and attack Syrian torpedo and Osa-class missile boats moored at the facility. The mother ship was embroiled in navigational problems and was late in reaching their pre-described dropping off point. The operators assigned to the raid weren't used to the poor seagoing abilities of the ship and suffered from a serious case of seasickness. The boat also had difficulties in reaching the drop-off point close to the target and, as a result, Bin-Nun aborted the operation without the Pigs ever being lowered into the sea.

A raid against the small port facility at Baniyas, along the route of the Iraqi oil pipeline, was also aborted, because the task force commander failed to locate the port.

Flotilla 13's two most ambitious attempts were made against the Egyptian Mediterranean fleet.

Alexandria was the Egyptian fleet's primary naval facility and Egypt's largest commercial port. In terms of targets, it ranked on the Israeli top-ten list along with the Ministry of Defense in Cairo and the sprawling Cairo West, Helwan, and Luxor air force bases. Much of the Egyptian Navy's submarine fleet was stationed at Alexandria, as were most of its destroyers, frigates, and a sizable and daunting percentage of its missile boat fleet. Alexandria was also Egypt's primary sea access to Europe and, more important, the Soviet Union. The steady stream of freighters heading from Leningrad and the Black Sea ports, from Gdansk and the Baltic, carrying T-54/55 main battle tanks, MiG-21 fighter bombers, and artillery shells all docked at Alexandria. For the Egyptian war machine to be resupplied, Alexandria needed to remain open and unmolested from Israeli air and naval attack.

Alexandria also had a history with frogman attacks. The port was a natural horseshoe, and once the breakwater was entered, there were dozens of convenient targets and hiding spots for invading underwater saboteurs. Naturally, Flotilla 13 considered Alexandria to be a prize. Authorization to attack the Egyptian port came at noon on the afternoon of June 5.

The "mother ship" for the raid on Alexandria was the I.N.S. *Tanin,* and Rear Admiral Bin-Nun's prophecy of the ship playing a pivotal role in the "next" war had come true. The *Tanin*'s skipper, Captain Eivan Dror, had been at sea with a complement of operators since the middle of May, ready, at a moment's notice, to strike out at a series of targets the IDF/Navy considered worthy of Flotilla 13's attention. Unlike other targets assigned to the flotilla during the war, Alexandria was an IDF/Navy operation—one not requiring a General Staff thumbs-up. The I.N.S. *Tanin* had returned to Israel on May 24, refueled and had its equipment checked, and then returned to the depths of the Mediterranean again on May 25. There were eight flotilla operators on board the *Tanin,* and the flotilla's complement commander, Lieutenant Eitan Lifshitz, was assigned a difficult task. Lifshitz had with him some of the flotilla's finest operators—the men included Ze'ev Ben-Yosef (Lifshitz's No. 2), Gilad Shani, Ilan Egozi, Danny Baram, and Gadi Patish. The six were considered the finest divers in the flotilla, and both Lifshitz and Egozi were looked upon as possible future commanders of the unit. The "on-the-books" plan called for six operators to lock out of the *Tanin* and swim about two kilometers toward the northernmost section of the breakwater, and under the cover of darkness, swim into the facility in search of targets. They'd be carrying enough limpet mines to inflict serious damage to the Egyptian fleet. If all went well, they'd cross the breakwater undetected and rendezvous with the *Tanin* at a predesignated meeting point. Two pathfinders (trip-wires) from Flotilla 13 would remain with the sub and surface at the predesignated time to search for the six divers. They'd search for the six with night-vision equipment and, hopefully, be back in Haifa in time for lunch on the afternoon of June 6. If all did *not* go well, the *Tanin* would return to a different rendezvous location forty-eight hours later.

The raid on Alexandria was classic commando and classic frogman. It was also classic folly. Everything that could go wrong did.

It is never a good start to an operation when the enemy is out in force expecting an attack. The Egyptians weren't foolish. They knew that Alexandria was the premier naval target of the theater, and they knew that Flotilla 13 was "probably" out there. Fast attack craft patrolled a steady quadrant around the port—reaching fifty-five kilometers around the strategic harbor. An urgent IDF/Navy intelligence report, one listing the Egyptian Navy's disposition in Alexandria, never made it to the radio room of the *Tanin*. In order to alleviate the tension and anxiety, it was decided not to go over the targets to be attacked on board the submarine, but rather the force would follow Lifshitz inside the harbor waters.

Each frogman was to carry nearly four kilograms of explosives and navigational equipment with him en route to Alexandria, but the lock-out process was a bumpy one. The sea was rough and the waves crashed against the submarine in merciless fashion. Several of the operators felt that the delicate equipment might have suffered damage, but there was no time to return to the war room and double-check the gear. They locked out under the last embers of a retreating sun. Six black figures invisible from view used their well-honed bodies as a delivery vehicle for the rough and exhausting swim toward Alexandria. Several hours later, the two pathfinders locked out of the sub to position themselves in wait for the rendezvous. Their infrared filters, the key ingredient to the rendezvous with Lifshitz and his five operators, had been knocked out of their hands by the smashing waves and lost at sea; the red-light flashlight, instrumental in communicating with the frogmen, was lost, too. Perched near the periscope, the two pathfinders told Captain Dror about the situation and he ordered them to flash their own personal-issue flashlights directly toward Alexandria. The flashing light could endanger the submarine, but without a source of light revealing the *Tanin*'s coordinates, the six frogmen were doomed. By 02:00 hours in the morning of June 6, the sounds of gunfire and explosions were heard emanating from Alexandria. Something was happening but no one on board the *Tanin* knew exactly what.

The swim toward the breakwater exhausted the six, and the Egyptians were making things difficult. Sentries, armed with AK-47 assault rifles, manned the breakwaters and showered the approaching waters with beams of bright yellow illumination from mobile searchlights. Sailors on board small torpedo boats tossed dozens of anti-personnel depth charges into the deep water, and they fired incessant bursts of machine-gun fire into the afterblasts just in case any of the explosions caused the divers to surface. The concussion of the underwater blasts pounded the divers like a hammer to the groin, and the incessant pounding fatigued the six men.

By the time the six reached the breakwater, they were exhausted, in pain, and behind schedule. They were also off course and lost. According to their training, an assault on an enemy port such as Alexandria would take place hours before an initial air attack—they would be, in essence, the force tasked with drawing first blood. They had studied intelligence charts based on the lights and illumination around the port area. Because they went into action a full eighteen hours after a full day of Israeli air assaults against Egyptian targets, Alexandria was under blackout conditions. None of the landmarks that should have been lit up were illuminated. They were operating under complete darkness. As a result, instead of being close to the military basin, where the destroyers, frigates, and Osa-class missile boats were moored, the six found themselves at the southern entrance to the port, near a civilian vessel which they were under strict orders not to sabotage. The other two pairs met with equally dismal results. Lifshitz and Ben-Yosef, though, managed to affix several mines to some midwater construction equipment.

Realizing that the mission would not be successful, Lifshitz ordered his frogmen to retreat back across the breakwater for the rendezvous with the *Tanin*. Lifshitz removed his infrared equipment from his kit, but the device wasn't working and he couldn't see any beacons of light from where the sub was supposed to be. Fear turned to desperation, and the six began a frantic swim in the direction of the *Tanin*. They removed their regular-issue flashlights from their pouches, flashed their positions in coordinates away from Alexandria, and even began shouting in Hebrew, *"Eifoh Atem?"* ("Where are you?") at the top of their lungs. It yielded little results other than exhausting the six even further. They had already swum six kilometers toward their target and had been in the water for nearly twelve hours. They were running on empty and close to collapse, but they now faced an even greater challenge than mining Egyptian ships—evading Egyptian patrols until the second rendezvous thirty-six hours later. As the sun began to rise from its western perch, the six reached the breakwater undetected. They destroyed much of their top-secret navigational equipment in their swim back to Egypt and met in a small cave near a rocky alcove.

For the next nine hours, the six contemplated their next move. Awaiting the next rendezvous was risky—if it failed the first time, some of the operators argued, why would it succeed now? Some contemplated stealing an Egyptian boat and simply sailing back toward Israel; others thought of commandeering a radio and possibly calling in a helicopter. Most knew that they were in dire straits.

As the group prepared to sit out the exposing daylight hours, a small group of local fishermen looking for abandoned nets came across the cave. The six began to argue with the fishermen, pleading that they were British divers from a merchant vessel moored in harbor and were enjoying a break from their duties, but the Egyptian fishermen did not speak English and thought that the six, wearing wet suits and looking more like they came from Tel Aviv rather than Sussex, were the enemy. A mob soon assaulted Lifshitz and his men, but the Israelis put up a hell of a fight, punching the approaching fishermen and trying to buy time (without killing anyone). Patish and Egozi managed to slip away and remained hidden along the outskirts of Alexandria for the next twelve hours. By the morning of June 7, 1967, at the same time that the second rendezvous was supposed to take place, Eitan Lifshitz, Ze'ev Ben-Yosef, Ilan Egozi, Gilad Shani, Danny Baram, and Gadi Patish were en route to Cairo as guests of the Egyptian secret service, the notorious *Muchabarat*.

When the eight operators left Haifa on May 25, 1967, en route to their meeting with operational destiny and disaster, they met with Rear Admiral Erel and Commander Shapir. Shapir could detect a sense of fear and trepidation, and he promised his operators that upon their return from Alexandria, he'd authorize them to wear a red background to their bat wings; the red background to military wings, a symbol of an operational combat jump or dive, was a badge of honor, a status symbol in an egalitarian army void of tangible decorations of status. Instead, the six received a badge of honor made of shattered muscle tissue and bruised limbs. In Egyptian custody, the six Israeli frogmen faced a horrendous ordeal. The Egyptians were not fond of prisoners of war. Beatings and malnutrition were considered kind treatment and the Geneva Convention held little weight. Even thirty years after the incident, the survivors of the Egyptian interrogations find it difficult to talk about their experiences. Ilan Egozi, perhaps one of the bravest men to ever serve in the Israeli military and a man who personifies the definition of an operator, still winces ever so slightly when he discusses life in Egyptian captivity. For two endless weeks of incessant beatings and sleep deprivation, Egyptian *Muchabarat* agents interrogated the six Israeli frogmen. Interrogators, men with ice-cold eyes and brutal strength, strung up the captured Israelis, and employing a traditional Middle Eastern art form of sadism, beat the soles of their feet with an iron bar. Gilad Shani, in an interview with an Israeli magazine, also recalled how lit cigarettes were burned against their skin, and how nails were driven up their fingernails.[25]

The only consolation was the fact that they weren't seized by the Syrians. Syrian secret service officials have been rumored to castrate Israeli POWs, and even dip their bodies in acid.

Eight months after their capture, the six badly beaten frogmen were returned to Israel (along with four additional POWs, including the Mossad's legendary "Champagne Spy" Wolfgang Lotz) in exchange for 5,000 Egyptian prisoners, including a field marshal, held by the IDF. They endured hell, though they managed to hold out long enough so that the Egyptians never knew of the fact that the *Tanin* was lurking off the coast of Alexandria days after their capture.

Thirty years after the raid in Alexandria, there are those who downplay the "negative" concerning the ill-fated mission. Operation commander Eitan Lifshitz, a man who still bears the scars of the brutal torture at the hands of his Egyptian captors, now believes the raid to be a success. "The fact that Israel managed to penetrate an Egyptian home port undetected persuaded the Egyptian High Command to send much of its Mediterranean navy to Libya, to the ports of Tripoli and Tobruk, for safety and as a result not one Egyptian warship even came close to the Israeli shore during the conflict."[26]

There would be no hindsight for Flotilla 13's other planned attack against Egypt's Mediterranean fleet.

At the same time as the six ill-fated Israeli divers were headed toward Alexandria, another force of operators from Flotilla 13, a flotilla of Pigs, was preparing to attack Egypt's second-most-important naval target—Port Said. Port Said was the Mediterranean opening for the Suez Canal. Beyond its ultraimportant strategic value, Port Said was an essential facet of the stumbling Egyptian economy and its integrity was a vital objective of the Egyptian defense establishment.

The man tasked with the planned Flotilla 13 assault on Port Said was Lieutenant Commander Almog—a commander who had slowly but surely begun to leave his mark on the unit. A stickler for discipline and tenacity, especially when lives were on the line, Almog found the flotilla's lack of professionalism (marked by several training accidents) troubling, and left the life of a commando in 1966 for the life of a conventional naval officer. A man in love with the sea, Almog took command of a torpedo boat. Yet as war neared, senior naval commanders asked him to return to the flotilla. Almog agreed, but only on the condition that he be named the unit's operations officer, and that when war erupted, he wouldn't be banished to an office in IDF/Navy HQ. He wanted to command a strike against an enemy target.

On June 5, 1967, Lieutenant Commander Almog found himself on board the I.N.S. *Yafo* en route toward a mooring location twenty kilometers west of Port Said. Initially, General Staff planners had thought of mounting an amphibious landing along the Mediterranean coast of Sinai to block off retreating Egyptian armor units racing back to the canal. Israel had yet to mount a large-scale amphibious landing and it didn't even have a large number of landing craft that could be deployed to land more than a battalion of tanks or APCs. Any landing hinged on the neutralization of the Port Said naval facility. The landing crafts and slow-moving IDF/Navy destroyer, the I.N.S. *Yafo,* would be most vulnerable to attack by a small force of Egyptian torpedo boats and Osa-class missile craft. It was felt that the presence of an Israeli armada heading south would draw the Egyptians out on the attack, and naval planners thought of the perfect and poignant ambush—decimating the Egyptian fleet with a fusillade of MTM exploding-craft attacks. It had, after all, been in preparation for a major IDF offensive in Sinai that Yochai Bin-Nun was tasked with taking out the *Emir Farouk* in 1948. Unlike 1948, however, the IDF advance went off with lightning speed and was unforgiving.

Several MTM craft had been loaded onto the deck of the I.N.S. *Yafo* along with the crews on the morning of June 5, 1967, but as the reports of the first IAF air strikes filtered back to IDF HQ, and the news on the ground from Colonel Shmuel Gorodish's 7th Armored Brigade and Colonel Rafael "Raful" Eitan's 35th Paratroop Brigade made its way back to a euphoric General Staff in Tel Aviv, the planned amphibious landing was scrubbed. The MTM craft were quickly unloaded, their crews sent back home, and two fiberglass Pigs, quickly loaded on board the destroyer in their place. Also loaded on board the deck of the I.N.S. *Yafo* was a small high-speed insertion craft, basically an armed and armored speedboat, built by the flotilla. It was known as the *Tzipor* ("Bird") and was a small fiberglass boat, painted gray, armed with .50-caliber and .30-caliber heavy machine guns, grenade launchers, advanced communications gear, a homing device, and radar.[27] The "Bird" was a mother ship for small unit entries, and one of its most redeeming qualities was its ability to tow MTM craft and delivery vehicles.

The naval holding action against Port Said, including the Pig attack, was under the overall command of Captain Benyamin Telem, a German-born career naval officer who had studied at the Royal Navy's Staff College in Greenwich and was, at the time of the war's outbreak, in charge of the IDF/Navy's secretive missile boat program. The I.N.S. *Yafo* was serving as a flagship for the operations; it was the primary warship involved and was escorted by several torpedo boats. The flotilla attack against Port Said was to commence at 21:00 hours on the night of June 5, when the Bird and the Pigs would be lowered into the choppy Mediterranean waters. The *Yafo* would hold a position some thirty kilometers off the coast of Port Said and serve as a beacon for the underwater task force. The Bird towed the two Pigs to a point some three kilometers off the Port Said breakwater; once they reached the first rendezvous point, the two Pigs cut their lines and submerged for the precarious entry into Port Said. Almog, scanning the port from the Bird, manned a machine gun and hoped for the best.

Both Pigs managed to enter the harbor with little difficulty, but Port Said was abuzz with military activity. Sentries along the breakwater showered the water with floodlights. Patrol boats and torpedo boats cut their way slowly through the oil-filled water, dropping depth charges and searching for any telltale signs of underwater intruders. Evading the Egyptian sentries and patrol boats was like running through a blazing maze, but it had to be surpassed while at the same time searching for targets. Intelligence, which until now had been off for the entire unit, was again inaccurate for the Port

Said operation. There were no Osa-class missile boats in the harbor, and the only torpedo boats to be found were racing about the waterway in search of frogmen. The commanders of both Pigs were dumbfounded. "How could they send us to attack a port with no targets?" To get a better view of the port and perhaps find something they'd missed, the two Pig crews surfaced at the interior section of the breakwater. What they found was the fact that they were in the sights of a torpedo boat's heavy machine-gun sights, and the target of a too-close-for-comfort volley of 14.5mm fire.

For the next three hours, a Catch-22 series of miscommunications almost led to tragedy. The Pigs, unable to locate any worthy targets and forced to withdraw, had difficulty in communicating with the Bird waiting outside the breakwater; communications were eventually established using a closed-radio system enabling the submerged divers on the Pig to talk to Almog on board the "mother ship." Captain Telem on board the *Yafo,* fearing a surprise attack by Styx-missile-firing Osas and eager to leave the area, couldn't, for reasons unknown to this day, communicate with Almog in the Bird; he ordered Commander Itzik Qat, the *Yafo*'s skipper, to raise anchor and head back north at full power. At the same time, the task force, especially the escorting torpedo boats, encountered Egyptian patrol and missile boats, and a long-range battle commenced. The enemy contact only reinforced Telem's desire to break contact and retreat.

To avoid capture, of both the operators and their Pigs, the pre-planned destruction of the delivery vehicles was undertaken once all the operators were safely on board Almog's Bird. The operators were only one mile from the entrance to Port Said and any and all attempts to prevent the operators from becoming POWs was to be taken. The destruction of the Pigs, a most top-secret of Israeli-produced devices, was also all-important to prevent them from falling into the hands of the enemy; "The Israeli-produced Pigs," Ze'ev Almog points out, "were far more advanced than anything available at the time to other units around the world, even the aging Mk VIII SDV used by the U.S. Navy SEALs at the time, and were not to fall into enemy hands."[28] With

Egyptian shore batteries closing in on the Bird's position and the operators abandoned, Almog ordered the task force to make their way back to Israel, alone and dangerously vulnerable in the middle of the Mediterranean.

Eventually, the Bird and the *Yafo* linked up fifty kilometers east of the prearranged rendezvous point and only after Commodore Izzy Rahav, the IDF/Navy's deputy commander, *ordered* Telem back to the Mediterranean after the *Yafo*'s return to Tel Aviv so that the flotilla operators could be retrieved. Almog eventually located the *Yafo* on his radar, though initially thought the ship to be an Egyptian destroyer. The operators prepared for capture and the hell of being prisoners in the hands of the Egyptians. Much to their surprise—and relief—their rendezvous had *finally* arrived. The mission was a failure compounded by the destruction of the Pigs. "The commander of the IDF/Navy sent us, his soldiers, to an enemy position that was empty of targets!" recalled Ze'ev Almog, the anger and bitterness still fresh in his mind. "I still cannot comprehend how this could have happened and how the commander of the task force could have simply abandoned us!"[29]

There would be no other operations involving Flotilla 13 during the war. The unit had been given its golden opportunity to make history, and instead failed to successfully execute a single of its assigned objectives. To many in the IDF/Navy, it was an embarrassing performance that would be addressed "harshly" at a later date. They could not fathom how an arm of the Israeli military tasked with relatively conventional targets could fail to destroy a single of its prescribed targets. Others in the navy and the flotilla in particular were less critical of what had happened. "I think that we proved that we, as a small force, could enter into an enemy port when the enemy expected us, and survive. That is a major accomplishment that few in any conventional fighting unit could ever hope to understand. After all, they aren't the ones enduring the concussion blasts of depth charges pressing like a vice against their bodies."[30] For many of the operators in the unit, they had trained for years, both in Israel and abroad, in secreting themselves into a bustling port—one bigger than Haifa or the small fishing posts in Tel Aviv or Jaffa. "It was in France, in Toulon," remembers Ilan Egozi, "that we learned just what it is to infiltrate into a large port that we are unfamiliar with, and that training was essential for even getting in to Alexandria."[31]

For Flotilla 13, the unit's performance proved one thing—no matter how much a unit trained, its abilities or inabilities can only be measured by its performance in enemy territory during *real* assignments. Flotilla 13's lack of operational experience in peacetime marked it for failure in war. Even in failure, the unit maintained a defining professional character that was infrangible. In Alexandria, the six-man force was taken prisoner in many ways to give the I.N.S. *Tanin* a chance to leave the area unmolested. In Port Said, Ze'ev Almog's force of Pig operators managed to successfully rendezvous with the I.N.S. *Yafo* even though they stuck to their mission and searched the inner sectors of the port, then had been abandoned and left for dead. In retrospect, Flotilla 13's poor showing in the war was a symptom of a far more serious problem that was faced by its parent body, the IDF/Navy. The IDF/Navy was the only branch of the Israeli military to perform poorly in the conflict. In a war marked by brilliant success, dramatic achievements, and victory beyond the realm of the imagination, the navy failed to score a single successful mission throughout the six days of combat—from Alexandria to Latakia, from Port Said to the attack on the U.S.S. *Liberty*. While the joint Israel Air Force and IDF/Navy attack on the American intelligence-gathering ship, a tragic accident and case of "friendly fire" resulting in over thirty dead American sailors, has become the source of conspiracy buffs and theories galore, it was, according to one former Flotilla 13 officer and senior naval commander, "a symptom of the IDF/Navy being that bad, as opposed to capable of hitting a predesignated target."

The 1967 Six Day War has gone down in the history books as the war that changed the face of the modern Middle East, the war that transformed Israel from a regional player into a regional superpower, and a war whose aftermath impacted not only the Middle East specifically, but would impact the rest of the world in the years to come—from terrorism to oil embargoes, from future wars to superpower conflicts.

In looking back at the unit's performance during the war, perhaps its poor showing came from the fact that it had, since 1948, been nothing more than a paper tiger. It trained as hard and as earnestly as a unit could push itself and perfect its skills, but training honed one's body—swimming inside a Syrian port trained an operator's mind. "In a unit like this you need the pressure and tension of knowing that in a few hours you'll be on an actual operation, one under the enemy's eyes, to keep it capable," reflected Ilan Egozi, "for without it, well . . . look what happened in 1967."[32] For Flotilla 13, a fifty-man unit at the time, the war placed the unit straight atop the razor's edge. Either it recovered from the debacle or it allowed itself to self-destruct. The 1967 Six Day War was certainly a turning point for Flotilla 13. Its days as a footnote to the overall Israeli military effort had ended in tragedy and failure. Its time as the nation's cutting edge, the unit that actually made history rather than watch it happen was about to begin.

130

CHAPTER THREE

The Mission Impossible Years

Flotilla 13: 1969 to 1972

"He was without doubt the most important commander to ever take command of the flotilla. There is a difference between being able to and actually taking the initiative, and Ze'ev mastered taking the initiative like no one else. He literally raised an entire generation of Flotilla 13 officers and commanders, and he took a remarkable interest in the unit's equipment and raised the unit's standards far beyond anyone's expectations."
—Captain (Ret.) Izzy Rahav,
former commander of Flotilla 13[1]

"Israeli naval special warfare is Ze'ev Almog!"
—OC IDF/Navy Rear Admiral Amichai "Ami" Ayalon[2]

IF THERE WAS ONE MAN WHO WAS BITTER CONCERNING FLOTILLA 13's performance during the 1967 War it was Lieutenant Commander Ze'ev Almog. He didn't care about the navy's pride, or about the fact that the IDF/Navy was the sole arm of the Israeli military establishment to fail in the conflict.

Ze'ev Almog didn't care about the U.S.S. *Liberty* fiasco, or that naval commanders who oversaw the ineptness were sharing in the victory celebrations without having their careers sunk. His anger centered around the fact that six comrades, combatants he admired and respected, were in the hands of the enemy. While senior naval commanders drank champagne and had their backs slapped in jubilant parties, Lifshitz and his crew of five were having their ribs punched mercilessly, their skulls smashed against cold concrete floors, and were subject to endless acts of Egyptian torture too cruel to think about. Ze'ev Almog cared that as an operator, cutting through the waves near Port Said, he and his men were abandoned and left for dead on a mission other naval commanders cared little about.

It was just because of Almog's justifiable bitterness that he became an obvious—and incredibly brave—choice to succeed Commander Shapir as Flotilla 13's commander. In the first few months following the 1967 War, however, the IDF/Navy was reviewing its performance and attempting to find out what went wrong. Unfortunately, there would be little time for soul-searching and little time to initiate investigations. In October 1967, there would only be time to mourn.

The Middle East is a region of the world run by the currency of vengeance sometimes reinforced by token symbolism. Retaliation can come the next day, or a thousand years later—grudges are nourished in the Near East like no other place on earth. For the flagship of the IDF/Navy, the destroyer I.N.S. *Eilat,* vengeance came calling on the morning of October 21, 1967, with the ferocity of a missile salvo impacting dead center in the cross-hairs. Lieutenant Commander Yitzhak Shoshan, the skipper of the IDF/Navy's flagship, thought little of the autumn sunset as he patrolled a routine course in the Mediterranean. After all, Intelligence Branch information indicating a heightened state of alert in the Egyptian naval base should have reached the IDF/Navy and Shoshan, but it never did; neither did the reports of aerial reconnaissance over the sector indicating enemy activity.[3] But at 15:15 hours, two Komar-class missile boats maneuvered discreetly into firing range and launched a double-edged salvo of two Styx SSMs at the *Eilat* and its crew of 202 sailors. The bright flashing projectiles cascading forward the Israeli flagship had marked a crossroads for the IDF/Navy. A new era had dawned in naval warfare.

The IDF/Navy had extensive files on the Styx, each with a thousand pounds of explosives in its warheads, and greatly feared the weapon's potential. Shoshan, until a few years earlier the IDF/Navy's chief electronics officer, was considered something of an expert in electronic and missile warfare, and he was well aware that the *Eilat*'s anti-missile defenses were dangerously inadequate. Those inadequacies were manifested when the bright green flash of light appeared in the sky over the starboard side heading straight for the *Eilat*. Battle stations were sounded, the ship's 20mm and .50-caliber machine guns were fired in the direction of the incoming missile, but impact occurred seconds later. A Styx slammed through the bow of the ship and directly into the *Eilat*'s engine room. The blinding fireball threw anyone not killed by the initial blasts down on the hard metal floor with unforgiving force. Fire engulfed the center of the ship and a choking cloud of smoke made rescue attempts for those trapped below the fireline impossible. Eleven minutes after the attack, the *Eilat* began to list. Amid the chaos, the Egyptians launched a second Styx at the smoldering vessel.

Destruction was absolute and fast. Twenty minutes after having been struck, the I.N.S. *Eilat,* flagship of the Israeli fleet, was on its way to the bottom of the Mediterranean off the coast of Sinai. Before the flagship could completely go under, a third Styx was fired at the listing ship; the blast of the missile's impact was magnified underwater and scores of sailors precariously treading water were dragged under by the blast never to emerge to the surface again. A fourth Styx finished off the *Eilat* moments later. Of the 202 men on board, forty-seven were lost at sea. Rescue operations were mounted for the next forty-eight hours by an armada of patrol craft and helicopters.

News of the I.N.S. *Eilat* reached Israel several hours later—after families had been notified and after the censor's office, which restricts the flow of all military-related news, realized that they could not keep the disaster a secret from the Israeli public for much longer. Israeli Army radio, and the national *Kol Yisrael* stations, set the mood by playing somber songs of loss and death, and then announced the sinking of the naval ship. Coming so soon following the euphoric victory of the Six Day War, the sinking of the I.N.S. *Eilat* was a shock to the confidence of the Israeli military. The war had produced a feeling of invincibility in the ranks of the IDF—the Arabs had been thrashed in battle, beaten to the point of humiliation. Israel had gone from being a local player to becoming a regional superpower. It had occupied territory about three and a half times the original size of the country, and the length of its coast went from 150 to 700 kilometers. Israeli political leaders had hoped that the war's outcome would convince the Arabs that Israel was a reality on the map and that the resumption of hostilities was pointless. The Arabs had other plans.

Israeli overconfidence soon turned to arrogance. Israeli Defense Minister Moshe Dayan ordered the IDF/Navy to mount daring "show the flag" patrols right under the nose of Egyptian forces stationed on the west bank of the canal, and in the Mediterranean.[4] Dayan's statement of policy, carried out by a navy that had neither the ships nor the manpower to enforce it, was a strategic challenge that stretched the limits and abilities of the IDF/Navy far beyond their envelope. The Egyptians, initially, stood fast and responded with silence. Then in September 1967, in the Arab League summit in Khartoum, Egyptian President Nasser issued his legendary "three-no" proclamation concerning a possible settlement with the Jewish State—no peace, no negotiations, no cease-fire. The sinking of the *Eilat* was the first salvo in the Arab response to the Six Day War—a war of attrition meant to destroy Israel's resolve and ability to fight. The Arabs, resupplied by the Soviets, had both the manpower and material to wage an endless campaign of artillery barrages, air raids, and sniper volleys to wear down the mighty Israeli military.

In military terms, the loss of the *Eilat* forced the IDF/Navy to expedite its Gabriel surface-to-surface missile program, and the acquisition of the French-built Sa'ar missile boats under joint construction in the French shipyards in Cherbourg. By early 1968, the IDF/Navy was also to receive two British World War II-era T-Class 1700-ton submarines, the I.N.S. *Dakar* and *Dolphin* purchased from the Royal Navy. Crews of Israeli submariners had been stationed in Portsmouth since early 1967 and were eager to return to Israel after the lengthy studies abroad. On the night of January 25, 1968, the I.N.S. *Dakar* disappeared in the eastern Mediterranean never to be heard from again. Lost were sixty-nine sailors and officers, and a submarine whose disappearance remains a mystery to this day. Although the theories behind the *Dakar*'s disappearance range from technical malfunction to human error, to Soviet and or Egyptian submarines and frogmen, the tragedy was compounded by the fact that the ship was never recovered from the bottom of the sea. In fact, it has never been located.

Amid the tragedy and loss of life and ships, the IDF/Navy also faced the difficult task of dealing with the problem of Flotilla 13. Until the sinking of the *Eilat* and the loss of the *Dakar,* Flotilla 13 bore the brunt of the wrath laid forth by the Defense Ministry and IDF Chief of Staff Lieutenant General Yitzhak Rabin. The Six Day War was a monumental national victory for the Jewish State, and Flotilla 13 could not participate in the national celebration. There were those who demanded that the unit be disbanded. After all, they argued, commandos from *Sayeret Mat'kal* (the "General Staff Reconnaissance Unit,") a top-secret intelligence-gathering and counter-terrorist strike force that had proven their daring feats behind enemy lines on countless occasions—could easily be taught scuba, combat-swimming, underwater sabotage, boating, and beachline reconnaissance. Morale at the flotilla's base at Atlit was at an all-time low: fights broke out, commandos neglected the maintenance of their gear, and professional soldiers who had once dreamed of a career in the military now searched the want ads for jobs in the private sector. The operators felt that the IDF/Navy was the basket case of the Israeli military and that they were somehow responsible for much of the bad luck by failing in their missions during the Six Day War.

Miraculously, the order to disband Flotilla 13 was never signed. Instead, the IDF/Navy commander, Rear Admiral Shlomoh Erel, opted to hand the unit to the one man in Israel who he felt could save the force from extinction. Almog, the thirty-three-year-old rogue voice of professionalism in the flotilla, was as disillusioned with the unit's performance in the war as anyone—after all, "It was him and his men," he would later comment, "that was left abandoned in the waters off of Port Said in his Bird awaiting retrieval and rescue from the 'regular' navy."[5] In early 1968, however, Rear Admiral Erel informed him that in May of that year he'd take over the command of the flotilla. As angry as he was about what had happened off of Port Said, Almog was naturally honored by the opportunity to command a force whose true potential had yet to be tapped. Almog also realized the unit needed to be built up again from scratch, and it needed work. In a military where "a unit is only as good as its last operation," Almog definitely had his work cut out for him. There was a new sheriff in town and the flotilla finally had a professional soldier—and operator—at the helm who wouldn't put up with the bullshit and the self-doubt.

He began his tenure as flotilla commander with a catchphrase he wanted every operator to consider as holy: "Nobody returns to base unless they carry out their mission!"[6]

Months before he assumed command of the unit, Almog asked Erel for some time so that he could make the necessary preparations he saw fit in bringing the unit up to standards—his standards. First and foremost, Commander Almog created a course for "Flotilla Commanders," designed specifically for ensigns.[7] Many of the problems in the unit, he felt, originated with squadron commanders and their subordinates. Command, in naval special warfare, Almog theorized, required a different curriculum and a different leader than were found elsewhere in active duty. The disciplines, the conceptions, and the practical aspects all had to be taught from the beginning. The students would need to be motivated, of course, and that became a problem. Following the war, a good percentage of the unit transferred out, retired, or returned bitter and unwilling to accept blame for what had happened. As long as the malcontents and hangers-on who lingered through a career in the pre-1967 inactive flotilla, some even dating back to the *Pal'mach*, were still part of the unit, Flotilla 13 would never cross the threshold. Many of the remaining officers in the unit during the Six Day War either transferred out or were "asked" by Almog to pack their bags—an act that would forever earn Almog a long cadre of enemies that would dog him through his rise up the IDF/Navy's ladder of command.

This mini-purge left Almog with only a handful of men to work with, but it was all that he needed. He had with him an officer cadre he trusted, and the noncommissioned officers were the type of men who had managed to keep their dignity in the turbulent days of inactivity, men who persevered and excelled regardless. Ilan Egozi, fresh out of an Egyptian torture chamber and an Israeli military hospital, was one such man. He returned to Israel broken and a shell of his former self, but he was determined to remain in the unit at any cost. "I was bitter, and angry, and nowhere near the physical strength that I was that night in Alexandria," recalls Egozi, "but I needed to go back to the unit and start again."[8] Another crucial cog in Almog's machine was a gritty master sergeant named Ami Ayalon. Ayalon, a Kibbutznik who joined the flotilla in 1963, had slowly earned a reputation as a man who possessed the courage to lead and the charisma to insure that men followed. Although his military profile indicated "natural tendencies" for command, he had been in the unit for nearly five years and had yet to go to an officer's course. Almog saw something special in the lanky Kibbutznik and made sure that Ayalon began service in the "new flotilla" as an ensign. "Ami had special qualities," reflected Almog. "I had a feeling that one day he'd go on to command the unit—at least!"[9]

With a cadre of young officers who were dedicated, tenacious, and innovative, Almog had a base from which to build—his building material would come in the form of several classes of operators who were in a squad commander course with the paratroops during the Six Day War and had not been present during the dark days of June. They were young, many already had been bloodied in battle fighting with Colonel Rafael Eitan's paratroopers in Sinai, and they had escaped the negativity surrounding the unit's operations in Syria, Alexandria, and Port Said. Like Ayalon, most of these men were Kibbutzniks.

As a purely volunteer force, Flotilla 13 accepted only the strongest and most intelligent conscripts entering into their three years of mandatory military service. They all needed the basic faculties of command, as well as the courage and determination to survive the excruciating hell of basic training and beyond. In assembling this human ensemble for selection, the flotilla, like the other IDF elite units, enjoyed a talent pool so unique and so special that their ranks were filled with motivated, highly talented operators who viewed self-sacrifice with eagerness. To them, courage was a test of one's own worth rather than a measure of patriotism. Although Flotilla 13 had always recruited heavily among eighteen-year-olds coming from the Kibbutzim, the men recruited in the mid-1960s were simply remarkable. They were smarter, stronger, and, following the 1967 War, more confident than any generation in Israeli history. They felt invincible, and many proved to be just that. Even a French special operations officer visiting Israel in the late 1960s would revel at the motivation and mettle of those volunteering for service in the flotilla (and other IDF special operations units) at the time.

The Kibbutz, the socialist collective farm that is the true personification of Zionist beliefs and dedication to the land, is a unique and self-sufficient society surrounded by life in the larger Jewish State. A Kibbutz is like no other place on earth. Kibbutz children are raised not by their parents but by nannys working in a collective nursery, and the young Kibbutznik is taught the virtues of being a leader, a commander, a role model. Competitiveness is a religion in the Kibbutz, and although they are egalitarian souls who work well in a team, Kibbutzniks need to prove their worth whenever challenges arise. "We are the nicest people in the world," boasted Y.*, a Kibbutznik and flotilla NCO for over a dozen years, "as long as we are your friends and not poised against you." Their greatest challenges are not in the wheat fields or in the cow pastures, but in the IDF's elite units. One's status in life—one's ability to obtain a spot as a ruling member on a Kibbutz council, and even one's ability to marry the girl of one's choice—is dependent on the type of uniform, the type of insignia, worn home on leave. Being a pilot or commando is the most important achievement any Kibbutznik can hope for. Being a routine soldier, an infantrymen or, worse, a tank crewman, is tantamount to having the scarlet letter "L" painted on the "loser's" forehead. According to Commander (Res.) Yisrael Asaf, a twenty-three-year veteran of Flotilla 13 and a native of one of the most affluent Kibbutzim in Galilee, "Coming home to the community without being able to boast of being accepted into the unit was not in my vocabulary. It would have denied me an equal spot under the apple tree by the dining hall with my friends, it would have denied me respect and admiration. I was damned if I'd allow the naval commandos to break me and deny me my birthright. The flotilla needed me to be the best because that was what was needed for special operations, I needed to be the best because of the peer pressure from the Kibbutz. How are things in the flotilla, they would ask, what did you do there? I would never answer those questions because of security considerations, but the very fact that I could bring my finger to my lips and hush them off with a 'I can't tell you because that's classified' was an honor and a privilege and worth all the pain, suffering, and challenges. It was bravado and image, but it was how we lived. These guys were pilots and commandos, and were involved in more secretive crap than us, but the ability to hush them off, deny them being in the loop, could only happen to someone in an elite unit. If you weren't in such a unit, you might have well packed your bags and found a one-bedroom flat in Tel Aviv."[10]

When volunteering into the many elite units in the IDF's order of battle, the Kibbutznikim have inherent advantages over their fellow eighteen-year-old citizens from the cities. They are usually more physically fit, they are used to not having Mommy and Daddy around, and as a result endure the trauma of having been away from home for the first time under some very trying circumstances in the best possible light. States Colonel (Res.) Reuven Gal, a former chief psychologist of Flotilla 13 as well as of the IDF whose studies in military behavior are required readings at West Point and Sandhurst, said, "These men are not Rambos, and don't even look like the type of superman one could imagine storming an enemy position. They are not muscle-bound comic-book figures. Yet they do have an inner strength that can be honed and strengthened in a military atmosphere, where camaraderie tones that strength and military discipline causes it to excel. While city kids can have that strength, Kibbutznikim display it in remarkable, mind-boggling percentages."[11] On the now-legendary four-day march from Rosh Haniqra along the Lebanese border to the beaches near Gaza all the way to the south, many Kibbutzniks used to simply walk until they passed out. Many of the Kibbutznikim had rarely ever worn shoes, let alone boots (they were used to sandals), and simply traversed the obstacle barefoot! They were determined to reach their envelope of pain, surpass it, and when their legs gave out, they would rely upon willpower. Those who passed out during the march, interestingly enough, were viewed favorably by Flotilla 13's psychologists. Kibbutznikim were also super-patriots. Many viewed their lives as a Zionist working the land and a commando serving the state as the ideal virtue of being an Israeli. Israel's founding father, David Ben-Gurion, viewed the farmer soldier as crucial to Israel's plight for survival and a stoic statement of nation building; in the flotilla and the other commando units, the Kibbutznikim have taken that ethic one giant step forward.

Kibbutznikim are also, by nature, independents. They

have spent a good portion of their formative years living by themselves, working for themselves, and relying upon their wits. While Kibbutzniks are used to working for the collective good of their community, a good many of them are ego-driven individualists. "I am a super-individualist, perhaps even too much so for my own good," claims Commander Asaf, a native of Kibbutz Degania-Bet, along the banks of the Sea of Galilee, "and when I was conscripted into the IDF, I wanted to do (a) the most interesting thing available, and (b) something where me, the individual, would make a difference. I couldn't go to the Armored Corps, because the most basic fighting unit there is the tank and I didn't want to be a member of a crew. I wanted to be it. I wanted to matter and I wanted my abilities to determine the course of events. Flotilla 13 was the only place I found where the individual was *the unit!*"[12]

Many in Almog's Kibbutz talent pool had been conscripted into the IDF in 1966, and they were still in the infantry and parachute portions of their basic training when the war broke out and, as a result, fought with paratroop units, *as paratroopers,* in Sinai. Several of these pre-underwater training cadets were wounded in the battles for El Arish and Umm Katef, including Yisrael Dagai, a lanky and awkward mountain of flesh and bones, who took three bullets to the chest and yet was first on line in the flotilla's underwater course a few months later. Another "wounded" naval commando was Uzi Livnat, another lanky special warfare warrior who was struck down by an Egyptian sniper and yet escaped a hospital bed in order to assume a spot in the underwater phase of the flotilla training in November 1967. Their determination to remain in the flotilla guaranteed them the endearment of Commander Almog.

Almog's first priority in gearing the unit for combat assignments was to install a religious sense of professionalism in the unit's work, appearance, and attitude. Discipline would be rigid and unforgiving. "If a soldier did not button his blouse or have his hair trimmed properly," said Almog, "it meant a lax attitude that would inevitably be reflected in how he cared for his SDV, his underwater gear, and his weapons. It would lead to tragedy and I could not allow it to be tolerated."[13] It was a matter of command and regulations that many of the operators thought trivial, but Almog viewed it with greater seriousness—perhaps with more stringent eyes than any other special operations commander in Israeli military history. "It was a question of character in the man," Almog reflected, "if an operator would make an issue about cutting his hair or buttoning his tunic, then he would also make an issue about diving at the ordered depth, and maintaining radio silence. It means that the soldier feels *he* knows better, and when lives are on the line and national policies are at stake, an operator cannot feel that he knows best."[14]

Indeed, the laid-back egalitarian attitude that had come to personify the IDF—sloppy uniforms, long hair, and close-knit relations between commanders and soldiers—was nowhere to be found in the flotilla. Underwater special operations was deadly business, and that business involved desperate dangers, the lives of others, and the potential for political fallout that could lead to a full-scale conflagration—after all, one captured frogman on a covert assignment in Syria or Egypt or "beyond" could escalate into full-scale war. When Almog arrived at Atlit as the *Ma'Shat* (the Hebrew acronym for *Mefaked Shayetet* or "Flotilla Commander"), for example, he recalled how there was no standard for maintaining personal equipment—even wearing load bearing vests, securing flippers and buoyancy equipment, and holstering their sidearms. "Everyone did it *his own* way," Almog recalls, "because these guys believed that they were the best and nobody could tell them anything." Following orders was a problem for the unit—men who lived in a pressure cooker where they trained under the most dangerous of circumstances, often with live ammunition and live explosives, were very hard to direct. Almog insisted that his operators always report the truth in the post-mission debriefings and rehash every single aspect of the exercise or the mission. He also observed the operators after a mission or an exercise to see who felt good, who dropped off his gear in a supply room and then headed for the shower, or who, almost dead from exhaustion, was still maintaining his gear. Those who underestimated, exaggerated, and neglected their gear were swimming "in shallow water." Almog wanted only professionals. There would be no mistaking who was the boss.

Not that Almog didn't want his men to think—he just wanted them dedicating their talents and resources to the mission at hand and not doing things the way they were done before 1967. He took six commando operations that the flotilla participated in, named each one after one of the six men captured in Alexandria, and then ordered the men in the unit to come up with operational critiques of the raid—not only in terms of what went wrong operationally, but what went wrong in the preparatory stages. For example, a 1967 War raid was aborted near Minat el-Baida because the Zodiacs were too slow in getting to the objective, and they were off course. In examining what went wrong, Almog wanted his men to realize that it was imperative to discover that even the smallest factor can jeopardize an operation to the point where it must be aborted. In this case, it was discovered that the men trained for the raid without taking their weapons and ammunition with them. With a lighter load on board, the Zodiacs raced across the sea reaching their targets at the prescribed time. On June 5, 1967, however, the operators took with them Uzis, FN rifles, MAG machine guns, and bazookas. They also took with them enough ammunition to wage hell against a Syrian battalion. The extra weight carried slowed them down and made navigating difficult. It also made them distort the mission at hand. Their objective was to penetrate the harbor defenses and sabotage enemy vessels—it wasn't to let the bullets fly.

Professionalism in Almog's flotilla meant work, it meant an ethic. In this business, it was the difference between life and death. Almog also made his men study. Every one of Flotilla 13's debacles, from missions in 1948 to the capture of the six in Alexandria, were studied religiously. Commandos had to prepare reports on the missions providing solutions to the difficulties and dilemmas the operators faced in the water and their commanders faced on the insertion craft and mother ships. Almog wanted these brash and confident men to play armchair generals. It would let them analyze how mistakes led to tragedy, and how mistakes could kill them or make them the target of an interrogator's cruelty. It would humble them. Bring them down a peg.

To hone their conventional ground combat skills, Almog teamed up with his old friend from the lecture hall at Hebrew University in Jerusalem, Lieutenant Colonel Uzi Yairi, the commander of Sayeret Mat'kal. At Almog's insistence, the Sayeret had used the flotilla on several occasions for transport to and from their waterborne targets—the Mat'kal commandos were aces when it came to assaulting an enemy fortification, but they knew very little about the operation of inflatable boats or speed craft. The inevitable deal was struck between the two units: the flotilla officers would teach water skills to the Mat'kal commandos and Lieutenant Colonel Yairi and his staff of officers, taught Almog's underwater warriors how to fight on land, how to assault a target with deadly and accurate firepower, and how to race through a gauntlet of enemy fire with speed and dexterity—expending the minimum of ammunition and hitting the maximum of targets. Most important, the Mat'kal commandos gave the flotilla a professional and disciplined analytical approach to pre-operational planning. Sayeret Mat'kal was known to dissect each and every mission into a million and one contingencies. Everything that could go wrong was discussed, analyzed, rehashed, and then prepared for. The unit operated in what was known as *Tzvatim,* or teams, small self-contained entities similar to the "A Teams" in the U.S. Army Special Forces Groups (the exact size and configuration of a Sayeret Mat'kal team remains classified top-secret by the Israeli military). On any mission, each commando knew every aspect of his task on a particular operation, as well as that of every other fighter. He was prepared for *every* possible contingency—ready to assume the role of commander, radioman, or medic—all at a split-second's notice. A Mat'kal operator knew how to fire just about any weapon to be found in the region—from the

Israeli-produced Uzi submachine gun to the Mat'kal favorite, the Soviet-produced AK-47 7.62mm assault rifle.

The relationship between Mat'kal and Flotilla 13 was an informal agreement between the two units achieved without interference—or knowledge—from the higher ranks, though its effects on Israel's ability to wage a war characterized by special operations was of paramount importance. Sayeret Mat'kal, the IDF's "deniable" special operations force, found the War of Attrition a most challenging set of circumstances. In the north, for example, the targets were no longer restricted to the Golan Heights—there were terrorist and intelligence-related objectives throughout the region. Israel's elongated frontier with Jordan was now marked by the flowing waters of the Jordan River, an obstacle that often needed Flotilla 13's assistance in order to be traversed. And, along the Egyptian front, a front marked by the canal, various gulfs and lakes, and the Red Sea, virtually every target involved the crossing of a water obstacle. Heliborne insertions for Mat'kal were common, but before the advent of sophisticated night-vision flying goggles, low-flying choppers risked crashing into desert hills; medium-altitude insertions risked radar detection and the scorn of surface-to-air missile batteries. Zodiacs, the flotilla's inflatable taxis, were the insertion means in those very busy days during the War of Attrition.

To perform with Sayeret Mat'kal, Flotilla 13 had to modify its methods and its overall approach. The transformation from naval saboteur to full-fledged guns-ablaze commando was not as easy as one would think and presented Almog and his staff with a great challenge. For years, the flotilla motto was *silence, stealth, and secrecy.* Missions were supposed to be in-and-out affairs where the operators left no traces—nothing that could link their operations to the State of Israel. For twenty years, they had spent countless training hours involved in honing their stealthlike skills—entering a port or a beach unnoticed, after all, was the currency by which they lived. Their individual weapons training was intense, but always considered a last resort. After all, if an operator had to toss a fragmentation grenade and fire a magazine-emptying burst from his Uzi submachine gun, it meant that he had been compromised, the mission had failed, and he was forced to save himself and his comrades. Silence, of course, meant survival. Flotilla 13 was intended to operate very far from the Israeli national boundaries, sometimes hundreds of kilometers away. They operated in teams of two, or groups of six or eight. They never operated with a battalion of infantrymen held in reserve behind a hill, or a squadron of fighter-bombers to fly close air support.

Suddenly they were sent out on operations where only their arrival to an operation was silent. They were no longer concerned about retrieving any evidence of their presence in an enemy facility; now they wanted the enemy to know who had paid a visit. "It was a remarkable transition," offers Commander (Res.) Yisrael Asaf. "We went from being sneaky and invisible, to being noticeable and aggressive. Many of our people did not possess the killer instinct, they preferred the silent approach, but slowly and very effectively we were taught to be aggressive, to want to harm the enemy, and we were taught to focus on the skill of killing. I remember one exercise, a small example of how we were taught the discipline of killing, where we would race through an obstacle course firing our automatic weapons at a series of paper targets. As we raced through the twist and turns, officers would throw tennis balls at us to confuse and disorientate us. At first, we began to miss our marks and fire wildly. Then, we learned to ignore the balls and even ignore the twist and turns of the course and concentrate solely on putting the bullet square into the target."[15]

Flotilla 13 used its role as covert operation ferrymen to gain combat experience. Although there was little glamour in the work, and there was little contact with the enemy, the unit was operating behind enemy lines. Most of the missions, some carried out hundreds of kilometers from Israeli lines, went smoothly. Other operations were a little more eventful. One such mission occurred on the night of May 13, 1969, when a Flotilla 13 armada of Zodiacs ferried a Mat'kal task force to an ambush on the Egyptian mainland near the northern section of the canal; there were three

Zodiacs in all, and each inflatable carried eight operators and the one "driver." Earlier, a similar Mat'kal detail had ambushed an Egyptian convoy; nearly a dozen Egyptian soldiers were killed and several vehicles set ablaze. This night, however, Egyptian commandos were waiting for them. As the operators of Flotilla 13 guided their boats toward the Egyptian lines, Egyptian commandos opened up with a massive display of automatic fire. When the bullets began to fly as they waited inside their Zodiacs, they heard the sounds of dozens of heavy machine guns opening up near the ambush position. The naval commandos, responsible for the waterborne aspect of the operation, released their lines and retreated. The Mat'kal operators, sitting on the sides of the craft, responded instinctively to the Egyptian fire by bunching up in the back of the boat and then jumping into the water. One operator, the FN MAG 7.62mm light machine gunner, known in the IDF vernacular as the *Magist,* began to sink in the canal's waters; he carried nearly forty kilos of equipment on his back and he could not free himself from his load bearing equipment. Yisrael Asaf, the Zodiac's skipper, instinctively raced into the water, pulled the *Magist* up by the hair, and threw his almost-drowned body back into the Zodiac. Asaf ordered the *Magist* to hold on the life-line rope affixed to the side of the inflatable and quickly, with his Mat'kal cargo holding on to the boat in the water, retreated back to Israeli lines. All Israeli personnel reached friendly lines safely that spring night, except for one Mat'kal officer shot in the head (his body was returned by the Egyptians several days later).

There were many who thought that Asaf should have been decorated for his valor that night, but Yisrael Asaf was as modest an operator as could be found. In fact, following the Six Day War, Defense Minister Moshe Dayan ordered Flotilla 13 to send several Zodiacs sailing through the Suez Canal displaying a large Israeli flag, so that the Israelis could say that they, too, were using the waterway. Three teams of two sailed from the mouth of the canal all the way to the Gulf of Suez. Yisrael Asaf, just off his flotilla course, was one of the unfortunate six given the assignment. His Zodiac was the target of hundreds of Egyptian guns and miracu-

lously he succeeded in his assignment without getting a
hundred bullet holes in him. After the folly, the negligent
endangering of the life of a soldier for a half-assed public
relations gesture would have long-term impact on Asaf, who
would rise up the ranks to one day become the flotilla's
deputy commander. "After I survived the stupid mission,"
Asaf reflects, "I promised myself two things: one, I would
never go on another mission like that, and two, as a
commander, I would never ever send soldiers out on a
mission like that!"[16] The defense minister wanted to give
him a decoration for his courage, but Asaf refused. In fact, if
it were up to Yisrael Asaf, the story of saving the operator
from Mat'kal would have remained forgotten, but the
Magist was a young sergeant named Benjamin "Bibi"
Netanyahu, and at the time of this book's writing he is the
prime minister of the State of Israel.[17]

There were other "fascinating" operations, all relatively
small operations, in which Flotilla 13 slowly began to prove
itself to Almog, and to the IDF/Navy. Some involved
intelligence-gathering missions along the waterways of the
canal; others, according to published accounts, involved
covert operations involving Israeli intelligence. There were
operations against Palestinian targets, training and operational bases of Yasir Arafat's Fatah terrorist group, across
the Jordan River. Pathfinders from Flotilla 13 would cross
the harrowing waterways, secure a beachhead and a safety
line for the assault force, usually a reconnaissance para
troop or Golani infantry squad, and then make sure that
their return across the river was uneventful. There were also
beach recces where soil samples, possible landing zones
and enemy shoreline facilities were mapped and targeted.
Most of the missions were ambushes, however. A flotilla
team would reach the Egyptian mainland courtesy of a
submersible or a Zodiac, plant several anti-personnel and
anti-tank mines along a patrol path, a rail line, or roadway
and then slink back to friendly lines.

The small missions, courtesy of Flotilla 13's relationship
with Sayeret Mat'kal, had improved the unit's standings in
the eyes of senior commanders. The operators performed

148

well—they had acted with skill, discipline, and courage. Now Almog also had to change how Israeli military planners viewed naval operators. In the 1967 War, Israeli naval strategy was simple—the Israeli navy, with only two destroyers and a few torpedo boats, was numerically dwarfed by the Egyptian fleet. To even the score as much as a satchel of limpet mines would allow, Flotilla 13 was to enter the enemy ports and sink as many ships as possible. Naval special warfare, Almog argued to his superiors, was not an excuse for not having a vast armada of warships, but rather a tool to strike at an enemy's weak points, its nerve centers, and to cause the other side to dedicate vast assets and attention to rear areas as opposed to the front lines. Naval commandos, Almog argued, could achieve maximum effectiveness by dedicating efforts on a single *difficult* target, rather than go for broke in a large-scale strike. "You would have achieved the same effectiveness by going after one single ship in Alexandria," Almog would reflect, "rather than try and sink the entire port."[18] Commandos, according to the doctrine, were also tasked with weakening an enemy's resolve and morale, and this was achieved by attacking hard targets, heavily fortified ones, in the rear areas that the enemy thought of as "invulnerable."

Almog was also the first Israeli combat officer to ever lobby for work for his men. He routinely ventured out to the various commands, from the Southern Command commander to the chief of staff himself to volunteer his unit for operations. Almog's team of intelligence and operations officers routinely took it upon themselves to conjure up raids, and plead with their superiors to authorize the operations for the flotilla to execute. Female conscripts, serving as secretaries during their two years of conscripted service, knew that a visit from Almog meant trouble. A day's quiet routine of having a cigarette, typing reports, and flirting with an officer was often interrupted by Almog and his entourage, bearing maps, charts, and folders full of files, marching through the door asking, *"Efshar Ledaber Im Ha'Mefaked?"* ("Can we speak to the commander?"). Answers of no were rarely accepted. Almog wanted work for his men and didn't care who he had to nag in order to get it.

At first, Major General Yeshayau Gavish, the OC Southern Command at the time of the Six Day War, was the fortunate recipient of Almog's persistence. "Excuse me, sir," Almog would politely tell the general as he fumbled with his maps and charts, "yesterday Egyptian commandos crossed the canal and placed mines here, here, here, and there. I suggest retaliation and I suggest that the flotilla carry it out. I have selected a group of targets that are suitable, sir?" As Almog made himself known among the senior officers in the south, the first reaction was usually, "Who the hell are you and you are from flotilla what?" Soon, however, there wasn't a colonel and above in Southern Command who didn't know Almog's face and what he wanted. Almog made very few friends during his bid at being part commando, part public relations wizard; his annoying, though persistent, demeanor was unique. Generals remembered him, remembered the unit. Most senior officers considered Almog a *Nudnik,* the Yiddish term for pest, but he slowly was wearing his superiors down.

In 1969, the founder of Unit 101, Major General Ariel "Arik" Sharon, was named OC Southern Command. A larger-than-life figure, both in persona and actual size, Sharon was three things—a dynamic military officer with incredible charisma, an authoritative officer who tolerated little insolence, and a man who loved initiative. Had any other type of officer knocked on his door, Sharon might have tossed him in the stockade for a week and demoted him a rank or two. But Almog was looking to initiate, to strike back, and Sharon appreciated the cut of his mettle. After Almog made his initial pitch to Sharon, the general scanned out his window at the harsh desert sun, and asked Almog, "When can you be there?" "We are there already, sir," Almog replied quickly, always handing maps and intelligence reports as he saw a conducive ear buying the sales pitch. Sharon, impressed by the initiative, then looked at Commander Almog and, as if asking for some help, gestured: "And what do you want from me?" Almog responded, "I want you to bring up these operations to the General Staff and have the General Staff instruct the navy to

THE NIGHT RAIDERS

order us into action. The IDF/Navy will not, on its own, get us work!"[19]

Almog walked a tightrope when he played politician among the generals in search of assignments. Although a small army, the IDF is as bureaucratic as they come and filled with more egos than they have general ranks to fill. By going to General Sharon, Almog bypassed the local area commander (usually an Armored Corps), the divisional commander (a brigadier general), the IDF/Navy commander (a rear admiral), the Operation Branch commander (a major general), the Military Intelligence Branch commander (a major general who was also in charge of most Sayeret Mat'kal operations),[20] and the deputy chief of staff. At pre-operational briefings, in the days before Sayeret Mat'kal and Flotilla 13, most of these generals were usually present and many would look at Almog and his staff and say to themselves, "What the hell are these people doing here." Almog's lobbying angered many and none more than the commander of the navy. At one pre-mission briefing, Rear Admiral Avraham Botzer came up to Almog and asked, "How did they [the green army generals] know about you?" Almog laconically replied, "I guess *they* bothered to take an interest in us."[21]

In the summer of 1968, Flotilla 13 began its formally sanctioned operations with Sayeret Mat'kal. By the summer of 1969, Flotilla 13 was finally given a solo mission.

From the onset of the War of Attrition, there were several shoreline targets that IDF Southern Command viewed with great interest. These included artillery batteries, anti-aircraft surface-to-air missile batteries, and radar installations. The brunt of the fighting was being waged by the warplanes of the Israel Air Force—gaining Votour bombers and new A-4 Skyhawk fighter-bombers acquired from the United States. One target that required special attention was a surface-to-air radar facility on the Red Sea coastal area at Ras al-Adabia. Positioned on the west coast of the northern section of the Gulf of Suez, approximately forty miles from Suez City, Ras al-Adabia was a formidable

151

target not easily handled by the IAF. At first, Chief Infantry and Paratroop Officer Brigadier General "Raful" Eitan had wanted his boys, the paratroops, to carry out the raid, but preliminary intelligence-gathering efforts examining the target on the ground, probably by operators from Sayeret Mat'kal, recommended that a seaborne approach was prudent. The base was defended by approximately fifty Egyptian soldiers, it was fortified by machine nests and pillboxes, and nearby a battery of 130mm artillery pieces kept the surrounding areas of approach well within range. The radar facility controlled the entire surrounding waterway and the air approaches, as well.

"Raful," as Brigadier General Eitan was known to all, was a man who usually got his way—both on the battlefield and in the halls of IDF bureaucracy. He was also a man incredibly loyal to *his* paratroopers, and when it was suggested that a heliborne approach to Ras al-Adabia was not a safe means of insertion, he summoned Almog to his headquarters to talk about how the flotilla would transport the red berets to their target. A great field officer with unbreached courage under fire, "Raful" took a bullet to the head in Sinai while leading his 35th Paratroop Brigade in action. Never a man known to throw around an extra word unless he absolutely had to (sometimes he rarely talked at all), "Raful" found it hard to talk to officers he didn't know and whose abilities under fire he hadn't personally witnessed. Yet attending the meeting was Lieutenant Colonel Uzi Yairi, now the deputy commander of the 35th Paratroop Brigade, and he helped break the ice between "Raful" and Almog.

"So, how are you going to transport the paratroops to the target?" "Raful" asked as Commander Almog began jotting down notes in his small pad, "Rubber boats?" Stone faced, his stomach acid bubbling, Almog replied, "I am not transporting the paratroops anywhere. We should be given this assignment. We are more than up for the task!"[22] "Raful" wasn't used to insolence. He never tolerated it. His face turned the same crimson color of his paratroop beret and he ordered the pesky Flotilla 13 to "get the hell out." As Almog departed the office, a flabbergasted Yairi chased his about-to-be-in-deep-shit friend down and said, "Are you nuts? You can't talk to him like that!" "Uzi, you gotta tell him that we are able to do this mission by ourselves. Tell him. Please!"[23]

Over the course of the next several weeks, while the fate of Ras al-Adabia was debated, Flotilla 13 carried out reconnaissance of the target and effectively mapped out paths of attack, extraction points, and the disposition of attacking personnel to defenders. In the first week of June 1969, Almog and his senior officers had just returned to Israeli-held Sinai following a reconnaissance sortie against Ras al-Adabia, when Almog learned that a chopper was waiting to fly him back to Tel Aviv. Sliding out of his wet suit and stowing his gear away, Commander Almog put on his Class A's and flew the 600 kilometers to Tel Aviv for a meeting with Chief of Staff Bar-Lev and members of the General Staff. It was Almog's chance to present the top brass with his plans and to, once and for all, make a concerted effort to have the flotilla handle a major commando assault strictly on its own. With maps and aerial reconnaissance photos before him, Almog listed his battle plan. It was sound, effective, and daring, but many generals, themselves experienced infantry officers, took issue with his plan to bring only twenty operators. "Twenty isn't enough," some generals argued. "You need at least fifty?" Almog stood fast amid the criticism and second-guessing. "If you take fifty men, then you need more boats and our chances of discovery are greater." To hammer his point home with striking impact, Almog simply said, "Anyway, one of my men is worth five infantrymen, and if you want to see for yourselves what we can do, I invite you to the flotilla for a live-fire display!"[24]

The next evening, along the shores of the Mediterranean, Bar-Lev "Raful" and several other generals were treated to a masterful display of a unit hungry for work and recognition. "Raful" would write, "I can see twenty pirates emerging from the water, daggers between their teeth, capable of handling just about any mission assigned to them."[25] Although Almog had won the mission, "Raful" was still somewhat hesitant. After the display, the chief paratroop and infantry officer pulled Almog aside, and said, "Listen, you guys have no built-up area combat experience under your belt, why don't you take five paratroopers as backup?" "Absolutely not," replied Almog, "we have no built-up area fighting experience because nobody ever gave us the chance. The mission will be a complete success, I am absolutely sure of it, and if we take five paratroopers, they are certain to get all the credit. If, God forbid, the mission goes bad, which it won't, then everyone will say, sure things went wrong— there were only five paratroopers on board. I have an idea. I'll take *one* paratrooper with me, *you!* This way, once and for all, you can see what we are made of."[26]

"Raful," a commander who loved action, was issued an offer he could not refuse. He would go along as a "red beret" observer. In the IDF's Operations Branch computer, the raid on Ras al-Adabia was given the code name of "Operation Mania 5." It would be Flotilla 13's first solo. That night, Flotilla 13 was flown up to the Golan Heights for some intensive built-up area combat training. Over the course of the next seventy-two hours, over 10,000 rounds of ammunition would be fired amid the wrecked ruins of Syrian forts atop the volcanic plateau.

By the time the plans for Operation Mania 5 were handed down, morale in the unit equaled its high state of operational readiness. The unit was, after all, starting to get busy— they went from an entity that operated behind enemy lines once every ten years to one executing two operations a week. The target-rich environment of the Suez Canal was, by itself, 160 kilometers long; the Gulf of Suez, also filled with its share of tempting targets, was 300 kilometers long. Flotilla 13 had spent a good part of the spring and early summer of 1969 along the Suez Canal area—it was the "hot" theater of operations and nonheliborne strikes across the waterway required flotilla participation. There were areas along the waterways, between Port Fuad and Port Said, covered by thick and impassable swamps. They were ideal corridors of insertion to Egyptian rear positions that Sayeret Mat'kal, or one of the other paratroop reconnaissance units, couldn't master. Operators from Flotilla 13 though, in attack forces using the legendary British-built

Klepper canoes, had no problem silently slicing a path through the reeds and water-filled passages. And, of course, the busier they got, the more cohesive as a single unit they became. Even though it was a unit designed to be Spartan, Almog realized that even hard-nosed warriors need some creature comforts and he summoned the base master sergeant, a remarkable man named Musa Cohen, down from Atlit to be responsible for the operators' home away from home. Cohen, a bear of a man who was legendary for his rope work and participation in the excavations in the Judean Desert that uncovered the Dead Sea Scrolls, was what is known as a fixer. At the unit's forward camp at Ras Sudr, Cohen fixed comfortable living quarters for the men, along with comfortable latrines and working showers—a must in a desolate part of the planet where the daytime temperature dances with the 130-degree Fahrenheit mark. With Ras al-Adabia, the flotilla would need all the showers Senior Master Sergeant Cohen could arrange. Training for the mission would go on relentlessly nearly twenty hours a day.

D-day was the night of June 21, 1969, and because of the tides and the onset of daylight, the flotilla's time frame for carrying out the operation was limited; they possessed a stringent timetable and every second counted. The operators looked like a group of pirates in their black neoprene wet suits and their specially designed green canvas load bearing equipment. Most of the operators carried Uzis, some silenced, and all carried extra loads of ammunition and anti-personnel hand grenades. Commando daggers, sharpened to a razor's edge, were firmly nestled in load vests and ankle straps; field radios, tuned into secure frequencies, were covered by nylon bags and—hopefully—waterproofed for the mission at hand. Unit sappers, men usually accustomed to preparing explosives to take down enemy shipping, carried with them waterproof containers holding enough TNT to destroy the radar and any other building to be found at the base. Several of the operators carried FN MAG 7.62mm light machine guns, the IDF mainstay, as fire support weapons. It was hoped they wouldn't be needed.

The flotilla's attack plan called for the twenty operators to sail in Zodiac inflatables from their forward base at Ras Masle northwest, past the "Newport" boulder that protruded from the sea, and then head due west toward the target. The plan called for the assault force to land just due north of the target and then attack the target in five teams. Leading the assault was Lieutenant Commander Shaul Ziv, the flotilla's deputy commander. His task force's mission was to make entry into the camp and prepare the perimeter. The covering task force, led by First Lieutenant Amnon, was to set up a mini-defensive position throughout the camp and to cover the entire twenty-man team's withdrawal. One team, led by First Lieutenant Yoav Eitan, was responsible for the demolition of the towering radar and communications antenna, while another team, commanded by First Lieutenant Dov Bar, was to blow up the radar station itself and purify the facility's defenders. Finally a task force commanded by First Lieutenant Ilan Egozi was to blow up the garrison's living quarters. The raid itself wasn't expected to last more than several minutes.

Crossing the Gulf of Suez in a flotilla of Zodiacs was remarkably uneventful. Egyptian forces failed to notice the fast-moving group of rubber boats led by Almog and there were no technical or navigational problems. The rigid timetable that "Raful" demanded was already reaching its envelope, however. The departure point came several hours after the prescribed H-hour because of the slow advance of the force due to the unexpected Egyptian radar coverage and because the distances took longer to traverse than had originally been foreseen. The boats made it, though and Almog ordered the men into action immediately. Almog and "Raful," on an inflatable command post 100 meters offshore, watched as the operators left their boats for the swim to the target. Approximately 100 meters from the facility's outer perimeter, flotilla pathfinders identified two Egyptian sentries foolishly smoking cigarettes and chatting as if they were eating ice cream along the Nile and not guarding a front-line target. If the Israelis were close enough to see the Egyptians, then perhaps the Egyptians were close enough to hear the Israelis splashing about. As the combat swimmers reached the shallow shoreline waters, the order was given to crawl along the foot-high waters until land was reached. When the first team of pathfinders reached Egyptian Africa, on the other side of the Gulf, the Egyptians had no idea that there were intruders in their perimeter. Surprise, the flotilla's most lethal weapon, was in fine working order that summer's night.

Once the entire force had made it to dry land, the twenty operators assembled at an improvised staging area some twenty-five meters from the main gate. As they set out in bands of four, an Egyptian sentry walking a post thought he noticed movement from behind a few bushes and began to lower his AK-47 assault rifle from its slung position across his shoulder, but he was cut down by a burst of 9mm tracer fire from an operator's Uzi submachine gun. The five-round burst cut through the silence with acoustic thunder. The assault teams split up to their prescribed missions and commenced their attacks, weapons ablaze. Lieutenant Commander Ziv established a command post, and using coded messages, he relayed to Almog and "Raful" what was going on.

In methodical and well-rehearsed fashion, the operators moved about the facility as if the jerky motion of tossing a grenade, firing a burst, and then diving for cover was second nature. Ilan Egozi's team attacked the living-quarters area with unforgiving ferocity. A room's door was kicked down, a grenade was tossed in, and then the room was raked by magazine-emptying bursts of 9mm fire. Many of the Uzis began to malfunction, as sand particles gathered from the shallow-water crawl assembled in clumps inside the weapon's firing mechanism. Faced with little choice, the operators relieved the dead Egyptians of their "all-weather" and "all-condition" Russian-built assault weapon masterpieces, and used them in the assault. Lieutenant Bar's squad was facing heavy resistance in their concentrated attack on the radar station, but their well-choreographed advance proved too much for the Egyptian defenders. Scores of Egyptian dead littered the sands; others ran off into the night screaming and begging for mercy. The radar station and its generator were wired with explosives.

Yoav's assault team faced the stiffest resistance in their attack on the facility's towering antenna building. The antenna was at the far end of the base, and by the time the operators reached the building's entrance, the Egyptian defenders had time to wake up and grab their assault rifles and RPK light machine guns. A hellatious fire-fight erupted. It was close-quarter and it lit up the dark night with crisscrossing slivers of illuminating tracer round bullets traveling in a million different directions at thousands of feet per second. Lieutenant Eitam was hit by a bullet fragment, and another operator was hit by a piece of shrapnel. The battle was fought with grenades and rifle butts. In the end, Eitam's team persevered. The buildings were rigged with explosives and the Egyptian defenders were killed.

With the primary mission over, the task forces reassembled and then headed back for the waterline for the swim back to their awaiting Zodiac craft. The covering force mined the flotilla's path of retreat, and as they searched the horizon for targets, they were engulfed by a blinding light and thunderous blast as the explosives left behind razed the facility to the ground. The blast was the cue for the Zodiacs, moored off coast, to rev their engines and pick up the operators. There was no Egyptian attempt to intercept the Israeli raiders.

The sprawling Egyptian radar facility at Ras al-Adabia was destroyed in all of twelve minutes. In all, thirty-two Egyptian soldiers were killed in the fighting, and scores were more seriously wounded. Flotilla 13 returned to base without serious casualties. It was a striking victory that had evaded the Batmen for over twenty years. Most important, the raid on Ras al-Adabia had raised the stock of the unit not only in the eyes of the various regional commands that delegated their assignments, but it also caught the atention of the OC IDF/Navy, Rear Admiral Avraham Botzer, a "traditional" naval man and experienced torpedo boat and destroyer officer who had replaced Erel as commander of the IDF/Navy in September 1968. Botzer, trained by the Royal Navy's Staff College, was wary of the exploits of large-scale underwater assaults. Perhaps most important, the Ras al-Adabia operation proved to the General Staff that the naval commandos were far more than a force of "underwater oddballs," men who were segregated in the IDF by their skills, maneuvers, and specialized tasks. These warriors operated alone, in two-man teams, and with the minimum of rear support; this was all atypical military fare to many serving officers of the General Staff—men used to battalion-size assaults in rows of main battle tanks, not rows of Zodiac craft.

Ras al-Adabia was a rite of passage—a turning point. It transformed Flotilla 13's primary mission of intelligence-gathering, shoreline reconnaissance, underwater sabotage, and occasional ferrymen for Mat'kal to the surprise-attack *modus operandi* of full-fledged shock troops. Commander Ze'ev Almog realized that Ras al-Adabia was a most important victory not for the enemy forces killed or the radar station that was destroyed, but because it guaranteed more work for the flotilla. That, by itself, was an incredible accomplishment.

Almog and his officers reveled in their test under fire and studied the lessons learned from the operation with religious attention to detail. "What did we do right?" "What went wrong?" "Was the method of insertion correct, or could it have been improved?" "What do we now know about how Egyptians respond when attacked by surprise?" Each operator participating in the attack had to submit a report on the operation, with a list of conclusions he could draw on his, and the flotilla's, performance. The soul-searching was invaluable. Operators learned, for example, that their Uzi submachine guns, allegedly capable of firing when encased in mud, were jamming as a result of the fine shoreline sand filling its firing mechanism. As a result, since the Ras al-Adabia raid, all weapons ferried to a target are wrapped in plastic! Chief of Staff Bar-Lev, in a private meeting with Almog, also brought up some technical matters that were of concern to him. Bar-Lev had been troubled by the fact that the individual operators were not provided with communications gear that enabled them to report their progress to both Shaul Ziv's CP, to Almog and "Raful" moored 100 meters away, and even to Bar-Lev and the General Staff in the Kirya.

Technically speaking, Ras al-Adabia was a significant turning point in equipment, as well. When requesting equipment and the funds to purchase them abroad from the IDF/Navy, the standard response had always been, "Are you nuts?" Now, however, as shining stars in a navy desperately seeking heroes, the reply became, "Sure, what else can we do for you?" Ze'ev Almog had always been a technology-driven officer who believed that the tools of war were as important as the warriors. The designer of everything from load-bearing gear to, eventually, patrol and special operations craft, Almog believed that a unit could possess the greatest and most state-of-the-art gadget, but if that techno dynamo didn't fill the immediate needs of the person who used it (either in the civilian sector or for a soldier in battle) it was of little practical use. Prior to Ras al-Adabia, Almog faced enormous bureaucratic obstacles in getting his requests past the bean-counters in the IDF/Navy budget department. In acquiring the Dolphin, a French-built single-man delivery system, Almog fought long and hard to convince officers with little knowledge of special operations tactics why such a device was needed by the unit. Even in getting the flotilla's first high-speed boats, Cigarette boats that Almog named after a beguiling seabird, the *"Snunit"* (Hebrew for the maritime bird, the "Swallow"), he faced raised eyebrows and a twenty-month wait for the green light before he could authorize the purchase from Bertram Shipyards in San Diego. But the tight purse-strings were a symptom of the lack of respect the flotilla possessed for so long within the hallways of IDF/Navy HQ. When showing off the first Snunit to a close friend in the Israel Air Force, Commander Almog explained how it took him over a year and a half to get the $11,000 to buy the boat. "Eleven thousand dollars?" responded the IAF officer. "We spend more than that on jet fuel when we ignite our afterburners."[27]

Ras al-Adabia changed everything. Not only was Flotilla 13 given greater autonomy in acquiring material from

abroad, but they were also given greater access to the IDF/ Navy's technical research department. The IDF/Navy's chief electronic engineer, an admired genius named Tzemach, was quickly authorized to give the flotilla anything they needed, but his knowledge of the naval commandos, even their standards and practices, was extremely limited; when authorized to produce the waterproof communications device, he ended up conjuring up a radio packed inside an oval container—it looked more like a football than a commando's field radio. As a result, all technical requirements for the unit would be handled *in-house* by unit technical officers. Within weeks, Michael Avraham, Flotilla 13's legendary designer and chief technical officer, had modified a small field radio used by Sayeret Mat'kal for the flotilla's unique specifications.

With Flotilla 13 on the map, Ze'ev Almog had listed hundreds of potential targets worthy of Flotilla 13's attention in his reports to the IDF/Navy commander and Southern Command's operations officer. With Ras al-Adabia now marked off in red, the targets included a whole host of radar stations, naval facilities, and a man-made anti-aircraft position sitting in the middle of the Gulf of Suez known as Green Island. Almog thought that he'd be able to sit down, select the three or four sexiest targets, and then begin the lobbying process all over again.

Almog's desired target was Green Island, and he was already sending out feelers to his superiors about authorizing a raid. But Colonel Haim Nadel, the commander of the 35th Paratroop Brigade, was also lobbying the General Staff for work and a spectacular strike against a hard Egyptian target. Nadel's plan called for a seventy-man task force of paratroopers to be ferried to the shores of the Great Bitter Lake and attack an Egyptian officers' club. Of course, Nadel realized, he'd need the flotilla and its complement of Zodiac craft for the ride across the water obstacle, and he thought that the raid, one also involving Flotilla 13, would be to Almog's liking. Commander Almog hated playing second fiddle—especially to the paratroopers. In closed-door sessions in the Kirya, he told the General Staff that this mission, if eventually authorized, should be a Flotilla 13 operation, even though the unit boasted less than forty active duty operators. Much to Almog's surprise and Nadel's disbelief, the founder of the modern IDF paratroopers, Major General "Arik" Sharon favored using the flotilla for more than Zodiac drivers; so, too, did the deputy chief of staff, Major General David "Dado" Elazar. The debate continued over the course of a few weeks, but neither Almog nor Nadel would have a say in determining the next mission. That decision came from Cairo. The Egyptians were about to raise the ante in the war along the canal in dramatic fashion.

At twilight, on July 10, 1969, a platoon-size force of Egyptian commandos from the *as-Saiqa* ("Lightning Bolt") Battalion, the Egyptian version of America's Green Berets and the British SAS, launched several Zodiac dinghies from their concealed positions on the western bank of the Suez Canal and slowly made their way across the placid waters. Israeli sentries posted along the shore were unable to distinguish the low silhouette of the rubber inflatable craft as the commandos paddled through the mild surf. Hitting the "Israeli" side of the canal, the Egyptians quickly unloaded their gear and set out for the short slink through the pitch-black desert toward the night's objective: the Mezach Bar-Lev line position situated at the mouth of Port Tewfiq. Known for their dark green berets, and penchant for martial arts and removing sentries with razor-sharp Kalashnikov bayonets, the *as-Saiqa* commandos had built a daunting reputation among Israeli servicemen stationed along the canal. They had become increasingly bothersome to Israeli commanders, mounting hit-and-run raids against the loosely defended Bar-Lev line fortifications and rear-supply stations. On July 10, things would be different. It was the bloodiest commando attack the Egyptians ever mounted against an Israeli position. Seven IDF soldiers were killed and five were wounded in the raid; several were taken prisoner and dragged back to Egypt; in addition, the *as-Saiqa* force destroyed two Centurion MBTs (or "Main Battle Tank"). Israeli soldiers stationed along the canal buckled as news, and then rumor, about the raid filtered through the ranks. Seven dead, all killed at close-quarters, was demoralizing enough, but being dragged across the canal as a POW was a horrific fate. Many of the soldiers were reservists and were just as concerned about their wives and businesses as they were about the geopolitical struggle being waged along the Suez Canal. Morale nose-dived. Conscript units, on patrol or maneuvers elsewhere, were rushed to the canal to shore up IDF defenses.

The Egyptian raid had reaped the rewards of classic commando warfare. It also warranted an equally harsh Israeli response.

As far as retaliation was concerned, the IDF General Staff demanded a *naval* response, and they also demanded a response that would strike at the soul of Egyptian morale as the assault on Mezach had caused Israeli servicemen posted along the canal to be engulfed by fear and apprehension. Since the assault on Mezach, considered the most fortified of the Bar-Lev line positions, was assaulted by Egyptian naval commandos, Egypt's most fortified position would need to be assaulted. It was tit-for-tat on a bloodletting level, but such was the War of Attrition. Glancing at a map of the Suez front, one small mark on the map proved perfect. It was *Al-Ahdar* [or "Green Island"]: "The Monster!" A piece of protruding stone and concrete that the Egyptians affectionately called *their* "Rock of Gibraltar." Green Island was an impregnable fortress and symbol of Egyptian military prowess, and it was the one target in the Suez theater of operations were the Egyptians felt impregnable. Hitting an Egyptian officers' club along the coast of the Great Bitter Lake might result in a high body count and increase security around similar facilities in the area, but it would not hit the General Staff in Cairo the same way as if the Egyptian Rock of Gibraltar was hit and destroyed.

Following Ras al-Adabia, Chief of Staff Bar-Lev had all the confidence that Flotilla 13 could pull off such a daunting task. The objective of the operation was revenge—the killing of the Egyptian garrison. Blowing the place up was a secondary objective, and, should everything go well and according to plan, the Israelis were prepared to take a few prisoners back with them.

Green Island, located at the southern mouth of the Suez Canal (three kilometers south of Port Ibrahim), was built by the British during the Second World War to protect its ultrastrategic waterway from air and sea attack by Axis forces. Built on a bed of stable corals and made out of reinforced concrete, Green Island was a monstrous facility, which, at its longest point, was 150 meters long and, at its widest, eighty meters across; it was a single structure consisting of a one-story building with a large courtyard. At the end of the island, a concrete bridge jutted out into the water toward a circular five-meter-high tower supporting a radar site and two heavy anti-aircraft machine guns. A straight wall was built at the waterline, reinforced by thick rows of rusting barbed-wire concertina positioned to deter any intruder from attacking by sea. Its defenses were as formidable as its dominating position in the seemingly peaceful waters. Entrenched in the roof were four emplacements of 85mm heavy anti-aircraft guns and two 37mm gun positions; there were over a dozen machine-gun nests for 7.62mm light machine guns and 14.5mm heavy machine guns. A'man, Israeli military intelligence, reported that there were approximately 100 Egyptian soldiers garrisoned at Green Island, including *as-Saiqa* commandos.

Even before the Egyptian commando raid on the Mezach position, Flotilla 13 maintained an extensive and elaborate file on Green Island—it was an obvious target and a challenging one, as well. In April 1969, Yoav Eitam and Ilan Egozi led a four-man reconnaissance sortie to gather intelligence on the target. According to standard military practice, though, Ilan Egozi should have been nowhere near the Egyptian front; as a released POW from Egyptian hands, should he have fallen again into captivity, he wouldn't, under the Geneva Convention, have been considered a combatant anymore, but rather a spy, and the penalty for espionage during wartime was execution. Egozi, however, made it clear to Almog that he wouldn't accept a part-time role in the unit. Either he was a full-time player or he was out of the flotilla for good.[28] Almog needed men like Egozi and agreed to his conditions. Egozi was a fearless operator and an officer who possessed incredible charisma. He was

A special warfare visionary—Yitzhak Sadeh. Known as the "Old Man," Sadeh was one of the founding fathers of the Pal'mach, and the Pal'yam's underwater sabotage unit. *(IDF Archives)*

Captain Izzy Rahav, a former commander of Flotilla 13, as seen here during his tenure as commander of the Destroyer Flotilla. *(Courtesy: Ze'ev Almog)*

Rear Admiral Yochai Bin-Nun awards the newly issued bat-wings to the officers and NCOs of Flotilla 13, circa 1959. *(Courtesy: Ze'ev Almog)*

Israeli naval special warfare wings: *(top)* Unit 707 wings; *(middle)* Flotilla 13 operator wings; *(bottom)* Master Flotilla 13 wings. *(Sigalit Katz)*

The now legendary "dipping" ceremony for all new members of the unit who have passed through the grueling course, circa 1963. *(Courtesy: Ze'ev Almog)*

Zodiacs being para-dropped into the Mediterranean during maneuvers in 1967. *(Courtesy: Ze'ev Almog)*

The flotilla training with the Italian-produced MTM
craft during explosive boat exercises in 1969.
(Courtesy: Ze'ev Almog)

Commander Ze'ev Almog *(left)* jokes around with
Defense Minister Moshe Dayan and IDF/Navy
commander Rear Admiral Botzer in a briefing just
after the raid on Adabiya. *(Courtesy: Ze'ev Almog)*

Green Island—the monster. A formidable target for a brigade of men, let alone a twenty-man team of frogmen. *(IDF Archives)*

Operators from Flotilla 13 train in assaulting a target following a combat swim in the days prior to the raid on Green Island. *(IDF Archives)*

Chief of Staff Lieutenant General Haim Bar-Lev *(left)* awards the Medal of Valor to Lieutenant Ami Ayalon *(right)* and Exemplary Service Medal to Lieutenant Gil Lavi *(next to Ayalon)* for their heroism under fire during the assault on Green Island. Flotilla 13 commander Ze'ev Almog *(center)* looks on proudly. *(Courtesy: Ze'ev Almog)*

A moment of celebration following the successful completion of the first phrase of "Operation Escort" with Lieutenant Ayalon *(left)* and his "pig" crew: a moment of "mission well done" after the sinking of the targeted Egyptian torpedo boat. Hours later, joy would turn to grief as the dead and wounded from the second Pig's crew were discovered. *(Courtesy: Ze'ev Almog)*

Captain Ze'ev Almog, Red Sea Theater commander, accepts the surrender of the port of Adabiya from his Egyptian counterpart on October 24, 1973, the final day of the Yom Kippur War. *(Courtesy: Ze'ev Almog)*

Operators train in beach assaults along a stretch of Israel's Mediterranean coastline, circa 1979. *(IDF Archives)*

As commander of the IDF/Navy, Rear Admiral Almog greets Egyptian President Anwar el-Sadat only six years after Almog's successful naval special warfare campaign against the Egyptian fleet in 1973. *(Courtesy: Ze'ev Almog)*

IDF/Navy commander Rear Admiral Almog receives the Legion of Merit medal from U.S. Navy Admiral Thomas Heywood, in Washington, D.C., in March 1981. *(Courtesy: Ze'ev Almog)*

Operators head into the sea during an early morning dive off the coast of Atlit. *(IDF Spokesman)*

A mini-armada of Zodiacs and Snunit boats cuts a path across the Mediterranean during maneuvers with the IAF. *(IDF Spokesman)*

Operators, their faces concealed for security reasons, deploy from a Zodiac rubber inflatable during maneuvers in northern Israel. *(IDF Archives)*

also a brilliant man on a dark night and had, through his stories in and around Green Island, built an impressive and highly accurate dossier on the target.

As Almog and his team of officers went through possible plans for assaulting the rock, they estimated that they would need approximately forty men for the operation. Unfortunately, through attrition and Almog's vow to rid the unit of all those who did not fall in line with his program, Flotilla 13 consisted of only thirty men—from Commander Almog down to several students in the advanced underwater and boating stages of their training. More men had to be called in, and the only other unit capable of handling such a task were the commandos of Sayeret Mat'kal. In 1969, with Colonel Yairi now deputy commander of the 35th Paratroop Brigade, Mat'kal's command was in the hands of the wily wire-haired Lieutenant Colonel Menachem Digli. Digli's style of command was quite different from his predecessor's, and the chemistry that existed between Almog and Yairi no longer prevailed. In fact, combining the talents of both these highly specialized and, some would say, "high-strung" units into a coordinated effort was a most difficult undertaking—especially since Brigadier General Rafael "Raful" Eitan, the chief paratroop and infantry officer responsible for all commando strikes, gave Commander Almog only *one* week to draw up his plans (which had to be approved by various departments in the IDF), train his men, and execute the operation. Indeed, time was short and tempers were frayed.

Preparation for "Operation Mania 6," the IDF code name for the assault, was carried out with typical IDF intensity, and under the cover of supreme secrecy. While Brigadier-General Eitan was the operation's overall commander, planning and training for the assault was left in Almog's hands. Green Island was no stranger to the flotilla—it had been at the top of its target list since the outbreak of the War of Attrition, though it was considered such a "difficult" target that few flotilla officers ever thought the General Staff would have the "brass" to authorize its attack. Almog, having personally reconnoitered the area around Green Island several times himself while wedged inside the confines of a "Pig" SDV, knew that there was only one way the Israeli task force could reach the target undetected—*underwater!* Green Island's gun positions covered all possible approaches; any attempt to send in a force of speeding Zodiac craft would most certainly result in them being systematically blown out of the water by the dedicated Egyptian guns. *Swimming* to the target was also ruled out, since the overall state of alert in the Suez theater would have prompted positioned sentries to look out for frogmen, and, as a result, any swimmer closing in on Green Island would have become the target of deadly small-arms fire; even on a moonless night, there are compromising shadows which can reveal the warriors of the depths. As a result, the first wave of the assault, Flotilla 13, would have to approach Green Island underwater, emerging literally under the noses of the Egyptians at the base of the target. The violent transformation from stealth intruder to heavily armed attacker would have to be fantastic. The commandos would have to swim, underwater, at safe depths for several hours, laden down with ammunition, toward their target and then emerge from the placid waters and lay down enough firepower to secure a beachhead for the Mat'kal force, which would follow in on an armada of Zodiac craft. It was a method of attack never before attempted—either by Flotilla 13 or any other such naval special warfare force—in military history. Almog checked his history books and intelligence files. Perhaps this was folly. Perhaps this was a suicide mission.

Sitting inside the operations room at IDF HQ in southern Sinai at Sharm el Sheikh, Almog and his staff pondered the challenge: how can a group of approximately twenty frogmen reach their target underwater, together, and undetected? Plans were drawn up, sketches made and then burned, and various experts called in for their opinions; the operators even recalled secret training exercises that the flotilla had carried out with the Italian Navy's elite force of frogmen, the *Commando Subacquei ed Incursori* (COMSUBIN),[29] and assault training carried out with the Italians.[30] The solution was a thirty-meter-long piece of specially bound rope, with handles, that would allow the frogmen to swim underwater in a long line and approach the target in unison. The contacts with the Italians were very secretive, and few in the IDF/Navy knew about the hush-hush trip abroad and the purpose of the venture. The equipment was *immediately* tested in the waters off Atlit and given a rousing thumbs-up. It was, one of the operators would recall, as if the Italians had designed the rope specifically for use on Green Island.

"Moving underwater in unison is almost an impossible feat," reflected Ze'ev Almog when looking back at the operation. "It isn't like in a Hollywood movie where all the men swim in unison and move together."[31]

The entire operation, and the lives of the forty men who would participate in the raid, hinged on one factor—the element of surprise. The raid would fail, and the first wave would be cut down by enemy fire should they be discovered before the force could gain a foothold on the island. At first, there was talk about deploying an MTM-type exploding boat to mark an explosive introduction to the operation. Once the operators were at the barbed-wire fence, poised to attack, the MTM operator would guide his boat in the direction of the southern base and, after the ship's 300-kilogram warhead exploded and the Egyptian defenders raced toward the blast expecting an Israeli attack, the operators would move in, silently, from the northern entrance point. The exploding boats weren't foolproof, and in an operation like this, Almog felt, they presented just as many drawbacks as advantages. First, what if the MTM exploded prematurely? The Egyptians would have advance warning of an impending attack and certainly be able to deal with the exposed operators caught between a "rock and the barrel of an Egyptian AK-47!" There was also the chance that the boat would miss completely, its motor serving as a wake-up call to the Egyptian sentries. Green Island wasn't the type of target where a diversion was likely to work. It would be a point-blank face-off pitting courage against overwhelming enemy firepower pure and simple.

In drawing up the final plans of attack, Almog faced additional challenges. Because the flotilla operators were joined by their comrades in Mat'kal, the raid was, in reality, three separate operations. The first phase was the underwater element—reaching the target undetected; the second phase was the explosive assault and the gaining of the beachhead; and the last aspect was the entry of the Mat'kal commandos into the equation. Because they could neither swim nor dive, Digli's men had to be ferried to the target by Zodiac boats. The boats had to be far enough from the target so an alert Egyptian officer, possibly equipped with Soviet-produced night-imaging equipment, wouldn't see them in the distance. The farther they were from the objective, however, the longer they had to travel once the shooting started. That, in turn, meant that the twenty frogmen would be alone, outnumbered over twenty-to-one for several minutes before the reinforcements arrived. It was decided to moor the Mat'kal commandos 1,500 meters from the target.

The time of the operation was also a critical factor. To make the swim to the target easier, Almog and his staff concluded that H-hour should be at high tide, when the currents were weakest. That gave a window of opportunity between midnight and 01:00 hours. The absolute latest that the raid could begin was 01:00. The operation had to be over and the withdrawal complete by dawn's first light—otherwise the joint flotilla Mat'kal task force would be dangerously exposed to Egyptian gunners on the west bank of the gulf.

Not only did Flotilla 13 have to reach the target unnoticed, they also needed to designate and prepare a passage through three rows of barbed-wire concertina for the Mat'kal commandos who would race toward the island in the rubber inflatables once the first shots were fired, bringing with them the explosives needed to raze the position. The flotilla would also have to prepare their load-bearing equipment, ammunition, and weaponry to withstand the underwater conditions and pressure, so that their tools of war would be operational once they emerged from the water. Regular grenades, for example, were rendered inoperable by the pressure of a ten-meter dive, and special fragmentation grenades purchased from the Netherlands had to be modified by Michal Avraham and the flotilla's elite technical staff. The grenades were known to be water-resistant, but they were also small—much smaller than the M26 fragmentation grenades used by the IDF at the time, and, as a result, the operators could carry more of them. Web gear and other load-bearing equipment would have to be strengthened and waterproofed, and communications gear sealed. Each operator was offered the choice of what weapon he wanted to carry into battle. The AK-47, a weapon considered perfect by flotilla operators, was such a ballistic workhorse that it could fire after being submerged in twenty meters in filthy water; it was also a psychological weapon, as its captured status made it a good-luck charm of sorts. The Uzi was less reliable when wet, but it, too, was an all-condition weapon. Since it was considerably lighter than the AK-47, operators tasked with carrying field radios or loads of explosives opted to carry the indigenously produced 9mm submachine gun with them. The primary firepower problem wasn't the weapon but rather the ammunition. The underwater pressure rendered most ammunition inoperable and that nightmare scenario was too horrific for Almog to even contemplate.

Digli's force, on the other hand, had a somewhat easier go of it—from a training point of view, that is. Their unit had been expertly trained in assaulting heavily defended targets, in pinpointing their fire in shock assaults, and in seizing the initiative through surprise and firepower. Their training for Operation Mania, eventually joined in by Flotilla 13, was conducted at two facilities, a former Crusader fortress in Samaria, known as "Mickey Mouse" by the task force, and a police station in the Jordan Valley. Both were utilized as models for the combined Flotilla 13/Sayeret Mat'kal force to assault. In these initial stages of the training, Almog's men displayed their prowess and proficiency with devastating destruction. Their accuracy with the Uzi 9mm submachine gun and the AK-47 *K'latch* [the IDF's affectionate nickname for the "Kalashnikov"] 7.62mm assault rifle was remarkable. Grenades were also tossed with remarkable finesse and accuracy. The commandos, usually on the run, could toss a "fragger" through a small opening, such as a window on bunker perch, with little difficulty and with the finesse of a Cy Young award–winning pitcher. Although the Soviet-produced RPG-7 anti-tank rockets were very effective anti-tank weapons—captured in such numbers from the Egyptians and Syrians during the 1967 War that they became staple-issue items in elite unit arsenals—the Belgian-produced 3.5-inch bazooka, a staple of "regular" IDF ground units, would also be taken to Green Island because it was believed to be more reliable when wet. The bazookas were accurate, sturdy, and lethal against armor or fixed fortifications. The flotilla's commandos also put on a dog-and-pony show for "Raful," prompting his training officer to say, "Their marksmanship was remarkable, their firing skills and assault speeds unprecedented." Another staple brought along to Green Island were two FN MAG 7.62mm light machine guns. The MAG was a beloved tool of 7.62mm firepower—it was accurate, sturdy, and reliable. Israeli soldiers felt comfortable with the MAG—it provided them with a sense of security. Israeli soldiers were also expert in laying down blankets of covering fire with the Belgian-designed masterpiece. They could pepper a pillbox with hundreds of neatly spaced 7.62mm holes and turn an enemy position into smoldering ruins.

"Raful," a man rarely impressed by combat prowess, was moved by the flotilla's display. Pleased and offering a rare smile, he pulled Almog to the side and said, "If we had a brigade-size force of soldiers with these skills, we could be unstoppable!"

Through an exhaustive pace, one that neither Mat'kal or Flotilla 13 had ever experienced before, training proceeded. *All* mock assaults were carried out with *live* ammunition— the sounds of explosions and crackling automatic fire engulfed the training areas nearly twenty-four hours a day. To add an element of realism to the training, the Jordanians were kind enough to unleash a two-hour artillery barrage against the Jordan Valley police fort following a day-long incursion by Israeli paratroopers inside Jordanian territory. Had the assault force been issued with the luxury of time, they would have had the Engineering Corps build them a new training facility elsewhere. The operation's commanders liked the added bit of ordnance falling in the distance. It was an eerie sight. There were, however, certain controversies which needed to be ironed out. Like most combat units, the commandos involved in "Operation Mania 6" utilized tracer rounds to direct fire and coordinate targeting. The tracers, bullets which illuminated into a brilliant red or green line from point of fire to point of impact, allowed soldiers to see exactly where their bullets were impacting; the tracers also allowed the enemy soldiers to see exactly where hostile fire was originating from. This troubled "Raful," who feared that exposing his "Elite of the Elite" forces to added detection, risked increased casualties; these men were the best Israel could field and, as a result, their safety was paramount to the successful execution of the operation. "Raful," therefore, ordered that no tracers be utilized—an order which sparked outrage from both Almog and Digli. After a heated debate, in which shouting and profanity replaced reason, "Raful's" order stood until but a few hours before H-hour. Chief of Staff Bar-Lev, enjoying a last-minute cigarette break with the commanders, asked if there were any problems. Both Almog and Digli informed him of the "tracer" controversy and the order was quietly rescinded.[32]

There was also a very proactive intelligence-gathering effort mounted against the target. First Lieutenant Ilan Egozi, the fearless survivor of Alexandria, personally reconnoitered the target one night around 01:00 hours to see what the Egyptian defenses were like *at that hour*. Creating little noise with his closed-circuit breathing apparatus, Egozi was able to slink about the base of the island without the Egyptian defenders discovering him. Egozi was shocked to find Egyptian preparedness at a high level of alert; it was as if they were expecting the island to be hit. Sentries, carrying AK-47s and flashlights, combed the waters in search of Israeli frogmen. Many of the sentries carried antipersonnel grenades fastened to their utility belts. Sergeants and lieutenants walked around the island, barking orders and ordering their men to concentrate on the surrounding water. "This target is going to be difficult," Egozi thought to himself. Other operators had equal anxiety concerning the target. "Each time we went over the intelligence, each time we learned more on the target, the crazier this thing sounded—another machine-gun post here, another wall to jump over here, another cannon position here," recalled Captain (Res.) Uzi Livnat. "You don't need courage to attack the target, as much as you need nerves of steel just to think about it."[33]

Two days prior to D-day, the night between July 17 and 18, the task force was flown by IAF transport to Sinai, and the IDF/Navy facility at Ras Sudr. The base was engulfed by a tight security blackout, and in the operations room, each stage of the operation was reviewed, refined, and reviewed once again. Although every step was critical in such an operation and nothing left to chance, the commandos would be relying on an obsolete book on tide tables, published by the British Admiralty prior to the Second World War, to determine the strength of currents. Estimating currents is like picking a winner at the track. Sometimes luck isn't with you.

The commander of the first wave was Lieutenant Dov Bar, a burly bull of a man and a highly regarded officer who also commanded, and personally conducted, the arduous and highly selective naval commando training course. On his shoulders rested the difficult responsibility of navigating the path for his twenty commandos to the target, then positioning them for the assault. The naval commandos would attack in four squads—each consisting of two officers and three NCOs. The lead squad, commanded by First Lieutenant Ilan Egozi, was tasked with cutting through the barbed-wire concertina defenses, preparing a breech through which the beachhead would be exploited, then expanded and secured for the Mat'kal commandos in the second wave. While the five men cut the barbed wire, employing specially adapted cutters with rubber-coated elements which reduced noise, the remaining three squads would provide cover fire. Should they be discovered, the cutters were to be discarded in favor of bangelore torpedoes, "hijacked" from a Combat Engineer battalion and specially modified by the flotilla to operate underwater. Cutting through the wire was, unquestionably, the most precarious segment of the operation—the initial defenses, around the small entranceway, that needed to be breached included a two-and-a-half-meter-high wall, plus three rows of thick and impassable barbed-wire concertina. The entry position was a choke point where most of the fighters would be grouped together, treading water, and neither safely submerged nor on dry land, capable of waging a fire-fight. One burst of Egyptian machine-gun fire, or one well-placed grenade, could easily wipe out twenty of the IDF's finest fighters—the entire unit—in an instant of destructive ricocheting shrapnel. The man responsible for the demolitions work was the flotilla's most popular and soft-spoken member, the tall and skinny Yisrael Dagai, a man who bore the brunt of endless jokes comparing his physique to that of the thin and elongated torpedo. Dagai was the "typical" operator—he was lanky and wily, but what his body lacked in muscle and brawn, his mind more than made up for in perseverance and courage.

Once through the defenses, First Lieutenant Ilan Egozi's force would support the advance of the other operators, who would race up across the 2.5-meter-high wall, at a point near the walkway connecting the facility to the "dummy-radar" tower, establish a CP, and signal in the Mat'kal element. The second squad, led by task force commander Lieutenant Bar, would scale the roof of the complex and then command the landing zone for the Mat'kal commandos coming in on Zodiacs. To overcome the wall, Flotilla 13 would employ what became known as "Jacob's Ladder": the *back* of a frogman named Jacob Pundik. Bav's squad included First Lieutenant Amichai "Ami" Ayalon, who, while lying at the breakwater, was to lob fragmentation grenades into the tower to stun and terminate the sentries positioned there. The third squad was commanded by First-Lieutenant Amnon Sofer; his squad was tasked with seizing the opening at the front building and "cleaning out" the inner rooms that were behind the northern wall and that had access to the inner yard of the fortress. Finally, the fourth squad, commanded by First-Lieutenant Gadi Kroll, would charge north toward the main building from the breakthrough point. With a little luck, they would be able to secure a sizable chunk of the fortress in time for Lieutenant

Colonel Digli's force, who would terminate the remaining pockets of enemy resistance, allowing Flotilla 13 to fall back and prepare the sprawling fortress for detonation. Casualties were expected to be *very* high. After all, the Egyptians were trapped with nowhere to run. They could not surrender, as the Israelis weren't about to take prisoners (nor did they have the facilities to take soldiers into captivity); the Egyptians, Israeli intelligence estimates reported, would fight to the last man.

To ensure that his men were in the best possible physical shape to fight the battle, Almog ordered his trusted and legendary Master Sergeant Musa Cohen to build *hot-water* showers in the desert, along with functioning toilets and a top-notch kitchen. The unit's cook, the notoriously hot-tempered Sergeant Machluf, was flown to Sinai along with his refrigerator full of food; Almog wanted his men to eat home cooking and familiar items in order to prevent any outbreaks of dysentery. After a day of training, Almog would also have a *"Kumsitz"* with his men during meal-time, a Yiddish term for sitting around the campfire and simply bullshitting. Each commando spoke his mind as to questions and apprehensions. To lighten up the tense and anxious atmosphere, Almog also had his men converge around a record player during lunchtime, to listen to comedy albums and popular songs. On the whole, however, Almog and his men prepared for reaching Green Island, prepared for fighting an overwhelming and elite enemy, and prepared for undertaking a suicide mission. To make sure that the men were ready, Almog had them all turn in pre-op debriefing papers describing their roles in the mission, and explaining, in full detail, the tasks of each of their comrades.

A day before the attack, on Friday, July 18, the task force was taken to the Mezach Bar-Lev line fortification for a chance to peer through field glasses and observe Green Island firsthand. From nearly a dozen kilometers off, it did not seem too imposing, but bravado diminishes quite rapidly when a soldier is placed in machine-gun range. "An operator could train all day and all night in an obstacle course," a commando would comment, "but the moment he sees the water into which he'll dive into, with a pack full of explosives and nylon-wrapped ammo, a sense of trepidation engulfs your inner workings." Because the mission was considered so risky, so sensitive, and not given great chances for success, the IDF's top brass visited Sinai to inspect the commandos and share a few words with the men. Chief of Staff Lieutenant General Bar-Lev, Chief Paratroop and Infantry Officer Brigadier General Eitan and, ominously, the OC Southern Command Major General "Arik" Sharon, arrived at the base in a motorcade of jeeps and 4x4s. The sight of so many generals, so many campaign ribbons, and so many epaulets filled with crossed scimitars and leaf rank insignia daunted some of the commandos—it drove home the fatal fact that this was an extremely important operation, as well as an extremely dangerous one. "It was an odd sight," recalled Uzi Livnat, "since they put us, the soldiers, in the front rows to hear the chief of staff, and not in the back behind the generals, which is where we usually sat. This aberration drove the fact home to many of us that something was definitely special about this mission."[34]

Bar-Lev's pep talk, meant to instill confidence, did little to soothe nerves or increase confidence. The chief of staff reminded each fighter that *he* was the *best* in the IDF and that the nation would reflect on a victorious attack on the island with celebration and awe, and would understand any mishaps or failure encountered in this most difficult of assignments. Then, in a room engulfed by cigarette smoke and full of the commandos nervously twitching their knees and fingers, Bar-Lev shocked the gathered when he said, "This is not going to be an easy mission. *I can live with that!* The moment ten are dead, I am ordering the commanders to consider this raid a failure and pull back." The commandos sat awe-stricken, wide empty expressions filling their suddenly blank faces. Digli motioned to his men as if the chief of staff was losing it mentally, while Almog feared the words of apprehension and acceptable losses might destroy the morale of his men and their ability to mount the operation successfully. The moment Bar-Lev left the room, Almog left his monotone delivery and emotionally stated, "Do not become preoccupied with anything other than the

assault and advance on the target." You can either become
so concerned with the words of this general or stick to your
target, persevere, never stop the advance or let the enemy
recover, and prove him wrong!" A few smiles broke out, and
the commandos returned to their passionate discussions of
the best avenues of attack and the underwater methods they
would deploy. With the chief of staff heading back to his
quarters, Brigadier General Eitan, one of the flotilla's most
passionate supporters, quickly reiterated the need for
speed, firepower, and teamwork. They were less concerned
with the historical perspective and overall picture of the
raid—they wanted each soldier to remember his role, his
training, his weapon, and his capabilities. If the Mat'kal
force of reconnaissance paratroopers did not reach the
bridgehead in time, the members of Flotilla 13 were to seize
the initiative and assault the remainder of the island on
their own. This was supposed to be each unit's finest hour.
Almog ended the gathering by simply stating, "Remember
what our motto is: *Stick to your target!* Don't forget that,
never let it leave your mind. Your target is your existence.
Your mandate."

There was an electricity surrounding the task force at Ras
Sudr—a combination of fear, motivation, and gung-ho
morale. The night before the men were to head out to the
starting point, they refused to relax and kick back, wanting
instead to train some more and rehash their assignments by
a map and a blackboard. These officers and NCOs, acting
on their own, called themselves "the class" and didn't make
it to bed until they were damn sure that every single inch of
Green Island was etched in the back of their minds as
unforgettable fact. "The night before a big one you want to
think about nothing but the operation," reflected an operator still serving in the unit. "The morning before you want
to think about anything else."

The following day, D-day, several of the secular soldiers,
mainly technicians, decided that it was prudent to attend
Sabbath services in the base's synagogue; for many, it was
the first time that they had been in synagogue since their bar
mitzvahs. Mostly, though, the fighters kept to themselves.
Inside the small encampment each unit was provided with,

the men sat quietly and cleaned weapons, examined gear and wrote small notes to loved ones; newspapers were read and hundreds of "smoked to the filter" cigarette butts soon littered the Mezach base. Nerves were on a razor's edge: there were still too many unknowns, still too many things which could go wrong—especially with the underwater phase of the operation being so precarious. Yisrael Asaf, a boisterous and energetic figure, quietly cleaned his AK-47 and remembered the pleasures of his return visits to the Kibbutz, his beautiful girlfriend, and how much he loved life. Bar-Lev's analysis sobered him, quieted his demeanor. It caused him, for the first time in his three-year military career, to be really scared. Fear was neutralized, or placed on the mind's back burner, by endless preparation. "After all," as Almog would say to Ilan Egozi (a man who he knew did not experience the emotion of fear), "the guys can't be frightened if they're kept busy all the time."[35]

On the night of July 19, the task force left its touch-off point; the boats were in the water at 19:45 hours. The naval commandos wore only the top half of their black neoprene rubber wet suits (this provided buoyancy and warmth for the prolonged stay in the water) over their dacron olive fatigue blouses. Regular olive fatigue trousers were worn instead of the restrictive lower half of the wet suit, so as *not* to impede movement when thrusting out of the water into battle. The standard uniforms would dry quickly, and it was believed to be less distinguishable than a shiny wet suit in the nighttime fire-fight. Unlike the failed 1967 War raid against Minat el-Biada, this mission's objective was both to penetrate and to blow the enemy away—the more ammunition and equipment carried, the better. Each commando wore specially produced load-bearing equipment; vests, dark olive in color, carried ammunition (long rectangular magazines for the Uzi 9mm submachine gun or the banana shaped thirty-round magazine for the AK-47 assault rifle), grenades, waterproof first-aid pouches, canteens and a flashlight; the radiomen in each squad carried an infantry packboard attached to his vest which carried a water-proofed Motorola H.T. field radio. Fitted over the vest was what is known as the "Mae West" vest-type life preserver, dyed black. They wore commercial-bought canvas sneakers attached to their specially modified flippers and carried underwater masks and breathing apparatus systems.

Each fighter involved in the operation, from both units, entered the water with their weapons cocked and one bullet in the chamber.

Commander Almog knew that this mission was "the one" but also had, in the back of his mind, memories of his bitter experiences off the coast of Port Said. His primary fear, kept to himself, was that the first wave of operators would be cut down by Egyptian fire and cut off. Not wanting to risk a massacre, Chief of Staff Bar-Lev might have called off the second wave and aborted the mission. Almog was adamant about not abandoning anyone—especially his men. He felt that if he was in the second wave, personally commanding the boats bringing in the Mat'kal task force, he'd be able to make damn sure that if the mission was aborted, his men would be pulled off the island.

At 20:30 hours, the mini-rubberized armada, consisting of twelve Zodiac craft, set out into the contested waters toward the target. It was a beautiful summer's night, with many of the commandos, themselves from seaside Kibbutzim along the Mediterranean or Sea of Galilee, recalling their earlier days with either a fishing pole or girlfriend in hand. The Zodiacs belonging to the naval commando force proceeded first; following close behind was Digli's task force, along with Almog's top-echelon CP (command post), "Raful." In typical "Raful" fashion, he had attached himself to the operation and was in one of the Zodiacs, nervously looking on even though the chief of staff ordered him to observe the operation from a *safe* distance. "Raful" was many things as a soldier—a charismatic leader, a military tactician, and, most of all, one of the most courageous men ever to don the red beret. As the general in charge of all Israeli special operations, he often "attached" himself to missions—whether it be in a forward CP or dangerously close to ricocheting fragments and stray bullets. On many ops, "Raful" enjoyed strapping himself into a chopper and manning an FN MAG light machine gun in support of his troops. At the Jordan Valley training center, Almog and Digli could sense that "Raful" was dying to grab a *K'latch* and tangle with the Egyptians himself on Green Island. Bar-Lev, too, sensed "Raful's" adrenaline pumping as the hours to D-day grew closer and feared the possible worse-case scenario of "Raful" killed on the island—or worse, "Raful" captured and paraded in front of the cameras for Egyptian TV. He would have none of it. Taking his special operations czar aside, though within earshot of Almog and Digli, Bar-Lev simply said, *"Rafulchik, She'Lo Ta'iz La'alot Al Ha'Gag!"* ("Rafulchik, don't you dare go up to the roof [on Green Island]!").[36]

The armada's boats made little noise as their muffled motors churned a slow, though deliberate path, toward Green Island. At 22:30 hours, the armada reached a buoy moored one mile from the target. The menacing lights of Green Island were seen in the darkened background. Egyptian security was relaxed, but that was not surprising. Positioned inside the belly of "the monster" was all the psychological and physical security the Egyptian soldiers would need.

According to the plan, Flotilla 13 had between 00:30 and 01:30 hours on the morning of July 20 to reach the objective—the one-hour leeway was meant to compensate for shifting currents and the tides. After a last-minute weapons check, in which weapons were greased one final time and then inserted into protective waterproofed plastic cases, the twenty men of the deep jumped into the water, their thirty-plus kilograms of equipment plunging into the placidly moving waves and producing a loud and clumsy splash. Then they assumed their assault positions—the fighters swam in pairs and all clutched the station-keeping rope. With Green Island in the distance, the long trek through the chilling waters commenced. At first, they swam on their backs, but this proved slow and cumbersome—the heavy equipment they carried was too much for their well-honed feet, their sole source of propulsion, to provide consistent bursts of speed. For Lieutenant Bar, who continually examined the distance by turning over on to his stomach, they were not getting any closer to the target. The clock was ticking. They continued stroking through the waters, in four rows of five.

Thirty minutes to H-hour, 00:00, the naval commandos were still far away from their objective. As they struggled with the unforgiving current and uncooperative tide—so much for the bloody book by the British Admiralty!— Almog and Digli looked on through field glasses but saw a troubling nothing; no news was not good news. Apprehension began to set in, as did angst. Lieutenant Bar realized that it would be light by the time his men reached Green Island, dallying, on their backs stroking hard, so he ordered them underwater. Each commando removed the air from his "Mae West," spit into his mask, and readied his gear to venture into the murky depths. Underwater, chaos overwhelmed the divers struggling to assemble in a cohesive formation. The heavy weight of their equipment proved to be way too much. Expecting a hellish fight, most of the fighters carried twice the prescribed amount of ammunition—extra magazines were stuffed inside pockets and additional grenades attached to pistol belts—resulting in the diver sinking to dangerous depths; some were carried nearly forty feet down, an especially dangerous level considering the fact that they were breathing pure oxygen. At 01:00 hours, the first wave was still 600 meters off course, drifting south in the strong and dragging current. It was here that Lieutenant Bar decided to rally his men. He ordered them to emerge from the water, and, in a verbal volley of patriotism, he ordered his, "lazy, undisciplined and impotent ladies to get their asses in gear and get the goddamned mess over with." If they were tired, they could return to the boats and head back to a life of failure. *He* was going to go and get the job done—by himself if necessary." Most of the commandos could not hold in their anger that their commander had to talk with them like small children; others had to hold in laughter as a pep talk was whispered a few hundred meters in front of the most fortified target in all of Egypt. With little choice but to go on, they continued their underwater swim.

At 01:30 hours, Commander Almog rose from his craft and peered through his field glasses. Anxious, he uttered

"Madu'a Ha'Pe'ulah Od Lo Hitchila?" (or "Why hasn't the action started yet?")—a question which annoyed "Raful" and caused frustrated pangs in the minds of Digli and his men. A "strike force," one Pig led by Lieutenant-Commander Paz Paulin and two other operators, moored to a beacon 200 meters from Green Island and equipped with two 7.62mm FN MAG light machine guns for covering fire, and one Belgian Bazooka to hit the two 85mm gun positions atop the southern wall, radioed Almog, informing their commander that they were in position to provide a blanket of machine-gun fire to distract Egyptian troops when the assault at the other end of the island commenced, should the mission be aborted and the other Zodiacs need to be called in and rescue the swimmers. Lieutenant Bar's divers, however, swam at a brisk, almost inhuman pace; they returned to a surface swim, approaching from a parallel angle and then striking sharply toward the tower. Luck was on their side. They still possessed the element of surprise.

Only fifteen meters from Green Island, Lieutenant Bar slowly raised his head out of the water and noticed two Egyptians sentries—one on the tower and one standing stoically on the walkway. Even in the darkened sky, the Egyptian sentries were extremely visible in their light sand-colored uniforms and Cuban-style baseball fatigue caps worn smartly on their heads. Their AK-47 assault rifles were slung over their shoulders, indicating that it was unlikely that rounds were in the weapons' chambers; since none of the soldiers were wearing their helmets, it appeared as if they had not been forewarned of an impending attack. Realizing that even if discovered his force would have a two-second jump on the defenders, Lieutenant Bar rallied his men, even cursing at them in a display truly out of his soft-spoken character, and brought them to the waterline; the corals, tangible in the shallow waters, provided a brief rest to divers' weary legs. To ensure that the mission at this stage would not be aborted, Lieutenant Bar removed the earpiece from his radio—he eventually turned the device off altogether as they inched closer to the fortress walls. You couldn't disobey an order you couldn't hear, after all. To synchronize the assault, he ordered his men to submerge.

Underwater, he issued the silent order for his men to remove their diving gear, and the twenty silhouetted figures gingerly removed their oxygen equipment although air pipes were kept in each fighter's mouth. All packs were attached to the station-keeping rope (they would be picked up by the boatmen ferrying Digli's men); masks were lowered and placed on hooks; and flippers were removed and placed in a special pouch built into the load-bearing equipment. They would be needed later.

At 01:35 hours, Lieutenant Bar ordered his men to remove their air pipes and slowly rise out of the camouflaging depths. From beneath the tower and walkway, twenty figures emerged from the water, raising the barrels of their Uzis and AK-47s upward toward the sentries. One of the Egyptians was foolishly smoking a cigarette, the orange glow struck from his "Imperial" brand stub gave his position away in absolute terms. According to the attack plan, First Lieutenant Ilan Egozi led his "shock squad" forward by the walkway bridge. Yisrael Dagai prepared his modified bangelore torpedo while the others produced wire cutters from their gear and began slicing through the concertina. Egozi's men struggled with the wire, some became entangled in the labyrinth of prickly metal spikes, while others soon found themselves blinded by a film of oil and nauseating sewage; the Egyptians used this point of the fortress to dispose of their waste into the sea. As Lieutenant Bar and the remainder of the force clutched their weapons anxiously, Ilan Egozi suddenly noticed a sentry approaching his meager beachhead. Instinctively, he recoiled his arms, raised the Uzi toward his chest, and dropped the sentry with a quick burst of fire from his submachine gun. Immediately, another Egyptian soldier, wearing the tan-and-brown camouflage of the *as-Saiqa* commando unit, lobbed a grenade at the Israelis, its fragments injuring Egozi and two other divers. Green Island was ablaze with fire and engulfed in the deafening blasts of automatic fire.

"Kadima . . . Aharai" ("Forward . . . follow me!") was Egozi's cry as the four squads took advantage of the small opening established at the waterline to race toward the main facility. They encountered extremely heavy machine-

gun fire, but a well-placed fragmentation grenade, thrown by Egozi, destroyed the emplacement in a sparkling blast of glistening shrapnel fragments. One by one, Egyptian soldiers raced out of their barracks, stumbling to close their trousers and maneuver their assault rifles and slings into comfortable firing positions—they were cut down by merciless close-quarter bursts from the commandos' AK-47 rifles. The naval commandos hurled smoke grenades toward the Egyptian machine-gun nests, blinding their sights momentarily while the remainder of the first wave made it out of the water to engage the Egyptians.

With a pitched battle transpiring, the commandos made a terrifying discovery: much of their weaponry and ammunition was inoperable. Perhaps it was as a result of the depths their diving weights had dragged them to, or perhaps the water had seeped through the protective equipment. Grenades were not exploding and rifles were misfiring. Murphy's Law had set in. Now, when he needed it, Lieutenant Bar's radio did not work, either. Crouching behind a concrete block, watching fragments of his cover being chipped away by determined enemy fire, he produced a green flare from his ammunition pouch—the backup communications means agreed upon should radio contact be broken—and launched it into the black skies. Digli's men were now formally invited into the fray.

The Mat'kal task force should have been en route to the battle by the time the operators of Flotilla 13 emptied their first few magazines, but Digli's men were not called in by Bar the moment the operators came out of the sea. Instinctively and courageously, Lieutenant Bar ordered his men to not only hold the beachhead, but to attack and advance. The operators were in their diving gear, not prepared for a full-scale attack, but there was little point in waiting for the Sayeret. If Digli's men *weren't* coming, then their only chance for survival was to wipe out the defenders on their own. If Digli's men were held up for whatever reason, then laying in wait on a stretch of dry land waiting for the one well-tossed Egyptian grenade to wipe out all twenty men was not a good idea.

Compressing all their adrenaline, fear, zeal, and energy into an unstoppable push forward, the operators commenced their attack. First-Lieutenant Gadi Kroll, a bear of a man with the agility of a panther, seized the initiative and, with his AK-47 ablaze, headed for the bridge area cutting down any Egyptian unfortunate enough to be in his way. First Lieutenant Ayalon, in Lieutenant Bar's squad, also seized the initiative and tossed a grenade at a machine-gun nest. Jacob Pundik assumed his ladder position against the wall and allowed his comrades to climb up on top of him and gain access to the edge of the roof. Ayalon was the first one up, and he threw a smoke grenade while still standing atop Pundik's shoulders. Already, Green Island was engulfed by smoke, flying dust, and the spraying of blood and flesh. The Dutch grenades, those that actually worked, were proving to be nifty little killing machines and the operators were developing accurate pitching arms. The men moved about the positions with dexterity and incredible agility—especially considering the fact that many were already wounded by shrapnel and were in their diving gear. The standard practice was to toss a grenade, dive for cover, and then unleash small bursts of fire from the operator's personal weapon. The Egyptians were putting up a stiff resistance. They stood fast and replied to each grenade thrown with two of their own. Soldiers from the garrison in the courtyard below began to aim their weapons at the intruders moving about on the roof.[37] Operators who were wounded, which was just about every Israeli on the rock at the time, continued advancing even though many were covered in blood and some had fist-size holes in their midsections, legs, and arms. "It was," in the words of Yisrael Dagai, "absolute hell."[38]

An experienced combat officer, Almog had an instinctive sense that Lieutenant Bar's lack of communications had more to do with a junior officer assuming tactical command of a situation rather than any serious or fatal setback. "Stick to your target, Dov," Almog uttered silently to himself, knowing his trusted lieutenant would follow through as ordered. Even before the brilliant light of his flair was seen illuminating the Red Sea sky, Almog ordered the boats to fire up their engines and prepare to assault the island. Digli's commandos sat crouched inside their boats, weapons at the ready. Each commando checked his Uzi submachine gun one final time, insuring that the two thirty-round magazines attached by a special clip were firmly in place; those armed with AK-47s also checked their weapons once again, affectionately caressing the two banana clip thirty-round magazines they had taped together so carefully and then jammed inside the *K'latch*. The commandos also began to shake their legs in a hurried attempt to restore circulation to their cramped limbs; they had been sitting inside the constricting damp confines of the Zodiac for far too long. As the Zodiacs raced along the water, the flickering lights of automatic fire became pronounced—the sounds of battle were increasing in volume and ferocity. Breathing faster in surges of well-timed adrenaline, Almog's men and Digli's commandos prepared to spring off the Zodiacs the moment the craft hit Green Island's waterbreak. They would not have to wait very long.

According to the plan, the second wave was moored 1,000 meters away from the target and would fire their engines upon hearing Lieutenant Bar's coded message, the message being that the barbed wire was being cut; the task force was supposed to enter a holding position some 600 meters off the target until they learned that the landing site had been taken and Bar would summon them, by radio or flare, to join in on the attack. By the time the second wave was in midwater racing toward Green Island, however, the assault had developed into a full-scale ferocious fire-fight. The flotilla had seized the initiative and was assaulting bunkers and firing pits reserved for the Sayeret. The Egyptians, who in the first few moments of the attack were hunkered down in the barracks not knowing what fate had befallen them, had managed to mount a stirring defense. Crates of Soviet-produced F-1 fragmentation grenades were brought out from storage, and the Egyptians lobbed dozens of them at the small Flotilla 13 perimeter.

Casualties began to mount as the advance inched its way forward. Their wet uniforms were soon stained by blood. Two NCOs from Flotilla 13, Sergeant Yoav Shachar and Sergeant Haim Sturman, were killed by a grenade blast while a third, Danni Levy, suffered a direct burst of automatic fire and was blown off of a small roof housing gun emplacement "Six" (each anti-aircraft gun position was given a designation by the attack force); positions "Three" and "Four" had already been destroyed and taken. The naval commandos were outnumbered, running out of ammunition, and dangerously pinned down. From their positions atop the roof, they were absorbing wild and intimidating barrages of small-arms fire; whenever a commando rose to gain an advantageous firing position, he was hit from Egyptian fire originating from the courtyard. The *as-Saiqa* commandos proved to be tenacious foes, holding their ground until wiped out. Not a single Egyptian soldier or officer raised his hands in surrender. Surrender and being taken prisoner was out of the question for either side—this was truly a fight to the death. Seventeen minutes after the firing had begun, the Flotilla 13 commandos were close to overrunning a great deal of the island.

The sounds of the arriving Zodiacs, nearly muffled by the ongoing hellish fire-fight, was a welcomed relief. By the time Almog's and Digli's men reached the rooftop, the commandos, counting their remaining magazines and bandaging their wounds, had held their own in a most admirable fashion. Over half the first wave had been wounded, including First Lieutenant Ami Ayalon, who, after suffering shrapnel wound to both legs, was now struck in the throat with a bullet but still leading his men forward through the gauntlet of Egyptian fire. He was profusely bleeding and losing consciousness and yet refused to be evacuated to the Zodiacs for the urgent medical care he required. For his courage under fire during "Operation Mania," First Lieutenant Ayalon would be awarded the yellow ribbon *I'tur Ha'Gvura* (or "Bravery Medal"), the IDF's version of the American Congressional Medal of Honor and the British Victoria Cross. The medal, issued to soldiers who display the "ultimate heroism against enemy fire," is sparingly awarded by the IDF; in fact, only three IDF/Navy soldiers (including Ayalon) have received this most prestigious honor—all have been operators from Flotilla 13. According to the official version of the citation: "On the night of July 19–20, in the battle for Green Island, First Lieutenant

Amichai "Ami" Ayalon was the deputy commander of a band of operators in the assault. At the time of the attack, he tossed a grenade at the radar position, and during the assault moved ahead of his soldiers to lead the attack. When he climbed on the roof of one position, he suffered a shrapnel wound to the forehead, but still managed to hurl a grenade, even though it failed to explode. Under heavy fire, he continued his advance and killed two enemy soldiers. He continued his advance along with First Sergeant Zalman Rot, and wiped out a machine-gun nest. He later hooked up with another operator, and wiped out two more enemy positions. Leading the attack against a gun position, a grenade blast seriously wounded him in both legs, though he continued to fire his weapon at the enemy positions; another enemy grenade detonated near him, this time wounding him in the hand and neck. Severely wounded and bleeding profusely, he managed to continue his attack and only after the mission was complete did he inform his superiors of his wounds and evacuate himself."[39]

Another Flotilla 13 commando to be noted for his courage in Operation Mania was First Lieutenant Ilan Egozi, the rambunctious officer who, although seriously wounded, fought the enemy with cool and decisive leadership and "ordered" himself evacuated on the last Zodiac to leave the island. He received the blue ribbon *I'tur Ha'Mofet* (or "Exemplary Service Medal"), the IDF's third-highest award for battlefield courage. His citation went on to mention: "On the night of July 19–20, 1969, in the battle for Green Island, First Lieutenant Egozi was the commander of the squad responsible for breaking through the position's defenses. While cutting through the fence, he discovered Egyptian soldiers looking around the rooftop of their position, illuminating the area with their flashlights. Fearing discovery, he opened fire and ordered his men to attack. Seriously wounded in both legs by a grenade blast, he continued the attack, though was hampered by his grave wounds. Unable to fight, he assisted in the planting of explosives throughout the facility, and was on the last boat to evacuate the position."[40]

Remarkably, it would not be his last award for bravery.

Samuel M. Katz

There had been a directive issued by Chief of Staff Bar-Lev *forbidding* Egozi from participating in the operation. As a one-time POW, the IDF could have released him from active duty with a full pension; this was the type of mission where an operator falling into Egyptian hands was a definite possibility, and Bar-Lev didn't want Egozi's fate on his conscience—plus, if ever there was a mission where there was a chance of some men falling into captivity, this was it! Almog, as he knew from past discussion with Egozi, knew that nothing he could do or say would keep the brave first lieutenant away. He was in the loop no matter what the top brass would say, and Almog received special authorizations permitting Egozi to participate in the operation.

Digli's men prepared the explosives and also mopped up the inner rooms of the fortress. It was precarious duty. The deputy commander of Digli's unit, Captain Ehud Ram, was hit by a 7.62mm round in the head as he conferred with Gadi Kroll, while leading a charge against one of the Egyptian gun emplacements. The death of the young officer was a difficult blow for Digli's men to absorb and comprehend. They had felt that their mortality was solely in their own hands, and being forced to trek the body of their bright young commander to the Zodiac below, which served as a ferry vessel and mobile morgue, debilitated the men briefly. His death, however, prompted the Mat'kal commandos to push on harder—his death would be avenged! The Israelis controlled the upper section of Green Island, the perimeter roof, but it was clear to the commanders on the scene that the facility's total obliteration could not be achieved without terminating the stiff Egyptian resistance emanating from the courtyard below. Under heavy support fire, in which the combined Israeli force fired thousands of rounds of small-arms fire, tossed grenades, and launched PRG-7s down below, Digli's men, together with the few surviving and conscious naval commandos, slid into the courtyard utilizing collapsible ladders to engage the Egyptians "up close and personal." The ensuing melee was brutal and fierce.

The fighting inside the courtyard and the barracks was a harsh reminder to all involved as to how deadly close-quarter "bunker-purification type" combat can actually be. Once inside the facility, the commandos moved methodically through each room, each hallway, and each emplacement. The system was simple and effective. Commandos would line up along the hallway, stand with their backs against the wall, and then toss a fragmentation grenade inside the enclosed space. What was not killed by the grenade's blast was terminated by the commandos spraying the smoking aftermath with dedicated blasts of machinegun and automatic-weapons fire. If anything moved, even an Egyptian attempting to surrender or hide, it was blown away by a burst of fire from the hip—a commando specialty. The island was engulfed by a choking vapor of dust, decimated concrete, and cordite; the stench of dead and wounded soldiers was overpowering, and the screams of the hurt were chilling. Another Mat'kal commando was killed by a grenade blast, and another commando, an NCO named "Nimrod," lost a leg to a grenade—al-Ahdar had become a death trap. All of the Zodiacs were filled to capacity with men who were bleeding profusely or holding in their insides with improvised splints and web-gear pouches pulled tightly over gaping wounds.

Almog, Bar, and Uzi Livnat participated in purifying the Egyptian defenders. With many of his junior officers dead or dying in the "medevac," Almog rallied the survivors to seize the entire length of the island—AK-47 blazing away, and his right arm raised in a "follow me" posture. Then, without warning, the close-quarter melee was interrupted by an unexpected element to the equation. The Egyptians, realizing that Green Island was under attack and probably, considering past Israeli commandos' raids, overrun, ordered it shelled. Dozens of Egyptian artillery batteries on the West Bank of the Gulf of Suez let loose deadly bursts of 130mm shells onto the island, and wounded Egyptian defenders. The shelling was an "obvious" indication that it was time to get off the island quickly. At first, the shells fell clumsily into the Red Sea, flaming projectiles causing huge splashes in the still darkened water. Then, however, the acquisition skills of the Egyptian gunners improved—and improved markedly. Shells began to fall dangerously close to the "bridge" where the Zodiacs were moored; shells began landing on the island, as well. It was time to end the battle. From his mooring attached to the island, seeing Egyptian mortar rounds serve as range finders for heavier guns, "Raful" ordered his men off the island.

At 02:17 hours on the night of July 20, Almog and Digli ordered the evacuation of his task force. Through a megaphone both officers carried, a minor article of equipment an intelligence officer suggested be taken along, the words of *"Lahzor La'Sirot"* (or "Return to boats") were heard emanating from the roof. The combined commando task force had occupied two-thirds of the island; and after positions "Five" and "Six" were blown up, a few Egyptian commandos were still fighting back but the remainder of the garrison had escaped by jumping into the sea but were shot down by a force of operators led by First-Lieutenant Kroll, who blocked their escape. With the Israelis systematically destroying all resistance with small-arms and grenade fire, and Egyptian guns dedicating hundreds of shells to destroy the base, the beleaguered defenders had little choice but to flee. It would prove to be a wise decision. Three Israeli officers were frantically preparing 80 kilograms of high explosives concentrated on the northern wing of the fortress to ensure, through a thunderous blast, the IDF would never have to return to Green Island.

Remarkably, considering the circumstances and the continuous fire, the Flotilla 13/Sayeret Mat'kal evacuation was conducted in an orderly fashion. The fighters first loaded the dead and wounded on board the boats—there were fourteen wounded and six dead—and then the frogmen and commandos followed suit. The evacuation, what should be the most welcomed part of any mission into enemy territory, proved to be one of the most dreadful elements of the operation.

Initially all went well with the motorized sail back to Israel. As the Zodiacs—laden with dead, wounded, and physically exhausted fighters—slugged through the waters back to Israeli positions in Sinai, the explosives left behind on Green Island detonated in a wild and illuminating blast. The explosion was deafening, and the flash from the 100 kilograms of high explosives was blinding. The Egyptians, realizing that the Israeli raiding party was making its way back on the sea, dedicated *all* their available artillery assets to harass the retreating Zodiacs. Shells began to land dangerously close to the Israeli armada, which, discovered and exposed, were "rubberized" sitting ducks in a very large pond! One soldier, crouching in one of the lead Zodiacs, was critically wounded by a shell fragment. Another Zodiac, carrying Menachem Digli, was also struck—the slicing shrapnel ripped a gashing hole through the boat's rubber body and all its air was lost in a matter of moments. While Digli and a few of the wounded were transferred to another boat, the remaining commandos donned "Mae West" life jackets and grabbed their weapons, ammo pouches, AN/PRC-25 field radio, and jerrycans filled to capacity with fresh drinking water, then began to swim for home; most of the naval commandos, those with legs not sliced to shreds by bullets and shrapnel, threw on their flippers to make the arduous journey easier. Although his men were proficient swimmers, Almog realized that they could not swim very fast or for very much longer. Having left the island last with several officers, he sailed around the island to ensure its detonation, and then contacted the communications, command, and control center established at Ras Sudr specifically for the raid and ordered the IAF to send in helicopters to pick them up out of the fire zone at once. Almost every craft was holding at least one critically wounded commando, and the trembling water and slicing fragments of shrapnel flying past their eyes at hundreds of feet per second endangered the seriously wounded. Many lives were saved by Dr. Shimon Slayin, who treated the wounded during the battle.

The day's first light dawned upon the Red Sea, exposing the ragtag flotilla of rubber craft even more, offering the Egyptian gunners a greater chance of fixing their sights and scoring direct hits. The Egyptians had also dispatched several torpedo patrol craft into the "hot" waters in search of any stragglers from the raiding party. Against such heavy firepower, the Israeli Zodiacs would be blown out of the water with little difficulty. Into this developing melee entered flights of IAF Bell-205s, which dodged exploding puffs of anti-aircraft artillery fire to winch the wounded to safety. The courage of the naval commandos and reconnaissance paratroopers was now matched by the dedicated doctors and rescuers of the IAF's elite Aeromedical Evacuation Unit. By morning's full light, the force managed to limp back to Ras Sudr. The boats reached the shoreline's docking one by one, each craft filled with the debris of battle: bloodied equipment, mangled bodies, and the fallen. Several boats had stopped along an old quarantine station on the Sinai shore, originally established for Muslim pilgrims returning from the annual *Haj* to Mecca, before being picked up by helicopters and ships.

As the last of the commandos returned to Ras Sudr, there was no rejoicing and no jubilation. Operation Mania was history and Green Island had been destroyed after a few hours of absolute hell. The sight at Ras Sudr was one of exhaustion, relief to be alive, and quiet solitude. Medics and doctors tended to the wounded, and military rabbis sanctified the dead. Green Island had been a rite of passage. It had been an experience of terror, courage, and destruction. Following the raid, "Raful" would say, "The operation at Green Island had broken the back of the Egyptians in the War of Attrition." But, in retrospect, the raid had done much more. It put the entire Egyptian military on notice. Many positions, from the most secured radar and communications facilities embedded under hundreds of feet of rock and granite to Egyptian Army HQ in Cairo, could be assaulted and taken out. So scared was the Egyptian military of additional IDF raids that Egyptian positions all along the canal were heard firing into the night—shooting at shadows, shooting at what could be Israel's next Green Island. The raid had indeed shocked the Egyptians, who viewed their impregnable fortress as Cairo's "Rock of Gibraltar." According to published accounts, President Gamal Abdel Nasser telephoned the Soviet ambassador in Cairo following the raid and said, "These men are not ordinary soldiers, they are devils." Yet it was only after the 1973 Yom Kippur War that Israel learned the true and vast extent of Operation Mania. According to Egyptian military files captured on the road to Cairo during the war, eighty men, the entire garrison, died that summer night. News of the raid was suppressed by the Egyptian press for many years and is still considered a sore spot in Egyptian-Israeli relations today.

Green Island was the flotilla's battle of glory. The loss of the dead soldiers was a hammering blow, but the unit had performed in courageous and professional fashion; operators, eager for some sort of recognition, were concerned that Neil Armstrong, who had walked on the moon that very night, would steal some of their glory and attention. Yet Green Island remains a controversial operation in some IDF circles. Many veteran "green army" officers, especially veteran paratroopers, were jealous that this, the IDF's largest commando strike to date in the War of Attrition, was handed over to the navy. They were equally angry with the fact that Almog, not Digli, was the overall operation commander.

Operation Mania 6 formally and permanently cemented Flotilla 13's entry into the IDF's special operations order of battle with a ferocious bang. For the first time in its history, the naval commandos were openly talked about in the media, though specific details about the attack on Green Island were not publicly released for twenty-five years. Operation Mania 6 turned Flotilla 13 into a force that the prime minister wanted to know about, and calls came through from virtually every military attaché's office in Israel for foreign naval frogmen to come and visit Israel for exchange programs and joint maneuvers.

There would be time for overseas training and exchanges later. The War of Attrition had only just begun.

For Almog and the operators in the unit, Green Island was a bittersweet and painful victory. Three operators had died and over a dozen had been seriously wounded; nearly a dozen more required some time in the hospital. According to Ilan Egozi, "The flotilla was paralyzed for several weeks!"[41]

Being out of service was a physical reality of the ferocious fight for Green Island, but the War of Attrition intensified in the weeks following Operation Mania 6, and Flotilla 13 was on the minds of just about every general in the General Staff. There was still a lot of work to be done.

During the 1967 War, the IDF captured something other than land and scores of enemy prisoners. It captured an enormous supply of enemy equipment. This ranged from the AK-47s that would equip the IDF's elite troops for the next thirty years to jeeps and tanks. Scores of armored personnel carriers and main battle tanks had been abandoned in the Sinai Desert and atop the Golan Heights, and they had been repainted, cleaned up, and pressed into Israeli service. The IDF, after all, is a frugal army, and free hardware was always welcomed. The Russian-built APCs and main battle tanks were solid machines, but they were inferior to the British-built Centurion tanks and the American built Pattons; IDF technicians and tinkerers were already hard at work modifying and upgrading these spoils of war. Most of the captured equipment was relegated to reservist units, many positioned far from the front lines in rear positions.

Yet there were officers in *Aga'm*, the IDF Operations Branch, that felt that the captured booty wasn't being used to its maximum potential, and it was decided to use a small sample of the captured material on a most ambitious, some have even said downright cruel, commando raid against not only legitimate Egyptian targets, but against the Egyptian psyche, as well. Green Island had been a successful blow to Egyptian morale, but it didn't destroy the Egyptian's resolve to fight. In August 1969 alone, there were over 500 cease-fire violations recorded along the Suez front. Egyptian gunners lobbed mortar and 130mm shells into Israeli positions, snipers picked off Israeli sentries, and Egyptian commandos still crossed the canal in rubber boats in small-unit hit-and-run and sabotage strikes, though they never again mounted a large operation, the likes of which prompted the Green Island retaliation in the first place. The Egyptians were growing more arrogant with each artillery salvo, and something had to be done. To reek havoc in the Egyptian rear and bust their morale, and sense of security, wide open, the IDF General Staff came up with a brilliant plan. Repaint some of those captured T-54/55s in their original light sand camouflage scheme and Egyptian Army markings, ferry the vehicles along with a commando element across the Gulf of Suez, and have this masquerading armored task force blow the hell out of enemy rear missile and artillery defenses; the targeted area was inundated by Egyptian SAM, radar, artillery, and anti-aircraft gun positions, as well as scores of field ammunition and duel depots. Knowing how the Egyptian army operated, and what chaos such a deceitful plan could inflict, it was considered foolproof by Chief of Staff Bar-Lev, a former tank officer who—for once—was happy to see a commando strike involving armor, and most members of the General Staff. In the raid, six T-54s and three BTR-50 APCs in Egyptian colors would land and make a fast and unforgiving run down a seventy-kilometer-long stretch of the Egyptian coast destroying any and all targets encountered. To complete the masquerade, the tank crews would be issued with light sand Egyptian Army fatigues.[42]

There was one catch, however. The intended landing zone (LZ) for the IDF/Navy landing craft that were to ferry the task force across the Gulf of Suez was patrolled by two Egyptian Russian-built P-183 torpedo boats; the P-183, interestingly enough, had been brought to the area in the wake of the Green Island operation. Because the mission was supposed to be a covert insertion, the boats could not be picked off by IAF aircraft. Air strikes, even fast and lethal ones, leave telltale radar blips that alert entire sectors. The IAF dedicating two multimillion-dollar jets to the removal of two fairly unimportant torpedo boats would certainly have raised the red flags along the front that something was up. The torpedo boats, it was concluded, would have to be removed quietly and without an alarm being sounded in Cairo. Silent destruction meant Flotilla 13.

Commander Almog spent much of the summer visiting the families of the three fallen officers, and visiting his men recuperating in hospitals. It was a difficult time operationally, as a good percentage of his men were out of action, but for once Almog relished the quiet. He had known of the planned armored incursion into Egypt, and knew that it would involve the flotilla in one capacity or another. At first, though, he thought that the unit's role would be delegated to shoreline reconnaissance, gathering soil samples, and securing the beachhead. Removing the two torpedo boats was a bit more challenging—especially since the two vessels rarely dropped anchor and stood still in the volatile waters, in order to avoid getting hit by IDF artillery fire. Destroying a boat at sea meant a mine, and for that the boats need to be stationary. It also meant locating the boats. The P-183s weren't sitting in the middle of the Gulf of Suez with a big red-and-white bull's-eye across the bow and a sign saying "Kick me." They actively and aggressively patrolled their zones—often firing their 14.5mm machine guns into the surrounding waters to ward off any potential frogmen, and tossing in depth charges and grenades for good measure. It would be a difficult mission regardless of whether the boats were actually found, but a classic naval special warfare mission dating back to the Second World War and the Cockleshell Heroes.

Flotilla 13's role in the mission was code-named "Operation Escort"; the armored incursion was called "Operation Drizzle." The battle plan was for the flotilla's Pig unit to send two teams of operators toward a point in the Gulf of Suez where intelligence reports indicated that the P-183 were usually moored; a Greek freighter, the S.S. *Evangelas,* sunk in the 1967 fighting, remained semisubmerged four kilometers south of the Egyptian shoreline—a routine anchor drop for the torpedo boats. The operators would have to first locate the ships and then hope that the torpedo boats stayed there long enough for the limpet mines to be attached to their "wooden" hulls. Reaching the boats was one thing—locating the ships, even if they were moored, was more challenging. The entire region was under a wartime blackout, and the ships, of course, were running without illumination. As a result, Commander Almog told Chief of Staff Bar-Lev that the requirement for the mission was to go no later than August 28—when there would still be enough moonlight for the operators to "at least" see the silhouettes of the targeted vessels.

Commander Almog's primary concern was finding the manpower to take part in the mission. Green Island left three dead and fourteen wounded, and with twenty men still in the middle of their professional naval special warfare course, the talent pool had run thin. There were also additional operators, somewhat scarred by the hellatious fire-fight on Green Island and by a year of nonstop operations, who were mentally burned out and in need of a break. The men needed a break—pure and simple. Almog needed only eight operators for the underwater aspect of Escort, however, each Pig was capable of ferrying four men and their explosives, and an additional cadre of officers and NCOs were to remain behind at the shoreline command post. Additional operators were also needed to secure the LZ along the Egyptian coast at Mitham el-Hafir for Operation Drizzle.

At the unit headquarters, as Almog was juggling personnel files and evaluations to find men for the operation, a limping First Lieutenant Ayalon walked into his office and said, "I know that you are short of people for the raid, so count me in!" Ayalon, seriously wounded on Green Island, had undergone several operations and was nowhere near the advanced stages of his recovery and rehabilitation, but he heard from friends that came to visit him in the hospital that something was brewing, and manpower was short. Grabbing his clothes when the nurses were on a cigarette break, he escaped from the hospital and headed back to the unit.

To complete the roster, Almog gathered several operators who were in the unit but on extended leaves (either personal time or in connection with their education). One such man was Rafi Milo, an operator who took a year off to build a home for himself and his new bride. Another operator was Oded Nir, on leave to complete his high school equivalency, in order for him to gain acceptance into Tel Aviv University. Nir was special to Almog—they were together in the Bird off of Port Said when one of the engines began making noise and then died. Calmly, and with his characteristic hands of gold, Nir twisted a few screws, manipulated a few parts, and the Bird was back in business. Shlomoh Eshel, was another man outside the flotilla fold at the time who wanted back in. A lieutenant in Flotilla 13 up until the 1967 War, Eshel left the unit because of its poor morale and what he saw as a limited future. A Kibbutznik and a soldier with unquestionable courage and leadership skills, Eshel was caught between the life of an operator that he loved so much and the life of living among operators and hearing *their* war stories. "He was," Almog reflects, "dying to return to the unit but only on the condition that he be operational."[43] Following a visit to the IDF HQ in Tel Aviv, Almog drove past Kibbutz Shfeyim, near Herziliya, to visit his old comrade and offer him a spot in the unit. During their meeting, Eshel's wife, Esti, came into the living room and saw her husband, lit up by the prospect of getting back into the unit, and said, "Ze'ev, you aren't taking Shlomoh from me!" Not wanting to get in the middle of an argument between husband and wife, something that might be more dangerous than Green Island, Almog headed back to his jeep for the drive to Atlit. Eshel was back in the unit days later.

Because of the sensitive nature of the mission, and because of the inter-unit and inter-branch cooperation needed, security needed to be at its highest level. And as a result of the level of difficulty and complexity of the mission, discipline had to be above and beyond what had been the norm for the unit. On September 5, 1969, a day before the two Pigs were to be launched, Almog held a pre-mission briefing in which one of the operators, Master Sergeant Arieh Yitzhak, arrived fifteen minutes late. In Almog's view, being selected for a mission was a privilege and an operator who permits himself to be fifteen minutes late to an operational briefing would also permit himself to act negligently and sacrifice the entire mission. Even though he was desperately short on manpower, Almog refused to allow the NCO to participate. The commander's decision was infrangible and final. Even though some of the operators threatened a mini-mutiny, they understood that the mission was the most important result.

The man who replaced Yitzhak on board the Pig was an operator named Shmuel Tamir. Tamir, a capable and jovial operator, was unfortunate enough to be considered by the unit as a bad-luck charm—the soldier who, as the SEALs like to put it, "always attracts shit." Less than a year earlier, during an exercise, he was the only survivor of a four-man Pig crew killed in a horrific training accident. Superstition is as much a piece of equipment carried into battle as is a dagger or pistol, and Milo, Nir, and Eshel were concerned about Tamir being part of their team. "Bullshit," Almog replied, "just do your jobs." In the end, however, Almog relented and Yitzhak was included in the team as the driver of Pig No. 2 the next night.

With the landing craft and torpedo boats ready for the green light once the torpedo boats were sunk, on the night of September 5, 1969, the Pigs set sail for the long distance haul of nearly twenty miles. They traveled on the surface for much of the moonless night in search of the Egyptian boats, but found nothing. Suddenly, and to their horror, they realized that the Egyptian boats were sailing on top of them and were taking evasive action. Perhaps the Egyptians had picked them up on radar. Perhaps it was just Murphy's Law—again. Whatever the reason, the eight men returned to their base in Sinai disappointed and angry—after all, a unit catch-phrase had been that nobody returns to base without carrying out his mission.

Almog opted to send them out several hours later—in daylight—after the Pigs were taken care of and the men afforded a meal and a few hours of sleep. The Egyptians never activated their radar during daylight hours and the early A.M. send-off guaranteed the Pigs more nighttime hours in which to search for their targets. By 24:00 hours, they located their elusive targets.

Pig No. 1, commanded by First Lieutenant Ayalon, submerged at the sight of their target and two operators began the swim toward the base of the craft. Without making a noise or alerting the torpedo boat's crew, three limpet mines were attached to the hull (the means by which the magnetic mines were fastened to the wooden hull remains classified to this day) of one ship and two attached to the other; checking their handiwork and making sure that the limpets were securely fastened to the hull of the boat, both men gave each other a thumbs-up and rendezvoused with the Pig. First Lieutenant Ayalon, ready to head back to base, sent a coded message on the Pig's sophisticated—and classified—communications system back to an anxious Almog waiting on shore; "The ax is on the two dogs," read Ayalon's message.[44] The seven words were well received by the officers waiting nervously at the Sinai Desert CP.

Lieutenant Milo, the mission commander and in Pig No. 2, didn't pick up Ayalon's message and dispatched his divers to the target as well. The two frogmen saw Pig No. 1's handiwork, decided to throw in several more limpets for good measure, and then radioed back the same message.

Four hours later, one of the P-183s raised its anchor and began to begin its routine patrol, and moments after that it blew up in a thunderous explosion. The second boat, unclear about what happened, inched closer to the wreckage, but it, too, disappeared in a ball of flames. Operation Escort was a success. Operation Drizzle could begin.

The first two-thirds of Operation Escort had gone off remarkably well—the operators reached their targets and then obliterated them. Now came the most difficult part— returning to base. An element of the operation's objective was to run silent. The destruction of the two Egyptian torpedo boats was an opening salvo, but if Egyptian radar or Soviet-manned radio monitoring positions picked up suspicious activity, it would sound an alarm along the front and endanger Operation Drizzle. As a result, the Pigs were forced to return to base semi-submerged and separately. Almog's concern was that a rendezvous between the two Pigs would require radio contact and above-the-surface sailing; that risked detection and the compromise of the mission.

First Lieutenant Ayalon's Pig reached Ras Sudr, the staging area, several hours later to a hero's welcome by Almog and the IDF/Navy commander, Rear Admiral Avraham Botzer. Amid the happiness and celebration, there was a heavy feeling of concern. Last communication with Pig No. 2 was at 2:15 hours, reporting one coded word indicating everything was okay. As Milo's Pig headed back home, a limpet mine,[45] the Pigs' self-destruction device, detonated in a thunderous blast leaving all the operators critically wounded. The Pig was destroyed by the blast, but Yitzhak, the driver, was farthest from the blast. (The cause of the blast was later learned to be an engineering fault exacerbated by its prolonged exposure to salt water.) Only Milo had been killed by the blast outright. Eshel, mortally wounded, grabbed Yitzhak aside as they floated atop the Gulf of Suez warmed by their own blood and said, "Listen, I know I'm dying, please tell my wife and kids what happened and what I did."

For the next six hours, the severely wounded Yitzhak dragged his three dead comrades in a desperate and exhausting swim back to shore. A search-and-rescue chopper, with Almog on board, located the four bodies in the water and immediately retrieved them. It was a tragic end to a successful operation. As the news of the three flotilla deaths reached the unit at Ras Sudr, pathfinders from Flotilla 13 secured the beachhead at Mitham el-Hafir and watched as the T-54s and BTR-50s were off-loaded and sent into action. It would be a day the Egyptian Army would never forget. Never before in the history of the Egyptian Army, intelligence reports would later learn, had there been such chaos and confusion. Senior commanders thought it was a coup. Others believed the Russians, already in Egypt in significant numbers, were repeating a forced takeover of the country similar to what they pulled off in Czechoslovakia a year earlier.

Operations Escort and Drizzle were incredibly successful. The combined strikes resulted in over a hundred Egyptian soldiers killed, including a general; the death of the commander of the Egyptian Red Sea theater of operations (killed when his staff car was run over by a tank); the loss of two torpedo boats, seventy armored fighting vehicles, three APCs, seven observation and security posts, twenty-seven telephone posts, an entire military camp in Zafrana, and a radar position at Ras Abu Darj.[46]

In Cairo, the raid brought about the typical reaction from an incensed and embarrassed President Nasser. The Egyptian chief of staff and Navy commander were sacked, as were countless other staff officers. He was even reported to have suffered a heart attack upon learning of the incursion.[47]

On September 12, 1969, Commander Almog received a telegram from Chief of Staff Bar-Lev citing the unit for its valor and dedication in Operation Escort. The message read as follows:

Office of the Chief of the General Staff
12 September 1969

Commander, Flotilla 13
Commander, IDF/Navy

Subject: Operation "Escort"

The sinking of the Egyptian torpedo boats in the Gulf of Suez was a first-of-its-kind mission carried out by Flotilla 13.

The sinking of the Egyptian torpedo boats was the *condition* enabling the execution of Operation "Drizzle," which, too, was a first-of-its-kind mission.

The flotilla withstood the test, this time a professional test more difficult than most.

Not only professionals, but laymen, sensed the physical, emotional, and technical hardships the operators were faced with, and they appreciate the abilities, tenacity, courage, and dedication of those who took part in the mission.

With all the sorrow and the pain of the loss of Lieutenant Commander Rafi Milo, First Lieutenant Shlomoh Eshel, and Master Sergeant Oded Nir, who died because of a technical malfunction following the successful completion of their mission, I want to convey to you my appreciation to you and to the flotilla, and above all to the operators who participated in the mission, on their crowning achievement.

Haim Bar-Lev, Lieutenant General
Chief of the General Staff[48]

It had been a remarkable three months for Flotilla 13, and their operational successes were not lost to other naval special warfare units around the world—most notably the U.S. Navy's SEALs. In November 1969, Commander Ze'ev Almog left the wartorn landscape of the Sinai peninsula for the sixteen-hour flight to Coronado NAB, near San Diego, California. It was to be the first-ever *official* visit of an Israeli naval commando officer to his counterparts in the U.S. Navy, and this journey to the home of SEAL Teams One and Two was one of great secrecy and foreboding. Relations between the Israeli and American navies were not good—indifference had turned to outward hostility following the tragic attack on the U.S.S. *Liberty* toward the close of the 1967 Six Day War. Yet the *Liberty* had nothing to do with Almog's apprehension about visiting the SEALs. The visit, the gifts, the honors, the niceties—this was a mission of good will, after all, and one initiated by the U.S. Navy. It was, however, all a diversion. *His* place was with the remnants of his unit, with the wounded in hospital, and with the widows and orphans of those killed that summer. His role was to rally the survivors of his flotilla and make sure that their combat edge was not dulled by idle time, anxiously waiting for the new recruits and wounded comrades to return to the force and fill its depleted ranks. Almog's place was against the Egyptians in the canal and Red Sea, opposite the Palestinian terrorist bases in Jordan across the Yarmouk and Jordan rivers, and against Syrian port facilities, monitoring Soviet freighters and the comings and goings of terrorist chieftains. The commander's place was not in the soothing surf of the Pacific a few miles down the road from scenic San Diego.

Yet orders were orders, and after having seen the French and Italians in action, Almog was definitely curious about the Americans. The IDF/Navy was eager to forge closer, post-*Liberty* ties with its superpower partner in the cold war, and the SEALs, fresh off a few brutally fought tours of Vietnam, were buzzing with news of the visiting Israeli naval commando. Flotilla 13 had been something of a superstar that summer. Every naval commando force in the world, from the British Special Boat Service to the elite

West German *Kamphfschwimmers,* had been talking about Israel's Flotilla 13, and its visit to the rock; the assault on a formerly unheard-of island wedged at the entrance to the Suez Canal was now considered a turning point in the history of how the world's commando forces mount their covert special operations. The untested and the seemingly impossible had been executed at Green Island several months earlier in a trailblazing operation few could believe actually happened. Israel had revolutionized commando operations and naval special warfare in one single attack in a godforsaken stretch of the world, and everyone wanted to know how they pulled it off. At Coronado NAB, home base to the SEAL units not operating in Vietnam, the striking commander of Flotilla 13 was treated with all the trappings of a VIP visit—official guides, banquets, "dog-and-pony shows usually reserved for admirals," and the exchange of nonclassified ideas and techniques. He was even afforded a ride in a top-secret SEALs swimmer delivery vehicle (SDV) and allowed to fire every piece of ordnance in the SEALs armory. Yet Almog was more a focal point of intense curiosity than a spark for improving relations between the two units. The SEALs wanted to pick Almog's mind—to uncover the secrets, Ze'ev Almog's secrets, and to find out how the impossible became a page in history. No matter where he went on base, he was stopped by the inquisitive men of the trident and the eagle. "What happened at Green Island?" "You were there, right?" "Didn't you command the mission?" "How the hell did you pull it off?" "What was it like?"

Ze'ev Almog's visit to Coronado was a success—bridging a foothold of friendship between the two secretive units, and forging the basis for what would become a close-knit alliance in conventional and counter-terrorist warfare in the years to come. Contacts and friends were made with the CO, Captain Ted Fielding and Lieutenant Commander Lee Mansi, a prominent special boat expert—men who would soon come to command SEAL teams and rise through the ranks of the U.S. Navy's special operations community—from (future admiral) George Worthington to the man who would be Almog's host at Coronado (future admiral Irv),

"Chuck" LeMoyne. It was all, however, an unwelcome interruption from nurturing his men back to health following a summer of incessant operations and bloodshed. Throughout his first introduction to Morning PT SEALs-style, trying to down beers at the officers' club, and diving with faces and wet suits he wasn't familiar with, his mind was far from the calming Pacific surf. It was back under the cool desert moon and the blackened depths of the Red Sea and Mediterranean. "What was it like at Green Island?" The answer to that question defined a unit, a war, and a nation's unique ability to produce men willing to work hard and possibly sacrifice their lives in order to be a part of something special—to contribute, to be in the loop. Green Island, a desolate man-made oddity protruding from the shimmering waters of a Red Sea gulf, defined such a generation of Israelis.

In reflecting on Green Island, perhaps "Raful" said it best when he said that the operation would illuminate a path for the army and future generations of commandos to come. Yet perhaps the operation's true impact can be personified by the fact that of the twenty operators of Flotilla 13 who participated in the operation, eleven went on to become senior officers in the flotilla and in the IDF/Navy, including three commanders of the flotilla and two commanders of the IDF/Navy.

For the next year, Flotilla 13 continued to mount dozens of small incursions against Egyptian sea-hugging targets—both alone and in support of Mat'kal and *Sayeret Tzan-hanim* ("Paratroop Recon") strikes. Egyptian frogmen, however, were busy on their own plans to bring the war onto the Israeli rear, and on November 8, 1969, two Israeli merchant vessels were sabotaged in the port of Eilat—Israel's sole access to the Red Sea. By 1969, Egyptian special forces had expanded both in size (considered to number a brigade full of commandos) and in ability—they were trained, equipped, and, in many instances, supervised by Soviet Spetsnaz personnel. Over the course of the next eleven months, Egyptian frogmen, often operating out of secret bases in Saudi Arabia and Jordan (secret to both the Saudis and Jordanians in many cases), executed three additional attacks against Israeli shipping and were believed to have operated quite freely along the Sinai coast. Much of their activity centered around intelligence-gathering operations.

Flotilla 13 prepared many ambushes along the Gulf of Eilat and, according to reports, in Jordan and Saudi Arabia as well. Unit 707, the IDF/Navy's UDT entity, also operated quite extensively in ambushes laid against the wily Egyptian raiders. Until 1968, operators from Unit 707 were soldiers who were tossed out of the Flotilla 13 curriculum at such an advanced stage of their instruction that it didn't pay to send them back to a paratroop or infantry unit. Being known as an underwater leper colony was a poor way to raise morale, and in a prudent move, the IDF/Navy opted to recruit personnel directly into the underwater force. This raised morale and effectiveness, as volunteers flocked to its base—not rejects from Flotilla 13. During the War of Attrition, Unit 707 operated along the Suez Canal, preparing landing zones and performing engineering work along Israel's own seaside defenses.

By 1970, though, Flotilla 13 found a new theater of operations in which to test its metal and a new enemy.

During the same period, Flotilla 13 operated against Syrian positions, and across the Jordan River both against the Jordanian military and against the Palestinian guerrilla groups that had begun to use the Hashemite Kingdom as a staging area for attacks against Israel, but by 1970, the Jordanians and Palestinians were embroiled in a war of their own. In a broad sense, the 1970 Jordanian Civil War (better known as the *Ailul al-Aswad* or "Black September") was Lebanon's "Green Island"—a point of no return. The destruction of the Palestinian's Jordanian base of operations for launching strikes against Israel forced the different factions of Yasir Arafat's Palestine Liberation Organization to set up camp in Lebanon. With a weak central government and a poorly trained army, Lebanon was in a position to thwart the Palestinian invasion, especially since men like Arafat and Dr. George Habash, commander of the communist Popular Front for the Liberation of Palestine (PFLP), were supported directly by Egypt and Syria, and indirectly by the Soviet Union, the Warsaw pact, and the People's Republic of China. Dozens of training camps and operational bases for launching strikes against Israel were set up throughout Lebanon, many situated in the southern portion of the country opposite the Israeli frontier, inside Beirut, and along the cities of Tyre, Sidon, and Tripoli along Lebanon's Mediterranean coast. It was these facilities, with their potential for launching seaborne raids against Israel's very vulnerable coastline that worried IDF/Navy intelligence and operations officers. It was a great-enough concern to warrant intensive Flotilla 13 activity along the Lebanese shoreline and coastal region.

Just as he had done along the West Bank of the Canal and along Egyptian Red Sea positions, Commander Almog lobbied the General Staff for operations against terrorist targets. The desire to strike out at the terrorists was strong. Although the Egyptians were the enemy, they were soldiers and earned and received a grudging respect that combatants usually reserve for one another. Egyptian commandos attacked IDF positions, not schoolbuses full of kids. The Egyptians didn't use children as human shields. In operating against the terrorists, the flotilla (and the IDF in general) faced enormous hardships. Their assault training taught them to attack built-up targets in a fast-paced and unforgiving choreographed movement of constant advance. When attacking a building, for example, standard practice called for a grenade to be tossed in, followed by a volley of automatic fire. There was no need to think about who was hit, since anyone in an enemy base was an enemy soldier and a legitimate target. The Palestinian terrorists, turning Lebanon into their own mini-state, situated their camps near refugee camps where women and children milled about. There wasn't an operator in Flotilla 13 who wanted to have the death of a woman or a child on his conscience, so counter-terrorist operations meant trepidation and hesitation, and in this particular business, hesitation could result in death.

One operation that personified this problem, and dilemma, was known on the IDF Operations chart as "Hood 20."[49]

Lebanon presented challenges to the IDF, and it presented opportunities to the Palestinians. Instead of having to cross the Jordan River and fight IDF units in the Jordan Valley, they could now sail to the major Israeli population centers along the Mediterranean coast and bring the war for national liberation right into the living rooms of average Israeli citizens. Along the Lebanese coast, near Tyre and especially Sidon, various factions of the PLO began to set up seaborne insertion units and support facility; these terrorists were armed with light weaponry, RPGs, and explosives, but they had at their disposal scuba gear and Zodiacs and the same Soviet instructors teaching the art of commando warfare to the Egyptians (and Syrians). The Palestinians also had East German, Cuban, and North Korean instructors as well. The Palestinian "naval commando" bases were never extravagant facilities, nor were they well concealed. They usually consisted of several shacks and a few storage areas, had access to the water, and were almost always surrounded by civilians.

The IDF General Staff feared this seaborne potential growing to Israel's north and decided to strike back. It authorized a multi-unit raid, consisting of paratroopers and Flotilla 13, to attack several shoreline facilities and several training camps located inland around the village of Sarafand some thirteen kilometers south of Sidon. The paratroopers would be flown by helicopter to their targets; the flotilla operators would reached the Sarafand coast by Zodiac, attack the village's northern base, and also fulfill another objective—the assassination or abduction of the regional commander, a terrorist chieftain and Arafat confidant known by the *nom de guerre* of Abu Yusef. Abu Yusef's two-story house was located half a kilometer from the sea. It was surrounded by a banana plantation and several smaller houses where the field hands lived. The mission commander and commander of the flotilla's boat unit, Lieutenant Hanina Amishav, was to lead a task force of thirteen operators divided into three teams. The orders were *not to* harm civilians, though not at the risk of endangering anyone from the flotilla.

On the night of January 15, the operators went into action. The paratrooper's operation went well, and initially so, too, did the flotilla's mission. The operators landed discreetly, moving slowly and cautiously about the banana field until they made eye contact with Abu Yusef's house. Employing silenced weapons and getting their Belgian-made bazooka ready for firing, a brief fire-fight erupted between several of the operators and one of the Palestinian sentries. Enemy fire was coming from a casino located southwest of the operators' position. As the commandos moved into attack formation to enter the house, they heard the screams of several women emanating from inside the now-surrounded dwelling. Soon more voices were heard and women appeared on the scene, even though the area was under Palestinian fire. Unwilling to blow up the house if Abu Yusef wasn't home (they feared he escaped moments earlier in a staff car), especially with women and children inside, Lieutenant Hanina ordered his operators to withdraw back to their Zodiacs.

The following day, an outraged Chief of Staff Bar-Lev lambasted the young flotilla lieutenant over his failure to "stick to his target"; furthermore, Bar-Lev promised, Hanina would never become a high-ranking commander in the unit. Almog was outraged. Mainly due to the fact that he voiced such warnings about this mission before the operators left base. But the operators, especially the junior officers, were incensed. They rallied and promised Commander Almog that if Hanina wasn't good enough to be a commander in the unit, then neither were they. They threatened to resign and leave the unit for good. Almog's sentiments echoed his men's. He telephoned "Raful" and told him of the impending mutiny, adding that his name would be added to the list, as well. "Raful," by now a great fan of the unit, raced to Atlit to calm the situation down and even managed to get Chief of Staff Bar-Lev to recant his admonition of Hanina.[50]

Over the course of the next year, Flotilla 13's ambushes, intelligence-gathering sorties, and other counter-terrorist operations (a good many still not declassified) were mounted against targets in Lebanon. The war against the Palestinians ended three years of remarkable work against more conventional targets in Egypt and Jordan. For Flotilla 13, it was a period of rebirth, growth, and wonder.

In November 1971, Commander Ze'ev Almog was assigned to the missile boat Flotilla to be qualified as a missile boat commander, and in July 1972 he was promoted to Captain and named commander of the Red Sea theater of operations. His three and a half years and eighty combat special operations at the helm of the IDF/Navy's once-anonymous flotilla are characterized by both his admirers and detractors as the most impressive display of command ever witnessed in the history of Israeli special operations. He had brought a unit from the brink of disbanding and taken it to a level where the General Staff considered it Israel's premier commando force. He assumed command of a small group of disillusioned and beaten men, transforming them into warriors with more work than they knew what to do with. He had raised a generation of commanders and junior officers whose impact on the State of Israel, the IDF/Navy, and Flotilla 13 are still felt to this day. "He had," according to one retired U.S. Navy SEALs officer, "rewritten the rules and breached the envelope of naval special warfare as we know it."

Although promoted out of the flotilla, events would reunite Almog with his beloved Batmen two years later in a campaign that, many have commented, "would once again rewrite the naval special warfare rule book!"

CHAPTER FOUR

The Years of Vengeance

Flotilla 13: 1972 to 1975

"I always wanted to visit Lebanon. Eat its legendary fish, ski in its mountains, gamble in its casinos, and love its almond-eyed beauties. I never thought I'd see Lebanon from the insides of a fortress firing my Uzi like a madman!"[1]

GREEN ISLAND WAS A TURNING POINT NOT ONLY FOR FLOTILLA 13 but also for the entire Israeli special operations community. It was, at the time, the largest Israeli commando operation of the War of Attrition, and it was the kind of raid that raised the confidence and fighting spirit of an entire army. Green Island was a symbol of a war between two opposing armies separated by ideology, chauvinism, national loyalties, and the desire to do unto the other "SOB" in that strange-looking uniform before he did it to you. Even though Green Island was a ferocious battle where the bullet-torn tatters of men were littered about the rock, it had its elements of honor, too. It was a calling card that made a name for the unit and national heroes out of the operators. After all, every Israeli eighteen-year-old entering the IDF dreamed of joining the elite club of aces in the Israel Air Force, and all those who couldn't make the initial cut in the pilot's course then set their sights on the red beret and silver wings of the paratroops. Very few new conscripts dreamed of Flotilla 13—very few even knew the unit existed. According to an eighteen-year-old conscript in 1971, "The unit was an enigma concealed by secrecy; most new volunteers were recruited by flotilla officers scouring the main conscription and absorption base in search of talent, not by eager hopefuls walking through our doors."[2] That talent would be needed.

The war against the Palestinian terrorists would, indeed, see special operations similar in scope, imagination, and courage to Green Island, but there was something different about fighting the *Kefiyeh*-wearing terrorists who considered it a matter of pride to hijack aircraft, send letter bombs, and RPG schoolbuses full of youngsters. Waging war in this enemy's backyard meant trampling through clothes lines, wandering through refugee camps, and forcing an operator to think, for that all-important, potentially life-threatening split-second, whether the 7.62mm round he is about to fire from his AK-47 assault rifle will produce a cloud of pink spray from the head of a man in lizard-pattern fatigues holding a grenade, or whether it might accidentally kill a small child ducking for cover. Commando operations in the enemy's rear, when that enemy purposely employed innocent civilians as human shields, was an ugly, dangerous, and often heart-wrenching affair. It had no honor.

The transformation of Lebanon into a target state coincided with the transformation of Flotilla 13 as a true assault force. Since the first Palestinian hijackings and subsequent attempts—hijackings of El Al aircraft in July 1968, attacks that emanated from Beirut,—the IDF targeted the fledgling Palestinian terrorist presence with commando assaults. The most notable of these was the spectacular "Operation Gift" (December 27, 1968), when a heliborne force of commandos from Sayeret Mat'kal and *Sayeret Tzanhanim* (or "Paratroop Recon," the recce battalion of the conscript 35th Paratroop Brigade) destroyed thirteen planes belonging to Middle East Airlines as retaliation for Lebanese passive collusion with the terrorists by not prohibiting their actions. In the subsequent years, more conventional IDF strikes against terrorist targets in Lebanon were mounted, and a particularly brutal guerrilla war was waged in the mountainous region connecting Lebanon, Israel, and Syria around Mt. Hermon between Israeli and Palestinian forces; the area became known as "Fatahland." Yet it was only after Black September that Palestinian forces in Lebanon began their massive buildup along the shore, inviting attention from the IDF/Navy.

In July 1972, Commander Almog was promoted to command the Red Sea theater of operations and his deputy commander in Flotilla 13, Lieutenant Commander Shaul Ziv, assumed command of the unit. Captain Ze'ev Almog's appointment as Red Sea theater commander in 1972 was seen, in many ways, as a reward for the brilliant command of the flotilla from 1968 to 1971. Theater commands, followed by command of the Haifa naval base, were seen as the progressional march up the IDF/Navy's chain of command to that all-important position of *Mefaked* IDF/Navy, the rank of IDF/Navy commander known by its affectionate Hebrew acronym of *Ma'Chi!* Ze'ev Almog, in his almost four years of commanding Flotilla 13, had done more than be a unit commander; he had, in essence, become its soul and its personality. The volunteers who flocked to Atlit following the 1967 War were men personally selected by Almog. The operators promoted to senior NCO spots were approved by Almog. NCOs who went to the officers' course did so because Almog had given them positive reviews. In many cases, for men reluctant to become officers and sign on the extra time, Almog held their hands or lambasted them, pushing them toward officer rank knowing that they were officer material. When he took over command of the unit, he inherited a command shaken by failure, abandonment, and disillusionment. Thinking of the unit like a field ravaged by the elements, he personally tended the grounds, planted the seeds, and nurtured the first harvests. The unit may have had a new commander, but Almog's personal touch was still evident in the force from the executive officer down to the mechanics who maintained the Pigs, speed-craft, and other exotic gear the unit was known to bring to bear.

Born in Poland at the height of the Nazi occupation, Commander Shaul Ziv was a very different type of man than Ze'ev Almog. Ziv wasn't the dashing *Sabra* (native-born Israeli) who grew up in an established home and in an established environment of security. Ziv was a survivor and truly ideal material for an operator. Almog was stern and the man in charge; Ziv was more the populist, who cared as much about how much his men liked him, as well as how they performed at sea or in an enemy port. While Almog was an initiator, Ziv was more a responder to developing events—the traits of a survivor. Though the two men were at opposite plains of the command and personality charts, the unit remained relatively the same under the transfer of command. Almog's cadre of energetic young officers set the tone for the unit to proceed along its path of incessant training and nonstop across-the-border operations, and Ziv led them with charisma and courage. Ziv was a daring combat officer who had fought with the paratroopers and parachuted into the Mitla Pass in 1956.

By 1971, a cease-fire imposed by United States Secretary of State William Rodgers was holding quietly along the Suez Canal front, ending the 1000 days of the War of Attrition. It wasn't peace, but it meant a respite from the daily artillery barrages and mounting death toll. Israeli special operations continued, of course, as Secretary of State Rodgers had not negotiated a cease-fire with the PLO. Flotilla 13 was still busy. Its War of Attrition in Lebanon had only just begun.

Early probing actions by teams of frogment from Flotilla 13 painted a daunting image of the Palestinian seaside installations—especially those around Tyre and Sidon. Fortified and heavily defended, they were situated inside sprawling refugee camps, well protected—seemingly—from outside attack by a sea of innocent civilians. The refugee camps, especially those along the coast, were chaos-and congestion-filled ports, so that virtually anyone could mill about the area without suspicion. "After all," it was reported, "the camps are so teeming it is unlikely that anyone will suspect a few strangers walking about."[3] Indeed, there were several covert and disguised reconnaissance missions along the coast, but mainly the men of Flotilla 13 were dispatched to the shores of Lebanon on nighttime reconnaissance missions where harbor installations were examined and photographed and soil samples were gathered. Many of these missions were supported by Dabur patrol boats, armed with 20mm Oerlikon cannons and .50-caliber heavy machine guns, that took advantage of the nonexistent Lebanese coastal radar shield. On many operations, the operators were transported to their targets courtesy of the growing flotilla of Israeli missile boats, the Sa'ar-class ships smuggled out of the French shipyards of Cherbourg in 1968 and equipped with the compact, sleek, and lethal indigenously produced Gabriel surface-to-surface missile. The sea-skimming Gabriel, the end result of what had begun as a *Pal'yam* experiment with the "Shark" in commando operations, was a potent ship-killer that could be directed manually or via radar. With its warhead crammed with 150 kilograms of blast fragmentation explosives and an advanced top-secret electronic package, it was considered more than a match for the Soviet-built STYX SSMs. Yet on raids against Lebanon, squads from Flotilla 13 were less interested in the Gabriel than they were in the missile boats' main cannon—a 40mm gun that could provide immediate fire-suppression if a raiding party required offshore assistance.

One target that Flotilla 13 did not pay particularly close attention to was the northern city of Tripoli. Even though the various Palestinian factions had established quite formidable training facilities inside the vast network of interlacing refugee camps surrounding Lebanon's second largest city, Tripoli was over 100 miles from Israel's northernmost tip, and any *large-scale* reconnaissance endeavor was deemed too risky—especially since it would be encroaching dangerously close to Syrian territorial waters and any hostile engagements were to be avoided at all costs. That position ended as the Palestinian infrastructure in Lebanon grew at an alarming pace and Tripoli became home to an international brigade of terrorists, from South American leftists to the Japanese Red Army. Because it was so far from the Israeli frontier, Palestinian factions and their Soviet and East Bloc trainers found the port city conveniently beyond the reach of the Israeli military. KGB officials who ran many of the terrorist factions and supervised much of their training realized that they might be forced to endure the odd IAF air raid here and there (after all, dodging dive-bombing Phantoms was part of the job description that warranted their hazardous-duty pay from Moscow), but Tripoli was beyond the envelope of an Israeli commando strike. Russian officials in poor-fitting safari suits were seen moving about Tripoli without fear or impunity, as were East German instructors in fatigues, Cuban assassin-instructors puffing away on some of Havana's finest cigars, and North Korean and North Vietnamese officials who seemed comically out-of-place amid the backdrop of the *Suq* (Arabic for "Market") and the local sights, but who brought with them the invaluable lessons of successful anti-Western guerrilla conflicts. Heavily armed Palestinian guerrillas turned the once-thriving Lebanese city into a military camp. They moved about the city at will, often terrorizing and brutalizing many of the local inhabitants. Beirut might have been the Palestinians' capital in Lebanon, but Tripoli was their Pentagon and Camp Pendelton. In the IDF General Staff and Operations Branch, Tripoli was considered a major target. Because it was a port, it was considered the property of Flotilla 13.

Commander Ziv and his junior officers routinely reviewed IDF intelligence files on possible targets in Lebanon. Research was part of the job. If they didn't know what a target looked like, its disposition of forces, the layout of its defenses, and the proximity of a nearby refugee camp, they couldn't propose a raid to the IDF/Navy commander. Files were read and reread, accounts from assets reviewed and notes taken, and aerial reconnaissance photographs studied zealously. Some officers spent as much time with their eyes squinting through magnifying glasses as they did in the Mediterranean practicing mine-planting and sentry-removal. Ziv and his officers felt that any IDF raid along the coast should involve the flotilla and only the flotilla. If the unit had achieved anything during the War of Attrition, it was the right for exclusivity in the naval special warfare arena.

Flotilla 13 had, however, set a precedent by lobbying for work, and other units soon followed its lead—namely Sayeret Mat'kal, and the 35th Paratroop Brigade and its recon force. By 1972, Sayeret Mat'kal was commanded by Lieutenant Colonel Ehud Barak, a remarkable man of limitless courage who would go on to become Israel's most decorated soldier and chief of staff. Barak was daring, cunning, charismatic, and eager to test his men and the concept of a small and elite unit waged in a life-and-death struggle amid the shadows of the Middle East. "He was an officer," Ze'ev Almog recalls, "who could do just about anything."[4] With missile boats and new transport helicopters from the United States, namely the Bell-205 and the CH-53, a unit didn't have to sail up on an enemy coast in a rubber craft to necessarily achieve surprise. With the advent of the missile boat, these ground operators had a high-tech, heavily armed platform from which to launch a brief Zodiac ride to shore. The 35th Paratroop Brigade by 1972 was also under new command—under the helm of Ze'ev Almog's old college classmate, Uzi Yairi. Colonel Yairi had brought much of the Mat'kal swagger and over-the-top confidence with him to the conscript red berets, and he also brought with him the Mat'kal penchant for handling every operation, no matter how small, as if it were the "big one." Colonel Yairi was a great admirer of Flotilla 13, but he didn't wear bat wings on his chest. His loyalty was to the red beret, the brigade's emblem of the winged snake, and the men in his command—especially its reconnaissance assets.

Competition breeds excellence and sometimes cooperation. Sometimes, when the situation demands, egos and feelings take second seat when cooperation is needed to defeat the common enemy.

On September 5, 1972, terrorists from the Black September Organization, a covert special operations unit belonging to Yasir Arafat's Fatah faction, attacked the Israeli Olympic

217

team in Munich, as the squad slept at their residence at 31 Connoly Straße. The subsequent hostage drama—televised live to an enthralled international television audience of over one billion people—and botched rescue attempt by Bavarian police units led to the deaths of eleven Israeli athletes; two had been killed at the Olympic Village, and the remaining nine were massacred inside German Air Force helicopters at Fürstenfeldbruk Airport. The "Munich Olympics Massacre" was, in fact, the most infamous terrorist operation ever perpetrated. Clearly, the image of the hooded terrorist peering out of the Israeli residence remains imprinted in the minds of many when thoughts of terrorism in the modern age are evoked. Yet the massacre was more than a symbol. It was a turning point in Israel's war against terrorism. It transformed a small regional guerrilla war, one fought with small units on isolated hilltops in desolate locations, into a covert war waged on the streets of Europe.

After Munich, Israel declared full-scale war on Palestinian terrorists worldwide. Mossad hit teams, according to published accounts, made up of intelligence agents and Sayeret Mat'kal and Flotilla 13 commandos on loan, roamed the streets of Europe in search of the leadership of Black September responsible for the deaths in Munich. These men, distinctive in their olive complexion, off-the-rack suits, and Beretta .22s carried in rear-back holsters, were dispatched on a sacred mission of sorts, to exact an "eye-for-an-eye" justice on the men who, with ice water running through their veins, peered through the sights of their AK-47 assault rifles and sprayed 7.62mm rounds into the bodies of nine gagged and bound Israeli athletes. Israeli Prime Minister Golda Meir, a woman who viewed the attack as if it were her own children who had been massacred, ordered the nation's covert and military assets to strike at the terrorists in a way that would once and for all punish and deter. It would be a global effort. The Mossad, and the hit teams, would seek out the guilty parties in Europe. Israeli commandos would take care of the Middle East.

Following the Munich Olympics Massacre, Flotilla 13 was rumored and reported (depending on which source is believed) to have visited several nations where Black September was based, housed, and nourished—from points in Syria, Egypt, and even Libya.[5] All such operations are classified top-secret by the IDF, even twenty-five years later, and they are believed to have consisted primarily of intelligence-gathering forays; foreign reports indicate that they also involved the insertion and retrieval of deep-cover agents.[6] Lebanon was, however, the focal point of the flotilla effort and the operations were not solely limited to intelligence work. Operators from Flotilla 13 routinely ventured "up north" (as the sorties were called) for hit-and-run raids. They were small-time operations and all-important "hits," and they were designed to keep the terrorists off-balance. Three dead PFLP gunmen lying by a smoldering Zil truck by the side of a Sidon pier put the terrorists on guard. It made them mistrust their own, it left them scared and unwilling to venture out of their encampments after dark, and it caused them to fire wildly into the night thinking every howling wind and twisting branch to be an Israeli raider. Some of the raids, in the words of one Israeli operator, were designed on up-to-date intelligence—word that a terrorist leader would be driving from point A to point B, or in one case, that a terrorist commander would be having dinner at a seaside restaurant overlooking the Mediterranean. In that particular instance, the operators would swim to the pier directly underneath the dining area, locate and identify the targeted individual, and then hurl themselves up across the wooden fence and fire two 7.62mm rounds into the targeted terrorist's head. According to one retired U.S. Navy SEAL officer, who followed Ze'ev Almog's ground-breaking establishment of contact between the Israeli and American naval special warfare communities, "The Israelis followed a policy known in the business as 'ADD': Attack, Destroy, and Disengage."[7]

On February 16, 1973, the IDF General Staff met in a smoke-filled room at the Kirya and, in a lengthy deliberation marked by heated argument, aggravated egos and tempers, discussing a large-scale raid against Tripoli. This was to be no ordinary operation, and the piles of paperwork on the desk of Chief of Staff Lieutenant General David

"Dado" Elazar was larger than the usual assembly of top-secret reports from intelligence agents in Lebanon, black-and-white aerial reconnaissance photographs, and dossiers on the leaders of the Palestinian terrorist factions. Intelligence reports, both emanating from Mossad HUMINT assets on the ground, as well as military intelligence data, pinpointed the northern Lebanese port city of Tripoli, 180 kilometers from the Israeli frontier, as a prime target for a seventy-two-hour window of opportunity for action. Situated just north of Tripoli were two large Palestinian refugee camps, Nahar al-Bard and al-Badawi; both camps were home to a remarkable *seven* major terrorist bases and headquarters installations. These facilities, established with the advice and support of Soviet agents and personnel, were not only staging points for terrorist attacks worldwide, but also they served as training facilities for terrorists from Europe, Africa, Asia, and South America. In fact, a running joke in the Israeli intelligence community at the time was that there were so many "foreign" Western intelligence agents monitoring the two camps that a smart and enterprising Lebanese could make a fortune offering low-cost microfilm processing and shipping services.

Raiding the camps was viewed as an eventual necessity by senior Israeli military planners, but the intelligence coming from Lebanon was such that a raid against the facility needed to happen—and happen soon. Even to this day, more than twenty-five years following the raid, the veil of secrecy concerning the Tripoli operation remains strong. It has been reported that PFLP warlord Dr. George Habash, the man who brought about Skyjack Sunday and the Jordanian Civil War, and Abu Iyad, the de facto head of Black September, would be inspecting the camp that night. Few tears would be shed by many, had the two men been caught in the middle of a cross-fire during the raid. Targeting one or both could reap political and intelligence rewards beyond the comprehension of Israel's military leaders. Chief of Staff Elazar calmly told his generals that for the raid to take place, it would have to happen within the next few days—a surprise that caused the stomach acids of the navy, air force, and paratroop commanders to churn away without mercy.

Brigadier General Emanuel "Manno" Shaked, the man who replaced "Raful" as the chief paratroop and infantry officer, was named the mission's overall commander, and he at first shook his head with a throw of doubt, not believing that the training, assembling, and transport of the men and material required to assault both camps could be placed together within such a short period of time. Then, however, with the resolve of a man who feels he has nothing to lose, he turned Lieutenant General Elazar's office silent by saying, "If you want the raid, then I'll need the entire IDF under my command!" Shaked received all that he required. Naval and air units were placed under paratroop command, and Commander Ziv flew in his jeep back to Atlit from Tel Aviv to get his task force together. Having studied Tripoli as a freelance project, perhaps realizing that his men would one day pay a serious visit to the northern city, Ziv had done much of the work that might have otherwise taken weeks. Less than twenty-four hours later, an operational plan was on the chief of staff's desk in Tel Aviv.

Because of the distance between the two targets, the operation became in essence two separate, though inseparable, raids. The force that would attack the camp at Nahar al-Bard (Operation Hood 54) was commanded by the deputy commander of Paratroop Brigade, Lieutenant Colonel Amos Yaron, and was split into three attack forces: (a) a paratroop force, commanded by Lieutenant Colonel Yitzhak Mordechai, was assigned objective *Geulah 1*, Fatah's naval commando base where the international contingent of terrorists was trained; (b) a force from the paratroop squad leader's battalion, commanded by Major Doron Rubin, was assigned *Geulah 2*, the headquarters of the Popular Struggle Front, a pro-Syrian terrorist group that frequently mounted attacks against positions and settlements along the Israeli-Lebanese border; (c) *Geulah 3*, the headquarters of Dr. George Habash's Popular Front for the Liberation of Palestine (PFLP), fell to a force of operators from Flotilla 13 commanded by Lieutenant Commander Gadi Shefi, the unit's deputy commander.

The raid on the al-Badawi camp (Operation Hood 55), situated two kilometers north of Tripoli, was under the overall leadership of 35th Paratroop Brigade commander Colonel Uzi Yairi. Operation Hood 55 had four objectives: (a) *Ahuva 1* was a series of Fatah command, control, and communications installations that was entrusted to Lieutenant Colonel Amnon Shahak's 50th Na'ha'l Paratroop Battalion; (b) the destruction of *Ahuva 2*, the PFLP prison, as well as objectives *Ahuva 3* and *Ahuva 4*, the Fatah armory in the camp respectively, the heaviest defended targets of the entire operation, assigned to Major Avner Harmoni's reconnaissance paratroop force. Both camps were heavily fortified, and defended by hundreds of well-trained hardcore Palestinians equipped with a wide array of weapons, including anti-tank and anti-aircraft guns. To assist the paratroopers tasked with the *Ahuva* objectives, several operators from Unit 707 would drive the Zodiacs and make sure that the waterborne aspect of the insertion went smoothly.[8]

In historical terms, and as a forebear for future operations of its kind, Operation Hood 54-55 was the first large-scale IDF raid in which all three combat arms were represented. Although this was a year before the notion of "combined arms" would be initiated into the IDF's order of battle with one branch of the service completely in support of another, especially with its special operations assets, the raid on Tripoli was unique in that aerial support, naval transport, and ground forces were all under one unified command. All commands contributed equally to the logistics, planning, and execution of the raid. Time allotted to training for the raid was minimal. The paratroopers trained at a site near Jericho in a brigade-size exercise in the flowered hills of a Jordan Valley beset by a winter's rainfall. The combat elements of the exercises went extremely well—marksmanship scores were impressive, and even the commanders found that the required time hoped to be achieved on their stopwatches, and those actually performed by the "red berets" in the field, were close to split-second. The operators from Flotilla 13 participating in the joint exercises proved to be shining examples of ballistic proficiency. Yet Colonel Yairi remembered Shaul Ziv's recommendation that his paratroopers, men accustomed to

heliborne or mechanized assaults, might find it in their best
interests to undergo a few hours of "serious" amphibious
assault training; until the late 1970s, such instruction was
considered frivolous by IDF guidelines for their forces not
intending any major seaborne campaigns and more likely
than not to be engaged in either desert or mountainous
regions. Commander Ziv was concerned that the paratroopers might fall victim to motion sickness on the voyage from
the IDF/Navy base in Haifa to the shores of Tripoli, and be
too ill to perform their difficult combat assignments. Ziv's
apprehensions were incredibly accurate. During a pre-dress-
rehearsal, many of the paratroopers, bogged down by their
heavy gear and unaccustomed to the "Level 6" waves of the
stormy Mediterranean, found themselves suffering from
intense nausea and cramps even after only minutes at sea.
Clearly this was an operational hazard as great to the
success of the mission as a breech in security, and one that
had to be overcome. As a result, the flotilla commandos
were forced to take a break from their own instruction and
conduct basic sea skills for their paratrooper comrades.
This minor, though time-consuming, hindrance was at first
feared to remove the "edge" from the training regimen, as
well as preoccupy the task force with getting there, rather
than getting the job done. In reality, the paratroopers'
difficulties in coping with the waves of the wintry waters
helped solidify a camaraderie that might not have existed
otherwise—it certainly helped forge a few friendships and
allegiances that are crucial for a military force entering into
an assault deep behind enemy lines.

A day before the raid, the task force performed a full-scale
amphibious assault training near Haifa, supervised and
spearheaded by the men of units in Flotilla 13 assigned to
the operation (believed to have included nearly a third of
the flotilla), and performed under the complete cover of
darkness.[9] The operation was conceived and brought to its
pre-planning and functional fruition literally in a matter of
hours. Soldiers had but a few hours to sleep during the three
frantic days of preparation and were forbidden contact with
the outside world, but the practice assault, from journey out
to sea on a flotilla of missile and patrol boats, to the actual

landing and forced march toward the objective and the mock assault, with live ammunition in a wooden mock-up of the targets, went remarkably well. The task force lagged behind the estimates by only a matter of minutes, and these small delays were considered correctable. Such Spartan and immediate training conditions pointed to the importance of the preparations and the somewhat desperate nature of actually pulling off the operation as scheduled. By the morning of February 20, Brigadier General Shaked informed Chief of Staff Elazar that *his* forces were ready.

During the preparation for Operation Hood 54-55, Commander Ziv, through the inescapable reality of his presence, became Shaked's deputy, yet he was as equally concerned with the overall mission as he was with the welfare and readiness of his own contingent. "It was these qualities, of caring and worrying about his men, even under fire," according to an Israeli special operations officer, "that forever endeared him to his men."[10] He stood over the assault units with his trusty stopwatch until he was certain that landing, beachhead, and fire support for the reconnaissance paratroopers being ferried in on Zodiacs was carried out within the prescribed time limit—a split-second checklist that had to be perfected before he would allow his men to embark on this operation. Since both task forces would have to move through a formidable stretch of territory on foot before reaching their objectives, Ziv ordered his men to wear the regular-issue combat fatigues instead of neoprene wet suits. Wet bodies would shiver in the winter's chill, but fabric dried. The neoprene restricted comfortable movement, and the agility would save lives and allow the task force to reach the objective undetected. Ziv also requisitioned additional field radios for his assault teams—communications with one another would be crucial to the success of the overall operation, as well as ensuring that friendly forces did not engage each other on the unfamiliar Lebanese coast, instead of the Palestinians. Unlike what happened on Green Island, Ziv also demanded that his men move lightly. Heavy RPGs would be left at base, as would bazookas; a hardened target, such as an incredibly fortified pillbox, did not exist at the camps, according to the last-minute intelligence roundups, and there were no Lebanese armor units in the vicinity capable of reaching the camps in the time that it would take to pull off "Hood 54-55." It was also reasoned that should an unforeseen and serious complication enter the picture once the operation was underway, a flight of Skyhawks in the air and armed with everything from 20mm rockets to 500-pound bombs could be called in to action in a moment's notice. For the naval commandos participating in the raid, the standard weapon of the day, so to speak, was the flotilla's old and reliable AK-47 7.62mm assault rifle—a sturdy and robust weapon that was "user-friendly" when wet and covered in mud, yet incredibly gentle and accurate to trained hands; the squad support weapon was another "old reliable" of the IDF—the FN MAG 7.62mm light machine gun. The lead landing party, hitting the shore following a long swim and well ahead of the main group to ensure a "COLD LZ" would be armed with silenced Uzi 9mm submachine guns, as well as specially modified .22-caliber Berettas that produced only a muted thud on a calm day and were virtually noiseless in the wind and by the surf. To supplement their firepower, additional supplies of fragmentation grenades were handed to each commando. The raid on the camp was not a mission into an objective surrounded by innocent civilians where firepower had to be distributed with the utmost care. Anyone in the training facility was considered guilty, and as a result, the use of grenades was encouraged.

The armada departed Haifa at 12:55 hours on the afternoon of February 20, with very little fanfare from a base where all communications to the outside world had been cut. A steady stream of staff cars and important personnel with impressive decorations ferried about the base as if it were their own. The journey to Tripoli would not take very long, but once the flotilla of ships and commandos departed Israeli territorial waters, they would be extremely vulnerable. At 20:15 hours on February 20, however, the missile-boat flotilla ferrying the assault force reached the Lebanese coast just off Tripoli without incident, and without even encountering another vessel. The seven-hour voyage across heavy winter seas caused even the most seasoned paratroop veterans to "race for the buckets" and pray for land—even if it lay deep in enemy territory; the few hours of sea acclimation had not been enough. The naval commandos on board the Sa'ar craft chuckled at the motion-sickness victims, made a few jokes, and readied their gear. Many of the missile-boat crews looked on at the commandos of Flotilla 13 with a fair degree of envy; many had volunteered for the unit, but never made it past the *Gibush*. In reality, there would be nothing to be jealous of. Tripoli promised to be, in the military vernacular, "a hairy one."

Because of Commander Ziv's insistence that transport from ship to objective be a Flotilla 13 responsibility, Colonel Yairi's pathfinders were two flotilla frogmen, who emerged from the darkened depths to land on Lebanese soil at 21:50 hours. They had swum to the shorefront using a delivery mechanism still considered classified, patrolling the paratrooper's LZ with silenced Uzis in hand; this was not a situation where the Hollywood method of removing a sentry with a sharpened dagger would be employed. After uncovering nothing but a few illegally dumped piles of garbage, the frogmen signaled in the mini-armada of Zodiacs. As Yairi's objective was closest to the LZ, just due south of the al-Badawi camp, their trek was the shortest; the spread-out column of paratroopers, led by Colonel Yairi himself and the two frogmen, proceeded toward the target in a neat and orderly formation. The dozens of drivers of cars on the main road failed to notice the long row of heavily armed paratroopers, and the advance continued smoothly. Colonel Yairi led at a hectic pace through the barely passable rocky terrain, and many of even his most experienced officers were having difficulties keeping up. Because the attacks on Nahar al-Bard and al-Badawi were intended to begin simultaneously, Yairi was ordered on several occasions to halt his attack and wait for Lieutenant Colonel Yaron's force, which had been delayed by rough seas, to reach their targets. At 01:07 hours, an anxious Brigadier General Shaked, listening in from his command post aboard an IDF/Navy missile boat, ordered the attack to commence with or without Yaron![11]

Because *Ahuva 3* and *Ahuva 4* were considered the more problematic of the objectives, the *Sayeret* went into action first. *Ahuva 3* was attacked by eleven reconnaissance paratroopers led by the *Sayeret Tzanhanim* commander, Major Harmoni. The force entered the headquarters position raking the building with machinegun and rifle-grenade fire. Major Harmoni entered the building and eliminated a uniformed PLO sentry clutching an AK-47, but not before he got off a burst which hit Harmoni's right hand. By now the battle was in full swing. Grenades were thrown from all sides, seriously wounding Major Harmoni and three of his subordinates. After a heavy fire-fight, Palestinian resistance crumbled, and the *Sayeret* tended to its wounded, ransacked the building, and prepared its demolition. The attack on *Ahuva 4* was much easier, as most of the guards retreated at the sound of gunfire from *Ahuva 3*, and it was destroyed with little difficulty.

Lieutenant Colonel Mula Shaham's attack on the PFLP prison was conducted in true "commando" style. The combined force of Flotilla 13's operators and paratroopers had silently surrounded *Ahuva 2*, when thirty meters from the gates they encountered a PFLP patrol, and a firefight erupted. Lieutenant Colonel Shaham shouted a rousing "Follow me!" Then the ring of paratroopers closed in for the kill. Dozens of grenades were thrown at the building's defenses, allowing the attackers to enter the building unmolested. Leading the charge into the courtyard was flotilla operator Lieutenant Commander Kroll, considered one of the finest men ever to wear the bat-wing badge, and known as an absolute marksman with an AK-47. Firing his AK-47 in well-disciplined bursts of four rounds, Kroll managed to enter the courtyard with little difficulty. Yet once all the Israelis were inside the prison compound, a close-quarters battle developed in which the combatants literally fought each other eye-to-eye. In the darkness and confusion, the operators and paratroopers displayed remarkable marksmanship skills. In all, eighteen Palestinians were killed in the attack on *Ahuva 2*, and most of the buildings surrounding the base were destroyed in thundering explosions. Lieutenant Colonel Shaham's force was unscathed.

The attack on *Ahuva 1* by Lieutenant Colonel Shahak's Na'ha'l paratroopers was completed without incident. Its defenders had fled at the first sound of gunfire, and Shahak's force was afforded enough time to sift though the files and empty their contents in kitbags brought along for such a scenario, before sappers placed their explosive charges at strategic points throughout the area and then demolished the base.

Having encountered heavy seas and difficult terrain, Lieutenant Colonel Yitzhak Mordechai's attack on the Nahar al-Bard camp did not begin until 01:24 hours. His force entered their target, *Geulah 1,* after silently eliminating the base's two sentries and destroying the gate with Bangalore torpedoes. Surprise was total, and the fire-fight was quick and decisive. The elite el-Fatah frogmen chose to flee rather than fight and Mordechai's twenty-four paratroopers were able to seize the base and destroy it. Dozens of files, maps, plans, and photographs were seized and placed in secure waterproof pouches. After a quick head-count, the force withdrew to its rendezvous point to await their helicopter ride back to Israel.

Major Rubin's mixed forces of paratroopers and naval commandos had been lying in wait in a citrus grove near their target, *Geulah 2,* awaiting the order to attack. When shots rang out from the nearby el-Fatah naval base, they swung into action. The Popular Struggle Front's office building was surrounded by a stone wall, which was dealt with by a satchel charge. The explosion not only breached the wall, but destroyed a heavily armed jeep in the courtyard and killed three terrorists. As Major Rubin's force cleared the area of terrorists, a small naval commando detachment commanded by Lieutenant Commander Ilan Egozi came under heavy RPK fire from a first-floor window. One of Lieutenant Commander Egozi's men threw a fragmentation grenade at the window, but the grenade hit the window's bars and rolled down back among the naval commandos. Instinctively, Egozi first tried to kick the grenade away; then he made an attempt to reach for it and throw it far from the task force. Tragically, the grenade exploded, resulting in the loss of his right hand and eye. Four others were wounded by the grenade. Although seriously hurt, Lieutenant Egozi continued to give orders and calmly told the medic tending to his wounds to finish his mission before wasting time on him. After killing a total of seven terrorists, the office was razed to the ground.

Major Rubin frantically requested a doctor for Lieutenant Commander Egozi, who was lying in a puddle of mud, losing blood rapidly. A tourniquet was applied, as were massive doses of liquids administered through an intravenous drip. To keep their beloved officer warm, paratroopers and naval commandos alike shed their blouses, draping them over Lieutenant Commander Egozi's shivering body. For his bravery and self-sacrifice, Lieutenant Commander Egozi was awarded the *I'tur Ha'oz*, his second decoration in four years, in a military that rarely awards its heroes with ribbons and accolades. Sane minds would have thought that Egozi would have retired from active duty following his debilitating wounds and retired to a quiet life away from the military, but the IDF/Navy and the flotilla were in his blood—they were part of his psyche and persona. He remained with the IDF/Navy and the flotilla in a support capacity for the next fifteen years.

The final objective of the raid, *Geulah 3* was carried out by the Flotilla 13 contingent commanded by Lieutenant Commander Shefi and his team of operators. The force had moved silently through the brush, walking with what operators call "the cross-eyed waltz" (one eye peering down on the ground to make sure that the commando did not step on a twig or branch that would make a telltale sound and one eye motioning in a 180-degree span in search of enemy soldiers). Following a brisk forced march in which the operators slinked through the groves and roadside with stealth and incredible speed, the operators reached the staging area a few dozen meters in front of the base and commenced their attack. The point man took down a PFLP sentry with an accurate burst of 9mm fire from a silenced Uzi 9mm submachine gun; the shot to the head removing the *Kefiyeh* and much of the head of the unknowing Palestinian guard. With an obstacle removed, the commandos entered the compound and quickly seized control of the facility following a brief engagement. After a thorough search of the area for anything of intelligence value, the complex was destroyed. No casualties were sustained.

The paratroopers were evacuated by Super Frelon and CH-53 helicopters, while the commandos of Flotilla 13 returned to the waiting missile boats for the trip back to Israel. A'man estimated that thirty-seven terrorists were killed during Operation Hood 54-55, and approximately sixty-five were seriously wounded. Five terrorist bases had been totally destroyed, another two seriously damaged. Of the seven separate IDF attack forces, only eight suffered serious wounds. It was Colonel Yairi's first operation as commander of the 35th Paratroop Brigade, and it was a striking success. A souvenir which Colonel Yairi carried with him from the battle was an AK-47, taken from a dead terrorist. He would carry that weapon into many a future battle, and to his death two years later, leading the rescue operation against seaborne Black September terrorists, naval operators of a completely different sort, who seized Tel Aviv's Savoy Hotel in March 1975.

For the flotilla, the raid marked the end of an era—the loss of Egozi was a bitter blow to morale and to the feeling of invincibility that many of the younger operators possessed. To many in the unit, he was a symbol of perseverance and courage that could not be replicated or replaced. Many operators in the unit, in fact, remained in the unit only to be able to serve one day under Egozi when he became Flotilla 13 commander. Here was an operator who endured the hell of an Egyptian prison only to return to active duty and return to operations against the Egyptian military. He was an officer who, despite his suffering and lingering wounds endured at the hands of his sadistic interrogators, managed to swallow his fears and fight like the devil on operations deep behind enemy lines. On Green Island, he proved his mettle; in Tripoli, even though critically hurt, he cared less for himself than the welfare of his men and the execution of the mission. Bringing Egozi down was like striking down an icon, and his absence was seriously felt within the ranks. The loss of Egozi from the unit marked to many the true end of the "Almog era." Almog, the symbol of leadership and authority, was in Sharm el Sheikh in the Red Sea. His protégé, Lieutenant Ayalon—the Medal of Valor winner who personified the future of the unit to many of the men—was also in the Red Sea, commanding a squadron of Dabur patrol boats. Egozi, the heart and soul of the unit, many would say, was fighting for his life in a hospital bed near Tel Aviv. A true golden period had ended.

Militarily speaking, the raid on Tripoli was seen as a smashing success and a precedent—targets deep inside Lebanon were now not so removed from Israeli "treatment." It also sparked the imagination of many inside the halls of IDF HQ that bigger and more audacious operations were possible. More audacious meant only one thing—the "Paris of the Mediterranean." Beirut.

The IDF had already been to Beirut in spectacular fashion in December 1968, when the joint Sayeret Mat'kal/ *Sayeret Tzanhanim* task force was flown to the tarmac of Beirut International Airport to blow up thirteen Lebanese airliners in retaliation for that airport being a staging ground for terrorists heading to Europe to hijack and attack El Al airliners. "Operation Gift," as the raid was known, was truly a bold statement of a nation's resolve, as well as a TNT-inspired display of its innovative military abilities, but the Beirut of 1968 was not the Beirut of 1973. In 1968, Palestinian terrorists were an enigmatic presence in the Lebanese capital. They used the nation's airports, airlines, and facilities to mount attacks in Europe, but the Lebanese government, and its army and Gendarmerie, still controlled the streets. The Lebanese military and police were a small and ineffective force whose main concern was skimming payoffs made by casino owners, hashish smugglers, and wealthy Saudi and Gulf State businessmen involved in everything from vehicle thefts to white slavery. Fighting terrorism—and fighting the Israelis—was far beyond their abilities and desired agendas. By 1973, however, armed men wearing lizard-pattern camouflage fatigues and brandishing AK-47s became as much a part of the Beirut landscape as the high-fashion boutiques on the high-rent Aîn el-Mraisse and almond-eyed beauties roasting their olive skin on the flourlike sands of Dove Beach. The Palestinian factions moved into Lebanon—lock, stock, and barrel—following the Jordanian Civil War, and they brought with them all of their equipment and ammunition. The Lebanese Army was no match for the Fedayeen, and Beirut was an armed camp. Lebanon in 1973 was a different country. It was under new management.

By the spring of 1973, Lebanon became the one place on the planet where many in the Palestinian leadership felt safe. In Rome, Paris, London, and Athens, terrorist leaders were turning up dead. Seeing their comrades getting peppered by .22 fusillades or being blown up by booby-trapped telephone receivers had a sobering effect on the men who had planned and ordered the Munich Olympics Massacre. Indeed, the long arm of the Mossad had stretched far and wide, and most of the men on Prime Minister Meir's "hit list" had been eliminated. But as long as the list was not complete, revenge for Munich would be incomplete and barren. A raid on Beirut, Prime Minister Meir and Defense Minister Moshe Dayan concluded, would punish those responsible for Munich as well as light a fire for all the terrorists to see from their safe houses and heavily fortified camps: "Kill Israelis—and we will hunt you down wherever and whenever we choose!"

Initially, the raid on Beirut had not been intended to be a large-scale selective "hit" but merely a routine commando assault. As early as January 1973, there were reports of an el-Fatah explosives factory in southern Beirut, near the Sabra refugee camp in the el-Ouzai section of the city. The development of an indigenous Palestinian weapons manufacturing capability had ominous significance for the Israelis. Fifty years earlier, it had been the Jews' own minuscule weapons-producing industry that had been an important steppingstone on the road toward independence. It was rightly felt that the small factory in Beirut had historical similarities too close to ignore. The IDF General Staff had originally ordered Lieutenant Colonel Barak's Sayeret Mat'kal to carry out the raid, but they soon found themselves in stiff competition with Commander Shaul Ziv, who urged a central task for the flotilla. After bitter infighting uncharacteristic of even the IDF special operations planning and execution, persistence paid off, and the raid was given to Flotilla 13. It was considered a routine operation, but as the scope of the IDF venture on Beirut expanded, the raid on the munitions plant seemed less spectacular and more diversionary in nature. Nevertheless, the unit trained for the operation as it did under Almog's command—planning on a model, then incessant training in the water and inside the classroom. Beirut was the main topic of conversation at the Chief Paratroop and Infantry Officer HQ, as well. Brigadier General Shaked had long urged the General Staff to sanction a policy of hitting the terrorists in their "hearts and minds," spending many a sleepless night conjuring up contingency plans for such an eventuality. The success of the reported Mossad hit teams throughout Europe made it inevitable that the IDF's elite units would emulate them. The green light for an IDF "selective elimination" operation initiated numerous zealous ideas, including one by Lieutenant Colonel Shmuel Pressberger, the deputy chief paratroop and infantry officer, who had toyed with the idea of eliminating Yasir Arafat once and for all.

While PLO Chairman Arafat and PFLP warlord George Habash remained elusive targets, two "interesting addresses" in Beirut were discovered. One house, in the Rue Khartoum, was a seven-story headquarters and living facility for 170 terrorists of Nayif Hawatmeh's Democratic Front for the Liberation of Palestine (DFLP). The second address, two adjacent apartment blocks in Rue Verdun in the exclusive Ramlat el-Bida section of Beirut, was home to three of Black September's top leaders: Mohammed Najer (known by his *nom de guerre* of Abu Yusef), the el-Fatah operations and intelligence chief for worldwide terrorist attacks, as well as one of the leaders of Black September and planner of the September Munich Massacre; Kamal A'dwan, a senior el-Fatah officer, who was responsible for running terrorist cells in the West Bank and Gaza Strip; and

Samuel M. Katz

Kamal Nasser, the PLO's spokesman and a high-ranking Black September officer. This timely information brought new life to the prospects of a foray into the Lebanese capital.

In Israel, three death warrants had been signed!

Training for the raid into Beirut was attended to in fastidious fashion. This was to be the IDF's largest and most important commando raid in her twenty-five-year history, and nothing was left to chance. Many officers felt that since the IDF was attacking Beirut anyway, simultaneous attacks against other targets would prove economically as well as militarily necessary. The raid on Beirut expanded into a large, well-thought-out operation, once again encompassing joint IDF, IAF, and Navy cooperation. In March 1973, the IDF's computer came up with the mission's code name: "Operation Spring of Youth."

"Operation Spring of Youth" consisted of four primary objectives and one diversionary objective. The targets and executors, in order of mission importance, were:

- "Avivah," the assassination of Abu Yusef (the el-Fatah officer whom Flotilla 13 had failed to locate several years earlier in Lebanon), Kamal A'dwan, and Kamal Nasser by Lieutenant Colonel Ehud Barak's ubiquitous force of Mat'kal commandos
- "Gilah," the destruction of the DFLP's apartment complex in Rue Khartoum by Lieutenant Colonel Amnon Shahak and a force from *Sayeret Tzanhanim*
- "Vardah," the destruction of el-Fatah's headquarters responsible for the West Bank and Gaza, as well as the explosives factory at el-Ouzai by Flotilla 13
- "Tzilah," the destruction of a major el-Fatah ammunition dump located just north of Beirut's port, by operators from Flotilla 13 commanded by Lieutenant Commander Shefi, under the overall command, however, of Colonel Shmuel Pressberger
- "Yehudit," the diversionary raid against an el-Fatah ammunition dump north of Sidon by a force from

THE NIGHT RAIDERS

Sayeret Tzanhanim led by Lieutenant Colonel Amos Yaron.

"Operation Spring of Youth" was a gamble with fatal consequences. Should anything go wrong, the five separate forces would find themselves alone, far from friendly borders, and with little chance of returning home to Israel alive. In fact, Brigadier General Shaked was given authorization for the raid by Prime Minister Golda Meir only after he had promised her that "all the boys would come home."

Besides the essential pre-operation training, great attention was paid to familiarizing the volunteer force with Beirut's distinct geography. This was three years before Israel's friendship with Lebanon's Christians, and survival depended wholly on the commandos' wits, preparation, and proficiency. Brigadier General Shaked made it a point personally to quiz his fighters about street names, intersections, and local landmarks. A wall map of Beirut became the "Bible" for many soldiers during the month of March, and within a matter of weeks Beirut became as familiar as downtown Tel Aviv or Jerusalem. Military training was initiated at an intense pace. Models of each objective were constructed, and assault procedures were perfected to split-second timing, as well as the commander's own high standard of perfection.

Lieutenant Colonel Barak opted to train his unit in more realistic surroundings. In Tel Aviv's upper-class Lamed suburbs, Barak found a luxury high-rise apartment complex under construction that closely resembled *"Avivah,"* the houses in Rue Verdun. Without notifying the local police patrols, Barak's force landed on a nearby Tel Aviv beach from Zodiac craft and proceeded by automobile to their target—exactly as had been planned for the raid. Dressed in civilian clothes, the commandos perfected their assault techniques on the buildings, oblivious to their immediate environs. Many of Lamed's residents became frightened by the sight of armed men doing "strange things" in their peaceful neighborhood, and they summoned the police. Patrol cars were called in, and the night sergeant on duty was not appeased by Lieutenant Colonel Barak's tight-lipped refusal to explain the situation. After receiving orders from HQ to leave the site immediately, the now curious policemen left frustrated. Barak was then allowed to resume the training unhindered. So important was the *"Avivah"* objective that both Chief of Staff Elazar and Brigadier General Shaked took part in the training, in order to familiarize themselves with the intricacies of the operation.

Since the assassinations would entail a covert infiltration into a civilian housing complex, the Mat'kal commandos were ordered to wear civilian clothes, one size too large, in order to accommodate their ammunition belts underneath. During the first days of April 1973, dozens of commandos went on shopping trips throughout Tel Aviv to purchase their Beirut wardrobe. In one trendy Tel Aviv boutique, Barak and Shahak had to argue with a salesman, who insisted that their purchases were the wrong size. Undaunted, Barak and Shahak continued their shopping spree, buying women's dresses, impressive-size brassieres, and blond wigs!

On April 1, 1973, a thirty-five-year-old Belgian named Gilbert Rimbaud checked into Beirut's Sands Hotel, "in need of a few days' rest," as did a German tourist, Dieter Altnuder. The two men appeared not to know each other and they proceeded toward their sea-view rooms ignorant of each other's existence. Both took separate long walks into the city and night strolls along the Beirut coastline, and Altnuder enjoyed a particular nighttime hobby, fishing off Beirut's isolated Dove Beach. On April 6, the Sands Hotel received three new guests: two Englishmen, Andrew Whichelaw and George Elder, as well as Charles Boussaed, a Belgian national. These "tourists" were also quite interested in the beach, although their mannerisms, habits and *naïveté* aroused little suspicion. On that same day, a man named Andrew Macy with a British passport checked into the city's Atlantic Hotel. Uncharacteristic of the British, he was a good tipper, but he fitted back into character when asking about the weather thrice daily. All six men made extensive walking and driving tours throughout the city although concentrating in and around Rue Verdun and Rue

Khartoum. They rented strong and sturdy automobiles (three Buick Skylarks, one Plymouth station wagon, one Valiant, and one Renault 16), and appeared to be enjoying the as yet soft life of spring in Beirut. These tourists were, of course, seasoned Mossad agents, sent into the Lebanese capital to make the final preparations for the raid.

On the morning of April 9, an armada of nine IDF/Navy missile boats and two Dabur patrol craft left Haifa harbor bound for Beirut while two missile boats, the I.N.S. *Mivtah* and *Ga'ash*, ferried Lieutenant Colonel Amos Yaron's *Sayeret Tzanhanim* force to Sidon. The disposition of forces was as follows: the I.N.S. *Herev, Eilat, Misgav*, and *Sufah* brought Barak's, Shahak's, and Ziv's forces just off the el-Ouzai section. The I.N.S. *Miznak* and *Sa'ar* positioned Brigadier General Shaked's command group, plus a paratroop "rescue" force, off the Beirut coast, while the I.N.S. *Akko* brought Lieutenant Colonel Pressberger, Lieutenant Commander Shefi, and the operators of Flotilla 13 to Beirut's north. The fleet's radar had been turned off, and strict radio silence was observed. At 21:00 hours, the pre-civil-war Beirut skyline became impressively clear. The gray Zodiac craft were lowered into the water, and Brigadier General Shaked radioed Chief of Staff Elazar on a secure frequency. "We've arrived!"

The operation was brilliantly coordinated, allowing each objective to be executed separately, and in order of importance. The first to go into action were Lieutenant Colonel Barak's commandos. A few seconds before midnight, a small force of flotilla operators lowered their twelve Zodiacs into the choppy Mediterranean surf for the quick ride to the fashionable Dove Beach, where task forces *"Avivah"* and *"Gilah"* (Barak's and Shahak's men) were to land and meet the Mossad agents and their small fleet of rented vehicles. Following a brief exchange between the operators and the intelligence operatives, the force split into two, and three cars headed toward Rue Verdun, while the remaining three made their way to Rue Khartoum. The force of frogmen, their AK-47s hidden underneath field jackets, secured the beach in a covert and unobtrusive manner. Their mission was difficult and unnerving. While not participating in any of the direct fighting, they had to remain calm and cool while only imagining what was happening in the various targeted locations. Yet their safeguarding the landing zone permitted the task force a return to the missile boats, and it was to be defended at all costs. It was a difficult task and the chances for being discovered were high. It was one of those fine nights in the Lebanese capital that many of the operators had read about in Middle Eastern romance novels. A crisp chill in the air, the smell of fried falafel and coriander, the mesmerizing lights of a capital at play, and the hypnotic cadence of music emanating out of bars, casinos, and brothels. The Lebanese Gendarmes were out in force because of a series of student riots, which had plagued the city only days earlier, and also to ensure that the city's nightlife, the establishments that paid the Gendarmerie's second salary in kickbacks and bribes, was well protected from the civil unrest.

At 01:29 hours on April 10, Lieutenant Colonel Barak's task force left their cars just off Rue Verdun, near the Iraqi Consulate. The commandos carried a wide assortment of silenced weapons, Beretta .22-caliber MAC-10 submachine guns (a deniable weapon because it was politically prudent for Israel to deny any official visit to the Lebanese capital) all hidden beneath their sweaters, blouses, and blazers. Each hit team also carried suitcases full of explosive charges to be used for destroying the doors to three apartments, and to carry back documents found in the flats. The commandos wore civilian clothes except for their commander. The ever-innovative Barak was dressed in drag, complete with a blond wig and "impressive" false breasts. To complete their deception, Lieutenant Colonel Barak walked "arm and arm," romantically enthralled with Major Muki Betzer, both of whom entered the building first to make sure all was clear. While a small force remained outside the apartment block as cover, the hit squads entered the building.

The first slated for execution was "Abu Yusef." Majors Muki Betzer and "Yoni" Netanyahu, plus two other operators, raced up the six flights of stairs and reached "Abu Yusef's" apartment unnoticed. After breaching the door with an explosive charge, the five-room luxury apartment was searched. In the bedroom, "Abu Yusef" was found attempting to reach his AK-47, while his wife, Maha, tried to shield her husband from the inevitable. A twenty-round burst from Major Netanyahu's silenced Uzi killed them instantly. Following a thorough search of the flat for documents, the force headed back down the stairs toward the street.

Seconds later, the other two teams burst into action in the adjacent building. Kamal A'dwan's second-floor apartment was breached by a sharp kick, and he was found hiding behind the window curtain, firing his AK-47. He managed to wound one of the commandos, but he was eventually killed by a burst to his head and chest. His wife and two children, standing terrified in a nearby room, were left unharmed. Three suitcases filled with documents were retrieved from his flat.

Kamal Nasser was found sitting at his desk, writing a speech to be given the following day. Although a fully loaded Kalashnikov was against the wall, Nasser made little attempt to resist. Two magazine loads were sprayed into his body, and the PLO's spokesman was silenced permanently. Other team members searched the apartment and took away the papers.

Outside in Rue Verdun, things began to heat up. Lieutenant Colonel Barak's men were busy engaging a Lebanese Gendarme Land-Rover patrol, and in a quick exchange of fire its three occupants were killed. A second Land-Rover appeared seconds later, but it, too, was silenced by heavy machine-gun and grenade fire. Throughout the operation, the commandos' American-made MAC-10 proved a big disappointment. In engaging the Lebanese Gendarmes, the MAC-10 proved inaccurate at ranges as short as fifteen meters, forcing the commandos to allow the Lebanese to get dangerously close.

The entire operation at Rue Verdun lasted twenty-nine minutes. En route to the shore, a mere 200-meter trip, the commandos saw numerous Gendarme Land-Rovers heading toward Rue Verdun, but no attention was paid to their movement. The descent to the beach was made in such haste that one of the commandos left a suitcase filled with documents in the abandoned car. Lieutenant Colonel Barak did not allow him to retrieve the "merchandise," concentrating the unit's efforts in reaching the safety of the missile boats offshore. Minutes after Barak signaled the missile-boat fleet with his flashlight, six Zodiacs appeared from the darkness and carried the relieved fighters to safety.

Lieutenant Colonel Shahak and his force reached Target *"Gilah"* five minutes before schedule, established a command post in a nearby street, and made last-minute checks on their weapons and explosives. The twelve reconnaissance paratroopers and one naval commando officer under Shahak's command had been dressed in a wide variety of civilian clothing, ranging from that of well-dressed sophisticates to casually dressed hippies. The force was split into four teams of two, plus a command force consisting of Shahak, the team's medical officer, and, it is reported, the observing Mossad agents. Each team had one Motorola walkie-talkie, and each fighter carried a silenced weapon. At Shahak's signal, the four teams headed for the DFLP HQ.

The first team, which consisted of Avidea Shor and Hagai Ma'ayan, was dressed as European hippies and succeeded in approaching the target without arousing the suspicion of its four DFLP defenders. Shor pulled a cigarette out of his pocket, and in English he asked one of the gunmen for a light. Seconds later, the two DFLP gunmen were dead, hit in the head with well-placed .22-caliber bursts. Before dying, one of the gunmen managed to yell, *"Ya Allah!"* ("Oh God!"). Then DFLP guards arrived manning a Degtyarev 12.7mm heavy machine gun. They opened up on the two Israelis. Avidea Shor was killed instantly, and Ma'ayan was seriously wounded. Shahak received word of the operation's bad start and ordered the force into immediate action.

Within seconds, the house in Rue Khartoum was jumping and exploding to the sounds of automatic rifle fire. The Israelis were at a great firepower disadvantage, although they succeeded in getting into the building. While the cover force pinned down many of the DFLP gunmen firing from the building's windows, the attackers set off smoke-grenade canisters on the staircases, forcing the defenders to come down to street level by elevator. Foolishly, many did so only to be met by murderous Israeli fire. Not one DFLP gunman reached ground level alive by elevator—they were all cut down as its doors swung open. Nevertheless, the Palestinians put up a stiff resistance. They poured heavy and accurate AK-47 fire into the Israeli firing positions, as well as throwing numerous anti-personnel and anti-tank grenades down onto the street. Shahak responded with rifle-grenades fired into the building, causing thunderous explosions. Hundreds of residents in Rue Khartoum watched the fire-fight in awe from their balconies, snacking on figs and drinking tea with mint leaves.

The battle in Rue Khartoum was fierce, and hard fought. After five minutes, the Israelis had one dead and two wounded. One of the wounded, Yigal Pressler, was almost brought to safety by A., the force's naval commando. A DFLP gunman mistook Pressler for a wounded comrade about to be taken prisoner by the Israelis and whisked him off A.'s back. A vicious hand-to-hand battle followed, while Pressler tried in vain to summon Shahak with his Motorola, which had taken a 7.62mm round. With two fingers, A. pulled the magazine out of the gunman's AK-47 and managed then to retrieve Pressler's Uzi submachine gun. With the initiative lost, the DFLP gunman ran in panic.

Under heavy fire, the sappers prepared the 100 kilograms of explosives along the support pillars of the DFLP building. Under the cover of grenades and boxes of nails thrown onto the street, the force made its hasty withdrawal. Three minutes later, the DFLP HQ existed no longer.

The thunderous blast covered the withdrawal, diverting attention from the force assembling at Dove Beach for the short trip back to the missile boats. The entire operation had lasted thirty minutes and resulted in thirty DFLP killed. The Israelis lost two dead and three wounded, including Pressler, who was evacuated by helicopter for the quick ride back to an Israeli trauma team and the end to any official deniability by the State of Israel for launching the Beirut raid.

While the battle in Rue Khartoum was in full swing, Brigadier General Shaked ordered the flotilla operators into action. This was a brilliant stroke, confusing the Lebanese and Palestinian authorities about where the main burst of the attack lay. At 01:40 hours, on April 10, Commander Ziv's force reached the explosives factory at el-Ouzai, initiating the attack on Objective *"Vardah."* The objective, in fact, was split into two distinct components—*"Vardah A"* was an office used by Abu Hassan, one of the el-Fatah and Black September leaders, to direct attacks and intelligence-gathering efforts in the Gaza Strip. The destruction of the office, led by Lieutenant Commander Kroll, consisted of a force of fifteen frogmen from the "underwater" section of the unit, and they were under strict orders to make sure that their objective was empty of civilians before they engineered its ultimate destruction. As a result, the building had to be purified first before being prepared for demolition. To reach the building, standing near the munitions plant just overlooking the pier, the operators brought with them an indigenously designed collapsible ladder. The first man up the ladder, as was often the case, was Yisrael Asaf. With a flashlight attached to his AK-47, he slinked into the building to discover a Palestinian sentry. Three seconds and five rounds later, the sentry was eliminated, but the gunfire alerted additional Palestinian manpower. Peering through the sights of their weapons, the frogmen had little difficulty in spraying dead-on bursts of 7.62mm fire at the Black September gunmen, and soon they discovered that more than seven terrorists were dead. The building was readied with dynamite and razed to the ground.

Objective *"Vardah B,"* the destruction of the munitions plant, was tasked to Lieutenant Commander Eli Marek, commander of the Flotilla 13 boat section. A brief encounter with several armed Palestinian sentries ended without incident (to the Israelis, that is), and destroying an indigenously built Opel Accord armored car with a mounted RPG, the naval commandos set their charges in both installations and withdrew. Commander Ziv's intensive preparations had been well worth the effort. The naval commandos had been the last force to go into action and were the first back on the missile boats.

The attack on the el-Fatah ammunition dump north of Beirut harbor was also carried out without incident. Lieutenant Commander Kroll's force had been ferried to the mouth of the harbor by a Dabur patrol craft. While the conscript seamen nervously manned their 20mm Oerlikon cannon, the frogmen slipped into the water and swam the short distance. Soon a shattering explosion was heard and *all* the frogmen returned to the Dabur.

Lieutenant Colonel Amos Yaron's diversionary attack north of Sidon had also been executed brilliantly. They laid ambush to the Sidon–Beirut highway, poured nails over the road, and prevented any Palestinian reinforcements from reaching the capital. After destroying the ammunition dump, the force received its withdrawal order and returned to ship. No Israeli casualties were suffered.

Chief of Staff Elazar and Defense Minister Dayan were overcome with joy following the force's return to their home base of Haifa the following morning. Brigadier General Shaked had been saddened by the loss of two of his men and refused to partake in the post-mission press conference. Nevertheless, Lieutenant Colonel Barak's entire unit was awarded citations by Lieutenant General Elazar, and the other participants all received honorable mentions. For Israel, "Operation Spring of Youth" had been a remarkable victory, and one of the IDF's most audacious overt operations.

"Operation Spring of Youth" was the culmination of Israel's obsessive search for vengeance following the Munich Olympics Massacre. For almost a year, the entire Israeli defense and security apparatus had been mobilized for the destruction of the Black September international network. While their efforts had been impressively successful, and Black September had indeed been crippled beyond repair, Israel's immediate security concerns had also been crippled. The quest for revenge had so massively drained her intelligence capabilities that the threat from conventional enemies had been dangerously overlooked. A Mossad error in Norway in which an innocent waiter had been killed instead of the notorious Ali Hassan Salameh (the infamous "Red Prince," eventually assassinated in Beirut in 1979), had caused the Defense and Foreign Ministries to lose faith in its reports, while A'man had been tapped dry, assisting the special operations capabilities campaign against terrorism. Against this dangerous labyrinth of negligence, the success of the elite units in special operations had peaked in an aura of overconfidence and invincibility, born in the aftermath of the 1967 victory. Israel would pay a dear price for its poor judgment six months later on that day in Judaism when man and Creator settle all scores: Yom Kippur.

From his office overlooking the terrific blue waters of the Red Sea at Sharm el Sheikh, Captain Almog had known of the intense planning and preparation behind "Operation Spring of Youth," though he was somewhat disappointed not to be a part of it. After all, he had been to Beirut fifteen years earlier on a much smaller mission and was eager to see the city under very different circumstances. Sharm el Sheikh was as far removed from the war against terrorism as could possibly be found in Israel. Already a tourist hot spot, nude sunbathers from Europe and North America flocked to the sandy white beaches and energetic coral offerings. Bedouins sold hashish along the beachfront sleeping encampments, and a spirit of a far-removed paradise permeated for both Israeli and foreign tourists seeking a sun-drenched escape from life. Military service at Sharm el Sheikh was considered a reward—almost like winning the lottery. Sail by day, party by night, and for the reservists, this was a chance to be far from home and close to young women under an aura of free love, beer, and a paradise-like setting.

Almog, however, saw the true value of the area far beyond the free-flowing liquor and the eye-popping display of naked breasts. Should there be a next war between Israel and Egypt—and it was only a matter of when—along the Red Sea, Gulf of Suez, and Suez Canal, Sharm el Sheikh and the entire area would be a strategic ground zero.

Israeli naval assets in the area were small and unobtrusive. Several small squadrons of Dabur patrol craft were armed with nothing heavier than the World War II–era 20mm Oerlikon. The Dabur was a moderately fast ship ideal for counter-terrorist and patrol work, but it was not the type of ship that anyone would want when picking a fight with a missile boat or corvette. Augmenting this mighty Israeli naval presence were several landing craft, U.S. Army World War II–surplus LSTs; they were armed with 20mm Oerlikons and .50-caliber machine guns. With this massive naval might, Captain Almog was tasked with securing one of the largest and most important naval fronts in the IDF's overall scheme of things. Israel's Red Sea shipping, including its life-maintaining oil shipments from Iran, hinged on keeping the sea lanes open. Much of Israel's Sinai army was vulnerable to attack from the sea by Egyptian seaborne commandos or missile boats firing their Styx SSMs into strategic shoreline positions. A massive Israel Air Force network of Hawk surface-to-air missile batteries in Ras Sudr, a linchpin in Israel's defense of Sinai, was there for the taking to any Egyptian naval presence that was smart enough to attack it. From Port Said at the northern mouth of the canal in the Mediterranean to the Gulf of Suez and the Red Sea in the south, Israel's ability to hold Sinai was interlocked with Egypt's ability to gain control of the waterways. Unfortunately for Almog, two Sa'ar-4 missile boats, the first to be manufactured by Israel Shipyards, were *supposed to* have set sail from Haifa to Sharm el Sheikh (via the Horn of Africa) on October 15, 1973.

Captain Almog knew his responsibilities were not easy, and he realized that if war erupted, the General Staff would realize that Israeli naval assets in the theater were negligently inadequate. Plus, in the middle of a war, it would be impossible to send a missile boat sailing around the Horn of Africa to make it in time to participate in any of the fighting. Almog's plans and calculations, however, didn't anticipate Egypt catching the IDF by surprise. That would make a defensive—let alone offensive—campaign all the more difficult.

Egypt—and Syria—did indeed launch a surprise attack against Israel on the holiest day in Judaism: Yom Kippur, October 6, 1973, at 14:00 hours on a sunny and eerily calm Saturday afternoon. The intelligence services of the State of

Israel, the soldiers and spies who had performed so brilliantly in laying the groundwork for the surprise Israeli attack in 1967, failed with incredible inability to predict the war preparations of both Egypt and Syria. Perhaps it was that the Israelis had grown too cocky and arrogant for their own good, perhaps too much of the Israeli defense and intelligence community was mobilized for the fight against terrorism—both inside the Middle East and beyond. Whatever the reason, the breakdown was complete. Israeli warning of the impending attack was limited to hours, instead of days, and very few front-line units, mainly green conscript forces relieving reservist formations for the holiday leave, would soon be attacked by divisions of men and armor that had been preparing for an unforgiving assault of Arab revenge for well over two years. The subsequent surprise attack, one of the most complete in modern military history, overwhelmed Israeli defenses. Atop the Golan Heights, Israeli armored companies were smashed by attacking hordes of Syrian T-55s and T-62s. In the Sinai Desert, Egyptian UDT operators had disabled a medieval-like Israeli-built obstacle, a canal-long oil pipeline put in place to "ignite" should an Egyptian Zodiac ever enter the waterway en route to attacking the east bank of the canal, and water cannons, used to fight fires in most nations, were employed by the Egyptian military to obliterate Israeli sand defenses packed dozens of meters high along the banks of the canal. By late afternoon on October 6, Egyptian pontoon bridges were supporting the movement of entire divisions heading deep into Sinai.

For Israel, a military predicament more threatening than the fight-for-survival 1948 War loomed near. The Egyptian and Syrian advances were so fast and so unforgiving that on October 8, 1973, less than twenty-four-hours after the first shots were fired and the first Egyptian and Syrian shells landed on IDF positions, a panic-stricken Israeli Defense Minister Moshe Dayan, the symbol of victory in 1967, was quoted in press accounts as saying, "This is the end of the Third Temple," and he was reported to have suggested the use of Israeli nuclear missiles as a means of national last resort and desperation. The situations between the 1967

War and the 1973 War could not have been more opposite.
In fact, in another opposite between the two wars, the only
combat arm of the Israeli military that was prepared for
war, expecting it, and poised to fight back on even terms
was the IDF/Navy.

Led by Rear Admiral Telem, the IDF/Navy in 1973 was a
far cry from the destroyer-driven fleet sent into battle in
1967. It was equipped with a fleet of sleek and fast missile
attack craft, some built in Cherbourg, France (with many of
the boats spirited away in a daring part-espionage/part-
commando operation), and some built in Haifa by Israel
Shipyards. The IDF/Navy was a fast-sailing strike-first navy
that could reach most parts of the Mediterranean with
small ships that packed a punch far greater than any
destroyer, with greater maneuverability and guile than most
frigates and corvettes could muster. By October 1973, the
IDF/Navy fielded fourteen missile boats—all stationed in
the Mediterranean and working out of the ports of Haifa
(the navy's largest base and de facto operational headquarters) and Ashdod, to the south, halfway between Tel Aviv
and the Gaza Strip. Israeli naval policy was to strike at the
enemy far from the territorial waters of Israel—the best
defense was a Gabriel SSM-inspired offense. According to
one Israeli military historian, "If missile boats were launching Gabriels off the coast of Haifa, it meant that the country
was in deep shit!"[12]

On the afternoon of October 6, 1973, with the war less
than two hours old, the IDF/Navy's missile boats took its
new brand of war to the enemy. Five missile boats left the
safe confines of the sprawling naval facility in Haifa for the
trip up north toward the Syrian coast. The Syrian Navy
possessed nine Osa- and Komar-class missile boats and was
considered a most capable corps. It was led by Ba'ath-Party
loyalists, whose senior commanders were graduates from
the finest naval academies in the Warsaw Pact countries;
Israeli intelligence suspected that many of the ships were
piloted by Soviet or East German crews. The objective of
the Israeli naval task force was to shell the refinery at
Latakia and to sink enemy shipping. Contact was made at

22:58 hours, between Cyprus and the Levantine coast, between the Israeli armada and a Syrian torpedo boat on patrol. The patrol boat was first disabled by 40mm fire, then blown out of the water by a Gabriel. A Syrian minesweeper, too, entered the battle, and it was blown out of the water by a Gabriel fired by the I.N.S. *Reshef*, the newest missile boat to enter the IDF/Navy's order of battle and one built in Israel, no less.[13]

Although celebrating in their early victories and pushing due north toward Latakia, the missile boat task force had, in fact, sailed right into a Syrian ambush. As coded radio messages were dispatched back to Tel Aviv reporting the destruction of the two enemy ships, a barrage of bright orange fireballs appeared from the east. Four Styx missiles, with their warheads crammed with 500 kilograms of high explosives, were fired at the Israeli ships. None hit their targets, and in fact one was reportedly shot down by a missile boat cook manning a .50-caliber heavy machine gun. The Israelis had also invested heavily in electronic counter-measures to the Styx, a byproduct of the *Eilat* sinking. Once the missile boat commanders were sure that the Syrians had launched all their missiles, the boats were ordered into attack formation and the order of *Esh!* (Fire!) was issued to the fire controller holding the movements of the sleek Gabriel with their palms and their joysticks. The battle was one-sided and quick. By 00:40 hours on October 7, five Syrian warships, including three Osa-class missile boats, were at the bottom of the Mediterranean.

Over the course of the next two weeks, IDF/Navy missile boats waged a relentless campaign against the Syrian and Egyptian navies in which Israeli missile boat tactics—and equipment—achieved absolute victory. More than twenty Arab warships were sunk by Israeli warships during the war to not a single Israeli boat lost. The IDF/Navy's performance during the war was the one initial bright spot for the IDF in the bitter conflict.

An aspect of Israeli naval strategy, especially where its naval special warfare assets were concerned, was that sea-to-sea battles were designed not only to harm the enemy, but also, more important, to convince Arab admirals that it was prudent of them to keep their ships well protected inside harbors in Egypt and Syria. Of course, once Israeli naval intelligence determined that enemy shipping was moored inside seemingly hermetic ports, then Flotilla 13 would be ordered into action.

On October 6, 1973, Flotilla 13 consisted of more than 200 men (more when its reserves were called up) divided into the now conventionally separated frogmen, boat, and SDV units. Flotilla 13 possessed more than twenty Snunit fast insertion craft (including several being modified for remote-controlled explosive-craft operations); forty Zodiac Mk V inflatables capable of speeds in excess of twenty knots (thanks to two engines) and sturdy enough to carry up to twelve operators; and more than thirty Zodiac Mk III inflatables which were slower than the Mk Vs and could carry less men and material. The unit's technical section had also devised a small arsenal of classified gear and equipment, as well as upgrading existing material (such as the Pig and Dolphin) that enabled them to reach just about any target in the region.

That regional strategy, striking at the enemy's ability to wage the war, should have worked against the ports of Latakia and Tartus in Syria, especially since they were bustling with Soviet freighters bringing in tons of war material to replace the planes, tanks, and APCs lost on the battlefield. The strategy was attempted by Flotilla 13 at an old haunt of the unit—the Egyptian naval facility at Port Said. Following two disastrous engagements with the IDF/Navy, the Egyptian Navy's Mediterranean fleet was told to head for the safety of their home ports and to, in the words of a retired American naval officer, "Sit out the war quietly." With targets of a different variety at their disposal, Rear Admiral Telem summoned Flotilla 13's Commander Ziv to the war room at IDF HQ in the Kirya, in Tel Aviv, and authorized what would become known in the code book as "Operation Lady,"[14] an all-out unit raid on Port Said. For the Israelis fighting for dear life in northern Sinai, this was the most strategically important of enemy naval facilities. To say that Port Said was a target-rich objective was a gross understatement. It was a smorgasbord of missile boats, landing craft, and torpedo boats waiting to be blown up. However, Port Said, a failed objective of the 1967 War, was also, perhaps with the exception of President Sadat's war room, one of the most heavily defended targets in Egypt. There were P-183 torpedo boats, landing craft, torpedo boats modified to launch Katyusha rockets, and missile boats, too. There were also shore batteries consisting of 130mm and 100mm guns, and, it has been estimated, nearly 1,000 Egyptian sailors and military policemen safeguarded the base. Soldiers, armed with depth charges and grenades, chummed the water with their explosive bait hoping to send Israeli divers to the bottom in a horrible death of underwater concussion.

The Flotilla 13 battle plan called for four men, deployed on two Pigs, to reach Port Said's harbor, then sabotage as many ships as their limited supply of limpet mines would allow. It would be rough going, but if they managed to break through the enemy's defenses, they were expected to enjoy a night of destruction the likes of which the unit had never known. Unlike the classic definition of "underwater sabotage," the raid on Port Said was not meant to be a covert and publicly deniable mission. The Israelis wanted it to be loud, and they wanted the entire Egyptian defense establishment to be rocked by the fact that warships in a heavily defended port were picked off by a handful of brave men armed with nothing more than explosive charges and incredible physical and psychological stamina.

The two Pigs were to be ferried from the IDF/Navy base at Ashdod to a pre-positioned staging area along the Israeli-held coast of Sinai, and then the Pigs would set sail underwater toward the treacherous gauntlet at Port Said. The operators did not have a tremendously accurate listing of the targets to be found in Port Said, but they did know that there would be dozens of warships moored in the port and that missile boats and landing craft were to receive special attention. Pig No. 1 was piloted by First Lieutenant Oded Amiv and First Sergeant Eli Kimchi; Pig No. 2 was piloted by First Lieutenant Boaz Shakedi and First Sergeant Shayka Berman.[15] All four were experienced combatants;

several had entered the unit toward the end of the War of Attrition and had seen combat with Major General Ariel "Arik" Sharon in Gaza against Palestinian terrorists in one of the most bitterly contested counter insurgency campaigns ever waged in the Middle East. A brutal chess match of wills and firepower fought under the cloak of darkness and the guile of hunters seeking their prey.

As the two Pigs separated en route to the target, through the defensive nets and across the breakwater, they came across a military installation at the height of alertness. Egyptian sentries weren't sitting down awaiting any action—they were walking their posts with their AK-47s in hand, fingers on the triggers. Small patrol boats with powerful searchlights moved slowly through the port's murky waters in search of frogmen, and depth charges and grenades were generously tossed into the water for good measure. Incredibly, both Pigs managed to penetrate Egyptian defenses and proceed toward their targets. Pig No. 1 reached a Soviet-built landing craft and the crew began affixing limpet mines to the hull. While they were activating the timing mechanism and the locking devices, Egyptian sailors on board the landing craft, perhaps sensing intruders below, began tossing depth charges into the water. The blasts pounded the operators without mercy. "The depth-charge concussions are incredible," claims an operator still in active duty. "It's like getting hit in the midsection by a 2x4, and getting kicked in the balls by a soccer player wearing steel-tipped boots."[16]

By 04:00 hours, on October 17, 1973, Pig No. 1 departed Port Said to hook up with a Zodiac awaiting nearly ten kilometers offshore. Pig No. 2 had even greater success in locating targets within their allotted timetable, but they had missed their linkup with the Zodiac. Commander Ziv was already pacing around in the landing craft that had brought them to the departure point. The flotilla communications team, trying to raise Pig No. 2 on a secure frequency, could not reach the two operators. At 08:00 hours, already four hours late for the hookup, one of the Dabur patrol boats assigned to the "Operation Lady" task force picked up a small, though promising, radar blip near Port Said. It was too small to be a naval vessel, and there weren't any Egyptian fishermen in the water that morning. It had to be Amir and Kimchi. Shaul Ziv wasn't about to abandon two of his men in Egyptian waters without a major effort to recover them. He ordered a force of several Snunit cigarette insertion boats to fire up their engines and to enter the port along the path that Pig No. 2 took into the harbor. Racing a green-painted Cigarette boat into the heart of an enemy port, especially *following* a major sabotage strike, was nothing less than a suicide mission, but, as one operator would later comment about the type of work that the unit does, "Aren't all our endeavors suicide missions?"

The Snunit task force raced across the waves at top speed, believed in excess of forty knots, up until the first small breakwater, and they immediately found themselves the target of Egyptian 20mm cannon batteries. Egyptian fire was incessant and steady—nearly a dozen batteries were firing simultaneously, with many of the shells piercing the waves only inches from the bouncing hulls of the sleek elongated speedboats. Peering with their field glasses at possible hiding points along the breakwater and inside the port, the Snunit boats miraculously avoided Egyptian fire, but the fire was too heavy and the chance of retrieving the two operators from the barrage was not seen as promising. As the boats sped away toward the rendezvous point ten kilometers away, their withdrawal was followed by an hour-long barrage from Egyptian 130mm cannon batteries.

In the afternoon, at the low light of sunset, Commander Ziv ordered in a Zodiac team to search for Amir and Kimchi, but their efforts yielded nothing. Commander Ziv even received authorization to launch a search helicopter over the port, even though it would certainly be in the cross-hairs of Egyptian anti-aircraft gunners and the seemingly endless rows of surface-to-air missile batteries that ringed Port Said.

Pig No. 2 was lost and Amir and Kimchi remain missing in action to the time of this book's writing. Little is known about what happened to the two operators. Were they captured? Were they killed by Egyptian depth charges and cannon fire? Did the self-destruction mechanism of the Pig detonate prematurely? Yet the results of their actions are well documented. An IAF reconnaissance flight over Port Said the next day illustrated the results of "Operation Lady" to a happy General Staff—one destroyed landing craft, one seriously damaged torpedo boat, one seriously damaged patrol craft fitted with rockets, and one seriously damaged Osa-class missile boat.[17]

"Operation Lady" was the sole "known" Flotilla 13 operation in the Mediterranean during the entire 1973 Yom Kippur War. Although there were targets in Syria, Lebanon, Egypt, and points beyond in the Mediterranean Sea, Commander Shaul Ziv did not lobby for the flotilla to take part in any additional operations during the war. There was, however, another high-ranking officer who needed the services of the Batmen. His name was Captain Ze'ev Almog.

The situation in Israel's Red Sea naval theater was precarious, to say the least. The Suez Canal, Israel's one ultrastrategic buffer and bargaining chip, had been lost in the Egyptian blitzkrieg, and Egyptian forces consolidated their power along the narrow waterway from the Mediterranean to the south and the Gulf of Suez. One of the Israeli Bar-Lev line outposts, known as *"Mezach"* (the Hebrew word for "Pier"), had been completely surrounded by Egyptian forces on the first day of the war, and its defenders, mainly nervous and anxious conscripts who had run out of medicine and ammunition after a few hours of fighting, were holding on for dear life, and dear life was running out second by second. Many of the other Bar-Lev line positions had been abandoned, or had surrendered, without offering up too much resistance, so the Egyptians respected the upstart Israeli defenders enough to offer them the chance to surrender, but at first the white flags were met by Israeli .50-caliber machine-gun fire to which the Egyptians returned the gesture with a twelve-hour-long artillery bombardment. The Mezach position wasn't strategically important to the Egyptians. They had bypassed it and were pushing deeper into Sinai. It was, however, a matter of honor that no pockets of Israeli soldiers remain in liberated territory.

There had been attempts by both infantry and armor units to punch a hole in the Egyptian advance and make a mad dash in order to rescue the survivors of the Mezach position, but they all failed. By October 9, after the position's defenders had held out for over seventy-two hours, the IDF/Navy commander opted to make a tactical move to rescue them—after all, the position was a naval target right on the Sinai shore opposite the Gulf of Suez, with the city of Suez to the north and the bustling Egyptian naval port of A'ardaka to the south. But agendas and objectives do not always converge on what is expediently necessary. Rear Admiral Telem had originally wanted to send operators to the Suez Canal to blow up some of the pontoon bridges that the Egyptian military were using to send men and material across the waterway. The unit tasked with that operation were the underwater sappers of Unit 707, at the time commanded by Lieutenant Commander Dov Bar, and when the bridge mission was scrubbed, Unit 707 got the call to save the men of the Mezach position in a small flotilla of Zodiac inflatables. Two Dabur patrol boats, under the command of Lieutenant Commander Ayalon, would "ride shotgun," and they would act as backup and as fast-moving ambulances to ferry the injured defenders to a medevac position at Ras Sudr. The Daburs were to sail just up the range of the Egyptian 130mm artillery batteries set up in Sinai.[18]

The operation commenced on the night of October 11. The Daburs dropped anchor and observed as the operators began their move to shore. But before they could make any progress toward the coast, Egyptian artillery shells began to rain down on the operators in midwater. With a heavy heart, Lieutenant Commander Bar was ordered by IDF Southern Command to abort the operation, and the soldiers from the Mezach position, with little choice other than to surrender and live or to be overrun and die, opted to accept surrender.

The Gulf of Suez and the entire area from Suez city south to Sharm el Sheikh was a precarious front for regional commander Almog. Shedwan Island, a small and seemingly innocuous position on the gulf's southeast corner, was well within Egyptian control and was viewed as a convenient piece of camouflage which the fleet Komar missile boats based at A'ardaka could use as radar cover when launching hit-and-run strikes against Israeli naval assets in the area. A'ardaka was forty kilometers from Shedwan Island, and the small and unobtrusive isle was the limit of the coverage afforded by the Egyptian surface-to-air missile umbrella. There were reasons to fear an Egyptian missile ambush. One of the top-secret operational plans on the IDF's attack book, in preparation for the next war with Egypt, was a large-scale amphibious landing, one involving hundreds of troops and dozens of armored fighting vehicles, to the Egyptian mainland. There were two versions of the landing plan: the first version, the more special-forces-minded, involved a battalion-size assault involving commandos and T-54/T-55 tanks again disguised as Egyptian armor; the second version, favored by most armored generals, called for a force of "regular" tanks to land somewhere on the coast. The I.N.S. *Bat Sheva*, a Dutch-built 900-ton mining craft purchased from the South African Navy in 1968, was the IDF/Navy's largest landing craft and the pivot of its Sinai-theater naval operations. At 311 feet long and capable of holding sixteen T-54/55s, or twelve Patton or Centurion Main Battle Tanks, along with twenty-five APCs, plus 300 soldiers, the *Bat Sheva* was a slow-moving tempting target to any Egyptian fire-control officer. IDF plans were both preemptive and reactionary. In case a preemptive strike against Egypt was called for, as was the case in 1967, a landing could be a first devastating blow to Egyptian morale. Should Egypt draw first blood and succeed in crossing the canal, the amphibious landing was seen as a iron-fist alternative to crossing the Suez Canal for the lunge into the Egyptian mainland.

Whatever the version, whatever the scenario, the operation hinged on Israeli control of the Gulf of Suez and the Red Sea area. If one Styx SSM and its 500-kilogram warhead of high explosives impacted in the center of the I.N.S. *Bat Sheva*, over 300 men could be lost. It was a risk the IDF could not take.

Keeping the Egyptian missile boats out of the water and

held up in port should have been the work of a small armada of Israeli missile boats. As Almog only had Daburs and landing craft at his disposal, "special tactics" would be employed. Captain Almog would have none of it. As a theater commander he had a semi-independent free hand at running his zone of operations as he saw fit. Almog wanted to strike against the Egyptian Red Sea fleet and hit them hard. With nothing larger than a fleet of four Dabur craft at his disposal, he realized for Israel to win the naval war in the Red Sea, he would have to rewrite the books of naval warfare and pit men against ships, though this time on a scale never before attempted in the history of naval warfare. Captain Almog requisitioned much of Flotilla 13 to Sharm el Sheikh for operations against the Egyptian Red Sea fleet. Almog's vision was for a small force of underwater operators to mount a naval campaign against an entire fleet for control over a major waterway. It had never been done before, but that didn't daunt Almog. He sat down over intelligence maps and operational charts and began putting ideas to paper. Although a conventional naval officer, Almog's blood was that of an operator, and a special forces approach to even the most conventional of military problems was part of his persona. Once he assumed command of the Red Sea theater, Almog began preparing his operational books with plans and scenarios where Flotilla 13 could be deployed. Most red circles on Almog's detailed regional map were around the port of A'ardaka, and Almog had made his ideas known to both Rear Admiral Telem and to Commander Ziv. Both, however, turned down his ideas as impractical, since the flotilla did not possess boats strong enough nor adequately armed to support a withdrawal from A'ardaka should a raid be compromised, and the operators in need of some offshore firepower to cover their withdrawal. Zodiac craft, after all, were not armed, and the Snunit carried nothing heavier than a MAG 7.62mm light machine gun, or, in a pinch, a .30-caliber or .50-caliber heavy machine gun. Over a hundred kilometers separated the IDF/Navy's Red Sea HQ at Sharm el Sheikh and A'ardaka, and traversing such a distance on a Zodiac or Snunit was considered impractical, to say the least—impossible even under ideal conditions. Plus, skeptics of Almog's plans to attack A'ardaka with operators pointed out that there weren't enough hours of darkness in a night to cover the insertion and safe extraction of a force sailing by small craft from Sharm el Sheikh. By the time the operators reached the breakwater at A'ardaka and readied their limpets for action, Egyptian gunners would be able to see the intruders in clear sunlight and simply blow them out of the water.

Even though he encountered a wall of naysayers along the way to getting the mission against the Egyptian Red Sea fleet approved, Almog knew he had time on his side. In reality, the Egyptian Red Sea fleet not only threatened any possible Israeli counterattack, but also the missile boats and support craft threatened the very precarious Israeli presence on the peninsula. Without an Israeli missile boat presence in the Gulf, and with every man capable of carrying a rifle and every aircraft capable of carrying a bomb deployed over the canal, Sharm el Sheikh became a very tempting target for a large-scale attempt by the Egyptian military to initiate a second front in Sinai. If the Egyptians had opted to attack the southern tip of Sinai and push up the coast toward Eilat, they would have encountered smooth sailing in the naval channels and little opposition inland. Based at A'ardaka, the Egyptian fleet consisted of four Komar missile boats: the rest of the fleet, nine torpedo boats, four destroyers, two submarines, a minesweeper, and dozens of other smaller warships and fishing vessels converted for military use were positioned south, down the Red Sea coast at Safaga and other ports. The Egyptians had also used air attack with great force, and from the first moments of the war, had their MiG, Sukhoi, and Tupelov fighter-bombers launch air strikes against IDF positions throughout Sinai. Egyptian special forces, commandos who, too, had gained incredibly useful combat experience during the War of Attrition, were heli-lifted deep into Sinai, and they conducted sabotage strikes against IDF rear positions. Israeli intelligence estimates placed 1,000 Egyptian commandos in Sinai during the war, and should a second front be initiated, that number would have swelled fivefold.

The only formidable defense that the Israelis maintained along the coast in Sinai was a massive and highly integrated Hawk surface-to-air missile setup at Ras-Sudr. The Hawks prevented the Egyptians from developing complete aerial superiority during the first few days of the war, and IDF Operations officers feared that an Egyptian naval commando strike against the Hawks would be mounted sometime during the conflict. The Egyptians, however, wouldn't send in their commandos unless they possessed control of the water, and that meant a full-scale deployment of their Red Sea fleet.

Until Almog summoned Flotilla 13 to the theater, Lieutenant Commander Ayalon's armada of Daburs was the only Israeli naval offensive tool in the area. Ayalon, another officer with special forces thinking entrenched in his blood, had deployed his small Daburs in a highly mobile, highly effective killing pack that routinely attacked Egyptian shipping in the area and had destroyed over a dozen Egyptian vessels in hit-and-run attacks reminiscent of a waterborne "Long Range Desert Group" of World War II fame. Even in defensive operations, Ayalon's Daburs proved to be lethal foes and innovative sailors. They ambushed dozens of Egyptian commando attempts to land forces on the coast of Sinai. Sometimes, the intercept was large-scale: landing a small LCM ferry, a commando company would suddenly find itself in the cross-hairs of a Dabur's two 20mm Oerlikon gunners and end up in a ball of flames. The Egyptian landing attempts were often covered by Soviet-built P-4 torpedo boats modified to carry eight-barreled 122mm rocket launchers. The P-4s, too, tended to catch fire quickly after several dozen 20mm rounds struck the engine room and the main fuel tanks.

The Egyptians, always wary of an Israeli ambush, thought it prudent not to dispatch their larger warships into the fray, instead relying on shore batteries for deterring fire any time a Dabur was seen on radar. The minuscule force of Daburs, incredibly, served as a deterrent and managed to relieve, at least mentally, the Egyptian stranglehold over naval operations in the Red Sea and Gulf of Suez. With the enemy apparently neutralized, Almog contended, it was time to

THE NIGHT RAIDERS

"kick them in the nuts" and paralyze them—physically and psychologically. That meant hitting their sprawling, and seemingly impregnable, base at A'ardaka.

The IAF had once toyed with the idea of taking out A'ardaka, but the base was protected by nine SA-2 and SA-3 surface-to-air missile batteries. There was a large air base only a few kilometers from A'ardaka with a force of MiG-21 interceptors that could be scrambled at a moment's notice; the aircraft enjoyed a forty-kilometer zone of free operation in the area, since they fell within the Egyptian SAM umbrella ring around the ultrastrategic port. Major General Benny Peled, the IAF commander, in fact, told Captain Almog that in his estimation it would take a hundred Israeli warplanes to attack the target—assets not available for a single mission during the chaotic days of the war.[19] The Egyptian air defenses, which provided them with an aerial umbrella forty kilometers in diameter, also meant that any naval attack against A'ardaka would have to be executed *without* the security blanket of air support. Attacking the heart of a heavily fortified enemy target by means of an underwater commando operation is one thing. Doing it without an F-4E Phantom coming to your rescue is something entirely different.

From the third day of the fighting, Almog pressed Telem for authorization of the A'ardaka raid and also pressed Telem to send the flotilla south. A large contingent of operators did fly south to Sharm el Sheikh along with Commander Ziv, but before anything would be done, the senior naval officers did what, perhaps, Israelis do best—argue. In heated discussions, between all of the navy's high-ranking officers, A'ardaka was discussed. In typical Israeli fashion, the debates were heated—sometimes nasty. According to reports, Commander Ziv opposed the A'ardaka operation, considering it far too risky, and he lobbied senior naval commanders present at Sharm el Sheikh, like Bin-Nun and Botzer, not to authorize it. In operational meetings before the war, Ziv had opposed any talk of striking A'ardaka, and his resolve was only strengthened during the conflict. His opposition to the raid influenced the other naval commanders present at the meeting, and nothing was approved. Commander Ziv left a good portion of the flotilla behind at Sharm el Sheikh and flew back to Atlit to await additional assignments for the unit, while Botzer returned to Tel Aviv.

The senior Flotilla 13 officer remaining in the Red Sea theater was Lieutenant Commander Kroll, a popular officer from Kibbutz Kfar Giladi, who enjoyed the dichotomy of command few senior officers ever get to enjoy—he was loved by his men and respected by his bosses. Captain Almog, in particular, viewed Kroll as a superior officer and a courageous combatant. As commander of the flotilla frogman section, Lieutenant Commander Kroll's mindset was that of a saboteur. A silent intruder whose only traces were to be a target obliterated by a limpet mine. Kroll viewed virtually any operation through these polarized lenses—thinking not how a mission would be executed, but rather how he would get inside the enemy port. Almog's opinion of Kroll's men was equally high. After all, he had commanded virtually all of them only two years earlier. He knew each man's first name, where he was from, and what he was likely to do on a dark night when the tracers began to fly. It was Almog's intimacy with the unit that made even contemplating an assault on A'ardaka possible. Almog knew the men and knew exactly what they were capable of. If A'ardaka was, indeed, a suicide mission, as was suggested, then Almog would have been the first to realize that the men were *not* up for the job. The operators, on the other hand, knew Almog, as well. He was a strict officer, but he had never steered the unit in the wrong direction and had never dispatched them on missions beyond the unit's true scope and abilities. "If Almog said that A'ardaka was a doable objective," an operator would later reflect, "then with closed eye and a calm heart we were confident it was, too."[20]

The operators on hand at Sharm el Sheikh were split into two groups—those who'd be attacking A'ardaka, and those who'd be participating in smaller hit-and-run operations along the canal and on both sides of the Gulf of Suez (mining Egyptian roadways on the Egyptian side and ambushing Egyptian commandos on the Israeli side). Most of the operators wanted to join up with the hit-and-run attacks, because they wanted action, and they didn't think that the IDF/Navy had the "balls" to authorize a raid on A'ardaka.

Joining Almog and the flotilla operators in Sharm el Sheikh as part of the A'ardaka task force was, remarkably, Lieutenant Commander Ilan Egozi, still nursing his near-fatal wounds from the raid on Tripoli and obviously no longer fit for combat duty. Egozi, however, remained in the navy and in the unit—he was something of a grand council, an operator would later recall, a voice of reason and brilliance that everyone could listen to.

To get authorization for the strike on A'ardaka, Almog knew that he would have to have Lieutenant Commander Kroll express his faith in the plan to senior naval officers, and he knew he would have to circumvent the traditional IDF/Navy bureaucracy; after all, the raid had more or less been killed in its pre-planning stage by Ziv's refusal. Kroll not only agreed to promote the operation, but also he was adamant about leading it personally. That left Almog with only the bureaucracy to contend with. He placed a call to IDF/Navy commander Telem, but the rear admiral was out of the office at the time and instead Almog found himself talking to Commodore Tzvi "Hershel" Tirosh, the navy's second-in-command. Commodore Tirosh was an officer receptive to new ideas and initiative, and he had known of Almog's track record in getting the job done. "Anything you recommend, I'll approve," Commodore Tirosh told a stunned Almog. "Just remember," he added, "that any raid cannot include any assistance, direct or indirect, from the air force."[21]

A'ardaka was a green light. Almog decided to act before the raid could be turned down by an act of God or some other aspect of Israeli bureaucracy and D-day was set down as October 9. The raid was code-named "Operation Collection 10."[22]

The A'ardaka inlet is long and narrow like a pencil protruding from the sea. In order to reach the entrance of the dock and the enemy ships moored along the interior pier, any intruding frogman had to swim for nearly three kilometers. Insertion was one thing. Locating, identifying, and "handling" the enemy ships was another matter com-

pletely. The dock was well protected, both from the waves
and the wind, by a line of coral islands surrounding it from
the east, and the islands also protected the port from
commando attacks since every coral reef and island was
home to several batteries of 14.5mm and 20mm heavy
machine-gun and cannon positions to blow the unknowing
frogmen out of the water. Several of the islands also boasted
batteries of 120mm mortars that could cover a 360-degree
field of fire and truly decimate any intruding group of
raiders. Patrolling the corals were Egyptian sentries armed
with assault rifles, and another element to the defensive
assets that A'ardaka possessed was the clear, translucent
waters of the Red Sea. Rough seas outside the harbor made
small boat insertions a rough endeavor; the north winds
were always pushing the surf in violent contortions, though
inside the reefs the waters were smooth and calm, and that
made any underwater movement immediately noticeable.
According to one retired U.S. Navy SEAL lieutenant commander, a veteran naval special warfare officer who trained
with both the Israelis and the Egyptians in the Red Sea,
"The stormy seas are so rough in the Red Sea at times, that
they'd make even a fisherman reach for the bucket, and the
waters in the port areas are so placid, you'd find more
turbulent water in an old man's bathtub, and the water is so
clear, a sentry would have to be blind and stupid not to see
you!"[23]

Commanding the Zodiacs was Lieutenant Commander
Eli Marik, the commander of the boat section while Lieutenant Commander Godi Kroll was in charge of the strike
force with two pairs of frogmen. Two Zodiacs, supported by
a force of Dabur patrol craft sailing shotgun, til Ras
Mohammed would infiltrate the waters near A'ardaka and
then stand at the ready while teams of frogmen entered the
water and swam a three-kilometer path toward the port
area. The operators would be equipped, ready for battle.
Limpet mines, explosives, AK-47s and Uzis, and even
RPGs. In a worst-case scenario, if they were compromised
and forced to survive on their trigger fingers and wits, the
flotilla commanders wanted to ensure that the operators
were at least equipped to stave off a massive Egyptian

manhunt. The task force was to depart Ras Mohammed, the southernmost point of the Sinai peninsula, for the ninety-kilometer stretch toward their date with the Egyptian Red Sea fleet. Many in the IDF/Navy thought that the target was too rough for even the flotilla. Many in IDF/Navy HQ didn't even believe that the operators could even *reach* their target.

At Ras Mohammed, ten kilometers south of Sharm el Sheikh, just outside the range of Egyptian coastal radar, the Daburs cut their engines and stood by as the operators entered their Zodiacs. Darkness had just fallen and the fear of a barrage of Styx missiles suddenly falling from the horizon made all the sailors a bit on edge. But observing the calm demeanor in which the flotilla operators headed toward the mission made everyone feel a bit at ease. If the operators were anxious, they didn't show it. They disappeared into the black night silently and quickly.

From his HQ, Captain Almog sat anxiously by a set of radios awaiting word from the operators about their entry into the port—reaching the target, after all, was just as much an element of the mission as was the destruction of an Egyptian warship. When several hours later, Lieutenant Commander Kroll's voice was heard over the air affirming the entry into the dock, there was almost a feeling of celebration in the HQ's cramped C^3 center. "It is possible to get there!" Almog thought to himself. "They did it." But before backs could be slapped and hands shook, Lieutenant Commander Kroll informed relayed word that the force had just noticed an Egyptian torpedo boat at the line of the entrance to the port, and that any further progress with the boats under his command would lead to their being uncovered. The underwater aspect of the operation could not proceed until the torpedo boat left the narrow waterway, and it was showing no signs of going anywhere. As the minutes ticked away, and the extraction deadline came and went, it was decided to abort the operation. Entry was just too risky. "Collection 10" was an abort. Lieutenant Commander Kroll found the decision to abort a gut-wrenching one. As a first-sergeant during the 1967 Six Day War, he had been on a scrubbed mission along the Syrian coast, and not sticking to one's target was tantamount to personal failure. Making the mission's cancellation all the more painful was the fact that as the operators awaited the departure (or disappearance) of the Egyptian torpedo boat, they observed several Zodiacs, laden with Egyptian commandos, returning to A'ardaka following an attempted commando strike against Israeli positions along the Sinai coast.

Upon their return to Sharm el Sheikh and the immediate debriefing, Lieutenant Commander Kroll was disappointed about the order to abort, but Almog reassured the officer that he shouldn't make analogies between the failed mission and the Six Day War, since here, the enemy positions prohibited the operation. This wasn't a cancellation, but rather a postponement. The operators left no trace of their presence, and the Egyptians never knew they were there. The element of surprise was still there, and the decision to return to A'ardaka was immediately made.

In Operation Collection 10, IDF/Navy commander Telem had admonished Captain Almog for dispatching a Dabur so close to the enemy base "as an act of incredible negligence." The Zodiacs had run out of fuel and Almog, vowing never to abandon men in the field, simply towed the boats in to Sharm el Sheikh. Almog and Telem shared an uneasy history since Telem had "not picked up" Almog's Pig off Port Said during the 1967 Six Day War, and the lambasting of the theater commander was as much the result of personal dislike as it was a critique of the operation. For Operation Collection 11, Telem ordered that an additional Zodiac be deployed to act as a refueler and to assist in towing or the evacuation of any wounded personnel, and for no Daburs to be used. It was also decided to send only four men, two teams, into A'ardaka on the night of October 11–12, 1973, and not risk additional operators.

After sailing the hundred kilometers from Sharm el Sheikh in their Zodiacs, an incredible distance to traverse in such a small and exposed vessel, the attack force split into two for the entry into the dock—again, undetected by the diligent Egyptian defense. One two-man team failed to locate any targets and retreated back to the rendezvous point. Lieutenant Commander Kroll led the other team, and there was no way in hell that he was going to head back to base without executing his mission. Yet in carrying out Operation Collection 11, the second raid on A'ardaka, the task force was hampered by a lack of up-to-date intelligence. Although the Red Sea Command possessed pre-war aerial reconnaissance photographs of A'ardaka, the disposition of Egyptian ships on October 10 were unknown. When the operators entered a port, sticking a head out to find a good hull on which to attach a limpet was asking for a bullet in the face mask. Most of the searching had to be done underwater, and unless an operator had a clue about which direction he should be heading, finding a target was literally as difficult as finding a needle in a haystack. For this operation, however, Lieutenant Commander Kroll wasn't about to let anything like a lack of intelligence hinder his ability to make good on the mission. As he entered the dock and began to observe—and feel—the Egyptian defensive arrangements, he concluded that the area where Egyptian guards were tossing the most depth charges *had* to be the place where the missile boats were moored. Although voluntarily heading toward depths under heavy depth-charge attacks is not the act of a sane individual, it is a measure of an operator's professionalism and courage.

As Kroll and his No. 2 encroached on the thunderous depth-charge blasts and braced their neoprene-clad torsos for the impact of an underwater explosion's massive concussion, they managed to make a positive identification of what to them was pay dirt—an Egyptian Navy Komar-class missile boat. The Komar missile boat is eighty-seven feet long, its silhouette marked by the distinctive large tubes used to house the Styx SSMs. Up close, it was unmistakable, and even though Egyptian sailors were tossing depth charges into the waters below with incessant frequency, Lieutenant Commander Kroll and his No. 2 managed to affix several limpets to the Komar's wooden hull. Still undetected, the two operators headed back toward the open water and the linkup with the awaiting Zodiacs. As Murphy's Law often accompanies missions deep behind enemy lines, it reared its ugly head yet again on this operation. The four frogmen reached the anchored Zodiacs with little difficulty, but the long sail had rendered one of the Zodiac's outboard motors inoperable. Faced with a rubber boat and no engine with a hundred klicks to cross was not an ideal tactical situation for the four men—especially since a missle boat, and its fuel tanks and two 500-kilogram warheads, were about to blow up. A last-ditch attempt to start the engine failed, but the impotent roar of the horses not powering cut through the silent night like a cannon shot. Although they couldn't see the Israeli frogmen, Egyptian gunners heard them, and all hell broke loose. Red tracer lines illuminated the night, as the detonating bursts of close-call 20mm rounds began spraying the operators with massive bursts of water. With little choice, they ditched the Zodiac and transfered all their gear to the other two boats whose engines were operational. Within several minutes, the boats were blazing a path back to Sharm el Sheikh—out of range of the Egyptian shore batteries and hopefully still with enough fuel to make it back to base. As the boats raced home, an orange glow filled the sky from the direction of A'ardaka. The Komar had exploded and had suffered irreparable damage.

For the next week, IDF intelligence-listening posts monitored gleefully as Egyptian forces chased ghosts along their Red Sea coast almost on a nightly basis. So sure were the Egyptian regional commanders that Israeli commandos were striking at targets deep in the nation's heartland that commando companies, originally tasked with assaulting targets in Israeli-controlled Sinai, were sent back home in defensive ambushes.

Although "Operation Collection 11" was a success, Captain Almog realized that there was the definite strategic need for additional strikes against the Egyptian port. Israel was slowly turning the tide on the battlefields of Sinai, and the Egyptian advance was stalling. The shock of the October 6 attack had been washed away by the blood and anger of so many Israeli casualties, and the IDF was back to fighting with its now renowned fighting spirit and innovative manner. As part of the counterattack planned against the Egyptian 2nd and 3rd Armies entrenched, the IDF was either going to punch a bridgehead across the canal or land a significant number of troops across the Gulf of Suez on mainland Egypt. Even though a Komar had been destroyed in "Operation Collection 11," the Egyptian Red Sea fleet, at least in numbers, was still a force to be reckoned with. There were still enemy missile boats out there, and they still could, in the explosive arc of a missile being launched, place the entire national strategy in jeopardy.

For "Operation Collection 12," though, Captain Almog had a different sort of attack plan in mind. Flotilla 13 had just finished developing a new version of explosive boat built around the speed and maneuverability of the Snunit craft. By 1973, the MTM boats originally acquired from Italy had long since been retired (in explosive manner) from operational duty. The importance of destroying a multitude of targets wasn't as important as simply launching an attack. The Israelis had already caused the Egyptian rear garrisons to hunt down ghosts and see assaulting commando formations where there were none. This time, the ghosts would be real. They would be armed with speedboats and explosives, and they would leave a body count in their wake. It would prove to the Egyptians that the Israelis were not scared of attacking a heavily defended target expecting additional attacks, and it would cause Egyptian military planners to think that a major military move was being prepared far from the Suez Canal and cause them to commit armor and infantry units away from the front lines. Diversion, achieved with death and destruction in the enemy camp, is something that any military planner will accept. On the night of October 18, Rear-Admiral Telem arrived at the Red Sea HQ and on the ride from the airport to the naval base, Almog managed to convince his commander to authorize a third strike. D-day was set for the night of October 19–20.

The newer explosive craft were, of course, faster than the Italian kamikaze craft, far more maneuverable even though they still carried a whopping quarter ton of high-explosive payload. The only problem was that the boats were basically prototypes, and not all the kinks had been ironed out in tests. "What better way to test a new weapon than to deploy it against the enemy," Almog thought to himself, as he observed the boats being readied at a secluded section of the IDF/Navy base at Sharm el Sheikh. Commanding the operation was Lieutenant Commander Gadi Shefi. Two exploding boats would be used, and they would be accompanied by a small force of Snunit craft that would lay down covering fire with their twin-mounted FN MAG 7.62mm light machine guns, as well as collect the explosive boat drivers once they jettisoned from the speeding bombs and floated alone in the water.

An "operator" hoping to attach himself to the action was Rear Admiral (Res.) Yochai Bin-Nun. Although a former commander of the unit and the IDF/Navy, on October 6 Bin-Nun found himself a man with admiral ranks on his epaulets and no war to fight. He grabbed his uniform and his gun, picked up Captain "Yosele" Dror, another stalwart from the flotilla's "prehistoric" days, and drove down to Sinai and the Red Sea command where the two veterans knew there'd be work for experienced—albeit aging—warriors.[24]

The Snunit is a sturdy speedboat designed for long journeys in rough seas. At 03:00 hours in the early morning of October 19, Lieutenant Commander Shefi's attack force was poised to strike. The attackers moved in from the north, straight toward the main dock where the missile boats and torpedo patrol craft were moored—explosive boat No. 1 would attack first. Once its 300 kilograms of high explosives hit its mark and "woke the Egyptians up," explosive boat No. 2 would launch its attack. Explosive boat No. 1 was piloted by First Lieutenant Didi,* an operator who, as a result of wounds suffered at Green Island, spent a year in the hospital and was told that he'd never be able to return to the unit. Return he did, and he found himself once again too close for comfort. A heavy fog at A'ardaka that night made visibility along the waterway difficult. In his first run toward the targeted dock, First Lieutenant Didi had trouble locating his position and seeing where he was going. By the time he managed to decipher his bearings amid the fog and smoke, he realized he was far too close to the intended target in order to engage it in the explosive boat's characteristic high-speed run on the target. He regrouped his wits and his craft, then launched a second run.

Once again, Murphy's Law made an appearance in the waters of A'ardaka. Lieutenant Didi set his craft on course, readied the throttle and safety switch, and ejected himself from the speeding boat. A malfunction in the steering mechanism, however, caused the boat to move wildly in a circular path, instead of heading straight for the dock. In an almost comical sight, the explosive boat began moving precariously close to boat No. 2 and the Snunit boats awaiting offshore. Finally, miraculously, the one piece of equipment operating properly in Didi's boat was its self-destruct mechanism, and without warning the boat erupted into a blinding flash and a thunderous explosion that shattered eardrums and must have caused the Egyptians to think that they were under attack from the heavens. Egyptian gun posts began firing wildly into the night in a 360-degree radius; the flying tracer rounds illuminated the foggy sky in an eerie orange glow of impending death and destruction. The explosion of Didi's boat was the signal for boat No. 2, piloted by Lieutenant Yair Michaeli, an experienced boat officer who, in his spare time at his home of Kibbutz Sdot Yam, was the world champion in the sport of wind surfing, to head into action. Under intensive Egyptian fire, Lieutenant Michaeli managed to swerve around the exploding rounds and ricocheting bullets and aimed his boat at a Komar-class missile boat sitting helplessly along their pier. Dressed in full combat gear, from Mk 6 radio to assault rifle and survival gear, Michaeli jettisoned himself into the water and observed as his boat swerved ever so slightly off course and impacted against the pier instead of the Komar. The resulting explosion was enormous—the 300 kilograms of TNT turning much of the dock into splinters of wood and fragments of steel. The boat did miss the missile boat, but it did hit the pier and caused tremendous damage to the entire facility. The operators were retrieved by the Snunit craft and headed back to Sharm el Sheikh at full speed.

Common sense would have thought that the third raid on

A'ardaka would have been the flotilla's last. The IDF had crossed the Suez Canal on the night of October 15–16, establishing a bridgehead into Africa and pouring men and material into Egypt for a decisive and crippling pincer move against the invading Egyptian armies. Israeli armor was moving toward Isma'iliya and Suez City, and the Egyptian Third Army, nearly 100,000 men, were surrounded and at the mercy of a vengeful Israeli military. But as the Israeli military headed south, along the Egyptian side of the Gulf of Suez, the one remaining Komar missile boat still stationed at A'ardaka (many of the other vessels had been moved to safe harbor at other Egyptian facilities due south, near the Sudanese border) was still a threat. Rear Admiral Telem ordered the flotilla to return to A'ardaka and hit the missile boat with a new piece of hardware that had arrived from the United States. The order came in the afternoon of October 20, just as most of the operators were preparing to board a flight back to northern Israel.

When raiding a terrorist camp in southern Lebanon, the Soviet-produced RPG-7 had proven a more-than-adequate tool for removing vehicles, pillboxes, or sniper nests. Sturdy, accurate, and prestigious (they were captured weapons, after all), the RPG-7 was everything, but it wasn't reliable when wet and had been known to fail on certain missions when exposed to sea water. The Belgian-produced 3.5-inch bazooka that the unit used on Green Island was useful at close ranges, but it was hopelessly inaccurate at ranges of over a hundred meters. On October 21, 1973, a gift from U.S. President Richard M. Nixon and the American government arrived in Sharm el Sheikh. For the first eight days of the war, America had supported its Middle East ally with words and gestures, but the only war materials coming to the Middle East were Soviet in origin and they were landing in Alexandria and Latakia. On October 14, however, Nixon ordered the transfer of large stockpiles of U.S. tanks, aircraft, rifles, and ordnance to the IDF; much of the equipment was transferred from U.S. aircraft carriers (like the Skyhawk fighter-bomber) and from NATO stockpiles. The "Aerial Bridge," as the shipments were known, saved the State of Israel—ammunition supplies were depleted to the point where the IDF was going to run out of bullets in a matter of days. One American weapon dispatched in large crates was a tubelike expandable and disposable tank-killing device known as the M-72, that could fire a 66mm round capable of penetrating up to 305mm of steel-plate armor. It was more commonly known as the LAW.

Most of the LAWs went to front-line infantry and air-borne units waging a fight-to-the-death against Arab armor, but a crate of twenty LAWs reached Almog and company at Sharm el Sheikh, and it sparked a novel idea for the once-and-for-all removal of the Komar. It was mandatory to fire a LAW at the Komar's hull, argued Almog and Egozi, who had joined in on the planning sessions, since the warhead can cause the ship to explode into a massive and all-encompassing fireball. The Komars carried two Styx SSMs, and each Styx possessed a 500-kilogram warhead that, if hit by an anti-tank rocket, would cause a blast powerful enough to obliterate the Komar, the dock, and anything else within a hundred-meter radius. Also, should the second Styx detonate, the combined ton of erupting high explosives would not only destroy much of A'ardaka could but also envelop the operators in their Snunit boats, and care had to be taken. The IDF had not ordered the LAW rockets before the war, and the operators had never even seen one before the crates reached Sharm el Sheikh, let alone perfected their 66mm marksmanship skills. Many of the operators doubted that they could even hit the damn missile-boat—especially at night!

Ten LAWs were sanctioned for training—ten remained for the actual raid. Although many of the operators may have read about the weapon's use in Vietnam, the weapon was something of an oddity. There was, of course, no instructor to teach the operators what to do and all that was available. In fact, there were a few tattered manuals and the instructions stenciled on the actual launchers. To save time and ammunition, it was decided to allow only two men in the raiding party to actually fire the LAWs at the Egyptian targets. The men chosen to press the launching mechanism on their rockets were Master Sergeant Danny Eitan on one Snunit and Master Sergeant Uri Stein for the second boat.

At an improvised range near the Sharm el Sheikh facility, the operators who would participate in the evening's operation lined up for some target practice. Captain Almog would also come along for "Operation Collection 13," as would Rear Admiral (Res.) Bin-Nun, who, as fate would have it, was celebrating his twenty-fifth anniversary of the sinking of the R.E.N.S. *Emir Farouk.* "I thought it poignant to sink two enemy ships on the same day—even if it happened twenty-five years later," Bin-Nun would comment. "I thought it important."[25]

The ten LAWs launched were less a drill than an introduction. The range would not replicate conditions at night when firing the weapon, and of course it could not replicate what it was like to launch a 66mm anti-tank round from a boat that was rocking, rolling, and pitching excitedly. Many of the dozen operators participating in the raid were anxious about their chances of returning from the raid and anxious about going through all the effort and danger, only to not know how to fire these "damn American contraptions." Almog and Bin-Nun's participation in the operation calmed some jagged nerves, and it changed the overall atmosphere of the pre-raid briefing from an angry display of "Why the hell do we need to go back there again" to "Let's get this shit over with once and for all!" The chances of this mission succeeding were not viewed as high, and as a result, Captain Almog demanded that he be allowed to command the operation; he took his "demand" directly to Rear Admiral Telem. "I thought it immoral and unjustified to send the operators on an operation that was so dangerous and whose chances of success were so slim, unless I was the first one in the boat."[26] Telem agreed. Some later joked that Telem had no problem okaying Almog's participation in a mission with a very small chance of success.

In the meantime, making the mood of desperation and gloom more tangible, intelligence reports filtered to Sharm el Sheikh that the Egyptians were poised for an additional attack on A'ardaka, taking additional measures to protect the port's main dock; additional machine-gun nests were put into position, as were additional batteries of 14.5mm heavy machine guns. To achieve, at least, some measure of surprise, it was decided to attack at 04:00 in the early morning hours of October 22. That late H-hour gave the attacking party only sixty minutes of remaining darkness, but it was considered the one hour when Egyptian diligence would be at its absolute lowest. Attacking so late at night meant that the entire withdrawal, carried out over an area still under absolute Egyptian naval and air control, would have to be achieved under the brilliant morning sun. The flotilla officers felt that the lack of logic in attacking the Egyptians at such an hour would achieve absolute surprise. "From our experience with the Egyptians," Ze'ev Almog would reflect, "we knew that once they got hit, they linger around the targeted area and tend to 'lick their wounds.'"[27]

With this raid, Almog was also careful not to step on any toes or transgress the boundaries of any egos. He had his former commander along for the ride, and overall command of the mission was still, technically, the responsibility of Lieutenant Commander Shefi. Bin-Nun, on the other hand, was more problematic. There were the trappings of respect involved in giving the rear admiral everything that he wanted, but he was no longer a young man and not really part of the "crew." Plus, Almog realized, getting Bin-Nun killed or captured would cause "definite" and unnecessary "damage." Almog hoped that Rear Admiral Telem—a man with whom Almog was already in very shallow waters— would refuse the request, but Telem authorized it, much to everyone's surprise. Almog allowed Bin-Nun to command the evacuation Snunit that was supposed to position itself close to the opening of the dock, and its job would be to assist the force that would be active inside the target, in case the raiding force encountered difficulties. Bin-Nun's boat was also supposed to act as a technical reserve, but it was hoped that the mission wouldn't need a fifty-year-old admiral charging toward the target with his guns ablaze! "Imagine if he [Bin-Nun] would have fallen into the hands of the Egyptians," one of the operators recalled. "It would have been a disaster. They would probably parade him around, torture him, and then execute him for sinking the *Emir Farouk!*"[28]

Tensions at the final operational briefing were, to be

understated, high! Inside the briefing room, the operators were already dressed in their combat fatigues and carrying their weapons. Virtually all the operators chain-smoked endless cigarettes—some clutching a lit cigarette with their right hand, and lighting up another one with their left. Most of the AK-47s had two banana-clip magazines attached to each other, and some of the operators carried load-bearing gear filled to capacity with magazines and grenades. A heavy battle of some kind was expected and the operators wanted to even the odds as much as possible. The boats themselves were also loaded with extra weapons and ammunition. In additional to the extra belts of 7.62mm ammunition and additional grenades, satchel charges would also be carefully stored in the boats. The charges' twenty-eight kilograms of high explosives were to be used as toss-away charges should the ten LAWs all miss their mark, and in case the raiders were forced to abandon their ships and head for shore, the satchel packs would be most effective self-destruct mechanisms.

Almog, Bin-Nun, and Egozi couldn't help but notice the trepidation in the air. A similar air of despair existed before Green Island, but Green Island was a surprise attack. The flotilla had already been to A'ardaka three times in the last two weeks—the last time less than forty-eight hours earlier. They had inflicted damage, and the Egyptians were bound to be angry and bound to be waiting. Making the confidence level even lower was the last-minute intelligence that the Egyptians had positioned a high-powered beacon at the entrance to the harbor and were training it on the approaching waters. Prospects for even reaching the target weren't good. Chances of surviving the operation were even less promising.

The final briefing took place at 17:00 hours, but thirty minutes into the meeting, Almog received an urgent phone call from IDF/Navy HQ in Tel Aviv informing him that the mission was aborted. Rear Admiral Telem wasn't about to get into a verbal Mexican standoff with Almog, so he simply had the watch commander phone the message in. Almog couldn't let the operators know what was up—a cancellation from Tel Aviv would have resulted in panic and ruined any chance for the mission, or any derivative thereof, from being attempted again. So, with his men around him, Almog covered the receiver with one hand and acted like he was having a friendly chat with Tel Aviv, though in reality he was demanding to talk to Telem. Almog finally got Commodore Tirosh on the phone, and he informed his red-faced Red Sea commander that the mission was scrubbed because the air force couldn't send up a medevac chopper in case the attack force encountered difficulties. "What a crock of shit," Almog thought to himself, realizing that naval politics on the part of the IDF/Navy commander was rearing its ugly head. "The mission was built around the fact that the operators could not and would not have any assets at their disposal." To save "Collection 13," Almog informed Tirosh that not only was he not requesting IAF helicopters, but also Telem should be notified, that he would also refuse to accept them in his zone of operations. Faced with a de facto checkmate, Telem informed Almog, through his deputy, that the fourth raid on A'ardaka was, once again, a green light. Tirosh informed Almog that the raid was back to green-light status.

At 19:00 hours, the thirteen operators descended into their boats for an impromptu test-firing of "Practice-LAW-No. 10"; the nighttime launch was meant to replicate the sensation of launching the missile at night from the back-and-forth rocking of a moving vessel. It was decided that the maximum launching range would be *under* a hundred meters. The test-firing also proved to the nervous operators that the flash from the fired rocket was a brief burst of light and it did not leave a telltale illuminated path that Egyptian gunners could use to seek out the source of the launch. In fact, the LAW's flash burst was even dimmer than that of a MAG light machine gun when fired at night.

The task force of Snunit boats departed Sharm el Sheikh at 21:00 hours on the night of October 21, and after some rough sailing, they reached the staging area for the attack just before 04:00 hours. It was decide to once again attack from the north—Flotilla 13 had already attacked twice from a northern approach and Almog was sure that the Egyptians were expecting an attack from the southern approach this time. The boats passed Shedwan Island without being detected, and then they checked their bearings—only forty kilometers to go! Soon they'd be able to see A'ardaka silhouetted against the backdrop of targets, hit by the IAF, burning inside mainland Egypt. As the boats continued their move forward, however, an engine in Almog's boat malfunctioned. Bin-Nun, piloting the reserve boat, was ordered to change boats with the operators and take the damaged vessel back to Sharm el Sheikh. Rear Admiral Bin-Nun was none to happy about being removed from the operational team, but such was the life of the "reserve boat officer." Most of the operators were saddened to see Bin-Nun leave—he had been something of a good luck charm to the task force—though Almog was somewhat relieved. The chances of Bin-Nun ending up in Cairo's notorious el-Mazeh Prison were now slim. The chances of Almog getting yelled at, however, once the task force returned—*insh'Allah*—to Israel were high!

The raiding force, all nine of them, were now divided into two Snunit boats and they moved steadily toward the breakwater and the coral-reef entrance. The high-powered beacon, now at the southern end, proved that the Egyptians expected an attack from this direction. Lieutenant Commander Shefi, who was already familiar with the dock from the mission of the explosive boats, warned Almog of a trap. His gut feeling was that the Egyptians were letting the operators get in, so that once inside the dock, they could open up with everything they had. "It was too quiet," Lieutenant Yisrael Dagai observed. "Sometimes the sounds of a few gunshots make you feel at ease." As the two boats progressed toward the dock, a dark silhouette was becoming visible. At 800 meters away, it looked smaller than a postage stamp, but it was visible. At 400 meters away, it looked very distinct—two tubelike launchers, a mast, and a forward-mounted 25mm main armament cannon. It was the Komar—moored north across from the northern pier, located in the depth of the dock, approximately three kilometers from A'ardaka's main entrance. Lieutenant Commander Shefi became even more suspicious at this point. He feared the Komar to be bait, insisting that it was probably the boat that was struck and seriously damaged from Lieutenant Commander Kroll's mission, and because of its wooden hull, it was still managing to stay afloat. Lieutenant Commander Shefi feared that the Egyptians were drawing in the attackers with the damaged boat, and once they were deep inside A'ardaka's waters, the ambush would finally be sprung. Shefi's apprehension was good—it was the sign of a prudent commander. He was, however, wrong. The silhouette was a genuine operational Egyptian Navy missile boat—a Komar-class vessel that was just asking for a LAW rocket strike. The commander of Snunit No. 2, Lieutenant Yisrael Dagai, moved in, as well, at the identification of the boat.

The Snunit cut a smooth path through the still water, but at 120 meters from the target, a flash and a deafening explosion ripped across the silent desert night. Tracers emanating from Egyptian positions illuminated the black sky, and a full-scale battle erupted. The operators hunkered down inside their boats, moving fast into firing position, and at eighty meters out, Almog ordered Dagai to start firing and his operator Danny Eitan to start firing his allotment of LAWs; Sergeant Uri Stein sitting in Snunit No. 1 was also ordered to fire. The two "snipers" fired three missiles apiece. All missed. The two boats, still under hellatious Egyptian fire, moved up another forty meters, and Almog ordered each operator to launch a missile apiece. One rocket flew high, the other banked off to the left. The Komar's crew, now fully alerted, began firing madly toward the encroaching attackers. The main armament 25mm cannon was swung around to aim at the inlet, and it, too, began firing ten-round bursts at the two Israeli speed-boats.

Almog was angry. Only two LAWs remained, and he felt that the Snunits could move up right alongside the Komar and he would still not hit the damn thing. He told Danny Eitan that he was going to fire the boat's last remaining LAW, but Eitan resisted. "You don't have 'training' with the weapon," Eitan yelled at Captain Almog under the deafening blasts of Egyptian fire. "You won't hit it either." Before a struggle could ensue, Eitan assured his commander that

LAW No. 5 would be the charm. With Egyptian bullets flying only inches above the Snunit's silhouette, Danny Eitan stood up, extended the LAW to its firing positions, and peered down on its sights. At the same time, the "sniper" from boat No. 2 stood up as well. Incredibly, both men launched their last missiles simultaneously. The 66mm rockets departed their launchers and flew the short path directly toward the Komar's hull. Both rockets impacted dead-on, and the resulting fireball ignited the sky and virtually blinded the attackers. The Komar literally turned into a glowing fire-ball after being hit. Egyptian sailors, their uniforms on fire, began jumping into the water and screaming in a horrid high-pitched wail that comes when one's flesh is being charred by fire.

The operators viewed their handiwork for a brief moment—it was an awesome sight. It was also the ideal diversion to get their asses out of there as quickly as possible. Almog's Snunit driver readied the controls for a quick departure, but the water was all of a sudden filled with Egyptian sailors in a massive panic. They swam toward the two Snunit boats as if they wanted to be rescued, but there was no room for new acquaintances or prisoners. Gadi Shesi peered down the sights of the Snunit's FN MAG and began to fire, though he forgot to secure the gun's lock Almog's Snunit was also embedded on a coral reef and was stuck. Abandoning the boat and transferring to the other Snunit would take time, making the withdrawal a much slower one. Abandoning the boat and making it toward Egyptian soil, in the hope of an eventual Israel Air Force rescue, was also out of the question. With bullets whisking about, Almog raced to the front of the boat, to list the stern and release its stuck propellors but his foot activating an electronic switch that automatically fired the two FN MAGs mounted on either side of the deck. At 04:45 hours, with the operators in the water and the boat as light as it could be, the propellers were disengaged from the hold of the coral reef and the boat moved fast toward the Sinai peninsula.

The two Snunits raced away from A'ardaka, but the right propeller on Almog's Snunit No. 1 was hit by the coral reef, and the boat began to zigzag wildly. "What the hell are you doing?," Almog scolded Kleot, his Snunit driver, thinking the trusted operator was taking wild evasive action on his own, but the boat was slowly becoming unstable and losing all its steering abilities. A line was attached to Lieutenant Dagai's Snunit No. 2 and the slower withdrawal from the heart of the enemy base was attempted. The operators were exhausted and elated. The adrenaline rush that had swelled to their head had yet to diminish, but it appeared, even as the chasing Egyptian gunfire landed too close for comfort, that they had executed their mission successfully. At 07:00 hours, under a bright Red Sea sun, the boats passed Shedwan Island. They learned over the radio that both the Egyptians and the Israelis had agreed to an initial United Nations cease-fire. Amid the celebrations and hugs that the operators received upon their return to Sharm el Sheikh, the men received a bit of heart-warming news from the head of IDF/Navy intelligence. It appeared that the Komar struck at A'ardaka was one of the boats responsible for the sinking, six years earlier to the day, of the I.N.S. *Eilat.* Revenge had been long overdue, but was sweet nonetheless.

Following this mission, the Egyptians evacuated the port of A'ardaka, withdrawing their boats south to the port of Safga, some thirty miles from A'ardaka. Flotilla 13 emerged from the campaign without suffering a single casualty. By the dawn of October 23, 1973, the entire Egyptian front had collapsed, and by October 24, 1973, the war had come to an end. Although its battles had not been as large as some of the massive tank battles fought atop the Golan Heights or in Sinai, Flotilla 13 and a small force of Dabur patrol craft had succeeded in closing off an entire theater of operations to a vastly superior enemy force. For Almog, the war was a personal achievement few naval commanders ever get to enjoy. For Flotilla 13, it was the reaffirmation of a motto instilled in them during the War of Attrition—they stuck to their targets and achieved the destruction of over a half-dozen Egyptian warships. For the IDF/Navy, its overall success in the war exorcised the ghosts of 1967.

Israel lost 2,500 war dead in 1973—more than 10,000 seriously wounded. Its self-imposed aura of superiority and invincibility, which it had inherited following the 1967 War, had lasted all of six years. The IDF had staved off defeat and secured the national frontiers from collapse (therefore saving the Jewish State from destruction), achieving a miraculous military comeback. The IDF had been very lucky.

A year following the war, on Israel's twenty-sixth independence day, decorations for valor were handed out in an emotional ceremony at IDF/Navy HQ. Lieutenant Oded Amir was posthumously awarded the *I'tur Ha'Gvura,* Israel's highest decoration for valor, for his role in Operation Lady; Master Sergeant Eli Kimchi, was also posthumously awarded the *I'tur Ha'Oz,* Israel's second-highest decoration for battlefield heroism.[29] Also receiving the *I'tur Ha'Oz* decoration were Lieutenants Boaz Shakedi and Gadi Kroll; while Lieutenant Commander Gadi Shefi, Master Sergeant Dan Uziel, and Master Sergeant Shai Berman were awarded the *I'tur Ha'Mofet* medal, Israel's third-highest decoration, for their role in the war. Seven other operators from Flotilla 13 were awarded Chief of Staff citations, including the two LAW snipers and Lieutenant Yisrael Dagai.[30]

Peace is supposed to be the dividend following a bitter hard-fought war, but for Israel, anything but peace would follow the end of the 1973 Yom Kippur War. Israel may have won the conventional aspect of the conflict, winning back territory initially seized on the first days of the fighting, but they also suffered a tremendous morale defeat. Israel and the mighty IDF had been caught badly by surprise. The much-vaunted intelligence services had failed in monitoring developments in Cairo and Damascus, and they had not properly analyzed and disseminated that data down the chains of command and up toward the higher echelons of the military and political hierarchy. The State of Israel had been injured severely through the traumatic October 1973 earthquake, and the Palestinian terrorist groups operating out of Syria and Lebanon were determined to take advantage of striking out at their humbled enemy. On April 11, 1974, terrorists from Ahmed Jibril's PFLP-GC crossed the border from Lebanon and assaulted a block of flats in the northern town of Qiryat Shmonah; eighteen civilians were killed in the massacre, including fourteen women and children. On May 15, 1974, terrorists from Nayif Hawatmeh's Democratic Front for the Liberation of Palestine (DFLP) crossed the Lebanese frontier into northern Israel and seized a schoolhouse in the border town of Ma'alot. When Sayeret Mat'kal attempted to rescue more than a hundred children being held hostage, the terrorists turned their guns on the children. Twenty-five children were killed and more than seventy were wounded in the Ma'alot massacre. Bloodshed was continuing unabated.

There would be no peace in the Middle East following the Yom Kippur bloodbath. No period of recovery. A new full-scale war would erupt once again in the region, though this one did not involve conventional armies, and the targets weren't military in nature. Israel and the Palestinian guerrilla groups were about to go head-to-head in a war to the finish in which the only rule of engagement was to kill as many of the enemy as possible. Flotilla 13 was about to become very busy.

CHAPTER FIVE

The Years of Lebanon and Beyond, Revenge and the "Dream Team"

Flotilla 13: 1975 to 1996

"You don't learn this deadly business [naval special warfare] by sitting in a classroom and learning the business of assaulting a target from a textbook or from a manual. You learn by doing and you learn by seeing how others do. Even how we did Green Island came as a result of training we saw in Italy when the Italians attacked a target, underwater, in unison. You learn by crossing the frontier, even it means just crossing an international boundary marker, and bringing the war to your enemy."

—Commander (Res.) Yisrael Asaf[1]

FLOTILLA 13 HAD, BY THE MID-1970S, BECOME AN INSPIRATION to many naval special warfare units around the world. Green Island, Tripoli, and A'ardaka were studied by the British SBS, the German KSK, the U.S. Navy SEALs, and even the Soviet Spetsnaz. The Palestinians, too, had been inspired by the Flotilla 13 mystique—after all, they had seen the unit's handiwork firsthand and had grudgingly admired their skill and courage, almost as much as they hated their destructive aftermath. If Flotilla 13 did anything in its campaign against the Egyptians and Syrians during the War of Attrition, and then later against the Palestinians in Lebanon, it was that naval special warfare operators expanded a theater of operations to as many nautical miles as a Zodiac could sail and a frogman could swim. Israeli troops and Palestinian guerrillas could exchange gunfire along the border all they wanted to, but that was restricted to a grid, a speck on a map, along a section of frontier. Operators, men with black masks and silenced weapons, could hit targets hundreds of miles away. They could kill the enemy as they slept, sabotage their cars, and even whisk them away for interrogation. Operators terrorized their enemy—pure and simple—but it was in many ways a mental terror. Terrorists were after the real thing.

In the early morning hours of March 5, 1975, nearly two years to the day since Operation Spring of Youth, eight Palestinian terrorists from the Black September Organization sneaked through the Israeli coastal radar screen and landed two Mk V Zodiac craft along the beach just minutes from downtown Tel Aviv. The terrorists, on a suicide mission, proceeded to slink through the empty streets and alleyways, until they reached the sleepy Savoy Hotel, where they took the entire building over and made all of the guests hostages. They demanded that the State of Israel release hundreds of jailed Palestinians or else the hostages would be executed one by one.

Terrorist attacks were common against frontier settlements and towns, but never before in the picturesque Tel Aviv seaside—only a stone's throw away from the prime minister's residence and the Israeli Ministry of Defense. Hundreds of soldiers and border-guard policemen assembled outside the besieged hotel and secured a perimeter, while an impromptu rescue force was assembled outside the hotel. The assault squad that had been thrown together included operators from Sayeret Mat'kal, Colonel Uzi Yairi, who had just completed his tour of duty as commander of the 35th Paratroop Brigade, Commander Shaul Ziv and a group of operators from Flotilla 13. The men weren't summoned by an official call-up, but rather a good number of them lived nearby and brought their weapons and kit to the scene of the gunfire and police sirens. Later in the day, Colonel Yairi led an improvised force of Mat'kal commandos and flotilla operators inside the building to rescue the hostages. Yairi's attempts ended in disaster. He was fatally shot in the head by a terrorist bullet as he peered around a door, and the terrorists blew themselves up in the middle of the rescue attempt, reducing the hotel to a smoldering pile of ruins. In all, seven hostages died that wintry morning; one terrorist survived the melee and provided Israeli interrogators with a detailed outlay of Palestinian naval special warfare abilities: from training in the Soviet Union and Libya to their vast array of Zodiacs and speedboats. After all, much of the Palestinians' equipment, state-of-the-art and very expensive, was paid for by the hundreds of millions of dollars donated by Saudi Arabia and the Gulf States.

The Palestinian frogmen and naval assault units, primarily the PLO's "Force 17," were trained, until 1975, by the elite Egyptian as-Saiqa commandos, and then later by Soviet Spetsnaz personnel, East German Combat Swimmers, and even North Korean operators from the North Korean People's Army's "Amphibious Light Infantry Brigades."[2] North Korean combat swimmers and special boat personnel, among the world's busiest for their incessant insertion attempts into South Korea, are considered among the world's most experienced and ruthless naval special warfare commandos. The fact that the Palestinians had invested so heavily in naval commandos was worrisome. The fact that these men—and women—were more than willing to kill and die during the execution of their missions was daunting. The fact that the two Zodiacs, deployed from a mother ship outside Israeli territorial waters, had managed to sneak in through a hole in the Israeli coastal defenses was unacceptable.

The attack on the Savoy Hotel mortified the Jewish State—so soon after the October earthquake of the 1973

War and the Ma'alot massacre came a strike along the Tel Aviv promenade. Lebanon had become a naval base from which Palestinian raiders launched attacks against the elongated and vulnerable Israeli coast. Nearly two-thirds of the Israeli population lived along the coast, from Ashqelon in the south to Haifa in the north. Immediately, patrols of the coastline were beefed up, as were proactive patrols against shipping in Lebanese waters. Yet before the IDF and the IDF/Navy could retaliate forcibly against Palestinian naval assets and other targets inside Lebanon in retaliation for the Savoy Hotel attack, Palestinian guerrillas and Christian militiamen began fighting in the streets of Beirut and soon throughout the entire nation. The bloodshed was indescribable and wanton—far greater than anything the IDF would ever hope to dish out against her Palestinian enemies. Retaliation seemed pointless. The IDF hoped that the Lebanese Civil War would take its course.

The IDF was in no mood for a fight in 1975—the nation and its army were recovering from the bitter war fought two years earlier. It was rebuilding, revamping, and retooling. A war with terrorists up north did not fit in the overall scheme of reshaping an army for the next conventional war. Following the Yom Kippur War, the IDF/Navy had invested much of its budget and resources on the expansion of its missile boat fleet. Its record in 1973 had been impressive and its focus had been the conventional neutralization of the Arab fleets for the next conflict. Its record in combating terrorist infiltration wasn't very good, however. Missile boats and Daburs patrolled the elongated coast with aggressive vigor, but the IDF/Navy's counter-terrorist strategy was responsive in nature, and it was not linked to an overall strategy employing preemptive strikes or even the talents of Flotilla 13. It was believed that Rear Admiral Telem, because of his history with the unit dating back to 1967 and the raid on Port Said, was not the type of commander who would give the flotilla a green flag in operating along the Lebanese coast. He was a conventional naval officer who viewed Flotilla 13, and the type of warfare they excelled at, as a mere footnote to naval operations. Nothing more. Flotilla 13 operations, in fact, decreased in scale and in frequency;

even small unit incursions into Lebanon for intelligence-gathering purposes were scaled back. That situation wouldn't last long, however.

During the IDF's rebuilding process, Flotilla 13 commander Ziv, who had been in the flotilla for his entire career had openly lobbied for the IDF to create a large-scale Commando Corps—something akin to what would later be established in Great Britain with the Directorate of Special Force (DSF) and in the United States with the establishment of United States Special Operations Command (USSOCOM). Ziv's idea wasn't revolutionary. Many of the original founders of Flotilla 13 had openly called for such a creation where the talents and resources of many of the IDF's small reconnaissance and commando elements could be joined together. Ziv's ideas had definite merit. With regional interests from Turkey to Algeria, the IDF was faced with the possibilities of operating in mountains (some with snow), deep water ports, deserts, large urban environments and even, as was encountered in the fighting along the Egyptian side of the Suez Canal in the agricultural belt junglelike conditions. If an operation needed to be infiltrated by sea, cross a desert area, and then be forced to make its way up a snow-capped peak, not to mention be exfiltrated by chopper, it would require the combined talents of a half-dozen units whose training was markedly different, whose commanders were of a half-dozen differing personalities and temperaments, and whose agendas and objectives sometimes interfered (or "coincided") with the good of the overall mission. Each commando in Ziv's devised "Commando Corps" would be a professional operator, trained in all aspects of special warfare.

His plan ignored by the IDF General Staff and by senior officials in the Ministry of Defense, Commander Ziv retired from active duty. He was replaced by Captain Tzvi "Ca uzo" Giva'ati, an experienced officer considered a "diplomat" by many of the Batmen. Indeed, one of his primary objectives was to foster goodwill among his flotilla and the underwater divers of Unit 707. Like any unit resting on its laurels, Flotilla 13 was not forced to rebuild in any dramatic fashion following the 1973 War. It had lost two operators in Operation Lady, but its overall performance, especially against A'ardaka, had been stellar. It absorbed new weapons systems, continued to grow in scope and size, and was slowly expanding its ties with the new and formidable Israeli military ally—the United States. Contacts between Flotilla 13 and the U.S. Navy SEALs began to become regular.[3]

Perhaps more important, many of the unit's true stars, including Lieutenant Ami Ayalon, returned to active duty with the flotilla following stints in other naval units. Lieutenant Yisrael Asaf, already proving himself to be one of the unit's most charismatic and innovative officers, assumed command of the frogman unit and began to train his men in underwater-initiated assaults and underwater-initiated hostage-rescue operations.[4] Israel did not operate many passenger vessels, and a ferry service between Israel and Cyprus, not to mention Israel and Turkey and Israel and the Greek Isles, was not a popular means of travel. Many Israelis, however, possessed pleasure boats and even yachts, and these often sailed the Mediterranean freely and within the reach of Palestinian frogmen eager to seize hostages on the high seas. While much of this training remains classified top-secret to this day, especially insertion techniques and assault philosophy, the exercises centered on an operator being able to place his 7.62mm or 9mm round square into the head of the terrorist and not anywhere near a terrified hostage. Although the maritime counter-terrorism was extensive and geared specifically toward the objective of hostage-rescue, so many spent shells and exploded grenades had a profound effect on the combat proficiency of the frogman section. Soon, it developed into the most capable of assault squads in the entire Israeli military and police special operations community. This weapons proficiency, including the use of small arms, would prove beneficial in the many hit-and-run assaults that the unit would execute against the Lebanese coast. International counter-terrorist training between Flotilla 13 and other foreign units, including a "unique working relationship with the U.S. Navy SEALs," according to one retired JSOC officer, would come years later.[5]

Lebanon remained the flotilla's primary obsession, and operations against Palestinian naval targets along the entire Lebanon coast became commonplace— even routine. The raids were never large incursions similar to Green Island or Tripoli. They mostly consisted of small team insertions where a force of operators would sabotage Palestinian boats, Zodiacs, or seaside fuel pumps. Some of the operations were small "Psyop" endeavors, including spreading flyers in Lebanese fishing villages that stated that any cooperation with the PLO would result in "Flotilla 13 coming back to pay a visit."[6]

From 1974 to 1978 there were dozens of operations carried out by Flotilla 13 in Lebanon—the unit operated on a scale on par with their incessant work against Egypt, Syria, and Jordan during the 1967–70 War of Attrition. The unit was so inseparable from the Lebanese landscape that students in the flotilla naval special warfare course, in the advanced stage of their instruction, of course, were routinely sent into Lebanon—either to support ongoing operations or "just to get that feel of operating in enemy territory."[7]

Many of the operations were "intelligence" in nature. A Flotilla 13 team would simply perch itself underneath a pier or inside a parked fishing boat, sitting in position for a period of time and recording what they saw. They were gathering intelligence on the day-to-day habits of the Lebanese fishermen and the Palestinian terrorists who shared the bustling ports, and they also hoped to uncover the habits of the local PLO commander—find out which seaside restaurants he frequented, which seaside brothels enjoyed his business, and what time of night he usually visited his sentries. The operators knew more about the ports of Tyre, Sidon, Beirut, and Tripoli than did the harbor masters. Making many of these small recce missions possible were the Snunit boats. High-powered, equipped with radar and a fast-moving platform for machine-gun fire should a raiding party be compromised, the Snunit enabled operators to get in and out of a targeted location fast. According to one operator, "When bullets were flying and you were thirty klicks from home, a fast-moving delivery vehicle was a godsend."[8]

From 1974 to 1976, Flotilla 13, in the words of one of its officers, was "just about everywhere that the mind could imagine" in the region. One place they weren't, however, was in Africa. When, on June 27, 1976, Air France Flight 139 was hijacked from Athens to Libya, and then on to Entebbe, Uganda, the entire Israeli military and intelligence apparatus went into high alert. The flight had, after all, originated in Israel, and the terrorists were an international assortment of Germans and Arabs working for the PFLP. Originally, it was believed that the terrorists would divert the aircraft back to Israel and challenge Israel to rescue the hostages on board; and, indeed, Sayeret Mat'kal was summoned to Ben-Gurion International Airport to prepare for an aircraft takedown. But Entebbe complicated matters—it was a French plane, after all, and the targeted location was nearly 3,000 miles from Israeli airspace. When the terrorists released all non-Jewish and non-Israeli hostages, Israel obtained a free hand to move. While the politicians negotiated and postured, the commandos went to work.

Entebbe International Airport's main runway lies just a few hundred meters from the banks of Lake Victoria. While contemplating just how the IDF could infiltrate a force of commandos into Entebbe without alerting the authorities (who were acting in concert with the terrorists) and the terrorists, the Flotilla 13 commander at the time, Captain Gadi Shefi, and his counterparts in Sayeret Mat'kal came up with a plan of audacious innovation and with a credible chance of success. Operators from Flotilla 13 would parachute into Lake Victoria with their Zodiac rubber inflatables, position themselves for an attack, rescue the hostages, and seize the airport. Operators from Sayeret Mat'kal and other IDF reconnaissance formations would then be flown in and the hostages flown out. A "Murphy's Law" contingency to the plan was that agents from Mossad and officers from Flotilla 13 would rent a ferry boat and position in along the bank of Lake Victoria during the initial assault. If seizing the airport was impossible, then the hostages would be evacuated to Kenya on the rented vessel. Indeed, several officers from Flotilla 13 were flown to Nairobi in order to rent such a boat.[9]

Of course, as events unfolded, Flotilla 13 was the sole IDF special forces unit *not* to participate in "Operation Thunderball," the IDF code name for the Entebbe rescue. Intelligence revealed that large alligators called the banks of Lake Victoria home and that dropping nearly the entire flotilla into an alligator-infested waterway was too risky; the men were good enough to go against RPG-wielding Egyptian commandos, but not against four-legged creatures. It was also rumored that Brigadier General Dan Shomron, the chief paratroop and infantry officer named overall commander of the operation, was not the greatest admirer of the Batmen and decided to purposely exclude them from the operation.[10]

Operation Thunderball was, of course, one of the most spectacular commando operations ever staged in the history of modern warfare. On the night of July 3–4, 1976, the IDF simply flew C-130 Hercules aircraft onto the tarmac at Entebbe, and Sayeret Mat'kal operators handled the terrorists and freed the hostages, while recon commandos from other IDF paratroop and infantry units secured the runway and the rest of the airfield. All the hostages, with the exception of three killed in the assault, were freed. All the terrorists were killed, as were over twenty Ugandan soldiers. The sole Israeli military fatality was Lieutenant Colonel Yonatan "Yoni" Netanyahu, the Sayeret Mat'kal commander.

Entebbe was just the cure to remedy the ills of defeatism and anger that had overtaken much of the Israeli military community following the 1973 War. Entebbe, in fact, sparked the genesis of the golden age of Israeli special operations, where many of the nation's most famous and highly decorated operators were coming into their own as high-ranking officers. Even the IDF chief of staff at the time,

Lieutenant General Mordechai "Motta" Gur, was a red beret in heart and spirit, and he was a paratrooper virtually his entire military career. He was also the first "pure" paratrooper to become the IDF chief of staff; until his appointment in 1974, virtually all IDF commanders were tank officers. "Motta," as he was affectionately known, was a popular general faced with an incredible—some say impossible—task. Rebuilding the IDF into a modern force that would never endure the setbacks suffered during the first days of the 1973 War. The man who succeeded "Motta" in 1978 as IDF chief of staff was even more "commando friendly." On September 28, 1978, Lieutenant General Rafael "Raful" Eitan was named the IDF commander. "Raful" wasn't a great military thinker or brilliant tactician, but he was one of the bravest men ever to carry a machine gun into the abyss of a dark night in enemy territory. He was a soldier's soldier who believed in his men, the virtue of their tasks, and that the enemy was to be hit hard, hit often, and hit below the belt. Flotilla 13, along with the rest of the Israeli special operations community, was about to have its restraints removed and thrown away.

By 1978, the IDF/Navy was commanded by Rear Admiral Michael "Yomi" Barkai, a brilliant naval officer who commanded the missile boat fleet during the 1973 War and had been decorated for his cool and daring leadership under Styx fire. He was a conventional naval officer who was more interested in technological advancements in anti-missile defenses than he was with a Dabur crew's marksmanship with their 20mm main armament cannons. The Lebanese situation, and the Palestinian naval potential, was not seen as a priority—especially with Christian and Syrian gunners destroying more Palestinian boats and facilities in the open internecine carnage of the Lebanese Civil War than Flotilla 13 could ever have hoped to destroy.

In the spring of 1978, however, the Palestinians would prove that the Lebanese Civil War was but a diversion to them and that they were still a power to be reckoned with. The objective of Abu Jihad's operation was to once again display their ability to insert a large force of terrorists by

Samuel M. Katz

Zodiac craft onto the Israeli coastline, though this time the end result would make the Savoy Hotel incident look like a mere historical footnote. It was supposed to have been the best of times for the State of Israel—Egyptian President Anwar El-Sadat had already made his historic pilgrimage of peace to the Jewish State, and the Camp David Accords had set in motion the first-ever peace deal between Israel and one of her Arab neighbors. After thirty years of war, Israel had finally come to a point in its history where peace was within sight. On March 11, 1978, the only vision within view was blood and carnage.

Abu Jihad, the PLO defense minister (of sorts), had dispatched a suicide squad to Israel to see if the peace process could be torpedoed. Abu Jihad was a terrorist mastermind who had a penchant for amphibious operations; he had received his job in the wake of three job vacancies in the PLO hierarchy, courtesy of Operation Spring of Youth. He favored the spectacular operation over the routinely bloody, and for this unique step, he had assembled a thirteen-man force of terrorists specifically suited for the task at hand. Abu Jihad's mission called for his operators to seize a heavily booked seaside hotel in the Tel Aviv suburb of Bat Yam, take hundreds of hostages, and demand the release of hundreds of terrorists in Israeli jails. The terrorists were to plant explosives throughout the hotel and blow themselves—and their captives—up at the first sign of an Israeli rescue attempt. Remarkably, the squad was commanded by a woman, a twenty-year-old named Dalal Mughrabi, who was known to be even more vicious in combat than her male counterparts and who had been born in Israel and spoke fluent Hebrew.

On the night of March 11, 1978, the terrorists left their base just south of Tyre and boarded a Lebanese fishing trawler that would serve as a "mother ship." Just off the Tel Aviv coastline, the terrorists would lower their Zodiacs into the splashing waves and drive their motors hard toward the beaches of Bat Yam. Unfortunately for Abu Jihad's squad, "Murphy's Law" was a factor in the murderous plans of terrorists, as well. One of the Zodiacs capsized, and two of the terrorists, wearing nearly forty kilograms of equipment strapped to their bodies, quickly sank into the depths of the Mediterranean. The Palestinians' navigational skills were also off. The skyline they thought was that of Tel Aviv actually belonged to the northern port city of Haifa, and when they landed, they reached the shores of Kibbutz Ma'agan Michael, not Bat Yam. Incidentally, Ma'agan Michael was the home to Flotilla 13 founder Yochai Bin-Nun.

After encountering an American nature photographer in the marsh area near the beach and killing her, the eleven terrorists raced through the Kibbutz toward the bustling coastal highway where they fired wildly at the passing traffic and eventually managed to stop two buses filled with holiday travelers. Hoping to reach Ben-Gurion International Airport and commandeer a plane to Beirut, the terrorists packed the two busloads of frightened travelers—over a hundred men, women, and children—onto one bus and ordered the driver to race at full speed for Tel Aviv.

Israeli military and police units, including hostage-rescue specialists from the newly formed Israeli National Police counter-terrorist force, prepared a roadblock at the Country Club Junction at the northernmost outskirts of Tel Aviv. The Israelis weren't about to let a bus filled with terrorists enter its most populated city, and they were determined to end the ordeal at a point of their choosing. When the bus ran over snake-teeth spikes placed in the roadway to puncture its tires, one of the hostages used the diversion as an opportunity to end the ordeal himself. He grabbed an AK-47 from one of the Palestinians and began killing the terrorists. A fire-fight ensued, and the Israeli authorities, fearing that the hostages were being systematically slaughtered, ordered its intervention forces into the melee. There were several explosions on board the bus, then a massive fireball. In all, thirty-four hostages were killed and nearly seventy were wounded; several police officers and soldiers were also killed and wounded. Nine of the terrorists were killed, and two escaped the chaos only to be captured hours later roaming through a suburb with singed lizard-pattern fatigues. It was the worst terrorist attack in the history of the Jewish State.

An Israeli response was obvious, but both American President Jimmy Carter and Egyptian President Anwar El-Sadat urged Prime Minister Begin to act with restraint and caution. Four days later, however, the IDF invaded southern Lebanon. The invasion was known as "Operation Litani" and was designed to push the PLO mini-state in Lebanon north, beyond the Litani River, to a point where guerrillas would not be able to launch attacks against the Israeli frontier. In essence, Operation Litani succeeded in doing very little in neutralizing the Palestinian military presence in Lebanon. Attacks continued. Some were incredibly bloody and brutal.

The Country Club Junction Massacre, as the bloodbath was known, was a black mark against the IDF/Navy. And it should never have happened. Only several weeks earlier, on February 20, 1978, operators from Flotilla 13 attacked several Force 17 speedboats in what was known as "Operation Joy of Ages."[11] Apparently, the PLO's naval apparatus in Lebanon was so extensive that even a large-scale strike, like the frogman attack against Tyre, had little effect. But perhaps the IDF/Navy's failure to close off the sea to the Palestinians had just as much to do with the difficulty in sealing off such a long and vulnerable coastline as it did with the state of affairs in the navy at the time. Being unable to secure one's coast from terrorists was an indication that the coast was vulnerable to the possible intentions of a conventional navy. By 1979, Rear Admiral Barkai was forced to resign his command following a sexual-assault charge filed against him by a female soldier, and the Flotilla 13 chief, Captain Hanina, was ousted following the deaths of two of his men in a training accident. "Raful," an officer with an elephant's memory who recalled the tragic state of affairs with the corps in 1967, ordered immediate changes. Commodore Ze'ev Almog, one of the founders of the Institute for National Security (an IDF think tank and staff school) was named the IDF/Navy commander and promoted to the rank of rear admiral. Almog, many believed, was wrongly passed over for the position of navy commander in 1976; at the time, Almog was the commander of the the navy's largest facility, the Haifa Naval Base—a traditional stepping-stone for the rank of OC IDF/Navy. Almog had experience with just about every vessel in the IDF/Navy inventory, but his greatest passion and knowledge lay with his men and Flotilla 13, and the unit was in dire straits. Morale was at an all-time low because of the ouster of Hanina, and in order to keep the force from internal collapse, his first request of "Raful" upon learning of his appointment was permission to name Commander Ami Ayalon as the flotilla's skipper.[12]

For Israeli naval special warfare, the dream team was now in charge.

Almog's first priority was to close off the sea to Palestinian attacks, and time was of the essence. On the night of April 22, 1979, a heavily armed four-man terrorist squad from the Abu Abbas faction of the Palestine Liberation Front (PLF) managed to slip through the Israeli coastal defenses and land their Zodiac Mk V rubber inflatable along the breakwater on the picturesque beach of Nahariya, Israel's northernmost city, in search of committing a large-scale terrorist attack. The terrorists carried enough firepower and explosives with them to seize an entire apartment block, and that was, indeed, their mission. They entered an apartment block and began knocking on doors in an attempt to seize captives, but many of the building's residents had succeeded in reaching the bomb shelter located in the basement.

One family that failed to reach safety was that of Danny and Smadar Haran, a young couple with two small children. The terrorists grabbed Danny and his four-year-old daughter, but missed Smadar and their infant daughter, who hid inside a laundry cupboard. Tragically, while the terrorists searched the Harans' apartment, Smadar had accidentally suffocated her baby in the attempt to stifle the baby's crying. The terrorists were prepared to make a stand inside the flat, but they panicked at the sight of the oncoming police and army units. Police officers ringed the building while soldiers, summoned from nearby border patrol duty, prepared a perimeter and sealed off all possible escape routes. The terrorists weren't about to surrender, and they still thought it possible to reach their Zodiac moored at the breakwater and escape back to Lebanon. In a wild burst of gunfire, they managed to kill a police officer and race, with Danny and his daughter, to the beach. As the terrorists fumbled with their Zodiac, IDF units began to arrive. In an instant of final bravado, one of the terrorists took a boulder and smashed the four-year-old over the head, killing the young child instantly before her anguished father's eyes. Then, in an act of mercy, another terrorist placed the barrel of his AK-47 into Danny Haran's ear and blew his head off. In the ensuing fire-fight, two of the terrorists were killed and two were captured.

The attack mortified the Jewish State—the loss of the children was a particularly painful display of barbarism, and the government of Prime Minister Menachem Begin, a hardliner on terrorism, ordered the butchery to stop. Closing off the Palestinians' Lebanese sea lanes became a paramount military objective. Rear Admiral Almog was given carte blanche and a free hand in getting the job done. He mobilized his armadas of missile boats and Dabur patrol craft for proactive patrols of the coastline, both the Israeli and Lebanese, and ordered Flotilla 13 into action. For the next three years, there wouldn't be an inch of the Lebanese coast that the flotilla didn't come to know on an intimate basis. From Tripoli in the north near the Syrian border to Tyre in the south, if the Palestinians wanted to attack Israel by sea, they'd have to get by a Flotilla 13 ring of steel. The attack in Nahariya, it would turn out, would be the last time terrorists would succeed in landing on the Israeli shore and permitted to kill innocents.

There were dozens of operations that Almog immediately sanctioned. But just as he had closed down the Red Sea to the Egyptian Navy in 1973, Almog was determined to shut down the sea lanes for Palestinian terrorists using a combination of his assets, each specifically assigned a role in a triumvirate of defensive, offensive, and preemptive strikes. Stopping the terrorists at sea was a means of last resort. They were to be hit hard, hit where they lived, and hit with all the forces at the IDF/Navy's disposal from its large fleet of missile boats, some of which had already fired Gabriel surface-to-surface missiles at terrorist targets in the previous years.[13]

Almog's policy in sanctioning Flotilla 13's "hits" on terrorist targets revolved around a three-tiered solution based on flexibility, innovative strategy, and support from the highest levels of command in the IDF; with "Raful" as the chief of staff, authorization for special operations against terrorist targets would not be hard to obtain. Almog's plan called for the flotilla, and the IDF/Navy, to gather highly accurate, extremely up-to-date intelligence on the targets that would be hit; to hit the terrorists each time at a different place, a different time, and through different means; and to use every piece of equipment in the IDF/Navy's order of battle to disrupt the daily routine and schedules of the terrorists. If they were hit, hit hard, hit unexpectedly, and hit in a way that they could not carry out their training and preparations, Almog and Ayalon concurred that the terrorists would then not be able to strike at Israel.[14] During this "war of attrition" that was to be waged against the terrorists, Flotilla 13 was to be involved in four types of operations: ambushes, land assaults on shoreline targets, the sabotage and destruction of terrorist boats, and combined operations with Daburs, missile boats, and even IDF/Navy submarines against terrorist targets. There was one rule that Almog and Ayalon were determined to obey in this all-out war against the terrorists, and that was that civilians were not to be harmed on any strike.

One such successful combined-arms operation involved a circa-1980 raid against Tripoli, in northern Lebanon, where the headquarters facilities of Ahmed Jibril's Popular Front for the Liberation of Palestine General Command (PFLPGC) and Nayif Hawatmeh's Democratic Front for the Liberation of Palestine (DFLP) were to be hit simultaneously. The targeted buildings were not on the beach, but they were close enough to the Mediterranean that they could be seen from shore. It was too risky to dispatch the operators into the streets of Tripoli, alone and unprotected by large-scale backup (such as the manpower sent into the city in 1973), so a novel "combined-arms" approach was employed. According to Almog, "Flotilla 13 operators would infiltrate the beach and 'illuminate' the two targeted buildings, and then Gabriel surface-to-surface missiles would be launched from missile boats offshore and guided to the targets via the fire-control officer's optical control over the missile, onto their targets."[15] For obvious security reasons, the exact means of "illumination" cannot be discussed. The mission was a complete success, though the General Staff would only authorize the use of the Gabriel once it was "guaranteed" that only the two targeted structures, and not any nearby structures, would be hit.

The flotilla's favorite *modus operandi* was the ambush—over the course of a few months, the unit became expert in hunting its prey along the coastal roads and highways of Lebanon. Initially, due to logistics reasons, most of the ambushes were carried out around midnight; as the operators had to sail and deploy under the cover of darkness along the entire Lebanese coast, the earliest they could reach their objective and then march a kilometer or two toward a roadway was, in many cases, in the early A.M. hours. Lying in wait in the middle of enemy country is a daunting task—the dangers of being in a fire-fight against overwhelming odds can happen in the flash of a muzzle blast and the impact of an RPG. But beyond the dangers of engaging the enemy, there was the ever-present possibility of hitting a civilian truck or van. The Lebanese are the world's master-merchants, and even though an area could be under PLO control, with Syrian Army roadblocks, and under air assault from Israeli warplanes, the Lebanese would still pack their rusting vehicles with good wares and do their business—sometimes twenty-four hours a day. Forced to distinguish their targets ever so carefully, the operators became eagle-eyed in their marksmanship and frugal in the amount of ordnance they'd expend. By 1980, that flotilla had become so lethal in its use of firepower, so masterful in its combat skills, that in two-team ambushes launched along the coastal highway in Lebanon, terrorist targets were usually eliminated—completely and physically—by a remarkable *twenty-five* AK-47 rounds, one LAW rocket, and one RPG-7 grenade.[16] So good had Flotilla

13 become in ground operations, so advanced were their combat assault abilities, that "Raful," the venerable paratrooper who believed in his heart that the red berets followed no one into battle, sent operators from Sayeret Mat'kal, as well as commandos from various paratroop reconnaissance units.

Flotilla 13's ambushes were extremely successful in hindering terrorist movement along the coast—especially around bases where terrorist frogman units were trained and headquartered. In order to avoid ending up in the sights of a Flotilla 13 RPG, the terrorists changed their standard operating procedure and stopped sending vehicles out alone at night in the hopes that a reinforced convoy of several vehicles, with a complement of gunmen riding shotgun, would deter the Israeli commandos. Nothing, however, could have made Ayalon and the operators happier. "We were glad by this development," Almog said. "Instead of hitting one vehicle, we'd now hit two."[17] After each ambush, the terrorists would send their vehicles out earlier and earlier, hoping to do their business before the operators could land on Lebanese soil. Naturally, with a massive database of intelligence gathered on the terrorists and observation posts established on countless occasions, the operators knew a great deal about terrorist habits and trends, and they simply modified their own schedules accordingly. When the terrorists simply sent out their last vehicles at 18:00 hours, confident that the Israelis could never be on the ground so soon after sunset, Flotilla 13 simply began deploying their underwater delivery vehicles to get the operators to the targeted location.[18]

For the first time in the unit's history, too, sniper rifles were deployed with great frequency and with lethal results.

Almog had also wanted the flotilla to set up multiple ambushes, where one vehicle would be hit and then they'd sit back and wait until responding forces could be drawn into a fire-fight, but "Raful," hoping to avoid casualties, told his naval commander "not to be greedy." There was even concern that the amount of work being pushed on the unit was too much, and that the pressure, the fear, the constant adrenaline rushes, and the sheer physical exhaustion would one day—and possibly soon—takes its toll on the men.

In terms of seaborne assaults, the most successful Flotilla 13 raid of the period was "Operation High Voltage," an attack against the pro-Iraqi Arab Liberation Front (ALF) at their naval operating base at Ras as-Shaq, south of the Zaharani River tributaries, adjacent to the Sarafand refugee camp along the Mediterranean coast. The ALF had been very active in launching high-profile attacks against Israel's northern border, including a murderous attack against the nursery at Kibbutz Misgav Am in the spring of 1980, and intelligence received in Tel Aviv indicated that an eight-man squad was preparing a "major" operation against a civilian target in northern Israel that was to be launched from the Ras as-Shaq base. The targeted location was located just off the waterway leading into the sea, and the encampment was built around a small and shallow gulf of water. A two-story building served as HQ, while several smaller buildings and tents served as the living quarters, armory, and mess hall. There were more than forty terrorists calling Ras as-Shaq home, and all were heavily armed.[19]

Because of the inlet's shallow waters, and a series of OPs set up around the base, it wasn't possible to ferry in a company of paratroopers to the target and simply eradicate the facility. The IAF was hesitant about sending its fighter-bombers over the target, since it was surrounded by refugee dwellings and other civilian installations, including a school and a hospital. Stopping the ALF would require a "human touch," and it would have to be "up close and personal." The job fell to Flotilla 13. D-day was April 19, 1980.

"Operation High Voltage" would be, in the Flotilla 13 vernacular, "a big one." The force would consist of more than a dozen operators and would be ferried to the coast of Sarafand courtesy of a small armada of IDF/Navy missile boats. While a reserve force would await offshore in a defensive perimeter made up of Snunit insertion craft, the operators would reach the targeted beach by swimming to shore from their Zodiacs and establishing a beachhead.

Once the operators were safely on Lebanese soil, the task force would swim in the shallow inlet waters toward a lemon grove and attack the targeted facility while other operators, acting as a cover force, would lay down a barrage of intensive fire.

The insertion into Sarafand was achieved without incident and without the force being compromised. As the operators swam and marched into position, moving silently through the grove hoping not to give away their position by making noise or activating a booby-trap, two pathfinders discovered two terrorists leaving the HQ building. If they were going to go down, now was the time. The operators unleashed their AK-47s in a full auto blast of 7.62mm fire and suddenly the entire camp was ablaze with gunfire. As the attack force moved in toward the two-story building, carrying with them a twenty-kilogram satchel charge powerful enough to bring any building down, was tossed into an office window. In mounting the attack, the operators moved fast and without mercy. In well choreographed moves of disciplined movement, where the operators crouched into concealed positions, fired several rounds, and then continued their press forward, the attack was methodical and unstoppable. Grenades were tossed with accuracy and dexterity. Bursts of MAG fire sliced through the misty air, cutting down terrorists attempting to shield themselves behind lemon trees and tent posts. The fire-fight lasted nearly an hour. Before it was all over and the order to withdraw came in from the missile boats offshore, Flotilla 13 left Sarafand with a body count of fifteen dead terrorists, dozens more seriously wounded, and an infrastructure permanently destroyed.

In 1981, after two years of incessant operations against Palestinian targets in southern Lebanon, IDF Chief of Staff "Raful" Eitan bestowed upon Flotilla 13 the ultimate of honors—a Chief of Staff Citation to the entire unit. Such honors are rarely handed down to entire units, but the 200-plus men of the flotilla had, indeed, performed above and beyond the call of duty, and in the process of adhering to the professional guidelines of their work, they had rewritten the book on how Israel executes special operations behind enemy lines. For Almog, as IDF/Navy commander, and

Ayalon, his protégé, the unit citation was a sweet reward for a collective twenty-plus years of work with the Batmen.

In 1981, Captain Ayalon left the friendly confines of his beloved Atlit to attend the U.S. Naval Staff College prior to receiving command of a missile boat section. His deputy, Uzi Livnat, was promoted and named flotilla commander. Captain Livnat had joined the unit in 1966, and he had participated in the infamous march from Rosh Haniqra to Ashqelon with a young lieutenant named Ilan Egozi leading the rabble of zealous eighteen-year-old volunteers. Livnat was a charismatic officer whose popular and soft-spoken demeanor sometimes camouflaged the abilities of a natural-born warrior and combat officer. There were some in the Israeli special operations community who joked with Livnat that the flotilla had done so much in Lebanon that there wouldn't be much work left for him. They were wrong.

Lebanon in the summer of 1981 began to heat up until Israel's northern border resembled a war zone. IDF and PLO artillery batteries exchanged Katyusha and 155mm howitzer fire on a daily basis, the residents of northern Israel lived in their air-raid shelters, and Prime Minister Menachem Begin and new Defense Minister Ariel "Arik" Sharon, coming off a nation-elating first-strike destruction of the Iraqi nuclear reactor in Baghdad, were prepared to launch a full-scale war against the PLO in Lebanon to "once and for all" remove them from Israel's northern frontier. Only a superhuman effort by American Ambassador Philip Habbib managed to buy a year of relative quiet along the frontiers. A year was a long time in the Middle East.

On June 3, 1982, terrorists from the Abu Nidal faction critically wounded Israel's ambassador to the United Kingdom. Israel responded the way it did to any terrorist attack anywhere in the world—by launching a massive air and artillery assault against Palestinian targets in southern Lebanon and even in Beirut. The PLO, which coincidentally was also at war with the Abu Nidal faction, responded to the Israeli attacks in kind, with massive Katyusha barrages across Israel's northern frontier. This time, diplomacy would not soothe battered nerves and the march toward war. At 11:00 A.M. on June 6, 1982, over 50,000 Israeli soldiers crossed the border into Lebanon. The seventh full-scale Arab-Israeli War was under way. It was called "Operation Peace for Galilee."

The linchpin of Israel's strategy against the terrorists situated in the coastal cities from the frontier to Beirut was to have the IDF/Navy mount a large-scale amphibious landing at the Awali River tributaries, just due north of Sidon, in the hopes of cutting off large pockets of Palestinian forces within an Israeli stranglehold from the north, south, and east. The Awali beach was in the heart of terrorist country, and it needed to be secured. That task fell to Flotilla 13. Captain Uzi Livnat and his men had been to the beach dozens of times before in raids and ambushes, but this time they weren't playing hit-and-run. This time they were pathfinders, human trip-wires meant to check out the enemy presence, destroy it, and hold the beach until reinforced by paratroopers.

Already by June 5, twenty-four hours before the outbreak of the fighting, Rear Admiral Almog had mobilized the navy for war. With a large fleet of over twenty missile boats, dozens of Daburs, landing craft, and three relatively up-to-date submarines, an impressive armada of warships left the naval bases of Haifa and Ashdod that night—all prepared to close off Lebanon's sea lanes to the rest of the world. On board several of the missile boats was a large representation of naval commandos who would be landing on Lebanese soil hours later. The atmosphere at IDF/Navy HQ was tense on the morning of June 6 as the war broke out. The landing operation involved a large percentage of the entire navy, all sitting on warships around the coast of Sidon, vulnerable to Syrian missile-boat attack, or even the Syrian Air Force; the notorious Syrian SAM batteries in the Beka'a Valley had yet to be taken out and the IAF was forced to operate under the very real restrictions of being within range of nineteen surface-to-air missile batteries.

On the night of June 6, 1982, however, at 23:55 hours, a small of armada of Zodiacs began to appear over the horizon bouncing along the waves as they zoomed onto the Lebanese shore. The operators landed silently and in numbers that the unit had not deployed since Green Island. Establishing a small landing zone perimeter, a force of operators set up their FN MAGs and RPGs to create a defensive cross-fire (if needed), while the bulk of the sea-borne force fanned out into the surrounding foliage to establish a beachhead. The objective was *not* to engage the Palestinians in a pitched battle, since a large-scale fire-fight might send a red flag to local PLO commanders in Sidon (those who had yet to load their belongings into Mercedes automobiles for the mad dash to Beirut) and endanger the planned landing. In fact, a flotilla squad reaching the ditch at the bank of the coastal highway observed terrorist jeeps, laden with men and material, moving back and forth along the roadway. As they removed the safeties from their AK-47s and peered through the sites of their RPGs, the order to "break contact, continue to monitor" was heard over their headsets.

Thirty minutes after the operators landed, Rear Admiral Almog heard the words he'd been waiting to hear from Commander Didi, the flotilla's deputy commander in charge of the beachhead. "The beach is ready for the landing." Several Zodiacs filled with more operators from Flotilla 13 and supporting paratroopers were rushed to the beachhead as the cover of darkness remained strong. The following morning, over 5,000 pieces of equipment—tanks, artillery pieces, APCs, and jeeps—were landed from three IDF/Navy landing craft. It was the largest landing in Israeli military history.

For the next three months, the entire IDF/Navy was deployed off the Lebanese coast. Submarines served as coastal observation posts off the coasts of northern Beirut and Sidon, Dabur patrol boats hovered around the ports of Tyre and Sidon making sure that any terrorists hoping to escape in fishing vessels were cut down by well-placed 20mm fire, and the IDF/Navy's missile boat order of battle was deployed all along the elongated coastline as tactical backup for ground units fighting in the cities, in the refugee camps, and inside the Lebanese capital itself.[20]

For Flotilla 13, the primary task during the war was to prevent the terrorists from fleeing freely back to Beirut during the opening stages of Operation Peace for Galilee. Flotilla 13 was deployed in a classic full-fledged assault to execute dozens of ambushes against terrorist traffic along the coastal highway leading to the Lebanese capital. The ambushes were also of paramount strategic importance in at first preventing, and later deterring, terrorist forces from using the highway to head south and reinforce their comrades under attack by advancing IDF units. There were dozens of ambushes—some absolutely remarkable where several RPG rounds and a few dozen 7.62mm tracer rounds from a MAG lit up convoys of terrorist trucks like Roman candles. Other missions were smaller—some involving intelligence assets. A good deal of what the IDF/Navy and Flotilla 13 actually did during Operation Peace for Galilee remains classified top-secret to this day, though the corps did not suffer a single casualty to either ship or soldier during the conflict.

Israel's involvement in Lebanon lasts until this day—the adventure up north, at first pitting the IDF against the PLO, and then against a whole host of enemies, from Druze militiamen to the Shi'ite holy warriors of Hezbollah, has developed into a national quagmire. The results of the combined IDF/Navy and Flotilla 13 campaign against Palestinian seaborne terrorist attacks from April 1979 to February 1985 were amazing. During that period, not a single seaborne terrorist attack was perpetrated against the shoreline of the State of Israel, even though the terrorists tried, on countless occasions, to break through the hermetic ring of iron and neoprene wrapped around the Israeli coastline; more than twenty-five vessels, including those carrying suicide squads, were captured or sunk during this period. One of the most audacious attempts to break through the IDF/Navy's closure of the sea lanes came on the night of April 13, 1985, when the IDF/Navy intercepted a 1,000-ton, sixty-meter-long merchant ship, the S.S. *Attavirus*. The S.S. *Attavirus* had set sail from Algeria with a complement of nearly thirty terrorists from Abu Jihad's Force 17 in what would certainly have been the PLO's most spectacular attack ever against the Jewish State. The thirty men were to land rubber dinghies on the coast of Bat Yam,

Samuel M. Katz

south of Tel Aviv, and then they were to commandeer a bus
and drive toward the Kirya, the Israeli Ministry of Defense
and IDF HQ complex in the heart of downtown Tel Aviv,
and assassinate then Israeli Defense Minister Yitzhak
Rabin.

Force 17 would never make it to Tel Aviv. Approximately
a hundred miles off the Israeli coastline, however, the I.N.S.
Moledet, a missile boat commanded by a former Unit 707
officer, intercepted the *Attavirus* and, after being the target
of a half-dozen RPG rounds launched by the terrorists,
peppered the rusty freighter with an unforgiving blast of
20mm Vulcan fire, sinking the boat in minutes. In all, eight
terrorists were plucked out of the water. Twenty went down
with their ship.

That failed terrorist attack, in fact, would have major
repercussions for Abu Jihad three years later one quiet
spring night in the Tunisian capital of Tunis.

Israel circa 1988 was a land of despair and turmoil. The
Intifada, or Palestinian uprising, had scared the Jewish
State into a confused nation unsure of its direction and
doubtful of its future. The question of Palestinian rights,
their plea for self-determination, and their yearnings for
statehood were now removed from the small stage of a
regional conflict and propelled into the international spotlight. The Israeli leadership found itself the target of wide-
spread condemnation, much of it clearly biased, for its
handling of the uprising: the firebombing of a Jewish family
inside their car was viewed as an end result of tensions
allowed to fester for too long, while a rock-throwing Palestinian teenager shot and killed by Israeli security forces
became the centerpiece of a United Nations Security Council lambasting and inevitable condemnation. IDF officers
and soldiers, too, soon found their every action examined
under the scrutiny of the international press, as well as by
Israeli leaders eager to find unwitting scapegoats that would
deflect responsibility for the uncontrollable crisis from their
shoulders. Muddled and intentionally vague orders were
issued to the front-line personnel combating the uprising
including directives where riot ringleaders were to be beaten

with clubs and fists in order to break the bones, internally, of the Intifada. Inevitably, politically volatile court-martials were carried out for soldiers found guilty of administering undue force in their handling of the uprising. The very moral fiber of the IDF was challenged.

The uprising provided the PLO leadership with a tempting opportunity to assume unchallenged control of a struggle it had no role in initiating. The rock-throwing youths of the camps, the masked men of the Shabab (the Palestinian youth mob), who had tantalized the world's imagination with their tenacious challenge to Israeli rule in an epic David-versus-Goliath struggle, were, however, an uncontrolled and unguided force. They needed leadership, and they desperately required direction. Through glory-filled broadcasts via Radio Monte Carlo and fliers distributed throughout the territories, Arafat and his lieutenants in Tunis attempted to blaze a path toward Palestinian liberation. But it was the rock-throwing kids who were in the trenches, not Arafat. It was they who were assaulting Israeli troops, and it was they who were being killed in the ensuing chaos. For the PLO to lay a claim to the soul of the Intifada, rocks would have to be replaced by AK-47 assault rifles, and Molotov cocktails would have to be discarded in favor of five-kilogram loads of high explosives. The man to achieve this difficult task was Abu Jihad—Yasir Arafat's military mastermind and the man in charge of the Western Sector, the body responsible for executing terrorist attacks—and special operations—inside Israel and the territories.

Abu Jihad's career in Fatah had been a stormy and tumultuous tenure of missed glory. One of Fatah's founding fathers, Abu Jihad, had assumed a wide array of posts and tasks within the fledgling force of Palestinian liberation since 1964. Not as cutthroat as Abu Iyad, and as a result not placed in charge of the organization's dreaded internal security department, Abu Jihad was instead destined to formulate the organization's military character. Prior to the 1967 War, Abu Jihad had ventured to the far corners of the globe to obtain military assistance and training expertise for his fledgling Fatah liberation fighters. He traveled throughout the East Bloc countries, as well as the People's

Republic of China, North Korea, and North Vietnam. Throughout the tumultuous early years of Palestinian armed resistance against Israel, from 1965 to 1973, Abu Jihad had earned a solid reputation as a military planner and as an Arafat loyalist. Yet it was in the aftermath of Operation Spring of Youth, when Sayeret Mat'kal commandos assassinated Abu Yusef, a chief officer in Black September and director of Fatah operations inside Israel proper, that Abu Jihad was thrust into the forefront of the PLO leadership. It was an ironic twist of fate that the unit responsible in a roundabout way for promoting Abu Jihad would eventually be responsible for his elimination.

For the next fifteen years, Abu Jihad's signature adorned some of the most heinous acts of terrorism ever perpetrated against the Jewish State: the August 1972 takeover of the Israeli Embassy in Bangkok; the June 24, 1974, Nahariya Massacre; the March 5, 1975, seaborne attack against Tel Aviv's Savoy Hotel; the March 11, 1978, Country Club Massacre; and the April 1985 attempted assault on the Israeli Defense Ministry in which the S.S. *Attavirus* was blown out of the Mediterranean waters. Many analysts, in fact, have credited the failed 1985 raid on Tel Aviv as the Israelis' *causus belli* for terminating Abu Jihad, since it targeted Israeli Defense Minister Yitzhak Rabin for assassination. In retrospect, it was Abu Jihad's failed, though bloody, attempts to raise the Intifada's level of violence to extraordinary levels that eventually determined his fate.

In early February 1988, Abu Jihad dispatched three heavily laden Fatah terrorists across the Egyptian border into Israel. Their objective: to seize a passenger bus and take hostages inside a Negev Desert cooperative farm. Abu Jihad had personally designed the operation, a bloody undertaking bound to achieve notable media coverage, in order to propel the leadership of the uprising into the PLO's hands. The diabolical task failed miserably, however. The three terrorists managed to cross into Israel but were pursued for twenty-two hours by Bedouin trackers and reconnaissance infantrymen through the desert abyss of southern Israel. On February 11, 1988, the three Palestinians were cornered and, following a brief fire-fight, forced to surrender. It was a humiliating defeat for Abu Jihad, and one he vowed to avenge.

In the early morning hours of March 7, 1988, three heavily armed Fatah terrorists from Force 17 crossed the Egyptian frontier into Israel, commandeered a car, and raced through the Negev Desert toward the town of Beersheba. Their crossing had been discovered by an IDF unit, and a general security alert had been sounded throughout southern Israel. Ostensibly, the Israelis believed the terrorists were to attack one of the nearby agricultural settlements, and as a result, all the nearby Kibbutzim and Moshavim were sealed and secured by armed guards. Yet the terrorists hijacked an intercity bus carrying workers from their homes in Beersheba to the top-secret nuclear facility at Dimona. Special police and IDF units were summoned, and the bus was tracked down and subsequently immobilized. A standoff ensued, but after the terrorists murdered one of their hostages, the Ya'ma'm, the border guards' anti-terrorist hostage-rescue force, sprang into action. In a matter of seconds, the three terrorists were dead, but so, too, were three hostages—all women. The incident, known as the "Bus of Mothers Massacre," galvanized the Israeli leadership to act decisively. If Abu Jihad had ascended to the military command of the PLO through an Israeli commando operation, then he could be removed through similar means. Well after midnight on April 13, according to published reports, a small armada of missile boats secretly left Haifa.

In the late-night hours of April 15, 1988, a force of operators from Flotilla 13 landed on the shores of Ras Carthage, off the coast of Tunis. They reconnoitered in the area and were met by a group of Mossad agents in three rented vehicles. Once assured that the coast was clear, the naval commandos signaled to the spearhead of the operation, a task force of Sayeret Mat'kal commandos, who were brought ashore by means of Zodiac craft piloted by handpicked operators from Flotilla 13. The combined Mossad/Sayeret Mat'kal task force drove through downtown Tunis and on to the exclusive Siddi Bouseid suburb where many top PLO officials lived, including Abu Jihad. After staking out the luxurious villa for several hours awaiting the PLO deputy commander's return from a meeting at Arafat's headquarters, the commandos silently eliminated Abu Jihad's security detail and then quickly raced through the house in search of their target. Abu Jihad was killed in a matter of seconds, destroyed in a flurry of seventy-five bullets. According to several reports, the entire operation was videotaped by one of the Israeli commandos.

The Abu Jihad assassination was a large-scale covert operation involving IDF/Navy missile boats and two IAF Boeing 707 electronic countermeasure and C³ aircraft. According to foreign reports, the two planes provided an electronic blanket over much of Tunis, rendering Tunisian, as well as Palestinian, military and security communications useless for the duration of the raid. Nearly every aspect of Israel's intelligence community was involved in the operation, and it had been executed with brilliant precision. It was a daring display of a nation's resolve to pay back, with biblical justice, the perpetrators of terrorism.

Another perpetrator of terrorism that the State of Israel was after was Ahmed Jibril, the warlord of the Popular Front for the Liberation of Palestine General Command (PFLP-GC). Unlike the jet-setting Jihad, however, Jibril rarely ventured outside of Lebanon or Syria, and he was never without an extensive shield of bodyguards and Syrian military escorts. The only countries he would visit on official PFLP-GC business were Bulgaria (until 1991 a Communist Big Brother police state where Israeli operatives were not welcome), the Islamic republic of Iran (where Israel's intelligence operations were extremely limited since the expulsion of the Shah), and, of course, Libya. In his Lebanese and Syrian hideaways, Jibril might have been physically closer to Israel than Abu Jihad was in Tunis, but in reality he was in an envelope of invulnerability. Unlike other Palestinian officials that the Israelis had terminated in the past, such as the Black September officials responsible for the Munich Olympics Massacre, Ahmed Jibril was not the type of target to be removed by an assassin's—or an intelligence agent's—well-placed .22-caliber bullet; nor did his movements allow his vehicle or living quarters to be booby-trapped with a powerful explosive device. He was a man who did not follow a routine, did not travel to locations where there were large crowds, and never fell victim to the trappings of habit.

The spymasters at Mossad and A'man headquarters in Tel Aviv realized that accurate and timely intelligence would be crucial in any plan to kill Ahmed Jibril, but intelligence work alone would never achieve the task. The work of the intelligence-gatherers and analysts would have to lay the groundwork for some type of hard-hitting lightning military strike. In May 1988, Israel believed it had come across that very lethal combination that would turn a routine operation into a historic undertaking. A'man had learned that Jibril would be conducting an inspection tour of one of his western Lebanon bases south of Beirut. The IDF General Staff and IAF HQ had planned to launch an air strike at the exact time that Ahmed Jibril was walking past his legions and receiving the obligatory honor-guard parade; although not confirmed, it is believed that the IAF dispatched several RPV drones to monitor developments at the PFLP-GC base in Lebanon. At dusk on May 12, six IAF aircraft launched a Stukalike dive-bombing attack on the PFLP-GC base in Barja, sixteen kilometers south of Beirut, which was situated in the middle of a thick olive grove. Armed with rockets and air-to-surface missiles, the attacking aircraft launched a ten-minute attack on the base, even though Palestinian anti-aircraft fire, emanating from 23mm cannons mounted on flatbed Toyota trucks, was heavy. It has yet to be revealed if Jibril was indeed in the Barja facility, but if he was, he miraculously survived, for the Israeli pilots did report that they scored good hits on all the targets.

Clearly the Israelis were disappointed by this latest aerial failure to kill Jibril, even though the IDF spokesman never acknowledged that the objective of the air strike was the assassination of the PFLP-GC commander. It was clear to the IDF chief of staff, Lieutenant General Shomron; his deputy, Major General Ehud Barak, as well as the other members of the General Staff that if Jibril was, indeed, to be put out of action, it would have to be done on the ground and by a sizable commando force. Such an operation would require an elite force, adept at large-formation conventional fighting as well as lightning assaults deep into the enemy heartland. It would also have to be a force led by the most innovative commanders, known for their unyielding courage and decisive command under fire. In essence, the IDF General Staff required the services of its toughest conventional reconnaissance formation in the Israeli order of battle. That unit was an elite and highly heralded force with the affectionate nickname of the "Flying Tigers." The unit assigned to eliminate Ahmed Jibril was the 1st Golani Infantry Brigade's reconnaissance, *Sayeret Golani. Sayeret Golani* spearheaded Israel's assault on the Golan Heights on June 9, 1967, when its commandos, along with the brigade's Barak Battalion captured the Syrian fort at Tel Fahar, a seemingly impregnable gauntlet of rock and machine-gun nests considered the key to the overall defense of the Golan Heights. Dressed for battle in their lizard-pattern camouflage fatigues, the *Sayeret Golani* commandos were forced to use their Uzi submachine guns to launch magazine-emptying bursts of 9mm fire into darkened bunkers at point-blank range, as well as use their compact weapons as metal truncheons in the dozens of brutal hand-to-hand battles that raged throughout the cordite-engulfed fort. The unit's esprit de corps was epitomized by the fact that seriously wounded personnel "escaped" from hospital beds in order to participate in the fighting.

Just as *Sayeret Golani* would play an instrumental role in the capture of the Golan Heights during the 1967 War, so, too, would it play an instrumental role in its defense and eventual recapture. *Sayeret Golani,* in many General Staff circles, was considered the finest reconnaissance formation in the IDF.

Ahmed Jibril had been a thorn in the State of Israel's side for nearly thirty years, yet a spectacular terrorist attack he launched on November 25, 1987, against northern Israel, where a terrorist in a hang glider crossed the border and killed six Israeli soldiers, had marked him for death.

Such was the case on December 8, 1988, when a joint Flotilla 13/*Sayeret Golani* crew landed on the Lebanese coast, near Damur, for what was to have been one of the IDF's premier commando strikes—its code name was "Operation Blue Heat." The PFLP-GC complex at Al-Na'ameh, situated several kilometers from the shoreline, was a fortress, much of it built underground by Vietnamese engineers, and it was protected by a series of interlocking tunnels and trenches; a terrorist barracks was carved into the side of a hill, and Jibril's command complex, also located underground, was encased by cast-iron walls. To breach the terrorist defenses, the Golani commandos took with them a small force of trained Rottweilers, strong and sturdy dogs, whose backs would be laden with satchel charges of high explosives. The commandos would send the dogs into the tunnels and trenches, then detonate them from remote control.

The attack force was deployed from a missile boat moored off the Lebanese coast, which would also serve as a mobile command post for IDF Chief of Staff Shomron and IDF/Navy commander Rear Admiral Avraham Ben-Shoshan, a career missile-boat officer who had succeeded Ze'ev Almog. So professional was the Flotilla 13 landing that the Zodiacs were driven right up on the sand, and the Golani commandos didn't have to wet their uniforms. Soon, however, many Golani uniforms would be drenched in blood. The attack went well at first, but terrorist resistance was stiff, and Jibril's bunker was unreachable. Several commandos were seriously hurt, and the mission commander, Lieutenant Colonel Amir Meital, was killed. Under heavy terrorist fire, the commandos were heli-lifted to safety.

The war between Israel and the Palestinians, especially the one fought on the seas, would continue. On the early morning hours of May 30, 1990, nearly thirty terrorists from Abu Abbass's Palestine Liberation Front (PLF) prepared to launch an epic suicide attack against the Tel Aviv coast—beaches that were to be packed with nearly a quarter million holiday sunbathers. Trained near Benghazi by Libyan naval commandos, the terrorists were to be unloaded into the Mediterranean by a mother ship and proceed toward the shores of Tel Aviv on six high-powered motorboats; they were coated with rubberized paint to make them impervious to radar and armed with a variety of 23mm cannons and Katyusha rocket launchers. Luckily for the Israelis, four of the motorboats suffered mechanical difficulties in open water, and a fifth also had its engine break down after attempting to evade an IDF/Navy Dabur patrol craft that had attempted to chase it in vain just north of Tel Aviv. Only after interrogating the terrorists did the Dabur commander learn that a sixth boat was heading toward Tel Aviv, its target: the beachfront around the Sheraton Hotel. Immediately, the IDF/Navy mobilized Dabur patrol boats toward Tel Aviv, but the small radar blip fading in and out of their radar screens was moving at a speed of nearly thirty-five knots, and the Daburs were losing ground in every second of the pursuit. Israel Air Force attack choppers and light aircraft were called in to locate the speedboat and force it to beach at a secluded stretch of surf twenty kilometers south of Tel Aviv at Nitzanim, where a task force of reconnaissance commandos and anti-terrorists assault troops were awaiting it in the sand dunes. In the brief fire-fight, the terrorist squad was terminated and several terrorists captured. Tragedy had been averted, but only through the fortunate luck of faulty maintenance at the terrorists' base in Benghazi. "Luck," according to a frustrated Dabur commander, "was not an acceptable defense against seaborne infiltration."

Lebanon had traditionally been the staging area for seaborne terrorist attacks against the Jewish State, and it had borne the brunt of Israeli preemptory and retaliatory strikes. But would Libya be targeted in retaliation for the failed PLF raid? So far, nothing, to the date of the publication of this book, has publicly "blown up" in Benghazi or Tobruk had a Flotilla 13 address to it. Nor were there any reports of mysterious explosions in Algeria, Syria, the Sudan, or even the Persian Gulf. Even if there were some reports of sabotage so far from Israeli shores, the mission would, most likely, be deniable. "After all," claims one SEAL officer who had worked with Flotilla 13 in the black area of counter-terrorism, "in this type of business, if you don't hear about something blowing, some rag-head bastard getting whacked, or some bleeding-heart CNN reporter, usually with a British accent, talking about some martyred SOB who was blown to paradise, it means that it was a successful mission."[21]

It would be hard for the unit to remain an enigma, however, because on July 7, 1992, a tradition in Flotilla 13 would come full circle when Rear Admiral Ami Ayalon was named the commander of the IDF/Navy. With Chief of Staff Ehud Barak, Israel's ultimate commando warrior (and its most decorated soldier) as chief-of-staff and former Chief of Staff Yitzhak Rabin serving as prime minister, a new golden age of Israeli special operations had dawned. To the men of Flotilla 13 and Sayeret Mat'kal, there would be many sleepless nights in the months to come.

One sleepless night came on July 6, 1993, and it was known as "Operation Law and Order." In response to attacks by Iran's surrogate forces in Lebanon, Hezbollah guerrillas and terror warlord Ahmed Jibril's Popular Front for the Liberation of Palestine General Command (PFLP-GC), Flotilla 13 acted as a spearhead for an IDF assault on Tripoli. The mission was to inflict mayhem and destruction, both physical and psychological, on the enemy, and to make a statement that even though Tripoli is over 100 miles from Israel, it is still well within the domain of the flotilla. Being attacked by aircraft or gunships is an impersonal and distant strike that pits the guerrilla and his assault rifle against a Mach 2 jet fighter—these strikes are usually preceded by air raids and pursuing volleys of anti-aircraft artillery fire. Guerrillas view this warfare as unfair and unworthy of their skills; they usually race to improvised air-raid shelters to sit out the destructive blitzes. Being stalked by a commando, however, is what many Palestinian guerrillas in Lebanon fear most. If a bomb falls on them, *Insh'Allah*, it is God's will, but a garrote pulled tight around the neck, or a dagger lunged into their hearts, is a slow and paralyzing exercise in agonizing death. The darkness is their nemesis—its dangers and shadows cannot be seen. On this night, the guerrillas of the PFLP-GC would have much to fear. Flotilla 13 was no stranger to Tripoli.

The operators had their concerns about the raid, as well. Although they had trained for months for an operation of this sort, they were nervous that at the last minute the raid would be canceled. After all, Tripoli was as close to Syrian territorial waters as the IDF/Navy wished to venture, and an alert coastal radar operator could have endangered the entire operation. One hour prior to H-hour, the commandos, still living off of the endless pots of high-dosage coffee and endless chain of cigarette nicotine, were assembled in the forward living quarters of the rocking missile boat (doors closed to the ship's crew who do not have the clearance to overhear what will be said) for their final pre-mission briefing. Although each commando participating in the about-to-be-launched mission had been through the A-to-Zs of the operation countless times, a flotilla trademark is to have each and every possible and conceivable contingency answered for—there would be one more briefing. A map was examined *again*, a chart listing the objectives was studied one final time, and each commando had to verbally reiterate his tasks one final time. The briefing was completed without emotion or endearing pep talk. This was business—deadly business, but it was business as usual. The operators, already wearing the shorts of their neoprene wet suits and olive combat fatigues, gathered their specially modified black neoprene "Mae West" buoyancy vests and special nylon assault web gear, and then they tucked their black Nomex face masks inside their ammunition pouches. Leaving the forward cabin, they silently headed through the war room, across to the galley, and then up the narrow stairs toward the starboard deck. Standing aside a row of Gabriel and Harpoon surface-to-surface missiles in their tubelike launchers, the commandos performed one final weapons check on their Soviet-produced AK-47 7.62mm assault rifles, some fitted with silencers and others modified with M203 40mm grenade launchers, as well as their FN MAG light machine guns and RPG-7 anti-tank rocket launchers. As senior commanders looked on—including, it has been

reported, IDF/Navy commander Rear Admiral Ami
Ayalon[22]—the dark-clad men effortlessly lowered their Zodiac rubber inflatable boats (RIBs) into the choppy sea for
the ride to Tripoli.

The ride in the RIBs was short and uneventful. The
PFLP-GC sentries were not expecting an attack, and their
eyes and heavy weapons sights were aimed toward the
heavens in search of Israeli aircraft, not along the surf in
search of the dreaded frogmen. The operators landed silently and hooked up their craft at a deserted patch of
protective rock; specially modified single-lens night-vision
goggles, waterproofed and solidly constructed, were worn
over neoprene head covers and rebreather apparatus.[23]
Slinking across a narrow beach just north of Tripoli, they
quickly assembled in ambush position along Lebanon's
coastal highway—a stretch of road that ran from the Syrian
border all the way along the Mediterranean south toward
the barbed-wire fences of the Israeli frontier. With their
infrared sights and night-vision goggles, the commandos
were operating as if it were daytime, but the terrorists were
not. The first target was a PFLP-GC vehicle racing at high
speed from Tripoli to the logistics' base; it was marked for
destruction and obliterated in a ten-second burst of
machine-gun fire; the inhabitants of the vehicle, four men
clad in camouflage kit holding their assault rifles, were cut
down mercilessly. Satisfied but not done, the commandos
headed northward closer to the PFLP-GC base in order to
search for bigger and more lucrative prey, but the hunters
soon found themselves under the gun. A PFLP-GC patrol,
seeing their comrades erupt in a fireball down the road,
headed toward the highway with weapons ablaze. A pitched
battle ensued between the commandos of Flotilla 13 and
the gunmen of the PFLP-GC, but the battle was one-sided.
Three terrorists were killed immediately; nearly a dozen
more were cut down by the accurate bursts of AK-47 fire.
The assault team commander, Lieutenant Didi, radioed
back to the missile boat as the whine of silenced fire erupted
around him, and he said that his work had been done and
the rubber crafts would be heading back to ship shortly. In a

well-rehearsed and well-choreographed exercise, they withdrew toward the sea line. Two-man teams covered the retreat with well-placed, extremely accurate small-arms fire, with the occasional fragmentation grenade thrown in for good measure. By the time the PFLP-GC forces reached the shore, the RIBs were nearly hooked up with the missile boats. Several guerrillas brought out a North Korean 120mm mortar and attempted to hit the silhouette of a warship they saw in the distance, but their shells all fell short.

The Flotilla 13 commandos were inside the missile boat's war room, a bit more relaxed, when phase two of the mission commenced—the ship's 76mm main gun opened up a heavy artillery barrage. Additional terrorists were killed by the shelling, and installations inside the base were lit up by high-explosive shells. The commandos of Flotilla 13 had been able to gather invaluable targeting data on shore. By early morning, the ship returned to Haifa[24] and the commandos returned to their home base at Atlit just a few miles south of Israel's largest port city. The commandos returned tired and jubilant—it had been a good night's work—but they accepted their well-deserved rest with foreboding. It was only a matter of time before they would return to Lebanon.

Three months later, those same commandos sat inside the TV-and-recreation room at Atlit glued to a small 17-inch screen beaming history back to them. On September 13, 1993, Israeli Prime Minister Yitzhak Rabin and PLO Chairman Yasir Arafat achieved the impossible by not only cementing a deal where both sides appeared to recognize the legitimacy and existence of the other, but also they had stood side by side and shook hands under a brilliant sun on the White House lawn. It was absolutely breathtaking and inconceivable to most of the men in the room. But Flotilla 13 was not the type of unit that reaped the rewards of a peace treaty, and attention switched quickly to Beirut, where Hezbollah warned that Israel would now be destroyed in a firestorm of Islamic vengeance. Unconventional means, not only paradise-inspired attacks, were becoming part of the terrorists' arsenal. On the night of

October 21, 1993, according to Lebanese military reports, Flotilla 13 returned to the waters off southern Lebanon.[25] A week before, a suicide-terrorist emanating from the uncontrolled beaches of Sidon had attempted to infiltrate Israel courtesy of a Kawasaki jet ski; he was a frogman and part of an elite unit in Dr. George Habash's Popular Front for the Liberation of Palestine. Although he was picked off like a duck in a carnival arcade by a 20mm round fired from a Dabur patrol craft, this was too audacious an attempt to go unanswered. The Batmen were summoned.

At 3:00 A.M. on the night of October 21, 1993, three teams of frogmen emerged from the darkened waters and placed explosive devices, improvised limpets, to the hulls of three gigantic rafts used as buoys by terrorist forces.

By the time the rafts had erupted in a fiery ball hours later, the operators were sipping cups of Bedouin coffee and tea, safely inside an IDF/Navy vessel heading back to Israel.

The operation, spectacular and routine at the same time, took place on the forty-fifth anniversary of the sinking of the R.E.N.S. *Emir Farouk,* and the twentieth anniversary of the destruction of the Egyptian Komar missile boat in A'ardaka that was responsible, in part, for the sinking of the I.N.S. *Eilat*—also, incredibly, on an October 21, twenty-six years earlier.

There is a footnote to the saga of Flotilla 13 in the last quarter century worthy of a book of its own and certainly of mention here. Although the unit has been renowned for the last fifty years for daring underwater strikes, explosive assaults on enemy beaches, and a brilliant talent for terrorizing terrorists, one of the most poignant operations of Flotilla 13 in recent memory, one so connected to the overall mission of the Jewish State that the mission's successful—and covert—execution was by itself an epic justification to the very existence of the State of Israel, has recently been declassified. As early as 1980, the Israeli government had received reports that the Falashas, the Jews of Ethiopia, were in dire straits and suffering harsh treatment under the Communist dictatorship. A secret meeting of the Israeli cabinet voted to make an attempt to rescue the Ethiopian Jews, believed to be direct descendants of King

Solomon, once IDF/Navy OC Rear Admiral Ze'ev Almog assured them that such a mission was possible. Subsequently, a small army of Mossad agents were dispatched to Addis Ababa, where they established a diving resort, one geared for European tourists, along the banks of the Red Sea. While Sudanese officials thought nothing of the resort—they welcomed the tourist dollars and subsequent payoffs—the Mossad agents were using the facility as a way station for the smuggling of Ethiopian Jews to Israel. At night, while cocktails were being mixed and singers sang in the resort's nightclub, operators from Flotilla 13 would bring in small speedboats and provide a ferry service to an awaiting mother ship for the Jews brought to the resort under cover of darkness.[26] The operation was top-secret, with only a handful of officials in Jerusalem (and Langley, Virginia) knowing about its existence. It is estimated that nearly 1,000 Jews, brought out in ten waves, were smuggled out of Ethiopia this way. Thousands more would follow years later in massive airlifts.

From Sudan to Sidon, from Tunis to Tripoli, only one's imagination can tell where Flotilla 13 is operating today.

Postscript

The Human Element:
Men Made of Wits and Steel

"To do what we do one needs to be a truly unique—if not completely insane—individual. We are more than mere soldiers, more than neatly manicured machines marching in step, saluting with our rifles and shining our shoes. We are sneaky, we are ruthless, we are trained to kill, and we live according to our own frequency. We are all Rogue Warriors in a way—just like the book by the SEAL commander, Marcinko. We care little for authority or the rigid trappings of this society we call a military. We care that we are provided with a mission, and that we are provided with the freedom to successfully and safely—for us—carry out that mission. We care little for politics, public affairs, or bullshit. And, I should say, we are provided with the tools, and entrusted with the knowledge and the training and responsibility not to give a damn about the bullshit. We are anonymous and unforgiving. We are never there and we are always present. That's what we are all about!"

—Ensign D., June 6, 1996[1]

To become a *Kommando Yami,* a Flotilla 13 operator, an eighteen-year-old conscript into the ranks of the Israel Defense Forces does not need to be a ready-made Rambo, he does not have to be a champion weight-lifter, athlete, or martial artist, nor does he have to know how to swim or dive (knowing how to float, however, does help!). All those wishing to serve in Flotilla 13 *must* first be in good physical condition (a 97 medical profile, considered top-of-the-line, is required), must not have any medical problems that inhibit his potential underwater action (poor ears or vision requiring corrective glasses), and, most important, he must volunteer. Flotilla 13 does not recruit its personnel; those who want to become a member of the club must make the effort to volunteer and be ready to sign on for nearly two years of professional service in addition to the three years of mandatory service. Upon the conscript's arrival at the IDF's sprawling Absorption and Distribution Base where all Israeli teenagers undergo the uneasy transformation to teenage soldiers, all conscripts have already undergone their pre-military physical, psychological, and psychotechnical examinations. Each conscript has already amassed a huge and tell-all file in the IDF computer, and all this revealing data is awaiting the conscript upon his arrival at the base. Only those who have the basic faculties are even allowed to volunteer.

All volunteers participate in what is known as a *Gibush* or test-period, a week-long exercise in suffering that allows officers of Flotilla 13 to evaluate the commando candidates under extremely trying and stressful situations. There are grueling physical exercises that determine not the candidate's physical tolerance but rather his psychological endurance; according to former Flotilla 13 commander Captain (Res.) Uzi Livnat, "The most important muscle in any commando's body is his brain."[2] There is a point when the body quits but the mind takes over and provides reserve energy, reserve tolerance, reserve ability to continue and persevere. It is this strength that flotilla commanders look for among the hopefuls in the *Gibush,* and it is this strength that they seek. The flotilla's most intense means of viewing how the candidate can tolerate unimaginable suffering is the legendary and infamous march from Rosh Haniqra to Ashqelon: a tortuous 200-kilometer forced march along the Mediterranean coast from the Lebanese border at Rosh Haniqra to the barbed-wire frontier with the soon-to-be evacuated Gaza Strip. The number of hopefuls beginning the march at the Lebanese frontier might be seventy or eighty, but as the pace heightens and as feet accustomed to sneakers and sandals soon find how large blisters grow and flourish inside the sweaty confines of newly issued combat boots, the number of dropouts grows; an ambulance and a bus follows the long line of marchers awaiting those who, for physical or medical reasons, will not complete the course. Many just surrender because they cannot endure the pain, others simply realize that a life of suffering and challenges is too much for them—they are returned to Ba'ku'm with no marks against their records. Yet as the marchers reach central Israel, around Tel Aviv, the ranks separate and the assembled candidates become a loosely connected stream of slow-moving, heavy-breathing stubborn souls who are determined not to quit. The soles of their feet might be bleeding, joints and muscles pushed beyond the envelope of pain, but they are absolute in their resolve not to surrender. At this point in the march, with about half the hopefuls already gone, the flotilla instructors begin to apply their own personal pressure on the surviving few: "C'mon, you really want to quit . . . you've done well, but you can't make it, I can see how you are in pain . . . just quit and hop on the bus back to base . . . you still have sixty kilometers to go, you look like you can't go on for another sixty centimeters!" This personal egging on makes the remaining marchers spiteful, and it allows them to redirect their anger toward spiting the instructors and actually finishing off the course.

When the march from Rosh Haniqra to Ashqelon ends, and the temporary torture is complete, another bit of indigenous torture included in the Flotilla 13 *Gibush* is having the candidate, equipped with a snorkel and mask painted black, sit inside a pool filled with all sorts of crustaceans of the biting variety. Many hopefuls, only a few days in the army, find the underwater experience, enhanced by a sense of complete darkness, completely unnerving—the biting crabs and lobsters add to the feeling of utter fear and pain. Only half of those who started the process remain. The "survivors," as they are known, are then in a position to commence the long and hard road ahead of them. Obviously, much of the flotilla's training is highly classified, but the *general* path in the making of an operator has not changed in the past forty years. The first step in the path to owning the coveted bat-wing insignia is a seven-month-long paratroop-style basic infantry training. It is the exact same small-arms and combat instruction that paratroops undergo and virtually identical to the training that infantrymen in the Golani and Giva'ati Brigade receive, but the trainees of Flotilla 13 are segregated into their own platoon and handled somewhat separately than their red-beret brothers in arms. Officers and psychologists from Flotilla 13 generally visit these men in training to make sure that everything is okay and that they are surviving the training properly. Even at this basic phase of the long and arduous course, those not meeting the rigid flotilla standards are thrown out of the program—placed in a paratroop unit or offered the opportunity to volunteer for another elite reconnaissance or commando unit.

Basic training concludes with the commando candidate obtaining the rank of corporal and a visit to the Tel Nof air base and parachutist course. Each and every Flotilla 13 operator is parachutist-qualified. Only after the silver metal wings adorn the candidates' chests are they allowed entrance into the home base at Atlit for the aquatic phase of the training. It is here, according to Commander S. until recently the Flotilla 13 commander, "that the candidates stop being teenagers and start becoming potential commandos."[3]

The first phase of the truly naval aspect of this special warfare training is basic boating skills, rudimentary diving and advanced swimming. Commanders from Flotilla 13 through the ages realize that the underwater aspect of the training is a most crucial test of the candidates and the instructors. In the field, underwater, the commandos are faced with enormous hardships and situations in which they must change from the original plan and innovatively modify their approach. If the decisive and life-saving discipline of diving is not hammered into the heads of the men when they are impressionable and haven't learned from bad habit, underwater disaster whether it be while diving or while operating a SDV, is a tragic inevitability. According to Rear Admiral (Res.) Ze'ev Almog, a man who has, as Flotilla 13 commander and OC IDF/Navy, had to bury the dead of such training mishaps, "Diving accidents are a tragic example of poor discipline in the commander, the instructor, and the commando, and it cannot be allowed to occur in a commando unit such as the flotilla."[4]

The initial aspect of the diving instruction is one of the more difficult phases of the Flotilla 13 training, and this is where a good percentage of the candidates are forced out due to attrition. Failure to successfully master the art of scuba, deep-sea diving, and long-range swimming is not answered with a second chance slap on the back and a "Don't worry, you'll do better next time" to console a wounded ego. Any sign of failure guarantees immediate ouster from the unit and the abandonment for what to many is a life-long dream and aspiration. "It rocked my world as if I had just become homeless and rendered a cripple," claims a sergeant in the IDF Jump School at Tel Nof, who was dropped from the Flotilla 13 course in the underwater stage of his instruction. "I felt special, I felt invincible, and I felt like I was so important that the prime minister of the State of Israel would and could rely on me to carry out the most incredible assignments far from home and in the clutches of enemy territory. When you were in the training base, you felt like you were above everyone else. You were the elite. Everyone wanted to be like you. There is no room for imperfection in the elite society of the flotilla, though. One poor mark, a warning, and another poor evaluation in swimming technique, and you find yourself with a kitbag in one hand, your personal file in the other, and your damaged ego en route to a next assignment. Now I'm a parachute instructor. Some would consider the job daring and exciting. I consider it bullshit. A personal failure. I wanted to be underwater, with a pack of explosives in my hand and my heart in my throat. I wanted to be part of the club."[5]

The remainder of the Flotilla 13 curriculum is considered classified top-secret, though it is believed to include advanced assault training, firearms proficiency, rebreather proficiency, underwater demolitions and ordnance proficiency, fast craft instruction, Pig and Dolphin instruction, intelligence gathering, cold-killing, and other aspects of the naval special warfare A-to-Zs; some published accounts have even suggested that part of the instruction involves evasive driving skills and elements of the course provided to Israeli intelligence operatives.

Once in the unit for good, meaning that the operator has officially graduated, and the bat wings are worn on his Class A's, one's existence is divided into training, operational assignments, and additional training. The training is diverse and designed to provide the operator with nonstop work. Some of the training is heart-stopping and spectacular, such as a recent parachute drop into the Mediterranean in which forty operators dropped from 1,200 feet into the tepid waters of the blue sea in an exercise meant to see how quickly—and safely—an airborne water insertion could be executed; once in the water, the operators must swim to a rendezvous point where they are met by a small armada of Snunit boats.[6]

One officer that typifies the true essence of the Flotilla 13 operator in the 1990s is Commander D., until recently the Flotilla 13 chief, who by the age of twenty-eight was already a commander and the flotilla's deputy commander. Like many of his contemporaries and unit comrades, Commander D. is a Kibbutznik—a product of, according to former Flotilla 13 deputy CO, Commander (Res.) Yisrael Asaf, "The world's greatest commando talent pool."[7] Conscripted into the IDF upon his eighteenth birthday in 1972, he volunteered into a unit that was at its internal zenith; fresh off the War of Attrition and counter-terrorist forays, it was *the* popular unit to volunteer for. When he was conscripted, D. had no illusion other than that he would be volunteering for an elite combat unit; he knew that in the Kibbutz, if he didn't come back from his military units with wings (pilot wings, paratroop wings, commando wings!) he wouldn't be able to show his face. His father, a Holocaust survivor, wanted a son in an operational unit as a statement of the new Jew that Israel represented to the world. To D., his father's wishes were fine, but much of the talk at home of "us against everyone else" was just that, talk, until one year into his service when the Yom Kippur War broke out. "For the first time, I felt threatened, I felt under attack, I felt vulnerable as a nation." Immediately following the war, dozens of Flotilla 13 NCOs and officers signed on for additional service in the unit—including D.[8] Those years of additional service, as an NCO and an officer (with interlaced tours of duty as a patrol-boat and missile-boat officer), allowed D. to serve in the flotilla during its second "golden age" of operations, this time in Lebanon. Countless missions along a darkened surf opposite training camps and supply dumps, countless nights along the coast with a camera and a *K'latch*. "The whole essence of being a naval commando," according to D., "is to surprise, hit hard, and disappear! We don't measure the success of an operation by how many of the enemy we kill, but rather the level of surprise that we reached, and how accurate we were in hitting the targets we were ordered to strike. A successful operation, where we reached the element of surprise and hit hard has a greater morale impact than a military one. To overcome the fear of such operations, to be able to get right into the enemy's domain, right in his house, is only a commando's work."[9]

Virtually all past and present officers of Flotilla 13 agree on one thing: commando work, the commando way of life, is wild and abnormal. According to Commander S., until recently the commander of Flotilla 13, "Even today, after nearly twenty-five years of service in the navy and in the unit, when I sit in my office at two A.M. on a freezing winter's night and I hear the screams and the cries of the men, the new conscripts, undergoing their water training, I am convinced that this is madness."[10] It is, however, a necessary madness. It is also a well-disciplined madness.

There was a time when an operator remained in the unit until his retirement and then served on in a reservist capacity until his legs were too achy and bones too brittle to sit inside an SDV and have fun on a Lebanese beach. Today, however, there is a new trend. The IDF isn't letting its brightest and most successful officers vanish into the anonymity of being "naval veterans." To promote them quicker, and provide them with all-encompassing military skills and experience, many officers from Flotilla 13 are now serving as commanders in "green" army units. The trend began when, to initiate advanced urban combat skills into many of the flotilla's junior officers, many were sent to the West Bank and Gaza during the Intifada to serve in special forces and counter-terrorist units. Others soon followed suit, and others went on for stints with various paratroop reconnaissance units, infantry brigades, even tank companies. Perhaps Major General Matan Vilnai, at the time of this book's writing the deputy chief of staff, put it best when he said of these men, "If they aren't going to become the commander of the flotilla, then I want them in the green army!"[11] "These men are made of an iron will that this country is in short supply of," claims a retired Israeli tank general commenting on the success of the officers of Flotilla 13 in the green army. "All they want to do is serve, to be challenged, to be pushed, and most of all contribute."

Not only are former serving officers, still in active duty, continuing to serve in elite combat formations and even rise through the ranks of the green army, but also even many of the retired operators are continuing to make a difference in the defense of their country. They continue to contribute. Ze'ev Almog, after thirty-plus years in uniform, took his patents and innovative special operations mind with him to Haifa to head Israel Shipyards Ltd. His dream had also been to build a special operations and patrol craft so fast and so steady that not only could it outrun and outshoot anything in the terrorist's arsenal, but also it could be used to dispatch operators onto an enemy beach with speed, stealth, and, most important for a man who has had his insides bounced around like Jell-O from slamming the waves in a Snunit, comfort! Israel's defense industry has long been admired for its uncanny ability to produce weapons and equipment that is the byproduct of years of combat experience suited to the needs of a particular facet of the Israel Defense Forces (IDF). In the past, Israel's "soldier-friendly" weapons design philosophy has included the development and production of such varied weapons as the Uzi submachine gun, the Gabriel sea-to-sea missile, the Merkava main battle tanks, and the Galil family of assault rifles. Almog's vision, design, and prototype was the re-markable Shaldag (Kingfisher), an eighty-two-foot-long craft with a top speed in excess of fifty knots that was designed to become a "novel techno-operational solution for combating terrorism." It is also, in the opinion of many in the American naval special warfare community, the finest special operations craft ever designed. In fact, the Kingfisher almost became the U.S. Navy's SOC Mk V insertion craft.

For Rear Admiral (Res.) Ami Ayalon, the charismatic officer who had been pegged a future commander of Flotilla 13 and the IDF/Navy after his first interview at Atlit, he had decided to retire from the IDF/Navy in the summer of 1995 after an illustrious and remarkable career. Few admirals, with dress whites and all, can boast of wearing their nation's highest commendation for valor on their chests. It had been a remarkable run for a warrior with unlimited potential literally preordained to serve as flotilla and navy command-er. In his thirty-two years in uniform, Ayalon had seen the unit change from an asterisk on a naval order of battle to the first unit summoned when his country desperately needed a cool hand, a steady trigger finger, and nerves of steel. Ayalon, however, always a man to race headfirst into the fire, now finds his charismatic leadership abilities and cunning cool head more invaluable than ever.

On November 4, 1995, in the heart of downtown Tel

Aviv, Israeli Prime Minister Yitzhak Rabin was assassinated by a right-wing zealot opposed to the peace process with the Palestinians. Even though the gunman, a part-time law student named Yigal Amir, was known to the police and the General Security Service (GSS) as a man who had threatened the prime minister's life, he had managed to sneak past security agents and policemen to lie in wait for Rabin following a peace rally in the city's Kings of Israel Square. Amir was able to get within two feet of Rabin and pump several bullets into his back. For Israel, the murder of Rabin was an act of national uproar that could place the country on a march toward civil war—political assassinations, after all, happened in the Arab world and in the United States. For the peace process, it was a ballistic slice right across the soul of an icon, a fatherly figure of security, whose courage propelled a skeptical country to rapprochement with her Arab neighbors. For the General Security Service, the domestic counter-intelligence and counterterrorist service that, undercover, was the proverbial Rock of Gibraltar keeping Israel safe from her most despotic of enemies, as well as protecting the nation's leaders from an assassin's bullet, the murder of Rabin was a crushing blow that exposed an organization's inflated reputation and inabilities to a global audience. If the General Security Service couldn't protect the prime minister, then how could it protect the Israeli public?

Following the resignation of the serving director of the GSS, many in the traumatized Israeli government of Rabin's successor, Prime Minister Shimon Peres, realized that only one man in the country had the ability, experience, charisma, and courage to take the hot seat and assume command of the General Security Service. That man was Rear Admiral Ami Ayalon.

Over the course of fifty years, the man has become the machine in Israel's dramatic deployment of its naval special warfare forces—from the early days as underground saboteurs to a unit that even the U.S. Navy SEALs look at with pride and envy. Today, almost fifty years since it was created, Flotilla 13 remains an enigma, wrapped in a veil of secrecy, surrounded by a living organism, a covert cadre of professional operators, who know few limits to their abilities. They are an integral piece of the puzzle that keeps the Jewish State alive and, in the process, have become one of the world's top naval special forces. According to one retired U.S. Navy SEALs officer who had worked with Flotilla 13 on numerous occasions, "To the state they serve, they are just that important, to their enemies, they are simply that lethal, and to us, the people who ply this profession in the world's true hot spots, they are a true inspiration."[12]

On a dark night in the chaos of Lebanon, along some deserted stretch of beach in southern Lebanon near a terrorist camp, a small force of operators from Flotilla 13 are emerging from the surf, holding their AK-47 assault rifles with an iron grip, as they peer through night-vision goggles in search of a target. They could be on an intelligence-gathering assignment, or they could be out to attach a mine to a boat. They face death at every turn, and they must live off their instinct, wits, and courage to make it back to base. Many in the IDF have called Flotilla 13 a pressure cooker—a place where men and material are pushed beyond the envelope of human endurance. Yet perhaps Rear Admiral (Res.) Ze'ev Almog characterized the nature of the unit, and its operators, best while reflecting on the epic-setting campaign waged by Flotilla 13 against A'ardaka in 1973, a campaign that for the first time in the history of naval warfare saw an enemy fleet evacuate its port due to the actions of a handful of commandos. "No matter what the challenge, no matter what the hardships, *never say it's impossible!*"

For the last fifty years, Flotilla 13 has turned the impossible into the spectacular and the awe-inspiring.

Footnotes

Introduction

* Identity withheld for security reasons.
1 Interview, May 10, 1993.
2 Interview, May 30, 1993, Tel Aviv.
3 Videotape of the fiftieth anniversary celebrations, courtesy of the Flotilla 13 Foundation.

Chapter One

1 Interview, Kibbutz Ma'agan Michael, June 3, 1993.
2 Yigal Lossin, *Pillar of Fire: The Rebirth of Israel—A Visual History* (Jerusalem: Shikmona Publishing Company, 1983), p. 335.
3 Calev Ben-David, "The Wingate Papers," *The Jerusalem Report*, May 30, 1996, p. 40.
4 Ibid, p. 40.
5 *"Tamar Bergman, Bato Shel Me'Faked H'Sira, Katriel Yafa, She'Hayta Bat Shnatayim, Medaberet Al Avi'ha,"* Ma'ariv Mosaf Shabbat, May 17, 1991, p. 5.
6 Ibid., p. 5.

FOOTNOTES

7 Ibid., p. 5.
8 Alex Doron, *"Ta'alumat Yordei Ha'Sira: Ha'Tik Nisgar,"* *Ma'ariv Sof Shavu'a,* December 12, 1988, p. 31.
9 Interview, Ramat Ha'Sharon, June 11, 1993.
10 See Yigal Lossin, *Pillar of Fire,* p. 407.
11 Mike Eldar, *Shayetet Shlosh-Esrai* (Tel Aviv: Ma'aviv Book Guild, 1994), p. 65.
* Lieutenant Colonel Crabb was one of the most remarkable naval special warfare figures in the history of modern warfare. He disappeared in Portsmouth Harbor in 1956 after engaging in a secretive reconnaissance sortie of a Russian cruiser visiting the British port in the spring of 1956.
12 Interview, Izzy Rahav, Haifa, June 6, 1993.
13 See Mike Eldar.
14 See Mike Eldar, *Shayetet Shlosh-Esrai,* p. 69.
15 Interview, Izzy Rahav—Ramat Ha'Sharon, June 11, 1993.
16 See Mike Eldar, *Shayetet Shlosh-Esrai,* p. 76.
17 Interview, Ma'agan Michael, June 3, 1993.
18 See Yigal Lossin, *Pillar of Fire,* p. 443.
19 Andrew Mollo, *The Armed Forces of World War II: Uniforms, Insignia and Organization* (New York: Crown Publishers, Inc., 1981), p. 95.
20 Michael G. Welham, *Combat Frogmen: Military Diving from the Nineteenth Century to the Present Day* (London: Patrick Stephens Limited, 1989), p. 19.
21 Interview, Palmachim, Israel, June 6, 1996.
22 Shlomoh, Mann, "Yad Ha'Nefetz," *Yediot Sheva Yamim,* October 30, 1992, p. 33.
23 James Lucas, *Kommando: German Special Forces of World War Two* (New York: St. Martin's Press, 1985), p. 161; and see Mike Eldar, *Shayetet Shlosh-Esrai,* p. 138.
24 See Shlomoh Mann, "Ish Ha'Nefetz," p. 33.
25 Ibid., p. 35.
26 Ibid., p. 35.
27 Interview, Ma'agan Michael, June 3, 1993.

FOOTNOTES

Chapter Two

1 See Mike Eldar, *Shayetet Shlosh-Esrai* (Tel Aviv: Ma'ariv Book Guild, 1994), p. 175.
2 Interview, Ma'agan Michael, June 1, 1993.
3 Interview, Ramat Hasharon, June 1, 1993.
4 See Mike Eldar, *Shayetet Shlosh-Esrai*, p. 164.
5 Interview, Kibbutz Ma'agan Michael, June 1, 1993.
6 Interview, Ramat Ha'Sharon, June 1, 1993.
7 Interview, Haifa, May 26, 1993.
8 Interview, Haifa, June 1, 1993.
9 See Mike Eldar, *Shayetet Shlosh-Esrai*, p. 188.
10 Interview, Haifa, May 28, 1993.
11 Interview, Ramat Ha'Sharon, May 26, 1993.
12 Interview, Haifa, June 1, 1993.
13 Shlomoh Mann and Shani Payis, *"Shlosha Tza'la'shim Mi'Beirut,"* Bein Galim, No. 181, August 1990, p. 18.
14 See Mike Eldar, *Shayetet Shlosh-Esrai*, p. 199.
15 See Shlomoh Mann and Shani Payis, *"Shlosha Tza'la'shim Mi'Beirut,"* p. 20.
16 Interview, Ramat Ha'Sharon, May 26, 1993.
17 Interview, Ramat Ha'Sharon, May 26, 1993.
18 Interview, Ramat Ha'Sharon, May 26, 1993.
19 Interview, Haifa, June 1, 1993.
20 Interview (Ze'ev Almog), Ramat Ha'Sharon, May 26, 1993.
21 Interview, Ramat Ha'Sharon, May 26, 1993.
22 See Hirsh Goodman and Shlomoh Mann, *Heyl Ha'Yam: Tzahal Be'Heilo Entzyklopedia Le'Tzava Ule'Bitachon* (Tel Aviv: Revivim/Ma'ariv Library, 1982), p. 78.
23 Interview, Kibbutz Ma'agan Michael, June 3, 1993.
24 See Mike Eldar, *Shayetet Shlosh-Esrai*, p. 272.
25 See Peter Hirschbirg, "Operation Alexandria," *The Jerusalem Report*, June 4, 1992, p. 19.
26 See Peter Hirschbirg, "Operation Alexandria," *The Jerusalem Report*, June 4, 1992, p. 19.
27 See Mike Eldar, *Shayetet Shlosh-Esrai*, p. 291.

FOOTNOTES

28 Interview, Ramat Ha'Sharon, May 26, 1993.
29 Interview, Ramat Ha'Sharon, May 26, 1993.
30 Interview, Tel Aviv, June 1, 1996.
31 Interview, Kfar Ha'Maccabi, July 5, 1994.
32 Interview, Kfar Ha'Maccabi, July 5, 1994.

Chapter Three

1 Interview, Ramat Ha'Sharon, May 29, 1993.
2 Videotaped cassette of the fiftieth anniversary celebrations in Atlit.
3 Shlomoh Mann, *Hifkiru Otanu Le'Mavet," Yediot Sheva Yamim,* January 7, 1994, p. 2
4 Ibid., p. 4.
5 Interview, Ramat Ha'Sharon, May 26, 1993.
6 Interview [Yisrael Asaf], Tel Aviv, June 1, 1993.
7 Interview, Ramat Ha'Sharon, May 26, 1993.
8 Interview, Kfar Ha'Maccabi, June 4, 1994.
9 Interview, Ramat Ha'Sharon, May 26, 1993.
* Identity withheld for security reasons.
10 Interview, Tel Aviv, June 1, 1993.
11 Interview, Zichron Ya'akov, November 11, 1992.
12 Interview, Tel Aviv, June 1, 1993.
13 Interview, Ramat Ha'Sharon, May 26, 1993.
14 Interview, Ramat Ha'Sharon, May 27, 1993.
15 Interview, Tel Aviv, June 1, 1993.
16 Interview, Tel Aviv, June 1, 1993.
17 Amir Gilat, *"Mi Be'Emet Hitzil Et Bibi?", Ma'ariv Sof Shavu'a,* May 26, 1995, p. 35.
18 Interview, Ramat Ha'Sharon, May 26, 1993.
19 Interview, Ramat Ha'Sharon, May 26, 1993.
20 Samuel M. Katz, *The Elite* (New York: Pocket Books 1992), p. 111.
21 Interview, Ramat Ha'Sharon, May 26, 1993.
22 Interview, Ramat Ha'Sharon, May 26, 1993.
23 Interview, Ramat Ha'Sharon, May 26, 1993.
24 Interview, Ramat Ha'Sharon, May 26, 1993.

FOOTNOTES

25 Interview, Ramat Ha'Sharon, May 26, 1993.
26 Interview, Ramat Ha'Sharon, May 26, 1993.
27 Interview, Ramat Ha'Sharon, May 27, 1993.
28 Interview, Kfar Ha'Maccabi, June 4, 1994.
29 Interview, Italian special operations officer, St. Augustin, Germany, March 1, 1994.
30 Interview, Ramat Ha'Sharon, May 26, 1993.
31 Interview, Ramat Ha'Sharon, May 27, 1993.
32 Interview, Ramat Ha'Sharon, May 27, 1993.
33 Interview, Haifa, June 6, 1993.
* As A. is still in active service, a currently serving brigadier general, his identity is hidden for security considerations.
34 Interview, Haifa, June 6, 1993.
35 Interview, Ramat Ha'Sharon, May 26, 1993.
36 Interview [Ze'ev Almog], Ramat Ha'Sharon, May 27, 1993.
37 Abraham Rabinovich, "Assault on Green Island," *The Jerusalem Post Magazine,* July 28, 1989, p. 5.
38 Interview, Tel Aviv, June 8, 1993.
39 See Hirsh Goodman and Shlomoh Mann, *Heyl Ha'Yam,* p. 181.
40 Ibid., p. 1983.
41 Interview, Kfar Ha'Maccabi, June 9, 1994.
42 Ariella Ringel-Hoffman, *"Yam Ha'Mavet," Yediot Aharonot—Yom Kippur,* September 10, 1994, p. 4.
43 Interview, Ramat Ha'Sharon, May 27, 1993.
44 Lieutenant Colonel (Res.) Avraham Zohar, *"Escort, Raviv: Pshitot Be'Chof Mifratz Suetz—September 1969," Ma'archot,* No. 297, January 1985, p. 16.
45 See Ariella Ringel-Hoffman, *"Yam Ha'Mavet,"* p. 6.
46 See Lieutenant Colonel (Res.) Avraham Zohar, *"Escort, Raviv: Pshitot Be'Chof Mifratz Suetz—September 1969,"* p. 22.
47 Aluf Ben, *"Ha'Mivtza She'Garam Le'Nasser Hetkef Lev," Bamachane,* March 23, 1994, p. 87.
48 IDF document, M.S. 3405-24.
49 See Mike Eldar, *Shayetet Shlosh-Esrai,* p. 453.
50 Interview [Ze'ev Almog], May 28, 1993.
51 Interview, California, August 1, 1993.

FOOTNOTES

Chapter Four

1 Interview, Holon, November 1, 1994.
2 Interview, Tel Aviv, November 1992.
3 Interview with Colonel B., Tel Aviv, November 18, 1992.
4 Interview, June 1, 1993.
5 Neil Livingstone and David Halevy, *Inside the PLO* (New York: William Morrow and Company, Inc., 1990), p. 42.
6 Ibid., p. 42.
7 Interview, Los Angeles, California, March 3, 1996.
8 Mike Eldar, *Shayetet Shlosh-Esrai* (Tel Aviv: Ma'ariv Book Guild, 1994), p. 467.
9 According to "anonymous" intelligence sources, the Israelis have been able to obtain (probably as a gift from the Pentagon or Langley) a schedule of Soviet satellite flybys, and planned the mock assault in a black window when no unwanted intrusion from the heavens would tip Moscow to IDF intentions, and, as a result, tip off Damascus and then Tripoli.
10 Interview, Ramat Ha'Sharon, November 22, 1992.
11 See Uri Milshtein, *Historia Shel Ha'Tzanhanim (Kerech Daled)* (Jerusalem: Schalgi Publishing, 1987), p. 1255.
12 Interview, Tel Aviv, June 10, 1996.
13 Shlomoh Mann and Hirsch Goodman, *Heyl Ha'yam: Tzahal Be'Heilo Entzyklopedia Le'Tzava Ule'Bitachon* (Tel Aviv: Revivim Publishing, 1982), p. 142.
14 See Mike Eldar, *Shayetet Shlosh-Esrai,* p. 493.
15 Ibid., p. 495.
16 Interview, Tel Nof, June 5, 1996.
17 See Shlomoh Mann, and Hirsch Goodman, *Heyl Ha'yam,* p. 148.
18 See Mike Eldar, *Shayetet Shlosh-Esrai,* p. 498.
19 Interview, Ramat Ha'Sharon, May 28, 1993.
20 Interview, Lieutenant Y., Tel Aviv, June 1, 1993.
21 Interview, Ramat Ha'Sharon, May 28, 1993.
22 See Mike Eldar, *Shayetet Shlosh-Esrai* p. 22.
23 Interview, Los Angeles, September 28, 1996.
24 Interview, Kibbutz Ma'agan Michael, June 1, 1993.

FOOTNOTES

* At the time of this book's writing, Didi is Commodore Didi and fulfilling a post within the IDF/Navy hierarchy that forbids the publication of his full identity.

25 Interview, Kibbutz Ma'agan Michael, June 1, 1993.
26 Interview, Ramat Ha'Sharon, May 29, 1993.
27 Interview, Ramat Ha'Sharon, May 29, 1993.
28 Interview, Tel Aviv, May 31, 1993.
29 See Shlomoh Mann and Hirsch Goodman, *Heyl Ha'yam*, p. 148.
30 See Mike Eldar, *Shayetet Shlosh-Esrai*, p. 512.

Chapter Five

1 Interview, [Yisrael Asaf], Tel Aviv, June 1, 1993.
2 Ibid., p. 86.
3 Interview, U.S. Navy SEAL Lieutenant Commander (Ret.), Virginia Beach, Virginia, June 1, 1994.
4 Mike Eldar, *Shayetet Shlosh-Esrai* (Tel Aviv: Ma'ariv Book Guild, 1994), p. 523; and, Interview, Tel Aviv, June 1, 1993.
5 Interview, Los Angeles, March 1, 1996.
6 Interview, Tel Aviv, June 2, 1993.
7 Interview [Yisrael Asaf], June 1, 1993.
8 Interview, Tel Nof, June 6, 1996.
9 See Mike Eldar, *Shayetet Shlosh-Esrai*, p. 535.
10 Ibid., p. 535.
11 Samuel M. Katz *Guards Without Frontiers* (London: Arms and Armour Press, 1990), p. 160.
12 Interview, Ramat Ha'Sharon, May 29, 1993.
13 See Mike Eldar, *Shayetet Shlosh-Esrai*, p. 570.
14 Interview, Ramat Ha'Sharon, May 29, 1993.
15 Interview, Ramat Ha'Sharon, May 29, 1993.
16 Interview [Ze'ev Almog], Ramat Ha'Sharon, May 27, 1993.
17 Interview, Ramat Ha'Sharon, May 29, 1993.
18 Interview, Ramat Ha'Sharon, May 29, 1993.
19 See Mike Eldar, *Shayetet Shlosh-Esrai*, p. 572

FOOTNOTES

20 See Mike Eldar, *Shayetet Shlosh-Esrai,* p. 614.
21 Interview, Los Angeles, March 1, 1996.
22 Chaim Shibi, *"Pshita Be'O'ref Ha'Oyev,"* Yediot Aharonot, July 27, 1993, p. 9.
23 Gal Horenshtein, *"Avak Kochavim,"* Bamachane, November 10, 1993, p. 30.
24 Ibid., p. 9.
25 Arieh Kizel, *"Ha'Kommando Ha'Yami Potzetz 3 Asadot Be'Levanon,"* Yediot Aharonot, October 22, 1993, p. 9.
26 Uri Dan, "Israel Lifts Secrecy Veil on Rescue of Ethiopians," *New York Post,* March 19, 1994, p. 5.

Postscript

1 Interview, Tel Nof Jump School, June 6, 1996.
2 Interview, June 6, 1993, northern Israel.
3 Yisraela Gratziani, *"Ata Tzaf—Oh Holech Le'Ibud,"* Bamachane, June 20, 1990, p. 52.
4 Interview, Tel Aviv, May 27, 1993.
5 Interview, Tel Nof, June 6, 1996.
6 Various ed., *"Lochamei Shayetet 13: Svav Ha'Tznachot Me'Motesei Ha'Hercules,"* Biton Heyl Ha'Avir, No. 103, (204), June 1995, p. 16.
7 Interview, June 1, 1993, Tel Aviv.
8 Yisraela Gratziani, *"Cholem La'Hagiya La'Chalal,"* Bamachane, May 3, 1989, p. 11.
9 Ibid., p. 11.
10 See Yisraela Gratziani, *"Ata Tzaf—Oh Holech Le'Ibud,"* p. 52.
11 Yossi Levi, *"Tzolalim Kadimah,"* Ma'ariv Sof Shavu'a, January 19, 1996, p. 25.
12 Interview, Los Angeles, March 1, 1996.